THE
CHINESE
VIEW
OF THE
WORLD

THE
CHINESE
VIEW
OF THE
WORLD

EDITED BY

YUFAN HAO AND GUOCANG HUAN

PANTHEON BOOKS NEW YORK

Library of Congress Cataloging-in-Publication Data

The Chinese view of the world.

    Includes index.
    1. China—Foreign relations—1976-   . 2. China—
Foreign economic relations. I. Hao, Yufan. II. Huan,
Guocang.
DS779.27.C534   1989   327.51   88-43135
ISBN 0-394-57757-4
ISBN 0-679-72283-1 (pbk.)

CONTENTS

In memory of Ambassador Huan Xiang for his great contribution to international studies in China.

To our families.

PREFACE

During the past few years, great progress has been made in the West and Japan in the study of Chinese foreign policy. Yet, with a few exceptions, most of these studies are conducted by non-Chinese scholars, even though there has been a great increase in the number of Chinese scholars and students studying international relations abroad. One reason for this is of course that Chinese scholars and students have not been encouraged to write about their own country's foreign policy independently.

There is a wide gap between Chinese and Western views on Chinese foreign policy and other international issues, a gap that has strong policy implications, for scholars in both China and the West influence their own countries' foreign policy. Narrowing the gap would be a significant achievement.

There are over two hundred Chinese scholars and students in the United States studying international relations. They have become acquainted with American views and literature on Chinese foreign policy. A few of them have already written on this subject and have published widely in the United States. Nevertheless, there has not been a systematic study of Chinese foreign policy conducted by Chinese themselves and published in the United States.

To narrow the gap between Chinese and Western views of Chinese foreign policy and to develop the study of Chinese foreign policy, in the summer of 1986 we formed a working group to pursue this project, the "Chinese View of the World." Our purpose was to analyze various aspects of Chinese foreign policy and its future from a Chinese perspective. We also proposed policy directions that China should take on various international issues. The contributors have come from various Chinese academic and governmental institutions and are now studying in the United States. This book is the result. Nevertheless, it does not necessarily represent the Chinese government's views, nor does it try to reach a consensus. Rather, it is indeed a collection of independent analyses undertaken by individual scholars from China. Each contributor is fully responsible for his own work.

This book has its structural weaknesses, however. It does not cover all important aspects of Chinese foreign policy. For instance, there is no essay on China's policy toward Japan, a country increasingly important to China's national interests, although several contributors touch on this subject. Sino–West European relations are also not covered. Originally, we also planned to have an essay that analyzed the relationship between China's domestic development and its foreign policy, but we could not find the right person to write it at that time. Despite the weaknesses, this book is nevertheless a pathbreaking effort and presents a reasonably complete overview of Chinese foreign policy.

This study is the first research project sponsored by the Chinese Scholars of Political Science and International Studies, Inc. (formerly the Chinese Scholars of International Studies, Inc.), an independent academic association of Chinese scholars and students studying in the United States. As editors of this study, we are deeply grateful to the China Fund and the United Board of Christian Higher Education in Asia for their kind financial support, without which this study would not have been completed. Yufan Hao would also like to acknowledge the assistance he received from the Institute of Study of World Politics for his early research.

We have been encouraged by Professor Donald Zagoria of Hunter College in New York, whose advice and help have proven essential. Professor A. Doak Barnett of the School of Advanced International Studies at Johns Hopkins University and Dr. Harry Harding of the Brookings Institution have kindly provided their personal support. Professor Thomas Bernstein, Dr. Carol Hamrin, Ambassador U. Alexis Johnson, Professor Samuel Kim, Professor Kenneth Lieberthal, Professor Andrew Nathan, Professor Peter Van Ness, and Professor Lynn White have offered their comments on early drafts of this study. We are deeply grateful to all of them. Finally, special appreciation should be given to James Peck, a senior editor at Pantheon Books, whose editorial work has upgraded the quality of this study.

Y.H. and G.H.
March 1989

INTRODUCTION

CHINESE FOREIGN POLICY IN TRANSITION

Yufan Hao and Guocang Huan

I

Since 1978 the People's Republic of China (PRC) has started on a course of reform under the leadership of Deng Xiaoping. For the first time in the PRC's history, its leaders have set economic development as their principal goal in order to modernize the country. To carry out the modernization drive, China has pursued a policy of opening up to the outside world and of domestic economic reform. During the past ten years, the country has changed rapidly from a planned economy to a combination of planned and market economy, from ideological dogmatism to a more pragmatic approach, and from isolationism to active participation in the international community.

Meanwhile, Chinese foreign policy has also undergone significant changes. The country's foreign-policy–making has become less personal, less radical, less ideological, and more pragmatic and sophisticated. China's national interests are more specifically defined, and the pursuit of those interests has become more realistic and flexible.

During the past decade, China has significantly increased its participation in the international community and integrated itself into the global economy at large. While becoming active in over one thousand international organizations, including the United Nations, the World Bank, and the International Monetary Fund (IMF), China has rapidly expanded its economic ties with other parts of the world. During the past ten years, the country's foreign trade increased over 300 percent. China is now hosting over ten thousand contracted foreign direct-investment enterprises, mostly arranged in the mode of joint ventures with local groups, involving a total amount of US$23 billion in foreign private capital. By the end of 1987, over four thousand were in actual operation, and the total amount of capital involved came to more than $8 billion.[1] Meanwhile, over fifty thousand Chinese students are now studying in OECD (Organization of Economic Cooperation and Development) nations and thousands of foreign scholars and students are lecturing and conducting research in China. For the first time since 1949, Chinese society enjoys great access to information from abroad.

During the past ten years, China has reduced its ties with most national liberation movements. The Chinese government has significantly cut its support to revolutionary parties in other countries. While deemphasizing ideology in its relations with the Third World, China has rapidly expanded ties with many conservative developing countries, especially in the Middle East and South America. China has reduced its economic aid to developing countries. Instead, it places strong emphasis on expanding business ties with them.

For strategic reasons, China aligned with the Soviet Union in the 1950s and then shifted from that position to a de facto alignment with the United States in the 1970s. Since 1982, China has begun to readjust its position in the U.S.-USSR-PRC triangular relationship and to pursue an "independent foreign policy." The Chinese government has made great efforts to consolidate and manage Sino-American relations. At the same time, it has taken a low-key approach toward improving relations with the Soviet Union.

In the Asian-Pacific region, China has played a major role in maintaining stability. While continuing its support of resistance movements in both Cambodia and Afghanistan, China has made strong efforts to encourage North Korea and South Korea to further reduce tensions and increase contacts with each other. Compared to ten years ago, Sino-Japanese ties have become more manageable. In South Asia, China has improved its relations with India and continued its economic and political cooperation with Pakistan. In Southeast Asia, China has strengthened its ties with Singapore, Thailand, and the Philippines.

China's relations with Europe since 1978 have undergone similar changes. China has supported the North Atlantic Treaty Organization (NATO), and Beijing has been suspicious of some West Europeans' attempts at détente with the Soviets. Since 1983, however, some Chinese officials have begun to view Western Europe as the victim of the U.S.-Soviet conflict. Beijing has begun to support the peace movement and the efforts by West European states to lower tensions with the Soviet Union. In December 1988, Gorbachev proposed to reduce the size of the Red Army by a half a million in the following two years. Beijing immediately welcomed Moscow's initiative. To obtain capital investment and technology has been Beijing's key incentive to expand ties with Western Europe.

The move away from an anti-Soviet policy was also reflected in China's relations with Eastern Europe. With the exception of Yugoslavia and Romania, China's relations with East European countries were cool in the 1970s. Since 1983, with the reduction of tension, the growing trade relations with the Soviet Union, and Chinese willingness to separate economics from politics, there has been a significant increase in commercial and diplomatic activity between China and Eastern Europe.

China has also adjusted its policy toward the Third World. While taking a more realistic approach toward most of the developing countries in general, efforts to promote the South-South talks between Third World nations are being made. Since 1983 Beijing has tried to improve its image within the Third World, which had been tarnished in the 1970s when China was tilting toward the United States. While continuing its political support and reducing its economic aid to the Third World, Beijing has given more emphasis to expanding business relations with those countries. Having continued its efforts to counter Moscow's expansionism in the Asian-Pacific region, Beijing has become more critical of U.S. policy toward Central America, the Caribbean nations, and the Middle East.

During the past few years, the Chinese government has taken a more realistic approach toward both Hong Kong and Taiwan. It has signed an agreement with the British government, creating a model of "one country, two systems" for Hong Kong's future, and adopting moderate policies to deal with the local community in Hong Kong. Beijing has significantly changed its strategy toward Taiwan from the "liberation of Taiwan" to "peaceful reunification with Taiwan." Accordingly, it has reduced tensions and expanded economic and cultural relations with Taipei.

Four basic questions are raised here. In the first place, what are the driving forces behind these changes? Second, what is the nature of these changes? How should one evaluate them? Third, what are likely to be the basic trends in Chinese foreign policy in the coming decade? What are the basic policy issues that China will have to deal with? Finally, what are the basic policy options or policy guidelines that China will have in dealing with various international issues? These are issues each contributor to this book has addressed. Their analysis, we believe, offers a Chinese perspective for answering these questions.

Generally speaking, there are three major schools in the study of Chinese foreign policy. The first one explains Chinese foreign policy only by China's domestic changes and developments. In other words, it believes that, unlike other major powers' foreign policy, Chinese foreign policy is "domestically driven." It is determined by Chinese culture, tradition, leadership, ideology, politics, and economic development. No matter how the international environment changes, Chinese leaders would form and pursue their foreign policy only according to their own preference and perceptions of the world. Chinese foreign policy, this school believes, is a simple extension of the country's domestic development.

The second school believes that theoretically China's foreign policy is no different from any other major power's foreign policy. China's international behavior is determined by its position in the international system. Like any other nation, China has to define and protect its national interests: survival and economic well-being. No matter what is going on in the country's domestic politics and economics, China would have to act according to the dynamics of its international environment. Chinese foreign policy, the second school believes, is the country's reaction to its international environment.

The third school's approach lies somewhere between those of the first two schools. Chinese foreign policy, it argues, is determined by both its internal developments and its international environment. While carefully analyzing China's culture, tradition, politics, social development, economics, and leadership, the third school also looks at the dynamics of the international system with which China has to deal. As a nation-state, China cannot ignore the nature of the contemporary international system. To survive and pursue economic interests, China should act according to its position in the international system. Meanwhile, due to its specific internal structure and tradition, Chinese leaders have to balance their foreign policy with China's domestic developments.

For years, China specialists and the attentive public around the world have often been puzzled by the unpredictability of Chinese foreign policy. The major changes in Chinese foreign policy, especially those toward the two superpowers, were often unanticipated.[2]

For instance, in 1978, when the United States and the PRC agreed to establish formal diplomatic relations, one of the major objectives that Chinese leaders had in mind was to forge Sino-American strategic cooperation against the Soviet Union. But a few years later, the Chinese government publicly disavowed interest in cooperating with Washington against Moscow and began to pursue a policy designed to reduce tensions with the Soviet Union, although political consultation on various regional security issues in Asia and military exchange programs between China and the United States continued to expand.

One of the major weaknesses in the field of Chinese foreign-policy studies is that scholars have tended to analyze only what is going on in China, with far less emphasis being given to studies on how much other countries' policies toward China have changed and how these changes have affected Chinese foreign policy. By and large, Chinese leaders' perceptions of the world are still a mystery. So far, there have been no systematic and sophisticated studies on this subject. For most China scholars, the lack of a deep understanding of contemporary Chinese political culture has been another major obstacle to understanding Chinese foreign policy.

While Western studies on China's foreign policy are abundant, it is useful for people outside of China to know how the Chinese themselves understand their country's foreign policy and the changes. What have been the factors governing Chinese foreign policy since 1949? In this Introduction, we will address questions relating to the Beijing leadership's perception of the outside world, the way that Chinese pursue their national interests, changes in their approaches, and issues on which our contributors focus.

II

In order to understand the change in Chinese foreign policy one has to understand the basic factors that shape the continuity of the policy and the context of the change. A sophisticated analysis of China's foreign policy should indicate that the following factors have played vital roles in shaping the PRC's foreign relations since 1949: its historical legacy, its security concerns, its domestic need for economic development, and its international environment. These factors, we believe, will continue to govern Chinese foreign policy for the next decade and maybe even longer. Only when we understand these factors and interactions among them can we predict the future trend of Chinese foreign policy.

Historical Legacy and Chinese Perceptions of the World

Lessons that the Chinese draw from the country's foreign-relations experience in the modern era constitute one of the major elements that shape the thinking of the leaders of the PRC.

Chinese society retains a high degree of historical consciousness, and its long history as a grand civilization makes the Chinese assume the nation's greatness. This fact has led some scholars in the West to believe that there has been a Sinocentric perception of the world associated with the tribute system that has influenced the Chinese way of thinking and their conduct of foreign relations. While this proposition might, to some extent, have been applicable to Chinese foreign policy in the nineteenth century, its implications for contemporary Chinese foreign relations are very limited. On the contrary, we believe that a key factor in the modern history of China has been the foreign domination and humiliation of the Chinese people and China's anxiety to find its proper position in the international system.

From the Opium War of 1839–42 until 1949, China suffered miserably at the hands of foreign powers. By exercising their military power, Russia, Japan, and the Western powers forced China to sign a series of unequal treaties, in which the Ching dynasty agreed to cede huge pieces of its territory, pay enormous amounts of money, and to open almost all important Chinese ports to them. Besides extraterritoriality and the most-favored-nation principle, foreign powers obtained from the weak Chinese government various privileges, including control over the rate and collection of trade tariffs. By the end of the nineteenth century, much of China had been divided into competing spheres of influence between Britain, Russia, Japan, France, and Germany. Within these spheres of interest, the foreign power had complete jurisdiction, was free to establish military bases and exploit natural resources.[3] Although China was not a colony of any foreign power, its people suffered the worst type of denigration and exploitation. Even during the first four decades of this century, China was known as an "opium-eating nation," or the "sick man in East Asia"; in the big cities, signs put up by the colonial powers at clubs, restaurants, and parks read DOGS AND CHINESE ARE NOT ALLOWED.[4]

establishing a joint naval fleet
Zhou Enlai outlined five prin
ment stands in conducting fore
other's territorial integrity an
terference in each other's inter
fit, and peaceful coexistence.

The emphasis on national
hood could obviously be trace
ence. However, it also related,
goal of the revolution to constr
dence and sovereignty for Ma
formal international recognitic
ment. After all, as a semicolor
independent government reco
believed that the Chinese peopl
way without succumbing to fo
economic independence and th
out being beholden to externa
1950s, China was dependent on
antees, economic aid, and pol
heavy. The Chinese leaders fo
made it difficult for Beijing to
explains why Chinese leaders h
line of self-reliance since the mi
Sino-Soviet split was the questio

During the post-Mao era, th
although not as strong as that of
China still upholds the importan
and national sovereignty. This a
recent "independent" foreign p
the Soviet Union, in its policy to
in cases of renegotiating its bor
1970s, for instance, during t
negotiations, Washington expr
nounce its right to use force in it
the mainland. However, for its
its international credibility, Chin
right to use force in its domest
regard Taiwan as a province of
both privately and publicly expr
wan by peaceful means.

x

nd utilizing Chinese ports, Premier
ples that highlighted PRC govern-
gn relations: mutual respect for each
sovereignty, nonaggression, no in-
al affairs, equality and mutual bene-

overeignty and independent state-
back to China's past bitter experi-
it least before 1978, to the domestic
ct socialism within China. Indepen-
Zedong had meant more than the
a of an independent legal govern-
 China never fully lost its formal
nized by the foreign powers. Mao
should be free to develop their own
eign pressure and control. It meant
ability to determine priorities with-
benefactors.[7] In fact, during the
he Soviet Union for security guar-
ical support. But the costs were
nd that such a dependent position
eal with Moscow as an equal. This
ve held firmly to the concept and
-1950s. A major reason for the later
a of independence and self-reliance.
 influence of the historical legacy,
he early 1950s, has not faded away.
ce of independence, national unity,
titude has been revealed in China's
licy toward the United States and
vard Hong Kong and Taiwan, and
ers with its neighbors. In the late
e Sino-American normalization
ssed hope that Beijing would re-
attempt to reunify the island with
national sovereignty as well as for
 refused to renounce its legitimate
c affairs (both Beijing and Taipei
China), although PRC leaders had
ssed their hope of reunifying Tai-

Security Concerns

Obviously, the first objective of any country is to survive, politically and physically. In fact, during the first three decades of PRC history, China's foreign policy has been largely driven by its national security concern.

Since its founding in 1949, the People's Republic of China has gone through three major phases in its foreign policy: in the late 1940s and 1950s, China confronted the United States and was forced to ally itself closely with the Soviet Union; then from late 1950s to the late 1960s, China confronted both the United States and the Soviet Union and tried to build a third pole in the international community around the "newly emerging forces" of the Third World; and then in the early 1970s, when China perceived that the Soviet Union was the principal threat to its national security, it moved toward reconciliation with the United States, Japan, Western Europe, and other countries that might help it oppose Soviet hegemony.

Geographically, China has faced direct threats to its security from almost all directions since 1949: from the United States and Taiwan to the east, the Soviet Union to the north and northwest, Vietnam to the south, and India to the southwest. As Harry Harding once put it, "Few other major powers have felt as threatened, for such a long period of time, and by such powerful adversaries, as China has."[8]

Given the U.S. attitude toward the CCP during the Chinese civil war in the late 1940s, Beijing had reason to fear that Washington might intervene in that war on behalf of the Kuomintang* (KMT). This fear intensified when the United States sent its Seventh Fleet to protect the KMT in Taiwan in June 1950 and later gave substantial economic and military aid. This policy not only prevented Beijing from taking over Taiwan, but also created a serious threat to China's security.

In Beijing's eyes, the United States succeeded Japan as the major external threat to China's security. It might at any time encourage Japanese rearmament and support Taiwan or even invade the Chinese East Coast. This fear increased at times of crisis, such as the Korean War and the Vietnam War as well as the Taiwan Strait Crisis. In the late 1940s, China was in a shambles following decades

---

* The traditional spelling will be used throughout this book, although the pinyin "Guomindang" is sometimes encountered elsewhere.

of warlordism, civil war, and the war against Japan. The Chinese government urgently needed capital for reconstruction and outside support for their new regime. How could a weak China, which had just "stood up," survive without having reliable outside support? This was the primary impetus for Mao Zedong's decision to lean toward the Soviet Union.

Without going into details of the cause and the evolution of the Sino-Soviet rift, we can say that, by the early 1960s, the Sino-Soviet split stemmed from conflicts of ideologies and national interests. In the mid-1960s, Moscow began a military buildup along the Sino-Soviet border. By the late 1960s, when China itself was in deep internal political and economic crisis caused by the Cultural Revolution, political tensions and military confrontation with the Soviet Union increased sharply. While the Red Army developed a strong offensive capability against China, Mao and his colleagues regarded the Soviet Union as the principal threat to China's security. After the border clash in March 1969, Moscow threatened to launch a preemptive attack against China's nuclear facilities. In the early 1970s, Mao promoted rapprochement with the United States in order to counter Soviet military and political pressure. Due to his concerns about Western influence in China, Mao sought to build a strategic partnership with Washington that would call only for a minimum of economic and cultural ties between the two countries.

The forty-year history of the PRC has indeed been a history of struggle for survival. The Chinese leaders have had to deal with foreign pressure and threats almost all the time. Both superpowers tried to build up a strategic encirclement to contain China. Given China's relatively weaker economic and military power in comparison to the two superpowers, Mao and his colleagues realistically chose either to avoid confronting the two superpowers at the same time or to ally with one against the other.

Since the mid-1970s, the balance of power in the Asian-Pacific region has undergone major changes. Having lost the war in Vietnam, the U.S. gradually reduced its direct involvement in regional security affairs. Meanwhile, the Soviet Union rapidly built up its military forces, especially its air force, nuclear attack forces, and its naval fleet, in the region. On the Korean Peninsula, Moscow intensified its competition with Beijing for influence over Pyongyang. It created military alliances with both Vietnam and India and invaded Afghanistan, directly challenging China's western and southern borders. Meanwhile, Moscow began to expand its military presence in Cam Ranh and Da Nang bays, which threatened Beijing's interests in the South China Sea. Under such circumstances, in the late seventies Mao's successors decided to seek a strategic partnership with the United States against the Soviet Union. During his 1979 visit to Washington, Deng Xiaoping spoke of a Sino-American "alliance" within a global anti-Soviet united front. China thus became very much involved in the perilous game of big-power world politics.

The rise of China's international status helps explain the major change in China's foreign policy: its change from a revolutionary power to a pragmatic one. China's change came primarily after it had acquired a sense of national security and taken its proper and deserved place in the international system.

After thirty years of substantial economic construction and development, China has been transformed from a weak nation to a major power in the Asian-Pacific region. It now has the world's largest standing army, the third-largest navy and air force, the sixth-largest GNP, and the third-largest nuclear force. Moreover, Chinese resources are at the command of a powerful central government, in sharp contrast to the political fragmentation that characterized the country before 1949.[9]

In the early 1980s, when Sino-American relations became tense due to Washington's attempt to improve its ties with Taiwan, Beijing formulated a new approach in favor of the new "independent foreign policy." This policy was based on the following premises: (1) China needs a peaceful international environment in order to modernize its economy and defense. (2) Although the Soviet Union remains the principal threat to Chinese security, military confrontation with Moscow is unlikely in the near future. A moderate reduction of tension with Moscow would not only strengthen China's security, but also increase its leverage in dealing with Washington. (3) The United States does not present a threat to China's national security at present. Rather, it is a potential strategic partner in countering Soviet pressure. Therefore, maintaining good relations with Washington is important to Beijing's interests. (4) However, China does not want to be involved in the superpowers' global competition, in which China's relatively weak position makes its security uncertain. More importantly, as a regional power with global strategic significance, China's security interests are primarily concentrated in the Asian-Pacific region. Thus, it is not in China's interest to be locked into an exclusive alliance with either of the superpowers. Rather, China should cooperate with the United States on issues concerning Asian security while maintaining its independence.

Modernization

Beijing's other major objective is modernization. All Chinese leaders in the twentieth century have believed that modernization was essential if China was to enjoy security, independence, unity, and prestige in the international community. Without strong economic and technological power, there would be neither strong defense capability nor security. This objective has been a major consideration for Beijing's foreign-policy–makers.

Although there has been a consensus among Chinese leaders over the national goal of modernization, opinions and attitudes on how to achieve the goal have varied. How can China modernize without losing its national identity? What kind of national identity should China have? Should it forge a new identity? If so, what is the quickest way to do so? Chinese leaders have divided into different groups on the basis of their attitudes toward the nation's history and culture and their preferred strategies of economic modernization. Some within the Chinese leadership see power both internationally and domestically more in political and moral than in material and economic terms. They stress the importance of maintaining China's own culture, and thus prefer an isolationist foreign policy to prevent contamination by Western culture and values, though they want to strengthen China economically by using foreign technology and investment.[11] Others may be more tolerant of foreign influence and believe that Chinese culture should develop through interactions with other cultures.

Both approaches have their pros and cons. The first approach may lead to a further enlargement of the existing economic and technological gap between industrial and newly industrialized countries on the one hand and China itself on the other. Such a gap has already weakened China's position in the international system and will continue to do so. Nonetheless, it is difficult, if not impossible, after the Cultural Revolution and ten years of the open-door policy, to separate Chinese society from the rest of the world. The second approach, however, may temporarily weaken the Chinese government's position in managing China's domestic politics and dealing with foreign powers; rapidly spreading Western influence, together with difficulties from the ongoing economic reform, may create social unrest.

After the CCP's victory in 1949, Mao Zedong launched a series of socioeconomic changes aimed at transforming a largely illiterate, agriculture-oriented, and weak China into a modern, industrial, and strong power. During the 1950s, Chinese leaders carried out a modernization program that represented an effort to combine the Soviet model with certain Chinese characteristics. China's success in absorbing the Soviet technological transfer was to a large extent the result of an almost blind copying of many Soviet institutions, such as the economic-planning system, the educational system, and various state and local bureaucracies. Having received economic and technological aid from Moscow, China became heavily dependent on the Soviet Union politically, economically, and strategically. With the increased conflicts between national interests, as well as ideological differences between Beijing and Moscow, by the mid-fifties Mao began to worry about this dependency.

By the end of the fifties, Beijing and Moscow split. In 1960 Moscow terminated all its economic and technological aid programs to China and withdrew its experts from China. In addition, Moscow pressed Beijing to pay off the loans the Soviet Union had granted during the Korean War. Together with China's economic crisis, caused by the irrational economic policy of the Great Leap Forward (1958–60), Moscow's tough policy created an economic disaster in China. Ideological and political conflicts soon developed into strategic and military confrontations between the two countries. This history made Chinese leaders hesitant about turning abroad for economic assistance and advanced technology. Even those who have advocated doing so have often warned that China might become economically dependent on its foreign patron.

Since the death of Mao Zedong, the modernization approach has been fundamentally changed. As Deng Xiaoping gradually consolidated his power, he decided to open China to the outside world; this would be the central theme for the country's economic modernization. Deng and his colleagues believe that if China's modernization drive is to be successful, it has no alternative but to open its door to the international community. To narrow the existing economic and technological gap between China and the industrial nations, it needs access to foreign capital, advanced science and technology, and modern knowledge of management. Given the declining appeal of ideology in post-Mao China, this policy has the most widespread appeal for Chinese nationalistic feelings.

Despite the uneven ways in which the open-door policy and domestic economic reform have developed since 1978, China's participation in the international community has been significantly increased. Contracts with foreign firms for the installation of new machinery, factories, production processes, tourist hotels, and the extraction of coal and oil, to name a few, brought in not only capital and technology but Western values. The disillusion of many of China's young people with orthodox ideology and with much of the experience in Mao's era has been intensified by this foreign presence. People have begun to realize how far their country has fallen behind industrial and newly industrialized nations.

The current course of China's modernization drive has had and will continue to have a strong influence on Chinese foreign policy. Having rapidly increased its participation in the international community, the degree of interdependence between China and other parts of the world has increased significantly. A successful modernization program does need external assistance as well as markets abroad. The Chinese economy has become more dependent on foreign technology than ever. It will be difficult, if not impossible, for China to close the door to the outside world without paying a heavy price.

During the past ten years, Chinese society, including its leadership, has become well informed about the outside world. There has been a strong popular demand for high living standards as well as for individual political rights. Such demands have been associated with China's increased relations with industrial nations. Chinese leaders, especially the younger generation, have had extensive experiences of traveling in and learning from industrial and newly industrial countries. These experiences have improved their knowledge and confidence in dealing with their counterparts in foreign countries. On the other hand, the modernization drive may also create new problems for the Chinese leadership. During the past few years, the country's economic reform has had serious difficulties. Inflation has been high. The Chinese government has had huge budget deficits. Trade deficits, especially with Japan and other industrial nations, have increased. The income gap between those involved with foreign-related activities or businesses and the rest of the population has enlarged rapidly. There has been increased resentment against the foreign presence in China. If the Chinese government fails to manage these problems and loses control over the national economy, the nationalistic resentment within the society may force the government to reduce its participation in the international community.

International Environment

China's new foreign policy also reflects its leadership's reassessment of the international environment. In fact, since 1949, external events have played an important role in reshaping Chinese foreign policy: the emergence of the Cold War between Washington and Moscow, the U.S. policy of containing Communist regimes, Moscow's ambition to control the international Communist movement, the shifted military balance between the United States and the Soviet Union, and so on. Beijing's incentive to pursue the Sino-American rapprochement in the early 1970s was indeed a response to the Sino-Soviet military confrontation in 1969. At the same time, due to the intensified Soviet-U.S. competition and changes in the balance of power in the Asian-Pacific region, the Nixon administration took the initiative of knocking on China's door.

By the end of the 1970s, after the normalization of Sino-American relations and the collapse of the American-Soviet détente, the Chinese leaders seemed to conclude that it was time to build a united front against Soviet expansionism worldwide. Yet the Carter administration reacted coolly to Deng Xiaoping's proposal. From 1980 to 1982, due to President Reagan's pro-Taiwan policy, Sino-American relations were in deep trouble. By 1982, Beijing even began to downgrade the Soviet threat. While continuing to view Moscow as the principal threat to China's national security, Beijing began to reassess the changed Soviet-American relationship and the possibility of reducing tensions with Moscow.

The Chinese leaders' new perception of international affairs coincided with their awareness of the urgent need for China's economic development, which could be enhanced by a tranquil security environment and considerable international economic assistance. China's relations with the United States and the Soviet Union have been the crucial elements in achieving this goal, as both countries have been able to supply China with technology and industrial equipment, and both countries continue to provide a vast market for China's manufactured goods.

Although China is a regional and not a global power, it has played a key role in security and political affairs in the Asian-Pacific region. In this regard, two factors, the triangular relations between Washington, Beijing, and Moscow and the security of the Asian-Pacific region, are particularly important in reshaping China's foreign policy. As the weakest power in the triangle, Beijing does not have great resources to compete with either superpower at the global level. Yet it is in neither superpower's interest to drive China to the "other side." Such a position has given Beijing a certain leverage in dealing with both superpowers, especially when the competition between them has intensified either globally or regionally. It is in Moscow's interest to prevent the formation of a U.S.-China-Japan strategic partnership challenging its entire far eastern border. For its part, Washington is worried about possible improved Sino-Soviet relations, which could allow Moscow to increase its forces deployed against the United States and its allies. On the other hand, improved Soviet-American relations could reduce the incentive of both countries to approach Beijing. Yet Beijing could still benefit from either superpower's compromise made on regional security issues in Asia.

III

The fundamental reasons for the changes since 1978, we believe, are the change of PRC leadership, the rise in China's international status and self-confidence in its security, the urgent need to sustain the country's economic modernization as its highest priority, as well as the dynamics of China's international environment.

Among all these factors, the most fundamental one is Beijing's desire for a peaceful and stable international environment for its modernization drive. Obviously, China needs a fairly long period of peace in order to modernize its economy, and upgrade its industrial and defense capacity, so that it can become strong enough in the long term to defend itself in the face of external threats. For this purpose, Beijing needs to maintain political stability and unity at home and a peaceful external environment. To achieve this objective, Beijing has tried to improve relations with all of its traditional rivals, including India, Indonesia, and the Soviet Union, the only exception being Vietnam.

In the near future, it is unlikely China will face a major military challenge by either superpower. Yet the threat to China's national security will continue to exist. The Sino-British agreement in 1984 has decided the return of Hong Kong's sovereignty to the PRC, and

Taiwan will continue to be a major issue for territorial integrity. Moreover, the pace and direction of China's economic development in the coming decade will pose critical problems that will directly affect its foreign policy.

Questions concerning a forecast of China's future foreign policy appear particularly relevant now that China has attained substantial international status and become more active in the international economy. Will China turn inward again, for example, and, if so, to what extent will that influence future Chinese foreign policy?

As the world enters the 1990s, both China's international environment and its domestic affairs will continue to undergo major changes. Domestically, China will soon have a real change in leadership. Together with its open-door policy, China's economic and political reforms will likely face tough challenges. Internationally, increased protectionism will surely make it more difficult for Chinese goods to enter industrialized countries. While Soviet-American relations are likely to improve under George Bush's administration, Gorbachev will also probably continue his efforts to improve relations with Beijing. In Asia, Tokyo will continue its efforts to transform its economic power into political influence and military capability. The Soviet-American confrontation has, since the beginning of this year, undergone some subtle yet important changes. The Reagan-Gorbachev summit meeting in 1988 paved the way for the second Soviet-American détente. How will this development affect China's global policy? What will be the future trends in Sino-American relations? To what extent will the Taiwan issue disturb the bilateral relations between Washington and Beijing? Will the current Sino-Soviet limited détente continue, or will there be new tension in the bilateral relations? As a regional power, how will China deal with subregional security issues in East Asia? What will be China's policy toward Eastern Europe in the context of changing Sino-American and Sino-Soviet relations? Will China continue its open-door policy? How will China deal with the Third World? What will be Beijing's policy toward both Hong Kong and Taiwan? These are the questions that our contributors had in mind when they were writing this book.

This study is by no means a theoretical work. Nor have most of our contributors tried to use any single existing theoretical framework to formulate their analyses. Rather they have tried to build their own theories in their policy analyses. This is perhaps the most appropriate way to conduct policy-oriented studies.

Through their analyses, our contributors have demonstrated a few theoretical points that we believe are important in the understanding of Chinese foreign policy. In the first place, all of the contributors agree in their analyses that there is no single factor that determines China's foreign policy. In other words, the dependent variable, Chinese foreign policy, is "too big"; its nature cannot be explained by any single independent variable. Most contributors to this book use the following major variables: China's domestic economic and political development, Chinese culture and ideology, the Chinese leadership, interaction between China and other national states, and the dynamic of the international system. As most contributors demonstrate, for instance, China's domestic developments are important in shaping its foreign policy. Yet none of us believe that Chinese foreign policy is a simple extension of the country's domestic politics. Rather, we argue that Chinese foreign policy, as well as the foreign policy of other major powers, is determined by multiple factors, such as national objectives, other international players, and the dynamic interaction in the international system.

In the second place, all major variables that have shaped Chinese foreign policy in the past have been in flux. More important, the relations between these variables and the degree of their importance in determining Chinese foreign policy have also changed. Such changes have required new perspectives to analyze Chinese foreign policy. As most contributors to this book demonstrate, the degree of China's participation in the international community has increased significantly. The interdependence between China and other parts of the world, especially the industrial market economies, has also increased. As a result, in comparison to the situation ten years ago, when China was highly isolated internationally, interaction between China and other national states and the dynamics of the international environment have become increasingly important in shaping Chinese foreign policy.

The importance of ideology in the making of Chinese foreign policy is another example. In comparison with many foreign scholars, the authors of this book have given far less emphasis to this subject. This is because there has been a general process of "deideologizing" in Chinese society. The official ideology has undergone some important changes. As a result, not only has the importance of ideology in the country's foreign-policy–making declined, but also Chinese scholars have developed many new concepts and theories to define China's national interests and its new foreign policy.

Third, the authors of this book carefully and specifically redefine China's national interests. In particular, they demonstrate that under certain circumstances, the country's policy toward a specific issue can and should be relatively separate from its general foreign policy. In this regard, without a careful definition and analysis of China's specific interests, the Chinese government's official statements on its general foreign policy should not be simply applied to any of its specific policy actions.

The relationship between China's security policy and its general foreign policy is a good example. As our contributors indicate, China is a regional power with global strategic significance and political influence. China's basic security interests are largely concentrated in the Asian-Pacific region. China has indeed played a very active and important role in regional stability and security. Outside the region, as the largest developing country in the world and one of five permanent members of the U.N. Security Council, China does have strong economic and political interests. Nevertheless, China has neither the intention nor the capacity to play a key role in international security issues. This is a basic reason why the implications of the Chinese government's general statements on its foreign policy, such as those regarding the Third World, are often different from its policy actions in the Asian-Pacific region. This difference is also a key principle for guiding the studies of China's policy toward the two superpowers.

China is still at a historical turning point. By all means, its domestic economy, politics, and the dynamics of its international environment are likely to undergo significant changes in the coming decade. These changes will naturally reshape China's relations with other nation-states and the international system as a whole. By presenting this study, we hope to paint a convincing picture of what the basic trends will be in Chinese foreign policy and China's basic policy options. As such, this book aims to help people to understand Chinese foreign policy in the coming decade.

THE
CHINESE
VIEW
OF THE
WORLD

ONE

SECURITY
IN THE
ASIAN-PACIFIC
REGION

WEIQUN GU

In theory, the advent of intercontinental ballistic missiles (ICBMs) should have relegated the regional approach in security studies to a place of secondary importance, for ICBMs by definition acknowledge no continental barriers and hence are not susceptible to a regionally oriented analysis. However, the fact that no wars involving the use of ICBMs have been fought since their invention, while local wars fought with conventional weapons somewhere in the world have never ceased, has meant that the regional approach continues to play a central role in security studies and is likely to acquire even more prominence with significant achievement of nuclear arms control.

International security even without ICBMs can be said to be indivisible, given the interdependent nature of international economics and politics. Yet differences in intensity of economic and political interaction, history, culture, and geography are such that the world security system can be usefully divided into various regional security systems for analytical purposes. The Asian-Pacific security system is one such system.

CHARACTERISTICS OF THE ASIAN-PACIFIC SECURITY SYSTEM

Multipolarity

In contrast to the bipolarity of the European-Atlantic security system involving NATO on the one hand and the Warsaw Pact on the other, the defining characteristic of the Asian-Pacific security system is its multipolarity.

China is a major land power in Asia. Although poorly equipped, the People's Liberation Army (PLA) is the only military force in the world that has experience in combat with the forces of both the United States and the Soviet Union since the end of the Second

World War, and on both those occasions it did not fare badly. China has a population of over 1 billion, with an ample supply of manpower in case of a defensive war. It has developed a small strategic nuclear force whose second-strike capability is likely to become increasingly more credible. It has a long Pacific coast, two big islands, Taiwan and Hainan, and numerous small islands in the South China Sea, and shares sea borders with quite a few countries—hence its natural interest in the Pacific. It has built the world's third-largest navy and has in recent years developed the naval and air capability to defend its islands located in the southernmost part of the South China Sea. Though its share of the world product is only 3 percent right now, it may double by the end of this century. While per capita income in China is only around $300 per annum, the fact that the average life expectancy of the Chinese is sixty-nine years, not significantly lower than that of the peoples of developed countries, suggests that it is not as poor as its per capita income figure indicates.

Japan is a great economic power, with its GNP making up about 12 percent of the world product. Had it not been for its defeat in the Second World War and the constitutional constraints, it could well have become a military superpower. Being an island trading nation, it has great interest in the openness of sea-lanes, which are its lifeline. The U.S. government has been encouraging it to spend more on defense and the Japanese government has taken onto itself the responsibility of defending sea-lanes out to a distance of a thousand miles. Given time, and under certain conditions, the dynamics may be created for Japan to move in the direction of becoming a major sea power with certain self-imposed restraints.

The Soviet Union is both a major land power in Asia and a major sea power in the Pacific. It has deployed fifty-three divisions along the Sino-Soviet and Sino-Mongolian borders and on the Pacific approaches to the USSR, and its largest fleet, with its best naval officers and vessels, is in the Pacific. It has deployed 171 SS-20 intermediate-range nuclear missiles in the far eastern part of the Soviet Union. The GNP of the Soviet Union constitutes about 12 percent of the world product. However, the fact that it has two fronts to worry about means that it has to somehow divide its military resources between them, something which works against its overall force posture in the Asian-Pacific region.

The United States, with four states bordering the Pacific, a fifth, Hawaii, lying in the middle of the region, and numerous islands under its administration, is the leading Pacific sea power. Its GNP constitutes 24 percent of the world product, twice as high as the share of the next country down the line, Japan. It is also a major economic power in this region, conducting more than 30 percent of its trade and getting a higher return on its investment there than from that in other parts of the world. However, it also has to deal with the problem of having two fronts, which spreads its forces thin. Further, it does not have any significant number of ground troops on the mainland of Asia.

While China and Japan are regional powers with global interests, the Soviet Union and the United States are global powers with regional interests. As such, these four powers can be said to be in the same league as far as the Asian-Pacific region is concerned.

Besides these four, there are also certain subregional powers such as ASEAN (Association of Southeast Asian Nations), Vietnam, and North and South Korea that add further complications to the security scene in the Asian-Pacific region.

Even though none of the studies on the relationship between the structure of the international system and the frequency of conflict has been conclusive, the proposition that state behavior varies with, among other things, differences in the structure of the international system seems to be valid. A multipolar system certainly entails more sets of relationships than a bipolar or a unipolar system, and more centers that are in a position to take independent action, including the initiation of conflict—though there are more variables for them to consider (more systemic constraints) when they want to do so, which may work to reduce the intensity of conflict. (U.S. behavior during the Vietnam War, Soviet behavior in the border conflict with China in 1969, and the Chinese-Vietnamese border conflict of 1979 may be confirming evidence for this thesis.) One phenomenon that in part ensues from the multipolarity of the Asian-Pacific international system is bilateralism in security relations.

Bilateralism

In contrast with Europe, where multilateralism prevails in security relationships, bilateralism dominates the scene in the Asian-Pacific region.

Five out of eight U.S. bilateral security ties are with countries in the Asian-Pacific region. These are U.S. ties with Japan (1960), South Korea (1954), the Philippines (1947, 1951), Australia (1951), and

7

Thailand (1962). Besides, the U.S. offers foreign military sales credit to Indonesia and Malaysia even though they are not its allies. The Soviet Union has security ties with Vietnam (1978), North Korea (1961, 1984), and Mongolia (1966). China has security ties with North Korea (1961), de facto ties with Cambodia (1979), unwritten ties with Thailand (1980), and low-level military ties with the United States and Japan. Australia has security ties with New Zealand (1944).

There have been three exceptions to this dominant pattern of security bilateralism: the "U.N. Command" in South Korea: SEATO (abolished in 1977); and the Five-Power Defense Arrangements of 1970 between the United Kingdom, Australia, New Zealand, Malaysia, and Singapore, but these are either defunct or inactive.

The multipolar structure of the Asian-Pacific international system has worked to reduce the ability of any single power to construct a multilateral security regime. Another factor unfavorable to multilateralism is the diversity in the conditions and interests of the various Asian-Pacific countries. Differences in culture, political philosophy, religion, historical experience, level of socioeconomic and political development, and geopolitical positions have resulted in differences in ways national interests are identified and perceived.

Variegated Contradictions

The dominant contradiction in Europe is the East-West contradiction, a conflict in political philosophies, capitalism versus socialism, at least the Russian brand of socialism.

In the Asian-Pacific region, on the other hand, the picture is more colorful. There is the East-West contradiction. This includes the U.S.-USSR confrontation, a certain degree of mutual suspicion between China and the United States, and confrontation between the two Koreas, between mainland China and Taiwan, and between Vietnam and ASEAN.

There is the North-South contradiction. Trade problems between Japan and China, between Japan and certain ASEAN countries, and between the United States and mainland China, South Korea, Taiwan and Hong Kong belong here.

There is the East-East contradiction. Conflict between China and the Soviet Union, between China and Vietnam, and between Vietnam and Cambodia are cases in point.

There is the West-West contradiction. Trade problems between

Japan and the United States and between Japan and Australia, and the issue of naval ship visits in U.S.–New Zealand relations constitute such a contradiction.

There is the South-South contradiction. The problem of conflicting territorial claims existing between China and Vietnam, the Philippines, and Malaysia, between Vietnam and the Philippines, and Indonesia, and among various ASEAN countries are this type of contradiction. In a certain sense, it can be argued that the larger conflict between China and Vietnam, and between Vietnam and Kampuchea and Laos, while also an East-East contradiction, is more accurately put under this category (conflicting nationalisms between poor neighbors).

There is the oriental-occidental contradiction. Certain problems of communication and certain human rights issues that exist between China and the United States are of this kind.

And last but not least, there is also the intranational contradiction that has international implications. The conflicts between mainland China and Taiwan, between the two Koreas (also put under the category of East-West contradiction), between the New People's Army and the Filipino government, the Thai Communist Party and the Thai government, and the Burmese Communist Party and the Burmese government are of this type.

The dominant contradictions now in this region are East-West and East-East, which may in the long run give way to North-South and South-South ones. These different sociopolitical types of contradiction in the region's international relations have different origins and hence call for different solutions.

Volatility

Since the end of World War II, not one day has passed without a war, international or civil, going on somewhere in this region. During this period, two of the three major local wars in the world were fought in this area—the Korean War and the Vietnam War—with the latter using up several times more bombs than the whole of the Second World War. In this region, Communists killed Communists; the threat of the use of nuclear weapons over local wars and border conflicts was made five times;[1] the two most dangerous intranational conflicts, the Korean and the Chinese, remain unresolved; domestic insurgencies have fought governments longer

9

than anywhere else (Burma, the Philippines, Malaysia, and Thailand).

Unlike in Europe—where the Yalta system more or less held until it was replaced by the Helsinki European Security Conference regime and where the defense parameters of the two blocs, NATO and the Warsaw Pact, are clearly defined—in Asia the Yalta system came under challenge not long after it was created by rival political forces in China and Korea and was violated by its designers, the United States and the USSR. Even now the lines of defense of the various parties to the confrontation are not clear-cut.

In this region, major alignment patterns have changed frequently, with one major change virtually every ten years. China has changed its foreign-policy stance from alliance with the Soviet Union to hostility toward the Soviet Union and the United States, to alignment with the United States, to amity with the United States and near détente with the USSR.

In this region, where most countries are undergoing rapid socio-economic transformation and modernization, changes in the dominant values are not measured by generations. Before the relatively new values have time to take root in the minds of the elder brothers, the younger brothers jump onto something else.

This is a region where as a rule the life span of the charismatic leader is the best predictor of changes in government policies—that is, if the leader survives coups d'état, which are by no means infrequent.

There also exist numerous territorial disputes here. In all these aspects, the Asian-Pacific region is different from Europe.

The Prominence of the Navy and the Air Force

The role of the navy and the air force relative to the army and nuclear forces is greater in the Asian-Pacific region than in Europe, where the two enormous armies of NATO and the Warsaw Pact confront each other on land, with thousands of nuclear missiles deployed by both sides. In the Asian-Pacific region on the other hand, such factors as geography, the process of learning, the parties to the dominant contradiction, and the probable scenarios of future conflict point to a more prominent role for the navy and the air force.[2]

The Asian-Pacific region has many more important island countries and regions than there are in Europe: Japan, Indonesia, the

Philippines, New Zealand, Singapore, numerous islands in the South Pacific, Hawaii, Taiwan, Hainan, Sakhalin, and the Aleutian Islands. There are also several important peninsulas that give naval power an added advantage: the Korean, the Malay, and the Kamchatka peninsulas. Although Australia is a continent in itself, it can only be reached by sea and air. True, China, the Soviet Union, and the United States are continental countries; by virtue of the depth of their territories, they are also most readily accessible by sea.

In concrete military terms, the East-West contradiction manifests itself in the confrontation between U.S. and Soviet sea and air power. This can be shown from the way the navy is deployed relative to the army in this region by both powers in contrast to its deployment elsewhere. Calculated on the basis of figures contained in *The Report of the U.S. Secretary of Defense to the Congress on the Fiscal Year 1986 Defense Budget,* the ratio between U.S. forces on land and at sea in Europe and in Asia are 13 to 1 and 5.7 to 1 respectively, making the U.S. Navy in the Asian-Pacific region more than twice as important as the one in Europe in relation to the army in the two theaters. The Soviet Pacific Fleet in addition to being the largest fleet of the Soviet Union has two of the four aircraft carriers of the Soviet Navy.

Although the Soviet Union and China are confronting each other with land power, both sides have deployed their forces in a defensive manner—even though the Soviet Union has an offensive capability—and are likely to negotiate with each other on a balanced reduction of forces in the not-too-distant future.

The Korean and Vietnam experiences, particularly the latter, seem to have taught the United States a new principle in war: not to try to walk to the mainland of Asia.[3] In observance of this principle, the United States has adopted the strategy of limiting U.S. involvement in future conflicts on the Asian mainland to the use of naval and air power in support of indigenous ground forces.[4]

The more likely scenarios of conflict in the foreseeable future in the Asian-Pacific region are wars over the jurisdiction of islands in the South China Sea, conflict between mainland China and Taiwan, and a second Korean war. The first two, if they should really take place, would be naval and air wars and the third would again contain a significant naval and air component as in the first Korean War. Since no other conflicts seem to have a higher probability of occurrence, the relative importance of naval and air forces in the region is once again demonstrated.

The above description is not intended to belittle the role of the army in the Asian-Pacific region—after all, ferocious land wars have been fought in China, Korea, and Vietnam—but it is an attempt to bring into focus the special role of the navy and the air force in determining the outcome of conflict in the particular geographical and political context of the Asian-Pacific region.

U.S. Structural Superiority over the Soviet Union

The balance of forces between the United States and the Soviet Union in the world as a whole and in Europe (where the Warsaw Pact's conventional superiority is offset by NATO's nuclear strike capabilities) is one of essential parity. The balance of forces in the Asian-Pacific region on the other hand is one of structural disequilibrium in favor of the United States.

The balance of naval power continues to be strongly in favor of the United States. The Soviet Pacific Fleet is susceptible to blockade, and its major port on the Pacific coast, Vladivostok, the depots for the fleet around it, and the Trans-Siberian Railroad, which is the fleet's main supply line, are vulnerable to attack. Except for its facilities in Cam Ranh Bay, Vietnam, the Soviet Union does not have any forward deployment base outside its territories in the Pacific region, something which works to reduce the survivability of its fleet in a major war, since it lacks adequate seaborne aircraft capabilities. It has four allies in this region that are rather poor. The United States on the other hand, has an extensive network of forward deployment bases in the Asian-Pacific region—in the Philippines, Japan, South Korea, Guam, and so on—in addition to the Seventh Fleet, which is overwhelmingly superior to the Soviet fleet in terms of its seaborne aircraft capabilities. It has more allies, and stronger ones—Japan, Australia, South Korea, the Philippines, and Thailand—and even more friends, not the least among them, China. Although the Soviet Union has significant land power deployed in its far eastern region while the United States has only limited ground forces in South Korea, it is offset to a certain extent by Chinese land power and the Sea of Japan, which, as a German general once put it, is worth ninety divisions.[5]

The far eastern part of the Soviet Union has very long, cold winters and consequently a low level of development and low population density, a factor that defies human manipulation by and large. The Soviet Union has almost no economic interest in the Pacific except for the fish catches that constitute 40 percent of the total Soviet fish supply.[6] Even though richly endowed with energy resources, the far eastern part of the Soviet Union right now does not produce enough fuel even to meet the demand of its limited production facilities there. The Soviet Union's trade with the Asian-Pacific countries is comparatively insignificant. The United States on the other hand finds its best climate on the Pacific Coast, a region which is as rich as the Atlantic Coast, if not richer. It has extensive trade and investment in the Asian-Pacific region.

Last but not least, the Soviet economic and political model is increasingly losing, if it has not already lost, any appeal for countries in the region and even for itself. The U.S. economic and political institutions on the other hand seem to have become a major export commodity to countries of the region. It seems that the structural disequilibrium that exists in the balance of forces between the United State and the Soviet Union in the Asian-Pacific region will remain for the foreseeable future.

Absence of a Regional Arms Control Process

In Europe there are regional approaches to arms control, such as the Mutual and Balanced Force Reductions Talks in Vienna between NATO and the Warsaw Pact designed to negotiate a reduction of conventional forces of the two opposing sides, and the Conference on Confidence and Security-Building Measures and Disarmament in Europe. The Asian-Pacific region in contrast does not have any regional arms control process. The last arms control agreement that had a significant implication for the Asian-Pacific region was the Naval Agreement reached at the Washington Conference forty-five years ago among the United States, Britain, Japan, France, and Italy, setting a limit on the sizes of navies they were entitled to have.

The reason for the absence of a regional arms control process is not hard to identify. For much of the time after the Second World War, the United States had engaged in local wars in Asia and hence had no interest in arms control. Japan had few arms to control anyway as a result of its defeat in the Second World War. China had been isolated and later isolated itself from the world community and labeled all arms control efforts as imperialist and social-imperialist hoaxes. The Soviet Union, fearing a two-front war, after falling out with China, tried hard to build up its defenses in the Far East and hence was in no mood for arms control in the region. However, the degree of militarization is not as high as it is in Europe, hence there has been less need felt for arms control. Even if there were the will to engage in arms control, it might be harder to achieve in this multipolar environment than in a bipolar one.

POLITICAL TRENDS AND THEIR REGIONAL SECURITY IMPLICATIONS

Multipolarization

While multipolarization is a worldwide trend, it is particularly pronounced in the Asian-Pacific region. Having overtaken the Soviet Union recently, Japan has become the number-two economic power in the world and is moving in the direction of becoming a major political power and possibly a major high-tech sea power. Though much of the Japanese elite still regards Japan's ties with the United States as the cornerstone of its security, there are also those in the government who advocate that Japan become more independent of the United States, even to the point of developing an independent nuclear arsenal.

China has finally left behind the years of domestic political turmoil and set its mind to the singular pursuit of wealth, power, and international status. By the end of the century, a much stronger and confident China is likely to assert itself on the eastern rim of the Eurasian landmass. The ASEAN countries have also achieved tremendous economic growth and have developed considerable collective political clout.

Of course, the two superpowers, the United States and the Soviet Union, still play a very important role in the affairs of the region, but their actions in the region have increasingly been subject to regional international systematic constraints.

Neutralism

A trend related to multipolarization is the trend toward neutralism, a phenomenon of countries trying to disengage themselves from the bipolar rivalry between the United States and the Soviet Union.

The five countries of ASEAN (now six) started to assert neutrality as early as November 1971 and proclaimed in the Kuala Lumpur Declaration that they are determined "to exert initially necessary efforts to secure the recognition of, and respect for, South

East Asia as a Zone of Peace, Freedom and Neutrality, free from any form or manner of interference by outside Powers."[7] The declaration was issued only four months after Nixon announced that he would visit China, which represented U.S. acknowledgment of the growth of Chinese power. The ASEAN countries are likely to reemphasize this position once the Cambodian problem is solved. China formulated an "independent" foreign policy in 1982 that was clearly an attempt to disengage itself from the U.S.-USSR competition. Part of the benefit of this new policy was the savings on the 1 million troops that were demobilized in 1985–86. New Zealand's position in the ANZUS (Australia, New Zealand, United States) Treaty framework has come under increasing doubt. Both the Australian and Canadian governments made an effort to bring the U.S. and the USSR together again after the arms control talks broke down in 1983. Neutralist tendencies also exist within part of the Japanese elite. If the Soviet Union is really going to behave more moderately in the Asian-Pacific region in the years ahead, as Secretary Gorbachev's speechs at Vladivostok (1986) and at the United Nations (1988) seem to indicate, the neutralist tendency that already exists in the region may gather more momentum, something that may work to reduce the overall level of tension in the international relations of the region.

Democratization

A new wave of democratization is spreading in the Asian-Pacific region. Reemerging from the chaos of the Cultural Revolution, mainland China vowed to build a highly democratic society. The Democracy Wall movement, the active participation of students in local elections, the demands of intellectuals for freedom of expression and of journalists for freedom of the press, the efforts of people's deputies and congresses at various levels to exercise their rights to supervise the operations of the executive branch of government, the political obstacles to economic reforms, the student demonstrations demanding cleaner government and freedom and democracy—all these led to the official adoption by the Communist Party of the policy of instituting political reforms at the 13th Communist Party Congress in addition to the market-oriented economic reforms that have been underway for some time. In Taiwan the newly formed Democratic Progressive Party has gained about 22 percent of the votes, and power was transferred peacefully according to the constitution after the death of Chiang Ching-kuo.

In the Philippines, government tanks were stopped by "people power"—unarmed peaceful demonstrations—and the Marcos regime was voted out of office in a direct election. Under the influence of the triumph of democracy in the Philippines, a direct presidential election was held in South Korea.

Even Gorbachev could not remain totally immune to this new wave of change. Following what Deng Xiaoping did two years before, he called reforms in the Soviet Union a revolution and argued that they should not be confined to the economic realm but should be extended to the social and political realms.

The trend toward democratization has domestic as well as international systemic origins. Oppression, turmoil, and inefficiency "coming to a head" (the Philippines, China, and the USSR), rapid economic development, and a rise in the level of education and with it the consciousness of the possibilities of political participation are some of the domestic sources. Sino-U.S. rapprochement leading to a significant reduction of tension in the region, thus removing part of the rationale for tight government control in various countries; the visible demonstration of democracy through the wide spread of television; and Carter's human rights diplomacy and Reagan's foreign-policy emphasis on the promotion of democracy are some of the major international systemic origins for the change.

The implication of this trend for regional security is profound. Michael Doyle has found that although countries with democratic institutions do fight wars, they have never fought one another.[8] If Doyle's finding is relevant to the issue of security in the Asian-Pacific region, prospects for peace in the region in the long term are likely to be enhanced as a result of this trend, even though certain countries where the process of democratization is unfolding may be expected to experience some degree of domestic instability.

Decline of Ideology

International relations within the region have been significantly deideologized and foreign policies of the various countries rationalized. One no longer hears much of the rhetoric of the free world versus the unfree world, nationalism versus imperialism, or even socialism versus capitalism. Instead, concepts such as developed versus developing countries, market versus planned economies are becoming more popular.

The same Reagan who once vowed to wage a "crusade against communism" after coming back from a trip to China termed it "a so-called Communist country." International interdependence has become a catchword in China. Even Gorbachev found this term useful when he stated in his July 28, 1986, speech in Vladivostok, "Time is insistently demanding a new understanding of the current stage in the development of civilization; of international relations; of the world, of a world that is contradictory and complex but that is objectively united by ties of interdependence."[9] Not long after this, the Soviet Union decided to apply to join GATT (General Agreement on Tariffs and Trade) and explore the possibility of joining the International Monetary Fund (IMF) and the World Bank. China has also adopted a very pragmatic position on the question of Communist guerrillas in Southeast Asia and has called for the establishment of a nonsocialist system in Cambodia after Vietnamese troops are withdrawn. The Khmer Rouge has gone as far as it possibly can by declaring that it wishes to practice capitalist free enterprise after the departure of the Vietnamese. The process of national reconciliation has begun across the Taiwan Strait in spite of the official KMT "three nos" policy (no contact, no negotiation, no compromise;).

Sino-U.S. rapprochment also has had a role to play in the emergence of this trend. With mutual opening and increased understanding, people are making new and more accurate assessments of each other's societies, and find nothing lost and much to be gained by learning from the strong points of others. Deideologization will never lead to foreign policies that are value-free, but it does entail that rational, interest-oriented policies will have a greater chance to prevail, reducing the prospects of new forms of religious wars in an essentially postmedieval era.

Economics in Command

The economic component in international relations in the region is acquiring more and more prominence. Trade friction between the United States and Japan seems to have become a defining characteristic of their bilateral relations. Both the U.S. and Chinese governments have adopted the policy of giving economics a central place in their relationship. Notwithstanding the political and military competition with the Soviet Union, Reagan lifted the U.S. grain embargo against it. In its economic dealings with Japan, China has painfully learned what the term "economic animal" really means. Malaysia has decided to define its relationship with China solely in terms of economics. Singapore and China have set up trade offices in each other's capitals in the absence of diplomatic relations, and China and South Korea are about to do the same. Indonesia has decided to conduct direct trade with China, though it is not yet prepared to establish diplomatic relations with it. Mainland China has developed a rapidly expanding indirect trade relationship with Taiwan. Sino-Soviet economic relations are moving ahead full-steam.

This development is a corollary of the trend of deideologization. It represents the relative rise of Adam Smith and the fall of Machiavelli as the mastermind of international relations in the region today.

What implication will this trend have on the region's security? The assumption is that trade leads to peaceful relations, an age-old theory that has become dogma for some liberals and conservatives as much as Lenin's theory on economic competition leading to imperialist wars has become dogma for some Marxists. The causal linkage is not one that is completely free of problems, however.

International trade and investment are examples of the international division of labor; as such, they create mutual needs. When these mutual needs reach a significant level, as for example within the European Economic Community (EEC), countries grow together. Functional integration theorists such as Ernst Haas and Joseph S. Nye argue that cooperation in one issue area such as trade, can "spill over" into cooperation in other areas. Karl Deutsch suggests that trade can be construed as a transaction of information that furthers understanding and contributes to the process of integration and hence peace. While the absence of wars among West European countries after the Second World War offers some confirmation of these theories, contrary evidence also exists. The level of trade between Britain and Germany before the First World War, for example, was higher for each country than that with any other country. Economic ties were also very developed between the United States and Japan before the Japanese attack on Pearl Harbor during the Second World War. Perhaps it is safer to say that commerce by itself is neither necessary nor sufficient for peace and security, but under certain conditions it facilitates peaceful relations.

From Economic Bilateralism to Multilateralism

Political and economic ties among countries in the region are becoming increasingly multilateral and the demand for their institutionalization is becoming more and more vocal. The annual Foreign Ministers' Meeting between the six countries of ASEAN and five developed countries—the United States, Japan, Canada, Australia, and New Zealand—has been held for several years now. Concrete development projects such as the human resources development project have resulted from it, in addition to the general benefit to all parties of exchanging views and promoting understanding.

The concept of a Pacific Economic Community has fired the imagination of many in all countries within this region. Some in the U.S. government, declaring that the future of the world lies in the Pacific, are actively promoting the study of this concept. Also, the U.S. government has indicated an interest in the establishment of free-trade zones in the Asian-Pacific region. Japan, with its major economic interests in this region, is particularly eager to see this concept materialize in the form of an institution like the Organization of Economic Cooperation and Development (OECD). The ASEAN countries have tentatively endorsed this idea. Mainland China has great interest in this concept and would like to see it actualized in the framework of North-South cooperation, and would like to cooperate with Taiwan in this endeavor. The Soviet Union, very worried about being left out, expressed its "unprejudiced attitude toward it" and its willingness "to join in thinking about the possible foundations for such cooperation."[10]

The trend toward economic multilateralism is attributable to the explosion of production and the vast expansion of bilateral economic ties among nations of the region since the end of the Second World War. It is also a political reaction and alternative to the empire-building effort of Japan that led to the Asian part of the Second World War. Multilateral economic cooperation in the Asian-Pacific region is in the interest of all Pacific countries. It will facilitate interactions among its members through the reduction of "transaction costs" in dealings with one another, through a reduction in uncertainty resulting from a lack of information, and through creation of multiple issues through which mutually beneficial trade-offs may occur more easily.

The implications for Asian-Pacific security are significant. In a nutshell, it can provide a viable alternative to the further militarization of the region, through the establishment of what Karl Deutsch has termed a "security community" (defined as the attainment of "institutions and practices strong enough and widespread enough to assure, for a 'long' time, dependable expectations of 'peaceful change'" among its members). It was with this in mind that the EEC and ASEAN were set up. Their salutary effect on the relationship among their respective members since they were formed is there for everybody to see.

At present, the United States and Japan do not wish to take the lead in pushing for movement on the question of Pacific economic cooperation lest they be accused of attempting to dominate the region. Instead, they have asked ASEAN to take the lead. But the member states of ASEAN still do not see completely eye-to-eye on this question and are slow to act. The ASEAN countries do not have the resources, the will, or even the need to push for cooperation in as large a region as the entire Pacific, even though they have had some experience in the running of their own subregional organization.

The historical task of promoting Pacific economic cooperation falls on the United States and Japan, both of which have the resources and the need and can generate the will necessary for such an endeavor. In so doing, they should consult closely with ASEAN, China, Australia, Canada, and New Zealand. And once a certain framework, probably initially in the form of an information clearinghouse like the OECD, is set up, Taiwan, Hong Kong, South Korea, and North Korea should also be invited to participate. If the Soviet Union should radically alter its foreign policy in the world in general and in the Asian-Pacific region in particular, it should be welcomed to play a constructive role in Pacific economic cooperation.

Toward Negotiated Settlement of Disputes

Since the U.S. withdrawal of troops from Vietnam, the role of force in the settlement of international disputes in the region has declined somewhat, and more and more efforts have been made to try and solve disputes through negotiations. The restoration of Sino-U.S. relations is a milestone in the history of international relations, in the region and in the world. The signing of the Treaty of Peace and Friendship between China and Japan has equally been a stabilizing factor in the region. China and Japan reached agreement on joint suspension of claims on the Tiaoyu (Senkaku) Islands. The two Koreas are conducting bilateral talks, and China and the Soviet Union have been holding negotiations on the question of normalization of their relations. The Aquino government of the Philippines made an attempt to negotiate civil peace with the Communist guerrillas.

The exceptions to this pattern have been the Vietnamese invasion of Cambodia and the Chinese-Vietnamese border conflict. (The Soviet invasion of Afghanistan does not count, as the latter lies outside the region under consideration.)

If this trend continues and becomes more powerful, its implication for regional security is very encouraging.

Toward a Regional Arms Control Process

In recent years, with the reduction of tension in the region as a whole, largely a result of Sino-U.S. rapprochement and the initial thaw in Sino-Soviet relations, China has unilaterally reduced the number of its troops by 1 million.

Partly as a response to the Chinese initiative and partly to meet the Chinese preconditions for the normalization of Sino-Soviet relations,* Gorbachev declared in the aforementioned speeches that the Soviet Union is pulling out a considerable number of troops from Mongolia and is ready to negotiate with China on a balanced reduction in the level of land forces. He proposed talks on reduction of the activities of naval fleets in the Pacific and limitation on competition in the deployment of antisubmarine weapons. Partly in response to the new political development in the Philippines, he challenged the United States by alluding to possible withdrawal from Cam Ranh Bay if the United States should dismantle its bases in the Philippines. He declared support for North Korea's proposal on the creation of a nuclear-free zone on the Korean Peninsula, and he took note of the ASEAN proposal for such a zone in Southeast Asia. The SS-20s deployed in the far eastern part of the Soviet Union are to be dismantled. He voiced support for North Korea's proposal for tripartite talks among the two Koreas and the United

*The "three preconditions" to normalized Sino-Soviet relations (which remove the "three obstacles," another way of referring to the same set of ideas) are (1) a substantial cut in the Soviet troops along the Chinese border, (2) the complete withdrawal of Soviet troops from Afghanistan, and (3) the end of Soviet support for the Vietnamese occupation of Cambodia.

States. He declared the Soviet Union's support for the disbanding of military groups, removal of all foreign bases, and withdrawal of troops from the territories of other countries in the region. And he proposed that the Five Principles of Peaceful Coexistence, the Bandung Principles, and the examples of truce in Korea and the experience of the 1954 Geneva conference on Indochina be guidelines for international relations in the region.

Gorbachev's proposal constitutes the most comprehensive package of regional arms control measures that any country in the region has advanced so far. Whether or not the Soviet initiative will be endorsed by other countries in the region and a regional arms control process launched will hinge mainly on actual Soviet behavior in such areas as Afghanistan, Indochina, and in the Pacific Ocean.

CHINA'S SECURITY IN THE REGIONAL CONTEXT, AND ITS OPTIONS

In defining China's security interests, it is crucial that the characteristics of the Asian-Pacific security system and the political trends that have security implications be kept in mind. Even if the prevailing political trends today are conducive to China's security, they are not irreversible and there are always many factors beyond China's control. But China is not impotent. The adoption of rational foreign and domestic policies, which presupposes rational decision-making processes, would give China more control in an environment shaped by geography, history, and politics.

China shares a common land border with twelve countries and has sea borders with four countries. Besides, there are two colonies, Hong Kong and Macao, and one political entity, Taiwan, that are presently not under the jurisdiction of the central government of China. Altogether they add up to nineteen, two more than the number of neighbors of the next country down the line—the Soviet Union—a country whose territory is twice as big as China's. Out of these nineteen, eight have territorial disputes with China: the Soviet Union, Vietnam, Afghanistan, India, Japan, Malaysia, the Philippines, and Bhutan. No relationship exists between China and South Korea. Taiwan, which procures part of its weapons from the United States, continues to be a worry for the defense planners of the central government of China. Altogether, these add up to ten. In other words, China has problems with more than half of her neighbors. Among these ten countries and political entities, the ones that now constitute a threat to mainland China are fewer. They are the Soviet Union, and to a lesser degree Vietnam and Taiwan. The United States, by supplying highly sophisticated weapons to Taiwan, poses an indirect worry to mainland China. The severity and complexity of China's security environment, rarely found in other countries, cannot be overemphasized. China has fought in Korea, in the Taiwan Strait, against the Soviet Union, India, Vietnam, and South Vietnam (the Chinese–South Vietnamese naval conflict of 1974), but only once with each party (discounting minor clashes) since 1949. The geopolitical situation China finds itself in poses a great challenge to her defense and foreign policies and to the government's intra-Chinese policy.

The "Big Triangle"

China may be the only country in the world that has to worry about both the Soviet Union and the United States as far as its security is concerned. Such being the case, the skillful management of China's relations with the two superpowers is the key to the assurance of China's security.

In the past thirty-nine years, China's foreign-policy stance in relation to the Soviet Union and the United States has followed three patterns: balance of power (alignment with one power against the other, 1949–59 and 1971–82), opposition to both powers (1960–71), and asymmetrical rapprochement and neutrality in relation to the two powers (1982 to the present). During this period, the balance-of-power behavior has been the dominant pattern, prevailing over 53 percent of the time (twenty-one years), with the second and third types of behavior taking up 28 percent and 18 percent of the time (eleven and seven years) respectively.

The deep structural reason for the predominance of balance-of-power behavior lies in China's economic and military weakness in comparison with the two superpowers, hence its inability to safeguard its interests by relying on its own power alone. Besides, there is also the long historical tradition of "using foreigners to oppose foreigners." It can be expected that before China catches up with the USSR and the United States in terms of aggregate power (something that may happen during the years 2025–50), China's foreign-policy behavior vis-à-vis the USSR and the United States may move along a continuum of balance of power and neutrality. Whether it will move toward one end or the other, and if it does, what kind of balancing (balancing whom against whom) and neutrality (untilted or tilted toward whom) act it will be, will depend on such factors as the extent to which the Soviet Union is ready to remove the "three obstacles" to normalized Sino-Soviet relations; how well the Taiwan question in Sino-U.S. relations is managed; the extent to which Sino-U.S. relations become institutionalized and acquire a dynamic of their own; the extent of development of Sino-Soviet economic relations; the balance of forces between the United States and the USSR; the extent of Japanese rearmament; and political developments in China.

While China may obtain certain benefits through balance-of-power behavior, such behavior also has its costs. It may work to increase the overall level of tension in China's international relations, reduce China's room to maneuver, and sow seeds of distrust that adversely affect the long-term prospects of any healthy relationship. In view of this, China should avoid engaging in balance-of-power behavior to the extent possible and make an effort to develop Sino-U.S. and Sino-Soviet relations on their own respective merits and for their own respective values.

It is in the security interest of China and of the region that China continue to watch out for Soviet actions in the region.

Although it is inappropriate for the Chinese government to make a commitment to the U.S. government not to use force in the resolution of the Taiwan question, the use of force to reintegrate Taiwan with the mainland—the reopening of civil war—would be a national disaster. The threat by some leaders of the Chinese government to impose a naval blockade on Taiwan if the KMT refuses to talk peace is counterproductive and only serves to alienate the people living in Taiwan, hence retarding the process of reunification. The Chinese government should make an explicit declaration to our compatriots in Taiwan that under no circumstances shall force be used in the reunification effort as long as Taiwan does not become independent. Such a declaration will remove any rationale for the KMT authorities to continue to purchase highly sophisticated weaponry from the United States, develop nuclear weapons, and play the Soviet card, all of which can pose a threat to the security of the mainland. In order to accelerate the reunification process, the Chinese government may want to consider taking such radical measures as offering to sell defensive weapons to Taiwan; toning down opposition to Taiwan's procurement of limited defensive weapons from foreign countries; welcoming scientific, economic, military, legal and diplomatic leaders from the Taiwan government to come to work in the central government of China; and even allowing the Nationalist Party to come back to the mainland to run one or two provinces, with the Communist Party taking the role of opposition party (Fujian and Guangdong make good choices for such an experiment), and to compete peacefully with the Communist Party for political power at the national level.

International peace will also be well served if China continues to criticize certain self-righteous interventionist traits of U.S. foreign policy.

A vigorous expansion of China's economic ties with the United States and Soviet Union is in the interest of all three parties. China's security interest will be enhanced if American capital can merge with Soviet investment in China.

Northeast Asia

The Korean Peninsula is the most highly militarized area in the Asian-Pacific region. It is here where China got involved in the most severe military conflict in the history of the People's Republic.

Although nobody wants a second Korean war, the danger of another war exists. The problem is that all the relevant countries are still in varying degrees behaving as if nothing much has changed in the regional international environment since the last war. Every year, the United States and South Korea engage in what has now become the largest naval exercise in the world in waters not far from the Korean Peninsula. China and North Korea and the Soviet Union and North Korea try to keep the old memories alive by commemorating the anniversary of the establishment of their respective alliances. A state of "no war, no peace" prevails. Forces of inertia die hard.

To formulate a new policy on the question of Korea, the following changes should be taken into account: Neither North nor South Korea is a puppet of a foreign power; both have developed military capabilities that are in essential balance, reducing both sides' temptation, and ability, to solve the dispute by force; and both regimes have won some degree of domestic and international legitimacy. China no longer views the United States as wanting to use Korea as a springboard to attack her and is no longer in need of a buffer; the United States no longer views China as an expansive power; the Korean contradiction is now less one between the East and the West than one between rival political forces in Korea. Thus it is in the interest of everybody—North and South Korea, China, the United States, Japan, and the Soviet Union—that tension on the Korean Peninsula be reduced and the Korean question eventually be resolved and resolved peacefully. With these changes, it is indeed strange and abnormal that no drastically new policies have been adopted by anyone to try to promote an early settlement.

Instead of reemphasizing the alliance with North Korea in order to compete with the Soviet Union for its friendship, China should seize the initiative by establishing a commercial office and later a liaison office in Seoul. While encouraging North Korea to continue its bilateral talks with the South, China should urge it to agree to participate in a quadripartite conference on Korea attended by North and South Korea, China, and the United States—in essence not too different from the tripartite conference formula first put forward by the Carter administration and now agreed to by North Korea. At the same time, China should consult with the Soviet Union on ways and means to maintain stability on the Korean Peninsula and on prospective Soviet–South Korean relations, hence denying North Korea the Soviet card. China should encourage the United States and Japan to reciprocate this unilateral Chinese move by taking steps to open up similar relationships with North Korea, and should urge the United States and both Koreas to suspend military exercises in the meantime. It is in the best interest of the Korean nation that the final resolution of the Korean question be achieved in line with the formula of "one state, two systems" and eventually "one state, two (or more) parties."

Apart from the two Koreas themselves, peace and stability on the Korean Peninsula are of greater concern to China than they are to other major powers by virtue of geography and geoeconomics. History, culture, and geopolitics are such that China is now in the best position to take the initiative in pushing for an early equitable settlement of the Korean question, an initiative that should not await a second Korean war.

Southeast Asia

The main threat to international security in this region lies in Soviet-backed Vietnamese aggression against Cambodia. Such aggression has its origins in Vietnam's desire to augment its own power in order to balance the power of ASEAN and China. Besides, the large quantities of American weapons captured by Vietnam at the end of the Vietnam War provided strong temptation for their use.

China should continue resolutely to oppose the Vietnamese ambition to achieve hegemony in Indochina and should only normalize relations with Vietnam when its troops are pulled out of Cambodia. China should remain critical of the Soviet use of the facilities in Cam Ranh Bay and Da Nang and take a harsh position on the question of Vietnamese occupation of China's islands in the South China Sea.

The territorial disputes between China and the Philippines and Malaysia should be solved through negotiations, in accordance with international law. China should support efforts made by the Aquino government in the Philippines to reach a negotiated settlement with domestic insurgencies free from outside interference and should voice the same support if the other Southeast Asian countries that are faced with similar problems should decide to do the same.

Regional Arms Control

The Asian-Pacific region is now at a crossroads. It can develop either in the direction of formation of tighter military alliances and further militarization or in the direction of multilateral economic cooperation and arms control. China should opt for the latter. China should put forth a comprehensive regional arms control proposal that may cover, *inter alia,* such things as the reduction of Soviet and U.S. naval activities in the Pacific; the joint reduction of forces at the Sino-Soviet border; the withdrawal of troops from, and the dismantling of bases in, foreign territories; and the declaration of Southeast Asia and the Korean Peninsula as nuclear-free zones.

Pacific Economic Cooperation

Nonexclusive multilateral economic cooperation in the Pacific region is the wave of the future and offers a viable alternative to military rivalry in the region. As such, it should receive continued vigorous support from the Chinese government.

Domestic Reforms

The source of security lies not only in the external environment but, more importantly, in the domestic socioeconomic and political system. To replace the existing Stalinist war politicoeconomic system with neosocialism, which is defined as a free-enterprise economic system plus social security plus political democracy, would greatly enhance China's security.

The adoption of a free-enterprise, market-oriented economic system will help bring into full play the initiative of the whole people so as to more quickly generate greater wealth and power.

The adoption of a social security system supported by a modern progressive income tax system to guarantee the well-being of all citizens will contribute to social stability.

The establishment of a democratic political system, with a regular open competitive election system and government instead of party control of the military—supervised by the National People's Congress through the appropriation of defense expenditures and through sharing with the head of government the power to declare defensive war—will greatly increase the legitimacy of the government, hence promoting political stability and helping to identify more accurately where national interests lie. A government is strongest and the state most powerful when its legitimacy is based on a mandate from the people through periodic competitive elections rather than on a "mandate from heaven," blood ties, patrimonialism reflected in the words "With you in charge, I am at ease,"[11] revolutionary history, or a self-proclaimed and self-perpetuating leadership role by the few.

The situation of a nearly complete absence of open public debate on foreign and defense policy in China is most pathetic. Such a state of affairs is detrimental to China's security and is absolutely incompatible with China's status in the world. It is high time that this abnormal state of affairs was resolutely changed. Also, Chinese foreign policy should reflect the traditional values of the Chinese people. Such ancient Chinese precepts as "all men within the Four Seas are brothers," "the virtuous have no enemies," and "greatness lies in tolerance" should become mottoes for the foreign-policy decision-makers.

To sum up, what is advocated here is the adoption by China of a comprehensive security strategy—a grand strategy for the remaining part of this century and beyond. This strategy has six components: (1) continued improvement of China's relations with the United States and the Soviet Union on the basis of their respective merit and value; (2) commitment to a peaceful resolution of the Taiwan question as long as Taiwan does not become independent;

(3) seizing the initiative in contributing to the removal of "hot spots" and potential "hot spots" in Asia, Indochina, and Korea; (4) articulation of a comprehensive package of regional arms control measures; (5) vigorous support to, and serious study of, the concept of nonexclusive multilateral Pacific economic cooperation; and (6) completion of domestic economic and political reforms, and the reform and modernization of China's defense establishment.

What is needed is not just passive responses to the international environment but an active effort to seize the initiative to shape it with vision, resolve, and finesse.

TWO

CHINA
AND THE
TRIANGULAR
RELATIONSHIP

HONGQIAN ZHU

Ever since the People's Republic of China was founded, relations with the Soviet Union and the United States have occupied a central place in Chinese foreign policy. China's policy toward both superpowers can be satisfactorily understood in part through examining the triangular interactions of these three powers. While Beijing's policy has reflected China's response to American and Soviet policies, it has also reflected the responses of the latter two as well. During the 1950s, China allied itself with the Soviet Union against its principal enemy, the United States; during the 1960s, China gradually moved to an independent position against both the United States and the Soviet Union; during the 1970s, China improved relations with the United States in order to counter a perceived increase in the Soviet threat; and during much of the 1980s, China has followed a more flexible, independent foreign policy toward both the United States and the Soviet Union.

Changes in China's policy toward the superpowers over the decades raise two important questions. First, why did these changes occur as they did? Second, and perhaps more important, to what extent did these changes affect the triangular relationship? What kind of role has China played in the triangle? It has often been argued that China played a minimal role in the triangular relationship in the 1950s and 1960s, which was virtually dominated by Soviet-American relations. But this is not accurate. Even in the fifties and sixties, Chinese policy had a not insignificant impact on their policies. Since then, China has contributed, sometimes crucially, to the development of the triangular relationship. Indeed, "triangular politics" is a reality. The policies of each nation have been greatly shaped by the action of the others; each shapes policy with its consequence for the relationship among the three powers clearly in view. Today there has emerged a "positive balance" in the triangle. Serious disagreements and conflicts exist, especially between the United States and the Soviet Union, but the triangular relationship has become more mature, more stable, and more tranquil than in earlier years. At present, China is in the most favorable position it has occupied since 1949. In many ways, the current triangular structure provides more opportunities and potential benefits to China than to either of the other powers. Maintaining and strengthening this position will become a crucial part of Chinese foreign policy in the years ahead.

FIVE TRIANGULAR PATTERNS

1949–62: The First Pattern

From 1949 to 1962, the United States faced an alliance between the Soviet Union and China. In a triangular sense, it was in the interest of the United States to change its unfavorable position, altering its relations with either the Soviet Union or China. This prospect increased as Moscow sought to improve relations with the United States while Sino-American relations were in a state of tension.

Indeed, despite relatively high levels of tension in the late 1940s and early 1950s, the conflict between Moscow and Washington was noticeably restrained compared to what existed between Beijing and Washington. They avoided direct military confrontation and they continued to cooperate, though in a very limited manner, in areas such as the control of Germany. Neither side broke diplomatic relations nor was there a serious move to close the channel of access and communication through the United Nations.[1] Indeed, by the mid-fifties both realized that they shared a stake in consolidating and maintaining their respective areas of influence.

Tensions in Sino-American relations were considerably higher. The Korean War destroyed whatever hopes existed in the late 1940s for normalizing their relationship. Although starting in 1955 there were bilateral talks at the ambassadorial level, they simply reinforced mutual hostility. Deep suspicion and hatred on both sides prohibited any practical movement toward compromise or understanding. Washington's entire Asian policy was designed to counter the "China threat." The aim was to "contain" China, isolate it, reduce its influence abroad, and exert constant external pressure on it.[2] Taiwan became the focus of Sino-American tensions. The United States not only sought to encircle China ideologically and militarily, but actively blocked Beijing's efforts to reunify the country.

Inside the United States, ideology and domestic politics played a greater negative role in American policy toward China than toward the Soviet Union. Postwar anticommunism was accelerated by the victory of the Chinese Revolution in 1949. The subsequent McCarthyism and Korean War reflected the deep U.S. frustration over "the loss of China" in both its domestic politics and foreign policies. These events, coupled with the activities of the "China Lobby," made it impossible for the American government to adopt any policy that would lead to a normal relationship with China.[3]

In the mid-1950s, Soviet leadership changes brought about a substantial shift in Soviet foreign policy toward a greater emphasis on the relaxation of tensions with the United States. The positive response from the Eisenhower administration to the Soviet gesture of détente in 1955 presented a sharp contrast to its rigid rejection of Beijing's various efforts to find a common ground with Washington between 1955 and 1957.[4] Although the two "spirits" (the spirit of Geneva in 1955 and the spirit of Camp David in 1959) disappeared almost as quickly as they appeared, they nevertheless laid the foundation for the emergence of détente in the 1960s. In the meantime, American policy-makers believed that it was unnecessary for a superpower like the United States to negotiate with a militarily weak, economically backward Communist China. They saw the PRC as a virtual "client state" of the Soviet Union. They hoped that the new government in Beijing would be a "passing" phenomenon, and that continued United States political, military, and economic pressure would hasten its demise.[5] The PRC, for its part, was in a relatively disadvantageous position in the triangle. Its alliance with the Soviet Union, though offering many advantages, also restricted its foreign-policy options.

In reality, neither the Soviet Union nor the United States really recognized the strategic weight of China in the triangle. The Soviets wanted China dependent on the Soviet Union, while the Americans believed that China was an integral part of a "monolithic" Soviet-led bloc. Meanwhile, China allied itself with the Soviet Union and was thus no longer free to maneuver between the other powers. There is no clear evidence from American sources that the United States attempted to break up the alliance between the Soviet Union and China by improving relations with the Soviets. But Washington did hope that détente would encourage the Soviets to help them "contain" China. American policy-makers were delighted with Khrushchev's withdrawal of help for the Chinese nuclear program, his reluctance to back up the Chinese during the 1958 Taiwan Strait Crisis, and the Soviet refusal to take sides with China during the 1962 Chinese-Indian border conflict. In this sense, then, China constituted a factor in the development of Soviet-American relations, which, in turn, contributed greatly to the split between Beijing and Moscow, since any improvement in Soviet-American relations would be unfavorable to Chinese interests if it included continued American hostility to China. On the other hand, China's opposition put a brake, if only temporarily, on Soviet movement toward détente with the United States, in the late 1950s and early 1960s.[6]

1963–69: The Second Pattern

From 1963 to 1969, China confronted the enmity of both the United States and the Soviet Union; indeed, Beijing faced a relatively positive Soviet-American relationship and even a potential collaboration against China. The Cuban Missile Crisis in 1962 and the fear of a nuclear collision in the future made both the United States and the Soviet Union anxious to improve relations. Both sides seemed to realize that in a nuclear age practical steps had to be taken to control the arms race. The signing of the Nuclear Test-Ban Treaty in the summer of 1963 thus began a new era in Soviet-American relations in which talks on limiting nuclear weapons and arms control became important elements.

This Soviet-American détente effectively shattered the alliance between China and the Soviet Union. Beijing believed that the Test-Ban Treaty was an act of American-Soviet collusion to monopolize nuclear weapons and prevent China from developing its own. The treaty marked the end of China's efforts to stop the Soviet Union from seeking détente with the United States. Since compromise with either of the superpowers at the expense of its ideological and national interests was out of the question, Beijing had to take an independent course between Washington and Moscow. It then began searching vigorously for a third international force that could counter both "American imperialism" and "Soviet revisionism" and their growing relationship. China denounced both superpowers as enemies of national liberation movements and identified the underdeveloped countries of Africa, Asia, and Latin America as China's natural friends and allies. China's active contact with the countries outside the two military blocs formed by the United States and the Soviet Union began at the Bandung Afro-Asian Conference in 1955 in an effort to break American encirclement. Now this contact gained a new meaning and momentum. China not only greatly increased diplomatic exchanges with many of these countries but substantially expanded its economic assistance to them.[7] These contacts, though interrupted briefly by the eruption of the "Cultural Revolution," increased China's prestige and political influence in the world, shown in the the PRC's admission to the U.N. in 1971, a move supported by many Third World countries.

Beijing's dual conflict with Washington and Moscow, accelerated by the Cultural Revolution that started in 1966, put it in a very difficult and dangerous position. Strategically and militarily, it was faced with two threats: in the South, there were tensions with the United States, particularly over the Vietnam War; in the North, there was a dramatic buildup of Soviet forces along the border, which culminated in the 1969 border clashes that threatened to become a serious Soviet military conflict with China. The Soviets even flirted with the idea of collaborating with the United States for a strike against China's nuclear facilities.[8] Although the United States would not take the idea seriously, the fact that there were great tensions in Sino-American relations could only increase the Soviet temptation to take military steps against China. Therefore, national security had to take priority over ideology, domestic politics, and other considerations; the highly unbalanced situation had to be changed. Consequently, China sought to make the triangular structure more favorable to itself by changing its relations with Washington, since they were visibly less tense than the relationship with Moscow during the second part of the 1960s.

1970–75: The Third Pattern

Between 1970 and 1975, the triangular relationship changed dramatically with the Sino-American rapprochement. Countering the Soviet threat became the common ground for both to move together. For China it was vitally important to reduce the cost and danger of a possible "two-front war" by improving relations with the United States, so as to concentrate its resources against the bigger adversary, the Soviet Union. For the United States, it was necessary to reduce the cost of the "two-and-a-half-war strategy" by improving relations with China so as to concentrate its main military resources on deterring the Soviet Union.[9] The two powers also had some other concerns of their own. It was in China's interest to find some solution to the reunification of Taiwan with the mainland through Sino-American rapprochement. On the American side, the strategic motivation behind the rapprochement included capitalizing on the Sino-Soviet split to gain leverage over both the Soviet Union and China and heading off a Sino-Soviet rapprochement.[10]

The rapid improvement in Chinese-American relations had a profound impact on Soviet strategic thinking and planning. By the end of the 1960s, détente with the United States had declined to a new low level following the Soviet invasion of Czechoslovakia in 1968. The Soviets were facing a very tense relationship with the Chinese and a possible deterioration in their relationship with the Americans. The development in Sino-American relations naturally caused great alarm in the Soviet leadership at the possibility of a coordinated Sino-American strategy of a "two-front war" against the Soviets, and at the tendency to "be the isolated side of the emerging triangular relationship."[11] To avoid this, Moscow sought to step up its advances to Washington.

Washington evidently concluded that the strategy of increasing the leverage on Moscow through Sino-American rapprochement had worked. As Washington desired, Soviet-American relations rose to a level considerably higher than that of Sino-American relations, particularly between 1972 and 1975. During these years, Washington enjoyed the pivotal role in its positive relations with both Beijing and Moscow, while the latter were still in a tense relationship.

However, the United States did not retain this pivotal position for long. The cost of maintaining it was inherently high. One reason was that having developed its relationship with Beijing to the extent that it had generated a higher level of Soviet-American détente, the United States then turned its major attention to the relationship with the Soviet Union. This "card-playing" behavior naturally caused China to question American sincerity. As one prominent Chinese scholar points out, " 'Card-playing' will not win the respect of the other party; on the contrary, it will cause a crisis of confidence."[12] As the development of Sino-American relations lost its momentum, the Soviet bargaining position vis-à-vis the United States increased.

Even if the United States treated its relations with China and the Soviet Union in an "evenhanded" fashion, neither of them wanted to see the other develop a positive relationship with Washington, and instead, would do its best to hinder it. Moreover, neither would like to see Washington "sitting on top of the hill while watching the two tigers fight." The "romantic triangle"[13] would not be very stable.

In those years, China was in the most unfavorable position and consequently sought to develop its relations with the United States. But this proved most effective when there was a decline in Soviet-American détente, which increased the American incentive to develop a better Sino-American relationship. Therefore, from the early 1970s, China never stopped warning the Americans of the consequences of détente with the Soviets. Indeed, China strongly advocated that détente would only make the Soviets more aggressive and that only by strengthening the American military posture could Soviet expansionism be checked.

1976–81: The Fourth Pattern

Between 1976 and 1981, the Soviet Union, for the first time since 1949, was in the most negative position in the triangle. It had tense relations with both China and the United States, while being faced with new momentum in Sino-American relations. By 1981 the degree of tension between Washington and Moscow appeared to be greater than that between Moscow and Beijing.

The question of why Soviet-American relations so declined has been much debated.[14] Both Soviet and American leaders desired détente. Both wanted to avoid a nuclear war and hoped to benefit economically from each other. Apart from these, however, they had few fundamental objectives in common. In the words of an American scholar, the United States was basically the "status quo power" and the Soviet Union was the "revolutionary power" seeking to change the status quo.[15] Thus, their ultimate goals were understandably different. For the Soviet Union, détente would not only have made it an equal of the United States in world politics but would also have given it the opportunity to expand its influence to the areas where American interests were predominant. For the United States, détente represented a radical change as a means of American containment policy. "Whereas in the past containment had depended primarily on American power and Soviet caution, in the future it was to depend on Soviet restraint."[16] This shift from past policy, along with the overselling of détente by the Nixon administration, not only ran counter to the emerging dominant conservative trends in the middle of the 1970s within the United States but encouraged Soviet expansionist tendencies, which, in turn, further strengthened the conservative opposition to détente. Thus, it was understandable that President Ford finally dropped the word détente and at the beginning of 1976 decided to freeze the SALT process.[17]

President Carter sought to pursue an "evenhanded" policy, hoping that American interests would be best served by seeking to improve relations with both Moscow and Beijing simultaneously, and that this position in the triangle would provide incentives for the latter two to continue their forward movement with the United States.[18] Yet such a policy could not be successful when both China and the Soviet Union were in tension, for both would then resent such an American approach, from which only Washington could really benefit. As a result, the level of Beijing-Washington relations actually dropped in 1977, and no significant progress was achieved in Soviet-American relations. The failure of the policy resulted in a shift from Secretary of State Cyrus Vance's "evenhandedness" to National Security Adviser Zbigniew Brzezinski's "balance of power." "The Administration came to recognize that the way in which we sought to improve relations with the two would have to take into account the difference between the two countries and the threats they posed to us."[19] Again, China and the United States based the development of their relations on their common concern with the Soviet threat.[20] The Soviet invasion of Afghanistan further consolidated the relations by strengthening the military and security ties between the two powers, which many officials in Washington viewed as a principal way for the United States to respond to Soviet actions.[21]

Thus, China's position vis-à-vis the two superpowers in the triangle was noticeably strengthened. As one scholar has noted, the United States had irrevocably lost the positive pivotal seat in the strategic triangle; there was no longer any possibility of restoring détente with the Soviet Union and there was even less possibility of isolating the PRC, because the United States needed China as an ally.[22] This pattern offered China the greatest diplomatic opportunities it had had since 1949. To preserve its favorable prospects, China consciously kept a distance from the idea of forming a military alliance with the United States, even when it vigorously advocated the formation of a "united front" against Soviet expansionism. Indeed, China had just declared the official end of the Sino-Soviet alliance treaty signed in 1950, which had constrained China's diplomatic options. An alliance with the United States could only mean the loss once again of China's independence, maneuverability, and initiative.

It has been argued that China could have used the new triangular relationship after 1976 to cultivate new relations with the Soviet Union. But China could do so only if it had a strong relationship with the United States. Before the end of 1978 and early 1979, Beijing had been preoccupied with the normalization of relations with Washington and then the troubling relationship with the Vietnamese. Only well after the border conflict with Vietnam did China begin to explore the possibility of improving relations with the Soviet Union. This process, however, was soon disrupted by the Soviet invasion of Afghanistan, which was considered a serious Soviet strategic and security threat to China. Later, when negotiations with Moscow resumed, Beijing raised three preconditions for the normalization of relations between the two countries: withdrawal of a substantial number of Soviet troops from the Sino-Soviet and Sino-Mongolian borders; withdrawal of Moscow's support of Vietnam's occupation of Cambodia; and withdrawal of Soviet troops from Afghanistan. These preconditions, along with the initially strong response to the Soviet action, served as a warning to the Soviets that normalization would become impossible if similar events happened in the process of future negotiations. Therefore, a principal purpose of these preconditions was to guard against such future Soviet behavior rather than to cut off China's talks with the Soviets at the time.

On the whole, as Sino-Soviet relations remained tense, the decline of Soviet-American relations pushed the positive Sino-American relations to a new high level in 1979. Apart from the conclusion and signing of SALT II, Moscow did not behave very sensitively to the development of Sino-American relations when it took military action in Afghanistan in December 1979. The result was that both Sino-Soviet and Soviet-American relations declined even further. The unwise move into Afghanistan revealed the serious suspicion among the Soviet leaders of the potentiality of Sino-American strategic cooperation and their underestimation of China's role in the triangle.[23] But the strong Chinese and American reaction and their closer military ties in 1980 seemed to have convinced the Soviets that they could no longer ignore China's role in the strategic balance and the reality of triangular politics.

Since 1982: The Fifth Pattern

As Sino-American relations became more stabilized, Sino-Soviet relations improved rather rapidly. While some tensions still exist in Soviet-American relations, mainly in such areas as the arms race and competition in the Third World, frequent conversations and positive developments in economic and some other areas have substantially reduced tension and contributed to an overall "neither cold nor warm" superpower relationship in which the chance for further improvement seems to exist, as the Intermediate-range Nuclear Forces (INF) Treaty signed in December 1987 by the two powers has indicated. Indeed, in the past few years there appears to have emerged a *positive balance* in the triangle, with China occupying the most favorable position.

The crucial change in these years has been the noticeable improvement in Sino-Soviet relations since 1982. Although it considered its relations with the United States as most important, the Soviet Union nevertheless found it difficult in practice to improve them at the time. In the early 1980s, Moscow-Washington relations were tense, due largely to the Soviet invasion of Afghanistan and the Carter administration's strong reaction to it. The relations did not change much after Reagan came to office. Indeed, tensions remained relatively high, since the Reagan administration saw East-West, or more specifically Soviet-American, relations in strong ideological terms. In its first two years, the administration ruled out any quick improvement in Soviet-American relations.

On the other hand, Washington's unfavorable response to Moscow's gestures of improving relations made the latter more eager to improve relations with Beijing. As one observer has noted, the informal strategic linkage between China and the United States also "accelerated Moscow's efforts to foster a reduction of tensions in Sino-Soviet relations."[24] A hope might be lingering in the Soviet mind: A possible improvement in Sino-Soviet relations might improve Soviet-American relations while loosening the strategic ties between Beijing and Washington.

However, any change in Sino-Soviet relations now had to take place in the context of the Chinese adoption in 1982 of a more independent foreign policy.[25] The development of Sino-American relations in the first two years of the Reagan administration was not satisfactory to the Chinese. The administration looked at China as merely a regional power rather than one that played a strategic role in the world balance of power. This assessment led American officials to play down strategic cooperation between China and the United States. Reagan's anti-Communist rhetoric negatively affected Beijing-Washington relations. Taiwan again became the focus of Sino-American relations since at least for ideological reasons the administration tried to keep and even wanted a closer relationship with the "old friends" on the island. The result of all this was that by 1982 Sino-American relations, although positive, were at a relatively low level.

In addition, by 1982 China had realized that it could develop and maintain relatively good relations with both the United States and the Soviet Union. After all, the Soviet threat was primarily global and directed mainly against the United States and Western Europe. China was a target of secondary importance. Moreover, in the early 1980s Soviet assertiveness was significantly counterbalanced by the substantial increase in United States military spending, particularly during the early years of the Reagan administration. The Soviet threat still existed but had become less imminent than it was in earlier years. Under these circumstances, therefore, China could develop practical economic and cultural relations with the Soviet Union without upsetting the overall existing balance. On the other hand, Beijing had every reason to be concerned with a possible recurrence of tension with both Washington and Moscow. Such a possibility seemed to be increasing between 1981 and 1982. One way to prevent it was to have a more flexible foreign policy which, if managed well, could bring about relatively good relations with both of the other two powers.

Apart from strategic concerns, other factors were pushing the two sides closer together. Ideologically, China no longer described the Soviet Union as "revisionist" or "social imperialist." Each recognized the other as a socialist country, though differences still existed in some theoretical areas. Each now adopted an agenda of economic and political reforms. Diplomatically, China gradually abandoned the line of opposing whatever the Soviet Union was supporting and turned instead to improving relations with some of the countries that had good relationships with the Soviet Union. Economically, both sides had strong incentives for bilateral exchanges, particularly border trade that didn't require hard currencies. Similar interest also existed in increasing cultural and scientific exchange.

Thus, under the circumstances of the early 1980s both China and the Soviet Union had some strong reasons to improve their relations. As Sino-Soviet relations improved relatively rapidly after 1982, so did Sino-American relations. Interestingly, the most visible development in both Sino-Soviet and Sino-American relations has occurred in the economic, trade, and cultural fields.

Although it is hard to determine how much impact the development of Sino-Soviet relations had on Soviet-American relations, the latter nevertheless improved after 1982. Mutual accusations declined noticeably, while actual dialogue increased. In the last two years, the frequent contact between the two powers has also led to some concrete results, such as the INF Treaty and the Soviet promise to withdraw its troops from Afghanistan. Obviously, Washington did not like to see its position decline to the most unfavorable one in the triangle (this prospect seemed to be close in 1983 when both Sino-American and Soviet-American relations were at a low level and Sino-Soviet relations at a much higher level). Consequently, Washington tried to improve relations with both Beijing and Moscow. Indeed, after 1982 the United States appeared to have followed a line close to what Robert A. Scalapino has called an "equilibrium" policy—a strategy "based upon a conscious effort to keep relations with Russia and China in rough balance, cognizant of the fact that the two relationships must be significantly different. . . . This strategy requires that the United States avoid a sustained tilt toward either Moscow or Peking, eschewing the concept of alignment with one against the other. Rather, it is based upon the premise that maximum flexibility is preferable for the United States in both cases. The aim would be a broadening of each relationship but with a clear understanding that major differences between us will continue to prevail."[26]

Interestingly, the other two powers—China and the Soviet Union—have carried out a similar policy, particularly since 1983. Beijing's independent foreign policy indicates that it has wanted not only to continue to develop relations with Washington but also to reduce tensions and improve relations with Moscow. The same is true for Moscow.

However, a policy of relations in "equilibrium" here does not necessarily mean "equidistant" or "evenhanded." Indeed, none of the three powers has adopted an "equidistant" policy toward the others. Each relationship contains differences which vary in both degree and kind from those of the other two; each power evaluates differently the relative salience and importance of its respective relationships with the other two. In terms of security interests, trade, and technology, the United States is more important to China than the Soviet Union, thus China's foreign policy gives more weight to the development of Sino-American relations than to Sino-Soviet relations. On the other hand, the latter's improvement could stimulate the former, as trends since 1982 have shown. For both the United States and the Soviet Union, the management of their superpower relationship is more important than their respective relationships with China since each considers the other to be the major threat to its security and strategic interests and each has a similar nuclear arsenal that could destroy the earth many times. Hence each would calculate how much its relationship with China would affect its strategic balance with the other. This consideration sometimes leads them to give priority to developing relations with China in order to have a stronger position in the superpower relationship, as the trends after 1982 have also indicated.

In sum, in these years each member of the triangle has adopted a relatively balanced policy and more than ever has recognized the strategic salience and independent position of the others. All three subrelationships have close interactions with one another, each with a relatively high sensitivity to the changes in the others. In other words, the triangular relationship has become more mature, with each member knowing relatively well how to deal with the others in the triangle. As a result, the three powers have more potential for peaceful coexistence than under any previous pattern.

SOME REFLECTIONS ON THE TRIANGULAR RELATIONSHIP

A careful examination of the triangular relationship since 1949 helps us to see how and why each power might adopt different policies in different patterns. In particular, it helps us more fully understand why China has changed its policies toward the United States and the Soviet Union over the years. It also helps us comprehend the kind of role China has played in the triangle. China's role has been far greater than many people have thought. Any low assessment of China's role in the past triangular evolution may entail risky underestimation of its role in the future development of the triangular relationship.

Besides all this, it is also useful to look at some of the lessons from the past in order to understand the present and to try to predict the possible future course of the triangular relationship, and of Chinese policy toward the two superpowers in particular.

The first lesson is that when any of the three powers conducts its relations with the others in terms of ideology and/or too much under the dominance of domestic politics, there will be tensions in the triangle and the subrelationships will show less sensitivity to each other. In the 1950s, anticommunism in the United States, and the strong anti-American imperialist line and the "two-camp" theory adopted by the Soviet Union and China, contributed greatly to the political, military, and economic tensions between the Soviet Union and China on one side and the United States on the other. During the 1960s, the Chinese Cultural Revolution, in its drive for a pure ideological identity, exacerbated China's tensions with both the United States and the Soviet Union. Indeed, ideological and domestic political factors help explain why the changes in Soviet-American and Sino-Soviet relations seem to have had little immediate impact on Sino-American relations during the decade. In the early years of the Reagan administration, the ideological resurgence in American foreign policy partially explains why Sino-American relations developed slowly at the same time tensions continued in Soviet-American relations. "Experiences show that overemphasis on ideological differences, mixing them up with state relations, would do more harm than good."[27] Some American observers have also noted the incompatibility between ideology and reality. For the United States, one writes, "it is difficult to befriend China since the U.S. is subject to two conflicting impulses: anti-Sovietism and anticommunism."[28] The danger of ideological domination in foreign policy is that it "undermines the reality principle itself," and in the end national interests must set limits on ideology.[29] It seems that the Reagan administration has gradually realized this in its conduct of foreign relations.

At present, there is no sign that ideology will dominate foreign policy in any of the three countries in the near future. In the United States in recent years, the intensity of ideological rhetoric has been noticeably reduced. It is very unlikely that the Bush administration will ever be as ideological as the Reagan administration. Unless there is some big external event that affects the American public profoundly, domestic politics will not be strong enough to dominate the direction of American foreign policy toward the Soviet Union and China. In the Soviet Union, the chance of foreign policy being dominated by ideology or domestic politics is no greater than that in the United States. There has been "an erosion of the old ideological intensity" and "a good deal of what remains is simply a vocabulary in which Soviet leaders are accustomed to speak."[30] The three Soviet changes of leadership in the early part of the 1980s have had positive rather than negative effect on both Soviet-American and Sino-Soviet relations. Gorbachev seems to be more pragmatic and flexible in his foreign-policy approach than most of his predecessors. In China pragmatism and realism also prevail in the conduct of its relations with the superpowers. Beijing has become more flexible toward Washington and Moscow, trying to develop relations with both of them. In the meantime, political instability such as that caused by the Cultural Revolution is very unlikely to recur in the foreseeable future. Indeed, the pragmatic approach of all three powers is strongly reflected in their relatively balanced policies toward each other.

The second lesson is that a formal alliance creates rigidity and severely limits flexibility in one's foreign policy. In the 1950s and early 1960s, the alliance with the Soviet Union put China in a disadvantageous position and its interests frequently at the risk of being sacrificed by the stronger power, the Soviet Union. In addition, China found it very difficult to develop relations with the United States since the latter felt that it would be more convenient to deal with the Soviet Union and that China was merely a client of the Soviet Union. The Chinese experience has also indicated that the process of breaking from an alliance is hard, painful, and costly, and that any alliance between two powers in the triangle tends to prolong and even increase tensions in the triangle. Therefore, in order to maximize flexibility in foreign policy and to improve its position in the triangle and reduce tensions with the others, China will try to avoid forming an alliance with one against the third. Indeed, Beijing has more than once declared that it will follow an independent and assertive foreign policy and will not ally itself with one power against the other.[31]

The third lesson is that the change from one pattern to another has to do with the dynamic interactions between the power that occupies the least favorable position in the triangle and the power that has the most favorable position. In the 1950s, both the United States and the Soviet Union tended to seek improved relations with each other; their interactions eventually led to the second pattern. The interactions between China and the United

States in the late 1960s and early 1970s brought about the third pattern. When the United States failed to maintain its positive pivotal position in the mid-1970s, its interaction with China gave birth to the fourth pattern. The interaction between the Soviet Union and China in the early 1980s finally resulted in the fifth pattern.

These five patterns show that if there are substantial tensions in one or two of the subrelationships in the triangle, the interaction between the two powers occupying the most and least favorable positions becomes very crucial in generating instability in the existing pattern that eventually leads to a new one. The initiative is more likely to come from the least-favored power since such an interaction would improve its position vis-à-vis its major adversary. If there are no substantial tensions in any of the subrelationships, the power in the least favorable position will also seek to develop relations with the most favored power in order to push forward its relations with the third power, rather than to oppose it. In this latter case, all the three subrelationships could potentially improve as each state wants either to seek or maintain the most favorable position in the triangle by trying to improve relations with the others. The current situation, as revealed earlier in the fifth pattern, somewhat resembles this case.

OPPORTUNITIES, CONSTRAINTS, AND CHOICES

Foreign policy involves opportunities, constraints, and choices. Opportunity arises when a country can pursue and achieve its goals at a smaller cost. Constraints put limits on what one can pursue and achieve by either decreasing benefits or increasing costs. Policy choices are made according to the opportunities and constraints available to the policy-makers at the time. Within the triangle, then, what will China's opportunities, constraints, and choices be in the years ahead?

The manner in which Soviet-American relations develop will be crucial to the future of Sino-American and Sino-Soviet relations. In other words, the state of the relationship between the two superpowers provides opportunities for, as well as constraints on, Chinese policy. The following scenarios look at three possible developments in Soviet-American relations and at China's choices under these different opportunities and constraints.

A Rapid Deterioration in Soviet-American Relations

Under this scenario, the arms race intensifies (with an increasing number of nuclear tests, for example) and there is military instability between the United States and the USSR. Competition in the Third World increases with military interventions by either or both. Relations in economic, trade, cultural, and other areas decline. Dialogue between the two is substantially reduced; the volume of accusations rises. Under these circumstances, China for a while would occupy a positive position, enjoying good relations with the two while high tensions exist between them. For China, opportunities are great, with potentially high benefits; but constraints are considerable, with potentially high costs. Choices would not be easy to make. There are four strategies China might pursue.

MAXIMIZING STRATEGY. China might try to develop relations with both superpowers in such a way that they could reap the maximum benefits from any tension between them. In the short run, this could work. It might gain further concessions from both since they now need China much more than before. In the long run, however, there might be a backlash against Chinese interests. Neither of the superpowers would like to see China holding the pivotal position, gaining enormously from their hostile relationship. Each would want China to develop a relationship with itself rather than with the other. Increasingly, Moscow would consider any development in Sino-American relations as against its interests, and would take measures to block it. Likewise, any improvement in Sino-Soviet relations might antagonize Washington, thus affecting Sino-American relations. In this case, China would find itself in a position of potentially high benefits and high costs.

MAINTAINING STRATEGY. China might try to maintain the current level of relations with both superpowers. No further attempt would be made to push forward the relationship with either of them. Instead, China might privately and publicly urge both sides to reduce tensions through negotiation. However, unless it is joined with a similar voice from both American and Soviet allies and Third World countries, this policy may not be very successful in *persuading* the superpowers into reducing tensions.

PRESSURING STRATEGY. China might detach itself from both superpowers by reducing interactions with them, somewhat lowering the current level of relations with each of them, but not to the level of tension. In the meantime, China might publicly denounce both superpowers' policies and actions, warning the world of the possibility of war, and mobilizing world opinion against the two superpowers, in an effort to *pressure* the superpowers into reducing the intensity of confrontation.

BALANCING STRATEGY. China might tilt toward one against the other so as to keep a balance between the two superpowers. This balancing role would depend on Beijing's calculation of the respective military capabilities of the two powers, each one's threat to China's security and strategic interests, each one's influence in the world, the probability of each one initiating a war, and other factors. This policy might result in a substantial improvement in China's relations with one at the cost of deteriorating relations with the other.

Each of the above choices involves different benefits and costs to China. They also depend on how long the perceived high level of tension between the superpowers will last. If the tensions extend only for a very limited period of time, both the maximizing and the maintaining strategies could bring considerable benefits at relatively little cost. But if high tensions last for several years, as they usually do, a series of strategies may be needed. When Soviet-American relations begin to deteriorate rapidly, China may use the maximizing strategy. As tensions continue, it may then use the maintaining strategy, which may be followed by the pressuring strategy. When there occurs an increasing military imbalance between the two superpowers, the balancing strategy may be applied.

A Rapid Improvement in Soviet-American Relations

In this scenario, the two superpowers reach a new level of détente. The arms race slows down; nuclear testing is suspended. Meaningful agreements on arms control are reached. There is also a visible restraint on competition in the Third World. Accusations are rarely heard on either side. Relations in economic, trade, cultural, and other areas noticeably improve. There are frequent high-level contacts in a good, if not warmly friendly, atmosphere. Under these circumstances, China would lose its most favorable position in the triangle. It could be reduced to the least favorable position if the level of Soviet-American relations is substantially high. China's position would be made worse with the possibility that both superpowers may now need China much less than before as they focus on and enjoy a better relationship with each other than with China. Thus, China would have to try to regain its favorable position. However, opportunities would be relatively few, with only moderate benefits; constraints would be great, with considerable costs; and choices would be both limited and hard to make. Overall, China may take the following three policy directions.

SIMULTANEOUSLY IMPROVING STRATEGY. China might try to improve its relations with both superpowers simultaneously in an effort to push the levels of these relations once again above the level of Soviet-American relations so that it could regain the most favorable position in the triangle. But this means that China would have to endure substantial costs—costs that may be much higher than those paid by the other two powers. China would have to make more concessions, since both superpowers would need China much less than before. Each of them might be more reluctant to resolve existing problems with China. In a word, the more China pushes forward its relations with the other two, the more costs it would bring. Indeed, with increasing costs, it would still be uncertain whether China could regain the most favorable position.

DIFFERENTIATING STRATEGY. China might calculate the differences between the two superpowers and concentrate on developing the relationship considered to entail less cost. This would be the relationship with the United States, since it is currently much better and therefore easier to develop than the relationship with the Soviet Union. This strategy might help strengthen the United States' most-favorable position but at the same time China might avoid the least favorable position in the triangle. In the meantime, it could increase Soviet incentive to develop relations with China, but the extent of such an incentive is difficult to determine. Undoubtedly, this strategy could also be quite costly, but not as costly and uncertain as the first strategy.

WAITING STRATEGY. However, China might just try to keep relations with the other two unchanged and do no more, with the expectation that détente between the two superpowers would not last very long.

51

Of course, these strategies are not totally exclusive of each other, and they could be used interchangeably.

Neither Cold nor Warm Relations Between the United States and the Soviet Union

The arms race continues at a relatively moderate level. Nuclear testing may be conducted, though infrequently. There is a rough military balance between the two. Arms control agreements are difficult to reach, but talks nevertheless continue and neither side wants to deny access and refuse dialogue. Competition in the Third World is maintained at a relatively controlled level, but some hot spots remain for potential confrontation. There are some positive developments in economic, trade, cultural, and other areas. There are exchanges of visits and meetings at high levels, though the results often indicate disappointment or failure rather than progress. Accusations are routinely heard, coupled with the expression of desires to improve relations. In short, tension still persists in some areas, cooperation in others. Competition goes hand in hand with negotiation and some relaxation of tension. The relationship has a tendency toward improvement, but it could also go in the other direction or merely remain with little visible change. The current level of superpower relationship largely resembles this scenario.

Today both superpowers need China (no less than China needs them) in order to strengthen their positions, but the need is not strong enough to force China to make a choice between them. Indeed, a tendency toward improved Soviet-American relations reduces much of the difficulty in China's conduct of relations with the superpowers. For China, opportunities are great; constraints are relatively low. Choices can be made with more subtlety and calculation, designed to maintain and strengthen China's favorable position.

"STATUS QUO" STRATEGY. China might seek just to maintain the current levels of relations with both superpowers and do no more.

DUAL-TRACK STRATEGY. China might try to further develop relations with both superpowers at the same time. Neither superpower would be offended since both wish to improve relations with each other as well as with China. This strategy could also better prepare China to deal with a possible deterioration of relations between the superpowers. It could achieve all this by creating as wide a distance as possible between the level of Soviet-American relations and the levels of China's relations with the two. This requires that the latter must rise faster than the former. The problem with this strategy is that China's relations with the superpowers may not always be smooth. On some issues China may have to be prepared for the reluctance of each superpower to make a quick concession, or to make much concession at all.

STIMULATING STRATEGY. The limitations of a dual-track strategy might be partially compensated by another strategy—that is, pushing forward one relationship through developing the other.[32] This is actually what happened after 1982. It might be applied in the future because it could provide China with much beneficial flexibility and power of initiative in the triangle. Its success, however, depends much on the sensitivity of one superpower to the development of the other's relationship with China and on the speed and extent of such a development.

PRIORITY STRATEGY. China may give priority to the development of one relationship over the other, depending on the influence each superpower has on China's interests and its respective differences with them. Currently, China and the Soviet Union are still in the process of normalizing relations with each other. The three obstacles are being slowly removed, but some differences between the two sides are yet to be resolved. On the other hand, both Beijing and Washington continue to have a strong convergence of security interests in the Asian-Pacific region. Moreover, China needs advanced Western technology and management expertise for its modernization, which cannot be gained from the exchange with the Soviets. Thus, there is a strong reason to believe that China will continue, as it has done in the recent years, to give priority to developing its relationship with the United States, though some obstacles—the Taiwan issue, problems arising from the different social and economic systems, and trade issues—may emerge from time to time and haunt both sides.

The current Chinese policy appears to be a mixture of the second, third, and fourth strategies. It hopes to develop relations with both the United States and the Soviet Union, but it gives priority to Sino-American relations. At the same time, China also wishes to stimulate its relations with one power through developing

53

its relations with the other. In order to understand more clearly the future direction of the Chinese policy under the current situation, let us look more specifically at Beijing's policy choices toward Moscow and Washington.

Moscow

For convenience, policies toward the Soviet Union will be considered first.

A "HARD LINE." Under this policy, China would emphasize the three major obstacles, insisting that without their removal any improvement of relations in other areas would be impossible. Under the third scenario, such a policy could only create rigidity and inflexibility. On the one hand, Beijing would forego some rare opportunities in the development of its relations with Moscow, which might bring to it considerable benefits. On the other, it could not be sure whether Moscow would yield to such Chinese pressure without some kind of concession from Beijing. Indeed, since 1982 China has not followed such a policy.

"LIMITED DÉTENTE."[33] China would improve economic, trade, cultural, and other relations with the Soviet Union while leaving major political and security issues unresolved. The question is whether development in other matters would not be severely hindered by serious differences in some major areas, or whether there would be no correlation between the former and the latter.

"GRADUAL NORMALIZATION PROCESS," A RELATIONSHIP OF "GOOD NEIGHBORS, BUT NOT ALLIES."[34] Beijing would continue to improve relations with Moscow in economic and other areas, at the same time also trying to resolve their major differences. It might use the former to quicken the process of the latter. The normalization process would be slow— not only because China's status as a political equal of the Soviet Union must be recognized and secured, but equally important, because China's priority of developing relations with the United States should not be upset by its relations with the Soviet Union. For China, then, the issue would not be whether it would normalize relations with the Soviet Union, but how to control its pace. When Soviet General Secretary Gorbachev suggested in August 1986 that the Soviet Union would withdraw "a substantial number of troops" from

Mongolia, China's reaction was both positive and cautious: It welcomed the Soviet proposal, but at the same time it reminded the Soviets that China's major concern was Soviet support of the Vietnamese troops in Cambodia.[35] Furthermore, Beijing restated that China would not waver in its support of Democratic Kampuchea's struggle against the Vietnamese occupation.[36] For the Soviets, this issue appears to be most difficult to resolve. Meanwhile, it gave a signal to the Americans that the pace of development of Sino-Soviet relations would not be fast. Indeed, more than two years have passed since August 1986, and the Cambodian issue is still the major obstacle to the development of political relations between the two countries.

However, there is strong reason to believe that if Soviet-American relations continue to show signs of further development, China may seek the opportunity to quicken the process of normalizing relations with the Soviet Union, with little negative effect on Sino-American relations.

Washington

In this context, then, what are Beijing's policy choices toward Washington? They would be different from those toward Moscow since the main concern here is not to normalize but to ensure a stable and strong relationship. Three possible directions may be noted.

RESOLVE THE TAIWAN ISSUE. China might give priority to resolving its differences with the United States on the Taiwan issue, based on the rationalization that only with the disappearance of this major obstacle would a stable relationship be possible. But overemphasis on this issue might negatively affect the overall relationship, since Washington has been reluctant and unwilling to settle the issue quickly.

STRESS SECURITY ISSUES. China might instead emphasize the security and strategic aspects of the relationship with the United States. It could mean a substantial increase of military cooperation between the two. This would become very likely if China perceived a growing Soviet threat. Since the Soviet threat is now considered less acute and there is an improvement in Sino-Soviet relations, a strategic relationship would become less urgent—particularly when there are no high tensions between the two superpowers.

55

STRESS NONSECURITY ISSUES. A more likely direction would be an increasing stress on economic, trade, and other nonsecurity relations. This appears to have been the tendency in the past few years. Considering the current state of both Soviet-American and Sino-Soviet relations, this may be a better and more logical way to stabilize, consolidate, and further develop Sino-American relations. It would yield numerous benefits. Of course, this does not mean that settlement of the Taiwan issue is not important. But a strong security tie is still a necessary and crucial part of the overall relationship. Beijing will continue to pressure Washington on the Taiwan issue, especially when the latter is considered to be retreating from the provisions of the three Sino-American communiqués concerning the issue.

Generally, the Chinese are quite optimistic about China's role in the triangular relationship, and to a broader extent in world affairs. At the same time, the Chinese are pessimistic about the nature of Soviet-American relations.[37] There are ample reasons for this dual optimism and pessimism. In the triangle as well as the world arena, the PRC has been playing an ever-growing role since its founding. That role can be expected to expand further as China's economic and military capacities increase. The Chinese believe that China, together with other countries, will be an increasingly important force in both checking the warlike tendencies of the two superpowers and defending world peace.[38] From the history of the triangular relationship, Soviet-American relations have been much more unstable than either Sino-American or Sino-Soviet relations. High-level détente is abnormal and usually does not last long, while confrontation in the midst of conversation, competition in the midst of cooperation, have become the basic norm which also characterizes the current state of superpower relationship. "In the near future," one Chinese observer notes, "the two superpowers will, most likely, continue their current pattern of confrontation and conversation. When they rival with each other, they will see to it that their confrontation does not run out of control; and when they engage in dialogue, they will continue to scramble for that extra edge over the other."[39]

THREE

CHINA'S FOREIGN ECONOMIC POLICY

QINGGUO JIA

Nearly ten years have passed since China adopted an "open" foreign economic policy in 1978. Great changes have taken place since then. Never before had the People's Republic of China developed such extensive and wide-ranging contacts with foreign countries; never before had it felt economically so closely linked with and in competition with the outside world; and never before had foreign relations so deeply affected various aspects of the People's Republic's social, economic, and political life.

THE OPEN POLICY

Beijing describes its foreign economic policy as one of *kaifang*, or openness. Literally, *kaifang* means "open and release." Like other fashionable Chinese political terminology, the term is couched in the particular historical setting of China's political, ideological, and economic reality. Here *kaifang* means removing all obstacles, including such ideological and political taboos as that China must not allow foreign investment in China, so as to make the best use of foreign and domestic resources for China's economic development and progress. (Western commentators usually use the term "open-door" policy, which for the Chinese has unfortunate historical connotations; here "open" is preferred.)

Specifically, the open policy is designed to obtain foreign technology and capital. In order to achieve this goal, Beijing has taken a series of measures. To begin with, it has drastically expanded its economic ties with foreign countries and experimented with various possible channels to obtain advanced technology and capital. First, China has increased its trade relations with not only the Western and the developing countries, but also with the Soviet Union and Eastern Europe.[1] Hence China's foreign trade has experienced rapid growth. According to Premier Li Peng, the value of China's foreign trade for 1987 was as much as US$82.7 billion.[2] Second, China has reversed its previous practice of not borrowing money from the international money market. It has obtained loans and credits from foreign governments and international organizations and issued bonds in the Western countries. Between 1983 and 1987, China contracted US$15.38 billion worth of foreign loans.[3] Third, China has been encouraging foreign companies to make direct investments in China. Between 1983 and 1987, China absorbed US$8.78 billion of direct foreign investment.[4] Fourth, Beijing has sent a large number of Chinese visiting scholars and students to work and study in educational and research institutions in the West, mainly in the United States. It hopes that these visiting scholars and students will master the most advanced scientific and technical knowledge and bring it back to China. Fifth, Beijing has drastically expanded its tourist industry. Several tourist companies have been set up and many new hotels constructed. In 1987, China received 26.9 million tourists (person-trips) from abroad and earned US$1.84 billion from the tourist industry.[5] Sixth, China has competed for overseas construction projects and labor service. In 1986, it generated a business volume of US$950 million.[6] Finally, China has experimented with overseas investment. Between 1981 and 1985, China invested more than US$170 million abroad.[7]

In the second place, as China's foreign economic ties increase, it has made significant changes in its administration and management of foreign economic activities in China. China has reformed the old foreign-trade system. Since 1979, it has increased the independence of old local foreign-trade companies, established new export and import companies, with relevant manufacturing branches taking over export of a certain portion of products from conventional trade companies, and has allowed business units to retain a certain amount of foreign-currency earnings. More recently, in order to overcome problems such as ambiguity in the distribution of responsibilities, authority, and profit, and the weak linkage between production and export, China adopted additional reforms, including separating administration from business in trade institutions; streamlining bureaucracy; implementing an import-export agency system; strengthening the links between technology, industry, and trade and between export and import; and improving business and financial management of foreign-trade firms.[8] In addition, to increase China's export competitiveness, it twice significantly devalued renminbi, the Chinese currency.

In order to attract foreign investment, China has also granted tax relief to joint-venture companies, reduced its control over their import of machinery, equipment, and raw materials and over export of products by these companies, and waved taxes on their import of equipment and raw materials related to investment. It has also decided to supply raw materials to joint-venture companies at domestic prices.[9] China established four special economic zones (SEZs), fourteen open cities, and three open economic zones.[10] Recently, China has been planning to separate Hainan Island from China's Fujian province and make it a special economic province, open to the outside world.[11]

In the third place, since 1978, China has introduced and adopted over 110 laws and regulations to protect interests of foreign as well as domestic investors.[12]

Finally, China has reevaluated the role of foreign economic relations in its economic development. Prior to 1977, with the emphasis on self-reliance, China did not permit the presence of foreign capital in China. Foreign trade was largely supplementary to China's economic development. "For a long time," Teng Weizao, vice president of the World Economic Research Society of China, points out, "we have neglected the importance of foreign trade and placed one-sided emphasis on the policy of independence and self-reliance. We have regarded foreign trade merely as a supplement to make up for the gaps in our economy and we have failed to use it to its fullest extent as a means of maximizing our comparative economic advantages and our best interests."[13] While still maintaining the principle of self-reliance, China now attaches high importance to its economic relations with foreign countries, regarding it as an important and indispensable component of China's economy. In a 1984 article on utilizing foreign investment, for instance, Wei Yuming, vice-minister of foreign economic relations and trade, points out that utilization of foreign capital has already become an important part of China's long-term and annual economic plans. He urges local governments concerned to incorporate foreign-investment projects into their economic plans so as to enable these projects to acquire the matching funds, equipment, and raw materials they need.[14]

The open foreign economic policy constitutes an unprecedented, bold, and comprehensive attempt on the part of Beijing to promote China's economic development. Such an attempt involves fundamental changes not only in China's economic thinking but also in the Chinese way of life.

THE ORIGINS OF THE OPEN POLICY

The open policy is a product of combined political, economic, ideological, and international pressures of the mid-1970s.

Emerging from prolonged ultraleftist domination, intense intra-party political rivalries, and severe natural disasters in 1976, the new Beijing leadership was confronted with a grim economic, political, ideological, and international reality. As a BBC summary of a world broadcast on China of 1976 puts it, the year 1976 was "the most traumatic for China since the founding of the People's Republic of China."[15]

Economically, the country experienced little or no growth that year because of political rivalries and natural disasters. Combined with the poor economic performance of the previous few years, China's economy was verging on complete collapse.

Politically, Beijing was confronted with widespread disillusion and cynicism. The shadow of the Cultural Revolution chilled the hearts of millions. Horrifying stories about the cruelty and sadism committed during previous mass political movements traveled rapidly from house to house. The state of the economy and the long period of subsistence-level living standards contributed to widespread and increasing dissatisfaction. Many seriously doubted the intention as well as the capability of political leadership. Demand for redressing grievances of the past, for punishing the executors of "erroneous" policies, and for restructuring Chinese politics was intense and highlighted by the emergence of the Xidan Democracy Wall in Beijing. The "wall," among other things, demonstrated people's discontent with the new leadership in addition to their hatred for the purged radical leadership. With the suppression of its political opponents, the Communist Party's political prestige appeared to be at its lowest point since the founding of the PRC.

Ideologically, the Chinese people were at best confused. In theory, socialism appeared to be able to offer a more consistent and attractive alternative for China than other social theories. In practice, however, what had happened in China was not equally convincing. It was true that under socialism China had developed from a country of political disintegration with few modern industries to one of unity with a relatively comprehensive industrial structure in the previous twenty-seven years. But it was also true that other countries and areas such as Japan had experienced more significant industrial development than China without having to endure continuous political campaigns and subsistence-level living standards as China had. The harsh economic and political reality appeared to be the most potent threat to ideological appeals.

The threat appeared to be even more serious when the Chinese situation was viewed in the international context of the time. With the downfall of the "Gang of Four," a new awareness of China's backwardness vis-à-vis other nations was increasingly felt by the Chinese elite and the masses alike. Japan, which had been regarded by China as sharing a similar economic level of development in the early 1960s, had become an economic giant in the world economy by the late 1970s. At the outset of the 1960s, its GNP was only 10 percent of that of the United States; by the 1980s, however, it was nearly 40 percent. Following Japan's economic take-off, South Korea, Singapore, Taiwan, and Hong Kong achieved rapid economic development. Other Asian countries also enjoyed high economic growth. Rapid economic growth led to a substantial rise in per capita income in these countries and regions. "In 1962," as Peter Drysdale noted, "per capita income in Japan was 54 percent of the average for advanced industrial countries; in 1982 it was 92 percent. For Hong Kong, Korea, and Taiwan over the same period, per capita income rose from about 10 percent to 21 percent of the average for advanced industrial countries, while those of the ASEAN countries rose from 5 percent to 7 percent." Despite its success in development, mainland China's GDP per capita in 1982 was significantly lower than those of Japan, South Korea, Taiwan, Hong Kong, and the ASEAN countries.[16]

Viewing this situation, leaders in Beijing could not help but feel the pressure for change. An editorial in *Renmin Ribao* in 1979, for example, acknowledged that, although China had made significant economic progress, its level of development was still quite low. And compared with economically advanced countries, China's economy was still backward. In most areas of study, China's level of scientific and technological development lagged behind the world by fifteen to twenty years. Therefore, China had to develop at a higher speed than others in order to catch up with economically advanced countries. One major reason Japan caught up with and surpassed many economically advanced countries in the 1950s and 1960s, the editorial

**1. GROSS DOMESTIC PRODUCT
PER CAPITA IN SELECTED
ASIAN COUNTRIES IN 1982**

Japan	$10,080
Hong Kong	$5,340
Singapore	$2,500
Taiwan	$2,400
South Korea	$1,910
Malaysia	$1,860
Philippines	$820
Thailand	$790
Indonesia	$580
China	$310

pointed out, was that it had absorbed all the latest scientific and technological achievements from around the world and applied them in its economic development. For China to catch up with economically advanced countries, therefore, it must adopt a similar attitude and strategy.[17]

The pressure for change was particularly acute in view of Taiwan's rapid economic development and comparatively high standard of living. For decades the Chinese Communist Party (CCP) had used the old image of corruption and inefficiency of Kuomintang rule on the Chinese mainland prior to 1949 to describe the regime on Taiwan and to support its own legitimacy to govern China. Now rapid economic development and improving living conditions on Taiwan have proved that the Taiwan regime at least was reformable and that unless something was done, Beijing might one day lose in its long-term political rivalry with Taipei.

Under such circumstances, Beijing leaders realized that they had to offer some new alternative in order to rebuild the morale of the Chinese people, to improve the CCP's political prestige and ideological appeal, as well as to realize the long-standing dream of the Chinese people to catch up with the advanced industrial countries. Influenced by leftist ideas, the new alternative adopted turned out to be an ambitious program of economic development under the name of Four Modernizations. This program was put forth as an answer to all the current economic, political, and ideological problems.

No sooner had the program been announced, however, than the CCP found itself in a Catch-22. On the one hand, in order to restore the confidence of the Chinese people in the CCP's leadership, Beijing had to implement this extremely ambitious if not completely impossible program. On the other hand, given China's economic capabilities, the realization of the program required a high level of accumulation which the CCP could not accomplish without imposing a low level of consumption on the nation, and which, therefore, at least in the short run, could only serve to damage such confidence. This reminds one of the difficulties the CCP had faced in the 1950s when it embarked on an ambitious economic program. In certain aspects, the new difficulties the CCP faced in the mid-1970s were greater than those faced in the 1950s. First, the CCP enjoyed much more political prestige and ideological appeal in the 1950s than it did in the mid-1970s. Second, the CCP enjoyed important assistance, however grudging, from its Soviet ally in the 1950s, assistance of a kind it could not obtain from any country in the mid-1970s.

Facing the difficult task of both ensuring rapid economic growth and maintaining people's confidence in its leadership, Beijing found it necessary simultaneously to adopt a comprehensive program designed to regenerate social and political harmony, to tap the potential of the existing productive capacity, and to create a peaceful international environment.

To begin with, politically, in order to rally the widest possible range of support from the Chinese people, Beijing tried to revive its old policy of a united front. Following the downfall of the Gang of Four, it made a lot of effort to redress people's grievances accumulated in the previous political and ideological campaigns. It released people arrested during the Tienanmen Incident in April 1976. It rehabilitated people killed, tortured, and labeled as class enemies for various trumped-up crimes during the Cultural Revolution, the Anti-Rightist Campaign, and other political movements. And it abolished discrimination of former class enemies such as rich peasants, landlords, capitalists, and bureaucrats who used to work for the Kuomintang government before 1949, and their children. In addition, while maintaining tight control over the public media, Beijing expanded the scope of discussion and demonstrated an increased degree of political tolerance. Moreover, it attempted to reform government by reinstating free local elections, though with very moderate success. Finally, it appealed to the Taiwan authorities to make an effort to unify the country by offering maximum political concessions, such as allowing the latter to maintain its political, economic, administrative, legal, and military establishments after unification.

Economically, Beijing tried to improve people's living conditions while avoiding a slowdown in China's economic development. On the one hand, it allocated precious resources to improve people's living standards through expanding production of consumer goods both in quantity and in variety, through significantly raising people's incomes, and through constructing new houses and other facilities. On the other hand, it resorted to a variety of means to minimize the impact of this diversion of resources from production to consumption through introducing competition, reforming existing economic structure and management, and encouraging technological innovation and scientific development.

Diplomatically, Beijing moved toward a foreign policy of reconciliation as well as independence, which encourages interactions with all countries. It endeavored to improve its relations with the West, particularly the United States. It made efforts to maintain good relations with most of the Third World countries. And more recently, it demonstrated a willingness to improve its relations with the Soviet Union and the East European countries.[18] The favorable international environment that Beijing has been cultivating has allowed China to reduce, or at lease not increase, defense spending and has helped alleviate the shortage of capital for its economic development.

Competition, reforms, technological innovation and scientific development, and limiting defense spending, however, were not sufficient to ensure rapid economic development. Beijing found it necessary to introduce foreign capital and technology in order to generate additional resources. A consensus began to form in Beijing that foreign economic relations could be a useful means to achieve the dual goal of expediting China's economic development while minimizing its negative effect on people's living standards. Later in 1985, former Premier Zhao Ziyang expressed this consensus when he said that the realization of China's modernization program depends upon two things: domestic reforms and the open policy.[19]

THE CONTINUATION OF THE OPEN POLICY

Since the adoption of the open policy, three additional factors have facilitated its continuation: a helpful international environment, the gains brought by foreign economic relations, and favorable political development.

Helpful International Environment

The helpful international environment is chiefly reflected in China's relations with the superpowers. Despite his radical campaign rhetoric, Ronald Reagan did not resume diplomatic relations with Taipei after he came to the White House. After some brief rhetorical confrontation, Sino-American relations actually improved. In 1981, Moscow also decided to adopt a policy of reconciliation with Beijing. Not even the three turnovers of leadership altered this policy. Beijing's improved relationship with Washington and Moscow allowed China to acquire technology, capital, and markets from the West and at the same time keep its defense spending at a minimum, freeing additional resources for economic development.

Gains Brought by Foreign Economic Relations

With the open foreign economic policy, China has attracted a considerable amount of foreign investment and alleviated its capital shortage problem. During the period between 1981 and 1985, the amount of foreign capital China acquired was equivalent to 9 percent of China's total capital investment. "By using the medium and long-term loans provided by foreign governments and international institutions [between 1979 and September of 1985]," Liu Shulong of the Planning Department of the Ministry of Foreign Economic Relations and Trade wrote, "more than 150 construction projects have been arranged by the state in a unified way.... There are more than 50 big and medium-sized projects including 7 railway projects and 3,000 kilometers of new and rebuilt railways, which can increase the transportation capacity by 139 million tons a year, 4 hydropower stations with a capacity of 2 million kilowatts as well as 8 harbours and 28 berths with an increased annual handling capacity of 59 million tons."[20]

The policy also enables China to have access to many advanced technologies and equipment. As Liu Shulong put it, "A great number of medium and small sized enterprises have been transformed"; "some advanced technology has been imported"; and "a great number of projects with great investment, new technology and extensive influence such as the nuclear power station in Guangdong, the Pingshuo open-cut coal mine in Shanxi and the Shanghai Automobile Plant are under construction."[21] Thousands of Chinese visiting scholars sent to study abroad have returned home and brought back with them up-to-date knowledge of their myriad fields of study.

The investment and technology transfer have increasingly contributed to the development of China's economy. Important projects such as the Shanghai Baoshan Iron and Steel complex, the 1.7-meter rolling mill at the Wuhan Iron and Steel Company, the 300,000-ton ethylene project at the Daqing Oil Field, and the Pingshuo open-cut coal mine in Shanxi are being or will be built to be the backbone industries of China.[22] Take the Shanghai Baoshan Iron and Steel Works, for example. The recent completion of the first stage of construction has enabled China to produce 3 million tons of iron, 3.12 million tons of steel, .52 million tons of steel tubes and 2.12 million semifinished steel products annually. It will also help China save over $1 billion for import of steel products. When the whole project is complete, the complex will produce 6.5 million tons of iron, 6.7 million tons of steel, 4.22 million tons of steel products, and 1.22 million tons of semifinished steel products.[23] The impact of this input into China's steel industry and national economy is obviously significant.

Favorable Political Development

Beginning in 1980, the CCP's Central Committee decided to let a younger group of leaders take over leadership gradually. Since then, a massive transition of power has occurred in China, bringing a large number of reform-oriented leaders to powerful positions. A large turnover in the Central Committee took place in September 1985. During the 12th National Congress of the CCP, which was held between September 18 and 23, and the fourth and fifth plenary sessions of the CCP, ninety-one new Central Committee members and alternate members were recruited and sixty-four Central Committee members and alternate members, including such prominent figures as Ye Jianying, Deng Yingchao, Nie Rongzhen, Xu Xiangqian, and General Ulanfu, stepped down because of old age and other reasons.

The new generation of Chinese leaders are younger and more educated. They share the commitment to reforms and the open policy. As Kazuko Mohri noted, "Through this conference and the fourth and fifth plenary sessions of the 12th Central Committee on September 16 and September 24, respectively, the Party forged a central body dedicated to implementing the present leadership's basic policy of proceeding with reforms and opening doors to the rest of the world."[24]

The recent 13th Party Congress made even more progress in this direction.

CONTINUING WITH CHANGE

Although much has taken place since 1976, the nature of the problems Beijing was confronted with and the basic considerations that led to the adoption and continuation of the open foreign economic policy still remain. Despite rapid development in the last decade and in the years to come, China is likely to remain an economically backward country in the nineties, lagging far behind advanced industrial states. People's living standards will still be low compared with those of some of China's Asian neighbors, including Taiwan, let alone with those of the leading industrial states. Foreign capital and technology will continue to be badly needed to meet China's growing demand. And as expansion of China's foreign economic relations continues, increasing gains from such a development will serve as additional justification for the policy's continuation.

Politically, while the bitter memories of the Cultural Revolution are fading away, high expectations for reforms and improvement of the standard of living will continue to generate new disappointment and cynicism whenever Beijing's endeavor fails to meet them. Beijing is likely to continue to face, if not more acutely than before, the difficult and delicate problem of balancing between accumulation and distribution with relatively few resources at its own disposal. Foreign capital and technology therefore will continue to be critical to facilitate such a balance, keeping the negative effect of it to a minimum.

Internationally, an analysis of the present situation does not offer much hope for drastic change in China's foreign relations and thus in its foreign economic policy. China is likely to continue its present policy of political independence and economic integration

69

with the outside world. While the country will have various kinds of difficulties with the United States, it will probably continue to treasure its relationship with that country and try to avoid serious confrontation with it. The Sino-Soviet relationship is likely to improve further as the current border talks and other interactions continue, but, given China's strategic interests and its previous experience and dealings with the Soviet Union, it is likely to cultivate this relationship with great caution and within well-defined limits. Meanwhile, neither the Soviet Union nor the United States has good reason to go out of its way to push China to the other side at the expense of its own strategic and, secondarily, economic interests. Consequently, unless something unusual happens, the present structure of relationships between China and the United States and the Soviet Union will probably continue.

Since most of the major factors that were responsible for the policy's adoption and continuation are likely to remain in the years to come, one can argue that China is likely to continue the present open policy. This can be seen in Beijing's reaction to the decline of foreign investment in the first half of 1986. After realizing that foreign investors had been turned off by what they perceived as a poor investment environment, Beijing immediately undertook measures to offer more attractive terms to foreign investors instead of blaming them for their "inordinate" demands or retreating to its previous policy of self-reliance. It can also be seen in the importance Beijing attached to the role of foreign economic relations in its seventh five-year plan. The plan requires that China's economy between 1986 and 1990 increase 38 percent. That means an average increase of 6.7 percent annually, with an average increase of 4 percent in agriculture and 7.5 percent in industry. The total GNP in 1990 should increase by 160 percent over that in 1980. In order to accomplish this goal, total investment in fixed assets in state-owned companies will increase by 67 percent from that during the sixth five-year plan. Of this investment, that in capital construction will increase by 47 percent and that in the renovation of existing equipment by 87 percent. Under such circumstances, expansion of foreign economic relations is necessary. The plan therefore requires that China's foreign trade increase by 1990 to $83 billion, 40 percent over that of 1985, increasing by an average of 7 percent a year. Meanwhile, the scale of utilizing foreign capital and introducing advanced foreign technology should also be significantly expanded.[25] More recently, this can also be seen in Zhao Ziyang's call for further integration of China's coastal areas into the world economy.[26]

It is in view of these facts that leaders in Beijing repeatedly stress that the open policy is a long-standing strategy rather than a short-term tactic. According to Deng Xiaoping, China will rely on the open policy for its development not only during the remainder of this century, but also in the next century.[27]

FACTORS OF UNCERTAINTY

The continuation of the policy, however, could be significantly affected if not completely reversed, by three factors: (1) the way Beijing copes with the problems that are believed to be side effects of the open policy; (2) the state of the international economic system; and (3) China's political development.

A number of problems have emerged since the adoption of the policy. To begin with, in its drive for advanced technology and foreign capital, China has found itself increasingly dependent upon foreign markets for exports and imports and for foreign investment. To earn more foreign currency in order to import much-needed advanced technology and equipment, China has been quite successful in trying to expand its exports. This expansion, however, has also led to China's dependence on the international market for exports in certain sectors of its economy. For the first time since the 1950s, China began to feel significantly the impact of political decisions by foreign governments on its own economy. Take the Sino-U.S. textile dispute in 1984, for example. China had been very successful in developing its textile industry and increasing its export of textile goods. The income from this export constituted a large item in its foreign-currency earnings. When the American government decided to impose quotas on its import of textile goods from China in order to satisfy domestic political demands, however, China found serious repercussions in its domestic production of textiles.

China has also found itself increasingly dependent on the importation of foreign equipment and parts. In order to upgrade domestic production of certain commodities, such as TVs and automobiles, China has introduced some complete assembly lines from foreign countries and established some joint-venture factories. They are more efficient in production and capable of achieving better quality, but as production expands, these assembly lines and companies demand an increasing supply of parts and materials that China cannot produce. Under such circumstances, if these factories were unable to sell their products abroad, they would not be able to obtain hard currency to purchase parts and materials needed for production and would face bankruptcy. This was exactly the case with the Hitachi-Fujian Television Factory, the Beijing Jeep Factory, the Shanghai-Volkswagen Factory, and some others. Their bankruptcy was only prevented because political and economic considerations made bankruptcy unacceptable to Beijing. It diverted some of its valuable hard currency to these companies to sustain their operation.

In addition, China found itself increasingly dependent on foreign investment for expansion of production. Without continuous infusion of foreign capital and technology, Chinese economic development will be seriously affected. It was this dependence that produced China's rapid reaction to the decline in the volume of direct foreign investment during the first six months of 1986.[28] Immediately after Beijing became aware of the decline, Zhao Ziyang stated that China was prepared to study it seriously. After learning that the decline was caused by locally imposed high costs of operation and bureaucratic red tape, Beijing immediately set up a special group in the State Council to solve problems for joint ventures, comanagement enterprises, and enterprises with solely foreign investment.[29] A number of new incentives to encourage foreign investment were quickly offered.[30] Local governments also began taking measures to improve conditions for foreign investors so that they could make money.[31] Economic imperatives obviously explain this behavior of the Chinese government.

In the second place, in its drive for advanced technology and foreign capital, Beijing found itself confronted with greater unevenness of development between different geographical areas and greater disparity in distribution than before. The special economic zones and open cities enjoy more autonomy in decision-making than other areas in China, their export-oriented economies receive more benefit than other parts of the country from the new foreign economic policy, and the living standards in these areas are significantly higher than the average for the nation. The output value of industrial and agricultural production in the four special economic zones in 1985, for example, was 142 percent higher than that in 1984 and 6.3 times greater than that in 1979. Such growth was many times greater than that of the country's economy as a whole during the same periods. In 1985, 60 percent of the industrial products in Shantou and 43 percent in Shenzhen were exported. The percentages of industrial goods for export in the other two SEZs had also been growing.[32]

Uneven development can also be seen from a national geographical perspective. As shown in Table 2, economic growth in the eastern area of China, which has benefited most from China's open foreign economic policy, was significantly higher than that in the central and western areas. Between 1980 and 1985, while the total production value of the eastern area grew by 73 percent, that in the central area increased by 64 percent and that in the western area by only 61.3 percent. The eastern area's share of total production value in the national economy increased from 55.4 percent in 1980 to 56.9 percent in 1985, while that of the central area decreased from 29.8 percent to 28.9 percent, and that of the western area from 14.8 percent to 14.2 percent. Similar changes occurred in the growth rates and percentages of total industrial and agricultural output values.

Higher levels of growth in exports lead to higher living standards. This is what has happened. According to Chung-Tong Wu and David F. Ip, the average earnings of workers in Shenzhen were substantially higher than those in the country as a whole in 1983 and the difference continued to widen.[33]

2. TOTAL PRODUCTION VALUE BY AREA

	1985 (billion RMB)	Percentage increase over 1980	Percentage of total production	
			1980	1985
Total production value	1,216.8	69.1	100	100
Eastern area	692.7	73.7	55.4	56.9
Central area	352.0	64.3	29.8	28.9
Western area	172.1	61.4	14.8	14.2
Total industrial output value	925.5	76.2	100	100
Eastern area	566.4	79.5	60.0	61.2
Central area	245.7	71.6	27.3	26.5
Western area	113.4	70.5	12.7	12.3
Total agricultural output value	291.2	49.8	100	100
Eastern area	126.2	51.8	42.8	43.3
Central area	106.3	49.5	36.6	36.5
Western area	58.7	46.3	20.6	20.2

Source: "Economic Growth in Different Areas," *Beijing Review*, no. 49 (December 8, 1986), p. 23.

Disarticulation (to borrow a term from dependency theorists) in China's economic development has presented still another problem. By "disarticulation" we mean a situation in which the introduction of certain lines of industry using advanced technology does not bring about development of related industries, because the development of these factories that import needed parts and export their products is not linked with, and has little substantive impact on, overall economic development in China. An illustration of this case is the Hitachi-Fujian Television Factory, which imports most parts for production and exports the products.[34] The argument is that even if it could sell its products abroad, the benefits China received would not go far beyond adding some hard currency. Even in terms of making money, one wonders whether this is the best strategy in the long run. First, it is not certain that China's investment, both in terms of money and time, in such joint adventures would bring about more benefits for China's economic development than would a different investment strategy. Second, given the uncertainties of international economics, there is no guarantee that currently profitable enterprises would continue to provide profits for China in the future.

Finally, in its drive for advanced technology and foreign capital, Beijing has been confronted with increasing economic corruption, crimes related to the management of foreign economic relations. Among these crimes are the illegal appropriation of foreign currency by the Food and Edible Oil Import and Export Corporation of Liaoning province and a Shenzhen trade company; the massive importation and smuggling of automobiles, TVs, and other consumer goods on Hainan Island; and the coastal petroleum black market.[35] The scope of involvement has been significant. Take the Hainan scandal, for example. By the end of July 1985, cadres from twenty-one provinces, municipalities, and autonomous regions were reportedly involved. China Daily reported on December 5 that more than sixty-seven thousand party and government cadres had been implicated in illegal transactions in the first nine months of the year.[36]

Along with increasing foreign economic relations came what Beijing perceived as "spiritual pollution": "unhealthy thoughts, unhealthy works, unhealthy performance . . . the decadent ideas of the bourgeois, exploitative classes."[37]

Such problems have caused serious concern to the party leadership. Addressing the Sixth Plenary Session of the Central Discipline Inspection Commission on September 24, 1985, Chen Yun, a most senior-ranking party leader, pointed out that the corrupt bourgeois idea of "considering everything in terms of money" was corrupting China's socialist values and the CCP's work style.[38] Deng Xiaoping also finds it necessary to carry on the CCP's antiliberalization campaign for "at least 20 years."[39]

Despite Beijing's determination to carry on the open policy regardless of the difficulties, it simply cannot ignore these problems. As the development of other Third World countries demonstrates, China's dependence on foreign investment will increase as its economic integration continues. It will not take long before Beijing has to make hard choices to balance between economic dependence and political independence. Also, it remains to be seen how much Beijing will be able to contain uneven development. But as geographical developmental disparity increases, its political implications will one day become serious enough for Beijing to make a major readjustment in its development strategy. If that happens, it is not likely that the present open policy will remain unaffected. The political implications of the corruption and "spiritual pollution" may be used as handy excuses against the open policy by its opponents when the time comes.

The October 1987 worldwide stock market crises raised another question related to the future of the open policy. Will the international economic system in the coming decade be as kind to China as it was during the past decade? If the U.S. government cannot significantly reduce its serious trade deficit and resist domestic protectionist political pressures, it is likely that it will have to adopt some protectionist measures, and these measures will eventually affect China's exports to that country. Since China's exports to the United States constitute a significant portion of its foreign-currency earnings, such a development would seriously affect China's foreign trade and foreign investment as a whole.

Finally, Chinese political development in the years to come will definitely have a significant impact on its open, or open-door, foreign policy. How much should China open to the outside world? How much economic independence should China preserve? What should China do to achieve effective utilization of foreign technology and investment while resisting foreign cultural and political values? How much Western-style democracy should China tolerate? How should one view a distribution of wealth that has become increasingly uneven, geographically and socially? Such issues have caused serious debate in previous years. The rise and fall of the antipollution campaign, Hu Yaobang's resignation, the recent CCP decision to expel Liu Binyan and others from the party, college students' demonstrations for democracy—all these reflect opposing interests in the Chinese reforms and different perceptions of the open policy. These different interests and perceptions will continue to generate different answers to the questions listed above. While the open policy may continue in the coming decade, whoever comes to power will offer his answers to these questions and set his limits to the form and content of the open policy.

FOUR

CHINESE NUCLEAR STRATEGY

X I A O C H U A N   Z H A N G

Some twenty-five hundred years ago, Chinese strategist Sun Tzu in *The Art of War* suggested for the first time the difference between what we today call "national strategy" and "military strategy." War, he wrote, is a matter of vital importance to the state; the field of battle is the place of life and death, the road to survival or ruin. Weapons are the ominous tools to be used only when there is no alternative. Today China seeks a reliable, serviceable, yet "ominous" strategic retaliatory capability should deterrence and diplomatic channels fail. This paper discusses this military strategy.

China has been striving for the enhancement of its influence in international affairs ever since the founding of the People's Republic in 1949. The development of nuclear force serves this consistent goal. Its nuclear force enables China to deter nuclear blackmail and intimidation. Its emerging global strategic importance was made graphically evident in 1980 when it became the third nation to test successfully a land-based intercontinental ballistic missile.[1]

Since the early 1980s, the Chinese leadership's assessment of the major threats to China's security has changed. While the Soviet Union is believed to be the most dangerous threat to China, Beijing has decided that this threat is not immediate. Furthermore, unlike Mao Zedong in his later years, the current Chinese leadership is optimistic that a new world war can be avoided, or at least postponed. Therefore, the reform-minded Chinese leaders have been able to justify a slowly paced military modernization and to focus on economic development much more than before. The economic reform, if it succeeds, may become the most profound of all the factors affecting military modernization in the years to come.

The first part of this paper presents an introduction and analysis of PRC strategic planning and policy rationale. The second section starts with new developments in China's nuclear program, follows with an overview of projected weapons systems, and concludes with the perceived nuclear-policy choices. The third part is a discussion of China's attitudes toward nuclear arms control and the implications of Chinese nuclear forces on American and Soviet interests. The final section presents foreign-policy options.

PRC STRATEGIC PLANNING AND POLICY RATIONALE

In comparison with the superpowers, China's strategic force is small. While pledging a policy of "no first use" of nuclear weapons (thus reducing the fear of nonnuclear states), China has maintained a relatively minimal deterrence: it employs a variety of weapons but does not strive for a large quantity of them. Not even in the relatively long-established category of medium-range weapons has China built up more than a minimum capability. Nevertheless, such a policy of minimum deterrence increases the risks to a potential enemy and thus decreases the probability that a small conflict of interest will lead to war. China's nuclear strike capability is sufficiently advanced so that there can be no Soviet assurance that a first strike will not lead to a Chinese counterstrike. On the other hand, China will hardly have a first-strike capability at anytime in the foreseeable future.

China's nuclear program has maintained a high national priority throughout its existence, almost unaffected by political movements and shifts in national policy. Chinese defense policy has long maintained a balance between two concepts: (1) nuclear force to deter strategic attack, and (2) "people's war" or mass mobilization of the population to deter or repel conventional invasion. The present Chinese defense policy argues that because of its huge rural population, the only way to defeat China is to invade it, and such an operation is deterred by the nonnuclear "people's war," a conception which itself has undergone several changes to take into account "modern conditions."[2]

This is not to say that China does not see any role for nuclear weapons. However, China's defense concerns are primarily in the realm of limited wars. If nuclear weapons are only required to deter limited wars, then China requires only a limited number of weapons. The wide range of possible threats of limited war, however, require a wide range of limited nuclear forces for deterrence.

Until recently, China's nuclear strategy has been predicated upon a belief that, with the world's largest population, the Chinese people are less likely to be entirely destroyed in a nuclear exchange.

In absolute numbers, millions more reside in the countryside in China than in any other nation. Moreover, China's economy is less industrialized than that of either superpower. Articulating such views, General Su Yu, former general secretary of the Central Military Committee, asserted:

> We do not deny that nuclear weapons have great destructive power and inflict heavy casualties, but they cannot be counted on to decide the outcome of a war. The aggressors can use them to destroy a city or town, but they cannot occupy those places, still less can they win the people's hearts. . . . Everybody knows that under the conditions when both sides have nuclear weapons, such weapons pose a much greater threat to . . . the countries whose industries and population are highly concentrated. . . . Our economic construction cannot therefore be destroyed by nuclear weapons.[3]

Any effort to assert the decisiveness of nuclear weapons has been challenged. Yet none of these analyses suggest that they would not be employed against China or that the nonindustrial population is invulnerable to nuclear radiation. In addition, several specifically note that China would respond by employing its own nuclear weaponry against any such attack. Given such views, China's nuclear program retains powerful advocates in Beijing, with calls regularly heard for an expanded and more sophisticated strategic arsenal.

Mao Zedong's belief that military struggle would continue and inevitably result in world war (conventional or nuclear) was abandoned in 1980 when the country adopted its open-door policy. Although conflict will continue, it is no longer necessarily of the military kind. Nonetheless, China continues to believe the conventional wisdom that the avoidance of war is best achieved by preparation for war. This was particularly true during the Cultural Revolution, when urban civil defense systems on the one hand, and nuclear weapons programs on the other were the national defense priority.

In China emphasis on the political basis and context of conflict and of military action dates back to at least Sun Tzu. Since 1949 this has meant that the response to military or security problems has been through a careful orchestration of political, military, economic, and psychological factors. Underlying that orchestration have been views, often of great force and subtlety, about the central role of man in conflict situations, rather than of means and methods, and about the advantages of ambiguity and uncertainty in conducting politicomilitary disputes.

Until his death, Mao Zedong seems to have maintained the view that the masses are, in the end, irresistible and that whether in nation-building or social arrangements it is men who are decisive, not technologies. The present Chinese leadership holds similar views. During his visit to Europe in June 1986, former General Secretary Hu Yaobang, in a major policy speech at the Royal Institute of International Affairs in London, said:

> Being realists, we are fully aware that as the danger of a new world war has not been eliminated, we must be prepared against any surprise attacks. . . . We shall not be intimidated if war is imposed on us. As a country with a vast territory, China has much room for manoeuvring and the populous Chinese nation is conscious and capable of fending off foreign aggression.[4]

In short, the Chinese leadership seems to believe that (1) a general war, either conventional or nuclear, is not inevitable; (2) a possible regional or limited war requires China to have only a minimal level of nuclear forces for deterrence; (3) China's national defense has never relied largely on its nuclear capability, but rather on other distinctive strengths of the nation; and (4) nuclear weapons may well be an economy measure in defense.

Trends in PRC nuclear deployment since the late 1960s suggest a modest program intended almost exclusively to deal with only such extreme contingencies as an irrational nuclear attack on China. Such limits suggest two possible considerations. First, the nuclear program and its technological and economic requirements could slow economic development, thus weakening the foundations of the nation's security.[5] Second, a larger nuclear program has significant consequences for China's relations with other states in East and South Asia. There is no evidence that Chinese leaders have sought to use their strategic forces to gain political advantage vis-à-vis China's nonnuclear neighbors, such as Japan and the ASEAN countries.

In the last few years, China has tested its first full-range ICBM (intercontinental ballistic missile) and a shorter-range but more adaptable SLBM (sea-launched ballistic missile). The full-range ICBM test and the development of solid fuels, used in the SLBM test, demonstrate China's intent to raise the capability of its nuclear force to the point at which it can become China's primary deterrent against the USSR or any other nuclear power. However, according to *Jane's Weapon Systems 1985–1986*, China's nuclear deterrent continues to rest largely upon delivery systems of Soviet design, some more than two decades old. The possible vulnerability of these systems—for example, intermediate-range manned bombers and vulnerable liquid-fueled missiles—remains a key issue. Chinese defense planners have sought to mitigate this problem by efforts at dispersal, camouflage, and mobility.

There had been expectations of a Chinese ICBM for well over a decade, but apparently the technological problems remained a major obstacle. There are some recent indications that the Chinese government has given more emphasis to research and development programs for nuclear weapons. On May 15, 1986, technological breakthroughs involving underwater submarine launching of a surface missile and development of surface-to-surface long-range missiles and carrier rockets won China's highest national award. The announcement of the awards marked the first time China has disclosed that work on sophisticated weapons had been honored.

The recent advances were probably encouraged by a perception that nuclear deterrence might be a cheaper defense option than massive spending on modern conventional weaponry. There is a notable parallel here to the Gaullist *"tous azimuts"* concept.

At the medium-range level, China has long had a major nuclear strike potential against the Soviet Union. The needs in this category could more easily be met; pictures and stories released in 1979 indicate that some Chinese MRBMs (medium-range ballistic missiles) are mobile (by road or rail), making a successful first strike against China risky. However, since all PLA ballistic missiles are liquid-fueled, reaction times are still measured in hours. Furthermore, being generally close to Soviet territory, missile sites are vulnerable to conventional attack. In the event of a nonnuclear invasion, Beijing must decide very quickly whether to initiate a nuclear war, or simply to allow much of its nuclear force to be overrun. This is a serious potential challenge to China's "no-first-use" policy. It casts the strategic importance of the CSS-X-4, which can be deployed deep in the Chinese interior, beyond the reach of such a conventional preemptive strike.

China has only recently begun to extend its capability in tactical nuclear weapons. Recent discussions have made it plain that China sees some utility in deterring Soviet tactical nuclear superiority by using its own tactical nuclear weapons.[6] By 1982 it was clear that PLA forces were training in a simulated nuclear environment resulting from the use of tactical systems.[7]

Furthermore, the dispersal of population that the Chinese leadership has been taking as a strategic advantage is now undergoing a seemingly fundamental change. Recent statistical data show that by the end of 1985 China's urban population had approached a quarter of the country's total (eight times as many as at the end of the 1960s).[8] By the mid 1970s, around 70 percent of the population was in the more densely populated areas, leaving vast stretches of land relatively empty, especially in the Northwest and West. In some of these same areas, there are stretches of flat country, often without ground cover. These factors tend to make China more vulnerable than before to city strikes. However, it is not likely that the Chinese leadership will change its defense strategy at this stage. The dominant schools of thought on politicostrategic matters still agree on two basic propositions. If a nuclear strike came, it would destroy China's industrial centers and many of her cities. But it still could not destroy rural China or most of the country's massive population. Furthermore, in almost all circumstances, a long-range strike would have to be followed up by an attempt to impose the attacker's will through occupation or the threat of it. Whether or not nuclear weapons were used, the political success of an attack on China therefore depends upon the credibility of an invasion by conventional forces. And against a ground invasion, China is, or might be made to be, unconquerable.[9]

THE PROJECTED EVOLUTION OF CHINESE NUCLEAR POLICY AND WEAPONS SYSTEMS

Even as "people's war under modern conditions" entered the lexicon of strategic analysis, it soon became evident that a massive invasion from the USSR was unlikely. Instead, the emphasis was placed on the need to defend against more limited Soviet objectives, particularly in North and Northeast China. By the late 1970s, the concept of a people's war was already being challenged in the debates surrounding the modernization of conventional forces. Modernizers argued that it was now necessary to "win in a war against aggression at smaller cost and in less time."[10] Their view is based on the assumption that nuclear weapons are so distinctly different from conventional ones in terms of their range and lethality that they require different strategic concepts. But the difficulty for moving in this direction involves a question of budgetary priorities. The deliberately slow pace of military modernization imposed by the priority given to other sectors of the economy remains in place. And recent speeches made by the Chinese leaders indicate that this situation will not change in the foreseeable future.[11] The Chinese leadership has apparently decided to persevere largely along traditional lines, making internal improvements only when it can be demonstrated that total costs will not rise drastically.[12] In the past five years, the leadership has been engaged in a slow and selective re-equipment program in an effort to turn the armed forces from a heavily politicized institution into a more professional one. This search for a leaner, better-equipped armed force is part of a rethinking of China's defense strategy. Rather than luring an attacker deep into the heartland of China and relying on a "people's war" to defeat him, doctrine now calls for meeting an attack close to the border and using swift counterattacks to repel it.[13] This requires a smaller, more efficient, better-equipped force of professional soldiers, and more effective nuclear weapons systems.

As far as the weapons systems are concerned, two areas of change in the future seem probable. First, although military spending will probably see no increase in the next few years, a greater percentage of it is likely to go to the development of a secure second-strike posture, which means more spending on such top-of-the-range offensive weapons as ICBMs and SLBMs, notably the DF-5 (CSS-3), the CSSN-1, and the HY-2 (CSS-NX-4). At the lower end of the offensive spectrum, further development of tactical nuclear forces seems likely, since no large scale conventional weapons program has begun. There is, however, little likelihood that China will build up massive numbers of weapons in each category.

However, since China's overall national power is likely to increase faster than that of its neighbors, the country will increasingly be perceived by its neighbors as likely to exert its power abroad. This is a potential challenge to the current leadership with regard to the implication of nuclear arms development for the country's foreign policy.

The current PRC strategic missile force consists of 6 ICBMs, including 2 DF-5s (CSS-4s), each of which ranges 12,900 kilometers, with a yield of 5 megatons, and 4 DF-4s (CSS-3s), ranging 7,000 kilometers, with a yield of 3 megatons. As for IRBMs (intermediate-range ballistic missiles), China has 80-125 DF-3s (CSS-2s), ranging 2,700 kilometers, with a yield of 2 megatons. Among the MRBMs, 50 DF-2s (CSS-1s) are operational, ranging 1,100 kilometers, with a 2-megaton warhead.[14]

New developments indicate that 4 SSBNs (ballistic missile submarines) have probably been deployed, with 12 HY-2s (CSS-NX-4s; modified DF-3s, with a range that varies from 2,200 to 3,000 kilometers and possibly a 1- or 2-megaton warhead).[15] According to the U.S. Defense Intelligence Agency, production of CSS-3 and CSS-4 ICBMs and CSS-2 IRBMs continues at a rate of 10 and 20 missiles per year, respectively.[16]

Numbers of ballistic missiles seem to have changed little since 1972, when there were an estimated 50 medium-range and 100 intermediate-range missiles[17] (the latter number may be an overestimate). The nature of this current force suggests that weapons are deployed to strike targets in European Russia. Notably, China successfully test-fired the CSS-4 intercontinental ballistic missile for the first time with multiple independently targeted reentry vehicles (MIRV)—a capability achieved in 1984 when it placed three satellites in orbit simultaneously with the launch of its "Long March" CZ-2 missile. It now gives China the capability, under certain circumstances, to launch nuclear strikes on at least twelve major Soviet cities, including Moscow.[18]

Moreover, China in 1982 also successfully test-fired its CSS-NX-3 intermediate-range ballistic missile with an estimated range of 2,200 to 3,000 kilometers. Combined with its two ballistic-missile submarines, China now has the components of an assured second-strike capability—a quantum leap in nuclear weapons strategy.

Indications that disputes about priorities in weapons system development are waning in China could be seen in the October 1, 1984, military parade in Beijing. This was the first public display of Chinese nuclear missiles and included CSS-1, CSS-2, CSS-3, and CSS-4 missiles, as well as two CSS-N-3 SLBMs towed on trucks driven by naval personnel.[19] The appearance of nuclear weapons in the public parade was indicative of increased emphasis on nuclear weapons in the overall defense program. While the military has received the lowest priority of the Four Modernizations, nuclear programs have received high priority. In addition, in June 1984 the government announced the establishment of a new Strategic Missile Force, which parallels the Soviet Strategic Rocket Forces, taking over the previous nuclear responsibilities of the Second Artillery of the PLA.

Of the Four Modernizations, military modernization is still fourth, and this is reflected in the limited investment available for the wholesale reequipment of the PLA that its leaders (and certainly the party leaders as well) would like. Deng Xiaoping and his colleagues think that it is more important to channel scarce resources into agriculture, industry, and science.

For years China has tried to limit defense spending, utilizing military industrial plants for civilian purposes. Military spending has clearly been the subject of restraint since the late 1970s. In terms of the official budget, no more resources were devoted to the armed forces in recent years than in 1984. Officially, the military has been receiving a declining share, less than 10 percent, of the central budget (17.5 percent in 1979, and 10.5 percent in 1985).[20]

In June 1986, Zhao Ziyang asked the national defense science, technology, and industry unit to undertake bold reforms and shift to serving civilian production better. The potential of the military is to be put at the service of national economic development and the modernization program. Although the defense industry had already started civilian production, such as motorcycles, it is argued that the existing administrative structure restricts it from doing a still better job in manufacturing civilian products. The government now urges military scientists and workers to use their advantages in technology and equipment to help solve key technical problems of civilian production. Otherwise, such problems will have to be solved through introducing technology from outside. As a consequence of this strategic shift, military production will be greatly reduced, and more military enterprises, workers, and technical forces can be put into national economic development.[21]

Under these circumstances, a strong defense capability is seen to require an emphasis on nuclear deterrence. Funds are therefore to be concentrated on the domestic production of guided missiles and bombs and on a streamlined, more professional armed service. In his 1986 speech, former General Secretary Hu Yaobang said:

Economic development requires huge investment while expansion of military strength needs all the more increased funds. The two are mutually exclusive and it is hardly possible to lay equal stress on both. To tell you frankly, China lacks funds in launching the modernization drive and it is not possible today nor will it be in the next several decades for China to spend heavily on expanding its military forces. After careful consideration, the right thing to do is to concentrate on economic development and gradually improve people's livelihood. On that basis, to strengthen our defense capabilities, we can only do two things: First, we must keep an eye on and study the advanced defense means of the world. Naturally, we also need to import advanced military technology from abroad with a view to strengthening our defense capabilities. We will not spend our limited foreign exchange reserves on buying weapons in large quantities.[22]

However, in order to "keep an eye on and study the advanced defense means of the world," China will most likely make more "window-shopping" excursions like those of the past few years.[23] Although "large quantities" are unaffordable, a small number of purchases are still of practical significance. Certain electronics, aircraft, helicopters, and missiles are being purchased from both the United States and France. Nevertheless, observers comment that since China already had nuclear know-how, a nuclear program may be cheaper than modernizing its conventional forces. Over the next ten years, nuclear weapons developments will likely focus on work on MIRV technology, continued deployment of the CSS-4, and the deployment of SLBMs.[24]

The XIA class of nuclear-powered submarines is one of the key factors in the deployment of the Chinese SLBM. The XIA program probably began about 1975, with the first submarine launched in 1981. By 1983 *Jane's Fighting Ships* confirmed that China had commissioned one nuclear-powered ballistic missile submarine, were building another, and planned to build six more. More recently, Chinese officials have suggested that up to four XIA-class nuclear-powered submarines are now in existence.

In late 1980, a Chinese official noted that the country was developing a nuclear-powered merchant ship. The program should provide the Chinese Navy with an option of constructing nuclear-powered surface combat vessels to complement its submarine component. Therefore, it would not be unreasonable to expect one or more nuclear-powered surface ships to become operational by the end of the 1980s.[25]

The Chinese bomber force is also being modernized. Around 1970 the Chinese aviation industry began producing an indigenous version of the subsonic (Mach 85), jet-propelled Tu-16 Badger bomber, designated B-6 in China. These aircraft were more effective than their predecessors. Production of both the Il-28 Beagle and the Tu-16 Badger bombers has continued, with about two hundred of the light bombers and sixty of the medium bombers currently in service. However, the Chinese leadership apparently has decided to concentrate instead on ballistic missiles for the delivery of nuclear warheads. Although they are slow and vulnerable, the Tu-16 and Il-28 have combat radii that give them capabilities beyond the tactical uses of frontal aviation. But "strategic" bombing is clearly far too ambitious for such a force at this stage.

The Chinese missiles share with the bomber force the potential for limited strikes against the Soviet Union. Indeed, reportedly six of the twelve nuclear devices exploded by China through 1980 were dropped by Tu-16/B-6 aircraft. Despite efforts aimed at the development of an SLBM, the Chinese appear to have concentrated on land-launched strategic missiles. Future Chinese research and development in the ballistic missile field can be expected to emphasize accuracy, engine efficiency, and multiple warheads.[26]

Although the official military budget fell in real terms and as a percentage of government spending, cost for major equipment purchases and military research and development are embedded in other parts of the budget. The Chinese philosophy is that it is necessary to "allocate" resources in various sectors of the economy so that a transition from peace to wartime production can be made smoothly should the need arise. In addition, the strategic shift to put more military production capacity into civilian economic growth was probably made in order to promote efficiency. In the long run, it also seeks to improve the ability to adapt advanced technical know-how from foreign countries, and develop, if possible, cooperative ventures in certain fields. The future of the PRC nuclear program and its ability to design indigenous, advanced weapon systems will depend largely on the country's ability to obtain and assimilate technologies available from abroad. Consequently, in order to increase the flow of military know-how into the Chinese arms industry, a general opening to the West will continue. Current investment in infrastructure, basic industries, technology absorption capabilities, and personnel training will to a large extent support the defense modernization process.

Military modernization is likely to remain slow. The most fundamental problem will be to incorporate new Western design and manufacturing facilities into a preexisting industrial infrastructure. To close the qualitative gaps, particularly in such high-tech areas as the nuclear program, requires more than funding, training of scientists, building the industrial infrastructure, or manufacturing advanced equipment. It requires design innovation, which means that China will have to engage in basic scientific research.

In the current situation, the quality and quantity of Chinese strategic weapons systems seem sufficient, especially for purposes of deterrence. But beyond their utility at a strategic level, such weapons would be difficult to use at the tactical level. As mentioned earlier, at the current time Chinese military leadership faces the difficult choice between positioning their shorter-range missiles near the border (and thus necessitating a quick decision on their use during conflict) or deploying them deep in the Chinese interior, thereby giving the leadership more decision time, but with the result that the weapons (even when fired to maximum range) could only be used against targets on Chinese territory.

Thus, there are substantial pressures for China to mount a nuclear effort far more varied, intensive, and hence expensive than has yet been undertaken. Up to the present, however, the dominant concept has remained one of limited deterrence, and it seems highly probable that such a concept will continue to prevail.[27]

China, in short, shows confidence in its nuclear forces. Its decision to reduce its military expenditures resulted from the reduced estimate of a Soviet threat. In addition, Soviet difficulties in Afghanistan have intensified the Chinese belief that China's very size precludes any invasion.

Nonetheless, as former Deputy Chief of the PLA General Staff Wu Xiuquan observed, China has neither the capability nor the funds to compete with the United States and the USSR in the development of nuclear weaponry. Even without competing, however, China continues to take steps that are designed to improve the range, accuracy, and survivability of its nuclear forces. Among other things, SLBMs deployed in nuclear-powered submarines would add significantly to the survivability of the Chinese strategic forces. Current Chinese programs, although not competing with the USSR, are clearly designed to improve the competence of the nuclear forces for both war and deterrence.[28]

Although the present Chinese nuclear force structure cannot do much more than launch a retaliatory strike against the USSR, the future structure raises complex issues. Currently, China appears to have the ability to target every major urban-industrial complex in the USSR east of the Urals, with an additional but limited ability to strike at targets in European Russia with the few multiple-stage IRBMs and ICBMs that are now deployed. This capability, combined with China's evident willingness to fight a conventional war in defense of its northern and northeastern provinces, provides the deterrent value of the current military posture adopted by Beijing.

Some analysts have suggested that China's deployment of the CSS-4, when combined with programs that are intimately related to the development of more advanced, accurate, and survivable nuclear weapons, takes China beyond a simple deterrence of the Soviet threat. If this is the case, then it would be incorrect to interpret future missile developments in terms of the Soviet threat. However, it is not feasible and not even desirable for the Chinese to seek a more general deterrence in a strategically bipolar world. As a matter of fact, the practical challenge remains the fiscal constraint, and how high a priority the policy-makers are likely to give to nuclear weapons development. And the most important of all is how the Chinese leadership perceives the international environment and the role China should play in world politics.

ARMS CONTROL IMPLICATIONS

China has repeatedly stated that the small number of nuclear weapons it possesses are purely for defense, that China would never be the first to use nuclear weapons, never sell or provide other countries with nuclear weapons, and never deploy its own nuclear weapons abroad. Obviously, each of the above pledges has its own challenge in practice, and it is difficult to keep them under every condition. However, any new interpretation of these long-set policies will require a fundamental change in China's strategic doctrine, for which the current leadership seems not likely to be ready.

China has also stated that it is ready to take appropriate actions and assume its own duties and responsibilities in matters of disarmament as soon as the Soviet Union and the United States have also agreed to the above-mentioned restrictions.

Recently, progress has been made in the international disarmament arena. At the Washington summit in December 1987, the United States and the Soviet Union signed the Intermediate-range Nuclear Forces (INF) Treaty, eliminating all their intermediate-range and shorter-range missiles, and instructed their negotiators in Geneva to work toward a reduction of strategic offensive nuclear arms by approximately 50 percent. According to the treaty, within the next three years, the Soviet Union will destroy some 1,700 SS-4/5, SS-12, SS-20, and SS-23 missiles, and the United States will destroy 800 ground-launched cruise missiles along with Pershing 1A and 2 missiles. While the treaty is a landmark shift from arms control to arms reduction, it only covers 3 to 4 percent of the nuclear arsenals of the two countries, which is certainly not a convincing number to attract the other three smaller nuclear powers, including China, to join the reduction. Although the distruction of 150 mobile SS-20 missiles deployed in the Far East are included in the treaty, as one Chinese expert points out, it makes no difference whether "China is attacked by sophisticated SS-20s coming from Siberia or old Soviet ICBMs launched from silos west of the Urals."[29] However, the elimination of such survivable, mobile, longer-range, and more accurate nuclear weapons as SS-20s is particularly in the interest of security in East Asia, given the relative conventional balance in the region.

As far as a 50 percent reduction in the superpowers' central strategic forces is concerned, it would be at most a psychological achievement in terms of the security of the United States and the Soviet Union, rather than a significant contribution in real terms to the security of the rest of the world. For their nuclear arsenals will still account for approximately 90 percent of the world's total, let alone their absolute superiority in quality. However, the 50 percent reduction may build up a momentum leading to an end to the testing, manufacturing, and deployment of nuclear weapons. Then there would be a constructive atmosphere for other nuclear states to participate in the negotiation process. At present, China has made clear its opposition to the general notion of eliminating its independent deterrent forces. The Chinese leadership seems to believe that China needs more missiles to ensure an ability to deter any potential nuclear attack. No controls on Chinese offensive weapons will be allowed in the atmosphere of an intense superpower arms race—for example, one involving space weapons and improvement of the current strategic weapons.

China also refuses to join the 1968 Nuclear Weapons Non-Proliferation Treaty. Though it is opposed to proliferation, China regards the treaty as discriminatory. It believes that nuclear nonproliferation should refer to both "horizontal" and "vertical" nonproliferation: nonnuclear countries should not acquire nuclear weapons, and the nuclear countries should not increase or improve their nuclear arms. The treaty, however, only forbids the spread of atomic weapons to the nonnuclear countries, and fails to prevent the nuclear signatories to the treaty from increasing and improving their arsenals. China argues that this is clearly unfair.[30]

China also believes that the continual improvement of Soviet and U.S. nuclear arms has become increasingly dangerous, and jeopardizes Chinese security. Therefore, the superpowers must halt the development of nuclear weapons and unconditionally undertake not to use nuclear weapons against the nonnuclear countries.

In addition, the international community should give greater attention to regional political-security issues, which are in many cases the main reason countries develop a nuclear capacity. It is clearly not in China's interest to support any of its neighbors' efforts to develop a nuclear capacity, though it is an awkward problem for China to persuade anyone not to do so. This is particularly true with regard to the Chinese response to Pakistan's nuclear program, which is largely justified by its relations with India. China has little influence other than encouraging and supporting efforts aimed at improving the relationship between India and Pakistan. In addition, the Chinese also believe that so long as the superpowers continue to keep a large nuclear stockpile there is no way to convince other countries that it is not good for them to have their own nuclear capacity.

It is necessary to address the issue of Chinese international weapons sales, particularly those in the Middle East. Although the sales do not affect Chinese nuclear strategy (thus they seem not to have to do with the theme of this paper), they stand out as some of the new initiatives taken by the makers of Chinese foreign policy in recent years, and particularly so with the direct involvement of the military establishment in this case. Such initiatives seem to rest on several considerations: (1) Arms sales would help China gain political influence in the region, given China's continuous support for the Arab countries. (2) In the case of a missile sale to Saudi Arabia, it would bring political pressure upon the Nationalist regime in Taiwan. Of the twenty-three countries who now maintain formal diplomatic relations with Taiwan, Saudi Arabia stands out as one of the biggest and most important missions and thus extremely valuable to Taipei. It is in this sense that the missile sale would afford Beijing an opportunity to improve significantly its relations with Saudi Arabia. (3) It would earn China much-valued foreign exchange, which is badly needed to finance the country's highly demanded import of advanced technology. One estimate provides that China's weapons sales represented 8 percent of its total export earnings in 1986. Overseas arms sales totaled at least $2 billion in 1986, with most of that derived from Middle East sales.[31]

However, these considerations can hardly be taken as indicating any fundamental change in China's foreign policy, because they are to a large extent still consistent with the major principles that Chinese policy-makers have followed for years. First, with regard to the pledge that China would never sell or provide other countries with nuclear weapons, the recent intermediate-range missile sales to Saudi Arabia and any other sales have a clear-cut threshold that China would not cross. Saudi Arabia has promised not to use Chinese missiles to deliver nuclear warheads. Second, since China has long strongly supported the Arab countries against Israel, a move that could work to their advantage in the regional balance of power is considered to be politically justified and hence reasonable.[32]

Nonetheless, the increase of arms sales in terms of both scale and scope do suggest some new dimensions in Beijing's perception of current international relations. First, the policy-makers seem to perceive the world in much more pragmatic terms. Compared to the radical approach before the mid-1970s—for example, providing free military aid to a number of countries based merely on political and moral considerations—the current approach gives increasing importance to economic factors. In other words, the world is perceived not only as a political arena but, more importantly, as a marketplace. Arms deals are internationally accepted and are normal transactions between states. Thus, so long as other countries are routinely engaged in the larger amount of conventional arms transactions, there is little practical reason for the Chinese to shut themselves out of the market. As a matter of fact, China has further strengthened its efforts to compete in the world market.[33]

The commercial implications of arms sales are obvious. Given the fact that China is still far from being in the same class with the world's top arms salesmen—the Americans, Soviets, French, and British—China would not have to risk its international image in pursuing commercial interest, and might well take advantage of its competitiveness in durable, easy-to-use arms at much lower prices than those charged for sophisticated Western weapons. In short, the whole process of arms sales, particularly those to Saudi Arabia, reveals little evidence that the decisions were prompt and merely opportunistic, but rather they were well-backed and grounded in the pragmatic policies that have quickly evolved in China in recent years.

Second, the fact that the negative response to the Chinese missile sales came primarily from the United States is self-evident of the nature of the issue. Recently, the U.S. government has sought to gain assurances from the Chinese leaders that they would curb their sales of missiles in the Middle East. Moreover, the Dole Amendment, using high-technology transfer as leverage, clearly seeks to enforce linkage politics. China responded that the sales were conducted with caution and responsibility. Furthermore, while the United States keeps quiet about its Western allies' much more lucrative arms sales in the region, let alone its own sales, actions by the U.S. government against China would be interpreted in Beijing as motivated by political differences rather than by national security concerns.

Notably, the firm Chinese position on the issue seems to indicate the Chinese leaders' perceptions of Sino-U.S. relations. On the one hand, Beijing sees that the bilateral relations are well grounded and able to stand occasional problems. The strategic interest that they share in East Asia and the increasingly close economic relationship from which both can benefit provide a price that is too much for both countries to afford should either of them severely damage the relationship as a result of some relatively minor issues such as arms sales to countries like Saudi Arabia. As a matter of fact, despite its repeatedly expressed concerns, the United States went along in early July with a decision by the sixteen-nation CoCom, the Coordinating Committee for Multilateral Export Control, to further relax restrictions on high-technology exports to China.[34] On the other hand, it seems evident that China does not have overexpectations concerning the further development of the bilateral relationship, particularly in strategic terms. To be realistic, it is quite natural to see problems occurring every now and then. No country can absent itself from frequent frictions and disagreements even with its closest allies. Of the Sino-U.S. relationship, had there not been the issue of arms sale, other issues, such as that of Tibet, would be noisier. Without the Tibet issue, the Taiwan issue still exists. The bottom line is that, given the Chinese emphasis on an independent foreign policy, there is hardly any significant development of the bilateral relationship that either side could achieve at this point in time. After all, the implication is that the Sino-U.S. relationship is as good as can be realistically expected.

The arms control or arms reduction arena is currently dominated by the two superpowers. So long as such dominance remains unchanged, China will continue on its present nuclear course. In the long run, China views its nuclear weapons program as the core of an independent defence capability that will permit Beijing to deter any adversary. Additionally, China also sees the disarmament forums as useful platforms for enhancing its influence and involvement in international affairs. If no dramatic changes take place in the next decade or even if there were to be further significant and verifiable reductions in the superpowers' arsenals, it is difficult to imagine the Chinese greatly altering their own strategic program.

An overall examination of arms control implications for Chinese nuclear development cannot be fairly concluded without discussing the Soviet attitudes toward Chinese nuclear forces and the U.S. view of this issue. The Soviet Union is the only nuclear power that must actively prepare for nuclear contingencies involving more than a single state. At present, China remains a subsidiary element in these calculations. So far, China's overall strategic effort remains too modest to necessitate a substantial redirection in Soviet allocations.

However, since the Chinese nuclear forces are oriented almost exclusively toward the Soviet Union, they represent a direct threat to the USSR that must be taken into consideration. In the SALT II deliberations prior to the Vladivostok meeting, Soviet officials initially "insisted that the American total [of delivery vehicles] include nuclear capable aircraft in and around Europe as well as British, French, and Chinese nuclear forces."[35] While Soviet arguments subsequently eased, such a negotiating tactic will become increasingly used over time. The Soviet Union is fully aware that China with its ICBMs, like Britain with Polaris and now Trident missiles, constitutes a challenge to its defense program and has the ability to ensure at least a minimum deterrence.

A brief retrospective view provides a picture of the increased Soviet nuclear deployment facing China. The Soviet 1969 inventory probably included no more than 250 to 300 ICBM warheads capable of being used in a preemptive counterforce role. Clearly, these could not all be made available for a strike against China. Nor were any of the medium- or intermediate-range missiles accurate enough for such a role. By 1977–78 the situation had markedly changed. The number of tactical warheads available to Soviet forces on the Chinese border had increased, and delivery vehicles included advanced MiG-27s and Su-24s as well as SS-1 and SS-12 mobile missiles with

respective ranges of 180 and 500 nautical miles. Nearly 200 medium-
and intermediate-range missiles have been deployed along the
Trans-Siberian Railroad, including some of the new SS-20 IRBMs
with their three independently targetable warheads and a CEP of
one-tenth of a mile.[36] In addition, the Russians have over 400
ICBMs and over 260 SLBMs based in the Far East, which are
capable of being quickly reprogrammed for use against China.[37] In
this sense, even with the INF Treaty verified in the next three years,
China will still be in the shadow of massive Soviet strategic forces.

The Soviet Union obviously will continue to obstruct any possible Sino-American strategic relationship. It is clear that the addition
to the global power equation of large numbers of Chinese conventional ground forces and a limited but growing nuclear missile
arsenal significantly impairs Soviet confidence in their ability to
launch an effective nuclear or even conventional assault in the future. The current obvious imbalance of Chinese and Soviet nuclear
forces can be summed up as follows: On the one hand, China cannot
be confident that launch preparations could not be aborted by Moscow's potential for a rapid reaction, a preemptive strike, or that its
missiles, once launched, could penetrate Soviet missile defenses. On
the other hand, the USSR cannot feel absolutely confident of its
ability to prevent a Chinese strike. That uncertainty is China's deterrent, one that Beijing at present deems sufficient.

For many U.S. officials, China clearly plays an important and
helpful role in U.S. global and regional strategic planning, especially
vis-à-vis the USSR. First, China assists the United States by tying
down Soviet forces and resources that otherwise might have been
focused against the West in Europe or the Middle East, and by
complicating Soviet defense strategy, notably by raising uncertainty
in the USSR about the security of the Soviet Union's Asian front
if conflict were to break out farther west. Thus, on the simple
principle, in a sense, that "my enemy's enemy is my friend," many
American strategists regard China as a strategic asset of the United
States.

Second, the relative weakness of U.S. land forces in Asia, and
the massive Soviet military buildup during the 1970s, have offered
powerful inducements for the United States to make common cause
with China on security. In addition to the military considerations,
the United States also has increasingly important economic interests
in the Asian-Pacific region that in many ways are dependent upon
a high level of regional security.

In sum, the United States will not avoid doing its share to offset steadily increasing Soviet military capabilities. Since U.S. strategy assumes that Chinese forces offset Soviet ground forces and some nuclear forces, the principal U.S. force enhancements probably will emphasize naval and air capabilities. So far, on the American side there are few discussions specifically on U.S. attitudes toward the Chinese nuclear forces, partly because Chinese nuclear weapons are small in number and primarily target the Soviet Union, thus are of little consequence to U.S. security.

CONCLUSION: FOREIGN-POLICY OPTIONS

The size and scope both of China's government, including its military establishment, and its economy give pause to any thoughts of sweeping policy changes. The basic options for the next decade are actually fairly limited.

The country can continue along present policy lines that focus on the following:

1. It can work to improve the revised nuclear strategy, which is designed to deny the Soviets or any other potential enemy any realistic chance of gaining quick military victory. To fulfill this objective, China should develop a sound, long-term posture through the next decade that seeks a credible deterrent backed up by its improved land- and sea-based missile forces. More emphasis should be given to the development of additional tactical nuclear weapons, which could make the existing deterrent more flexible, effective, and reliable.
2. China can oppose any possible U.S.-Soviet agreement on arms control that would permit either Moscow or Washington to enhance significantly its existing superior nuclear capabilities despite the fact that they have begun to cut their respective nuclear forces. Moreover, while the current relatively stable balance of forces along the Sino-Soviet frontier should be maintained, the tensions on the southern border with Vietnam should be reduced. Any impression of a threat to use nuclear forces on nonnuclear nations should be absolutely avoided. Otherwise, China's objective of further developing nuclear weapons could easily be distorted or misinterpreted.

3. China can continue its efforts to maintain the so-far-so-good relations with Japan and to improve the current unsatisfactory relations with Southeast Asian countries. Although they have reacted calmly, many Asians, both in Japan and in ASEAN, express reservations about the development of Chinese nuclear forces. They acknowledge that such forces are built up mainly to cope with the potential threat from the Soviet Union. They are anxious, however, that increased Chinese nuclear capabilities could provoke more Soviet nuclear deployments in the Far East, which heightens the danger of possible conflict in the region. Also, some Southeast Asian countries are concerned that Chinese nuclear forces are not necessarily defensive in nature. As Chinese nuclear stockpiles continue to grow, those who make Chinese foreign policy will have to become increasingly sensitive to their neighbors' security concerns. This will require continuous efforts by Beijing, while clearly stating the justifications of its nuclear program, to further improve its relations with those countries through, for example, closer economic cooperation and more involvement in settling regional political problems. The efforts in this respect, although not all directly related to nuclear strategy, or even security strategy, would contribute toward a favorable and more stable international environment for China generally.

Or the country can return to the "spirit" of the old policies:

1. Maintenance of emphasis on the "traditional" strategy, which depends largely on China's capacity to prepare and sustain in-depth defense along the most likely avenues of attack. This option requires an increase in defense expenditures from current levels in order to meet the need of a large-scale military buildup not only in nuclear forces but also in conventional forces. The most obvious cost of the option is that such a buildup would absorb a considerable portion of the country's raw materials, production capacity, and most proficient manpower, which are the key resources for China's modernization program.

2. Renewed efforts to achieve development through a policy of self-reliance. This option, while acknowledging China's need for indigenous defense-industry capabilities, emphasizes the importance of first assuring the high quality of new weapons systems.

3. Opposition to the nonproliferation treaty, and rejection of participation in any international nuclear arms limitation agreements at

this time. China can thus maintain its independence and continue to project its image as the only developing country so far that has nuclear weapons, thereby underlining its position as a possible Third World leader.

Within these two policy directions, China could focus on implementing a number of processes to ensure greater chances of success. These policies need not be exclusive of each other, since development does not happen in a vacuum. However, of the two options, it is fairly clear that the first is more beneficial to the country as a whole.

FIVE

SINO-SOVIET RELATIONS

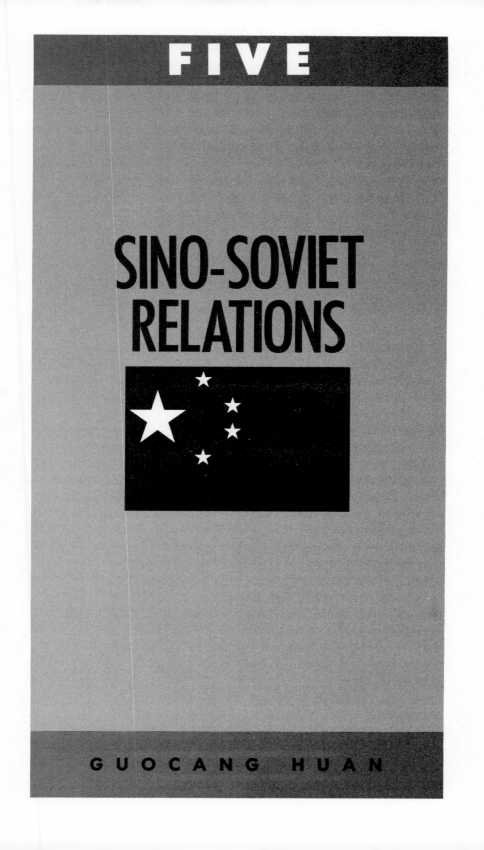

GUOCANG HUAN

Nineteen eighty-eight was a year of improving relations between China and the Soviet Union. For the first time since 1969, Beijing and Moscow expressed their strong interest in holding a summit, now set for May 1989. It has been reported that "the atmosphere of Sino-Soviet governmental consultations has improved dramatically." The Soviets now appear to be willing to hold serious discussions with China on the issue of Cambodia. The two sides have begun referring to each other as "comrades," a word suggesting that no serious ideological difficulties exist between them. Following the Geneva agreement, Moscow pulled out its troops from Afghanistan by the end of February 1989. It has negotiated directly with the representatives of Afghan resistance movements.[1] In March 1987, soon before the tenth round of Sino-Soviet talks, the Soviet Union withdrew one of its six troop divisions from Mongolia. During the recent Sino-Soviet border negotiations, Moscow made a significant concession by acknowledging Beijing's sole right over Zhengbao (Damensky) Island, where the two Communist powers had clashed bloodily in March 1969.[2] In December 1988, Gorbachev proposed to cut 500,000 of its troops, including those deployed in the Far East.

For its part, Beijing has welcomed Moscow's new initiatives. Deng Xiaoping has expressed his personal interest in meeting with Gorbachev if further progress could be made to end Hanoi's occupation of Cambodia, the most difficult issue among China's "three preconditions for the improvement of Sino-Soviet relations."[3] Beijing has become far less critical than before of Moscow's foreign policy, especially concerning matters outside the Asian-Pacific region. The Chinese media have published thousands of articles to introduce Gorbachev's reform program as well as his "new thinking" in international affairs. Meanwhile, Beijing has improved its ties with most East European states and reestablished relationships with most Communist parties in Western Europe.

Economically, Sino-Soviet trade has doubled during the past

two years and reached US$2.9 billion in 1987 and over $3.5 billion in 1988.[4] Moscow and Beijing have signed a number of long-term trade agreements. Soviet and East European technicians have begun to provide technical assistance to help Beijing replace 156 industrial installations imported from the Soviet bloc during the 1950s, which played the key role in China's process of industrialization. Senior officials in charge of economic affairs from both countries have visited each other frequently, exchanging views and experiences regarding their economic reform programs. In December 1988, the Soviet government even made a long-term loan in kind to the provincial government of Xingjiang. This is the first time since the Sino-Soviet split at the end of the 1950s that a Chinese province, located in a strategically important area, accepted a direct loan from Moscow.[5]

Cultural ties between Beijing and Moscow have also expanded. After a twenty-year break, the two countries have again begun to exchange students and scholars. Academicians in both countries have rapidly expanded their research and study programs about each other's economic development, politics, foreign policies, and other fields. More importantly, while Chinese scholars have been optimistic about Gorbachev's reform program, Soviet scholars have recently expressed more favorable views on China's economic reform and its open-door policy in over a hundred articles. In a newspaper interview, the Soviet ambassador to Beijing has openly supported China's economic reform.[6]

However, the strategic relationship between the two Communist powers has not undergone significant change. Moscow has continued to enlarge its Pacific Fleet, strengthened its air force in the Far East, increased its military aid to Hanoi, and expanded its military presence in Cam Ranh and Da Nang bays.[7] It has also deepened its involvements in subregional political and security affairs such as on the Korean Peninsula and in South Asia, where Beijing and Moscow have little common interest. The limited relaxation of tensions between China and the Soviet Union has not yet significantly altered Moscow's long-term strategic objectives: to push Beijing away from Washington and Tokyo and to contain China strategically through increased Soviet military power around China's peripheries.

For its part, Beijing continues to view the Soviet Union as the primary threat to its national security. Though Beijing has adjusted the "three preconditions" by not demanding that Moscow solve all three issues at once, its basic security and strategic interests have not changed: these are to reduce Moscow's political and military leverage over China and to break down Moscow's strategic encirclement around China. Beijing welcomed Moscow's withdrawal from Afghanistan in early 1989. But it has emphasized that the division of the Red Army that left Mongolia "had been stationed in the northern part of Mongolia, but not on the Chinese border."[8] In addition, Beijing has insisted that Moscow should more actively press Hanoi to pull out of Cambodia. China's strategic planners have continued to warn of the potential danger of the Soviet military presence in the South China Sea. As one Chinese strategic planner has put it, except for the removal of SS-20 missiles from the Far East, which is a result of the Soviet-American Intermediate-range Nuclear Forces (INF) Treaty, and not of changes in Sino-Soviet relations, Moscow has not yet made any significant move to reduce its military forces in the region.[9]

Beijing continues its efforts to develop political and military cooperation with the United States, especially with regard to the security of the Asian-Pacific region. Beijing has continued to play the role of major weapons supplier to the resistance forces in Cambodia and maintains political and military pressure on Vietnam. In addition, Beijing has expanded its political and military cooperation with Thailand. It has repeatedly expressed its interest in maintaining the stability of Northeast Asia. In South Asia, the Chinese government has continued its full support for both Pakistan and the rebels in Afghanistan, while making efforts to improve relations with India. The continued conflicts in security and strategic interests between Moscow and Beijing have not been dramatically reduced and will continue to influence strongly the dynamics of Sino-Soviet relations in general in the years ahead.

The development of Sino-Soviet relations has had and will continue to have a strong impact on the struggle between Moscow, Beijing, and Washington. It will also affect the balance of power and stability in the Asian-Pacific region. Furthermore, it will continue to be one major factor in reshaping Chinese foreign policy in general.

Three related factors will determine the dynamics of Sino-Soviet relations in the next decade: China's Soviet policy, the Soviet Union's China policy, and the dynamics of the international environment. This chapter will examine each of these factors, then discuss the possible developments in Sino-Soviet relations in the next decade, and finally suggest basic policy options that Beijing may choose in dealing with the Soviet Union.

CHINA'S DOMESTIC DEVELOPMENT AND SINO-SOVIET RELATIONS

In general, China's policy toward the Soviet Union is determined by its domestic development, the international environment, and Moscow's policy toward China. During the past two years, each of these factors has undergone significant changes, and the degree to which each affects China's policy toward the Soviet Union has also changed.

Domestically, the most important changes that have taken place during the past two years are the unstable developments resulting from the post-Mao political, economic, and cultural reforms. These developments have strongly affected Beijing's foreign policy, including its policy toward Moscow.

The reform group, led by Deng Xiaoping, has advanced a political reform program. This program, together with the government's economic reform and the "open-door" policy, has changed the following aspects of China's public life and political institutions.

- The personality cult and personal dictatorship, which was one of the key factors leading to the Sino-Soviet split during the 1960s and the first half of the 1970s, have been banned in China. Although Deng Xiaoping himself continues to play a decisive role in the decision-making process at the top, a multipolar power structure has gradually been established among the party and government institutions. The political struggle within the party no longer involves violent methods. The generation of the 1950s, many of whom were educated in the Soviet Union and Eastern Europe, has rapidly increased its influence within the top levels of the party and government establishment.[10]
- The relationship between the state and society has changed significantly. While the society has begun a process of "depoliticization," individualism and personal interests have become the core principle to guide social behavior in general. The degree of personal freedom, though not political freedom, has continued to increase. While the society has become increasingly alienated and independent from the state and there has been an increased tend-

ency to "noncooperatism," the credibility, authority, and capacity of the government to control and mobilize the society have been weakened. Through noninstitutionalized channels, various interest groups, especially the young generation and the intelligentsia, have begun to pressure the decision-makers. Due to the worsened economic situation and widely spread corruption, the government's credibility and authority has been increasingly challenged by the public at large.[11]

- Various political institutions have been reformed. Decision-making has been decentralized. Local authorities, notably at the provincial level, have been granted great political and economic power. The regional gap between the coastal areas and the inner parts of the country has significantly enlarged. There has been a process of professionalization of both civilian and military bureaucrats. A large number of younger, well-educated, and more pragmatic technocrats, many of whom have had the experience of either studying or visiting in the West, have replaced old and conservative political bureaucrats.

- The official ideology, which was another important factor leading to the Sino-Soviet split during the sixties and the early seventies, has changed significantly. The Chinese have already largely accepted the Soviets' views on many important theoretical issues with regard to international relations that were seriously debated between Beijing and Moscow during the sixties, such as war and peace, nuclear weapons and nuclear war, and the nature of international politics, the possibility of peaceful coexistence between capitalist and socialist states. Furthermore, the Chinese have studied and introduced many aspects of the successful experiences of economic, cultural, and political development of the Western countries, Japan, and Asia's newly industrialized nations. Meanwhile, the majority of the society has appeared far less interested in the official ideology.

The economic reforms have gone even further, although they have experienced some serious difficulties.

- Following the successful policy of decollectivization of the people's commune system, the Chinese government has encouraged several hundred million peasants to develop local industries, based upon a newly expanded private ownership. The free market, which is mainly operated by peasants, has become a major source of supplying consumer goods, especially foodstuffs. This policy has undercut the party organizations in rural areas and created a new peasant-industrial elite.[12]

• In both rural and urban areas, the government has continued to encourage the development of the private sector. In 1987, the Law of Bankruptcy was passed. Thousands of factories that were not profitable have been leased out to private individuals. Since early 1988, following the efforts to change state ownership into shareholder ownership, a number of major cities have set up stock markets. As a result, millions of NEP men (for New Economic Policy, a term used in the 1920s to refer to private entrepreneurs in the Soviet Union) are now operating their own businesses in China.

• The government has altered its developmental strategy; it has put strong emphasis on the production of consumer goods. While slowing down the development of military and heavy industries, the government has diverted more resources to light industry.

• The government has deepened its reform of the central planning system, allowing local authorities greater flexibility in making their own decisions. It has furthered price reform and the reform of financial institutions, aimed at developing the market mechanism and creating a "mixed economy." Further, the management has been professionalized, enterprises have been granted greater autonomy, and the Communist Party's control over enterprises has been weakened.[13]

Further, the Chinese government has continued its open-door policy.

• It has put strong emphasis on the development of export-oriented industries along the Chinese coastal areas. To integrate the Chinese economy into the world economy at large and to expand China's economic ties with industrialized and semi-industrialized nations have been regarded as the country's basic principles of economic development. China's foreign trade has continued its rapid growth, now amounting to roughly 8 percent of its GNP. The government has put a high priority on importing technology from industrial nations.[14]

• China has become more active than before in world financial markets and international economic institutions such as the World Bank and the International Monetary Fund (IMF). While increasing its commercial borrowing from abroad, China has increased its sales of bonds and the export of labor service to other countries.

- The Chinese government has continued to make great efforts to attract direct foreign investment. Besides four special economic zones (SEZs), fourteen coastal open cities, and Hainan Island (now becoming a province), most cities and provinces have also set up joint operations with foreign corporations. By the end of 1988, over ten thousand foreign-involved enterprises were operating in China. The degree of interdependence between the Chinese economy and the world market, especially the OECD (Organization for Economic Cooperation and Development) nations, has continued its rapid increase. In the summer of 1988, the central government decided to open Shandong province to South Korean investors. Efforts to gain more technology, industrial equipment, and capital investment, and to expand foreign trade have become increasingly important to the foreign-policy–makers in Beijing.
- The government has continued its policy of sending students to Western countries and Japan for study and training.[15] Thousands of foreign scholars have been invited to China to give lectures and seminars on various subjects—science, technology, business management, law, and the humanities. The Chinese government has significantly reduced its restrictions on the flow of information into China. Western cultural influence has spread rapidly and widely.

Nevertheless, domestic developments in China have not been stable. Rather, there have been many difficulties, frustrations, and even crises. In the long run, these problems, if they get out of control, may undermine the political stability and re-shape the country's foreign policy, including its policy toward both superpowers.

In the first place, the forthcoming succession remains uncertain. It is uncertain because the reformers have not been able to institutionalize and legitimize their policies fully. The conservatives, who want China to return to the so-called "golden age between 1949 and 1956," and have wanted to pursue a Soviet-type system with Chinese characteristics, still retain their strong influence within the top leadership circle. More importantly, conservatives have appeared capable of challenging not only the reformers' policies but also their political power. In December 1986, under the strong pressure of the conservatives, General Secretary Hu Yaobang, one of the leading reformers and Deng Xiaoping's successor, was ousted. A repressive political campaign against intellectual freedom was launched. In the summer of 1988, a similar attempt was made against Zhao Ziyang, now the party's general secretary. Although Zhao has survived, the conservatives have strengthened their position within the party and the central government, notably in the areas of ideology and the economy. These political changes have weakened the reformers' position, damaged their credibility, deepened tensions between the state and society, and increased political uncertainties.[16]

In the second place, reformers themselves have imposed certain restrictions on the reform program. Politically, they are not able to reform the political system in a pluralist direction, nor are they in the position to create a new generation of technocrats to support its policies in the near future. They have not had much control over the party's ideological affairs, nor have they created a new ideology to justify their policies. Instead, under strong pressure from the conservatives, they have periodically vacillated in one or another direction.

Third, although the agricultural reform has been quite successful, the urban industrial reform and the open-door policy have appeared to encounter increasing difficulties. During the past two years, inflation rates have remained high; the central government has had difficulties in managing the scale of national investment and the money flow.[17] There have been neither mechanisms nor policies to coordinate the reform programs in different economic sectors. Nor has the central government been able to carry out an effective political reform that can moderate the conflicts between the ongoing economic reforms and the existing political institutions. Besides bureaucratic politics and ideological constraints, the major reason for such troubles is the lack of knowledge on "how" to reform.

Fourth, the open-door policy is facing challenges, too. Politically, the conservatives have launched strong attacks on the open-door policy, calling it "Westernization." Culturally, the conflicts between traditional Chinese values and the conservative views of the party, on the one hand, and the newly imported Western culture, materialistic youth, and an alienated intelligentsia, on the other, have already increased tensions between the state and society. In addition, the adoption of the open-door policy has created new tensions between those who have benefited by the policy and those who have not. Economically, the lack of knowledge and experience in international business and the mismanagement of economic and financial policies have been the major factors jeopardizing China's investment environment and weakening its competitiveness in the international market.[18] In addition, the existing institutional gap between the Chinese economy and market economies abroad, the continuous political disagreements within the leadership, the frequent policy swings, serious bureaucratism, and the shortcomings of the country's legal institutions have continued to be major barriers to foreign investors' deep commitments to the Chinese market. Finally, the continued world recession, the decline in the price of raw materials and oil in the international market, and increased international protectionism in the industrial world against developing or underdeveloped nations have continued to restrict China's performance in the international market.[19] These economic difficulties have strongly affected politics and challenged the reform group, which was generally in charge of the economic policy-making until the summer 1988.

Fifth, the tensions between the state and society have intensified. Unsatisfied with the high inflation, the rapidly enlarged income gap, bureaucratic privileges, and widespread corruption, the urban population, especially the youth and the intelligentsia, has become increasingly impatient, demanding further democratic reforms. During the past two years, there have been more demonstrations and unrest in a number of major cities. Workers and students have reportedly tried to form independent trade unions and political organizations.[20] In Tibet, Inner Mongolia, and Xingjiang, there has been increased ethnic unrest and violence, challenging the central government's authority. If the economic situation gets worse, these developments may lead to a fundamental political crisis during the succession process, similar to what has happened in Poland.

Taken together, there are basically two possible future developments in China in the next few years. The degree to which each of them would affect China's policy toward the Soviet Union are different. In the first case, the reform program will continue. Following the implementation of Deng Xiaoping's succession, the reform group will further pursue its political liberalization and institutional reform. It will also continue its economic strategy and the open-door policy. As a result, China will enjoy greater political stability; the policy-making process will be further rationalized; the present political system may continue to move in a more pluralistic direction; and the society's participation in public life will increase while economic and cultural life will be further depoliticized. Economically, the country will enjoy stable growth and expanded cooperation with industrial-market economies. While the institutional gap between the Chinese economy and market economies will be narrowed, the degree of interdependence between the Chinese economy and the world economy will increase further.

In this situation, China will not have strong domestic incentives to develop "equidistant" relationships with the United States and the Soviet Union. Instead, strong economic interests will allow policy-makers in Beijing to move closer to the West, especially the United States. In political and security affairs, Beijing will continue to seek relaxation of tensions with Moscow and the reduction of the latter's military pressure on it, but not at the cost of jeopardizing its ties with the United States.

In the second case, the reform programs will be reversed, notably in urban industrial sectors, either by the conservatives taking over or by the reformers themselves. In this case, the course of political development in China will move in a direction similar to that in the post-Khrushchev Soviet Union. The present efforts to reform the political and economic system will cease, although it is unlikely that the government would be able to "bring" China back to the prereform period. The political system will be more repressive and less liberal. The government's political control over public life will be strengthened. China may alter its open-door policy and instead look for increased economic and technological assistance from the Soviet bloc. China's economic development will slow down. Given society's increased political independence of the state, this development is likely to jeopardize the country's political stability.

If the second possibility occurs, the conservative government will have strong domestic incentive to change its foreign policy—in other words, to cut back its ties with the West, especially the United States, and with Japan. To contain the Western cultural and political influence among the youth and the intelligentsia will become one of the top priorities on the government's political agenda. Beijing will certainly have strong political and ideological incentives to move closer to Moscow, as a Soviet-type political system can best serve its interests of repressing the society at large. Nevertheless, whether such an intention will alter China's security strategy toward the Soviet Union may largely depend on the further dynamics of China's security environment, especially whether Moscow would substantially reduce its military and strategic pressure on Beijing and whether the Taiwan issue would get out of control in Beijing-Washington relations.

CHINA'S INTERNATIONAL ENVIRONMENT AND ITS POLICY TOWARD THE SOVIET UNION

China is not a global power, but an Asian-Pacific power of global strategic importance. Its security interests concern primarily the Asian-Pacific region. Two factors in particular—the triangular relations among the United States, the Soviet Union, and China on the one hand and the dynamics of the Asian-Pacific region on the other—have appeared to be increasingly significant in determining China's foreign policy, notably its security strategy. During the past few years, both factors have undergone important changes, which have strongly affected China's foreign policy, including its policy toward the Soviet Union.

One of China's leading experts on international relations, Huan Xiang, writes: "Contemporary world politics is largely determined by the dynamics of the 'triangle' between the United States, China and the Soviet Union. The politics of the Asian-Pacific region is largely determined by the relations between four powers: the United States, the Soviet Union, China and Japan,"[21] which accurately expresses China's perspective on contemporary international politics and China's role in the international system.

During the past few years, the "big" triangle between Washington, Beijing, and Moscow has undergone the following important changes. These changes are likely to continue in the years ahead.

• The triangular relations have tended to be more stable than before. This is because both Moscow and Washington have made strong efforts to reduce tensions and improve relations between them. As a result, the need for Washington to develop a strategic partnership with Beijing against Moscow has declined. Beijing, the weaker power among the three, has chosen a more realistic approach to deal with both superpowers and has pursued its foreign policy in a much less general and simplistic way. All three powers have more clearly defined the balance of power among them, their specific interests in dealing with each other, and their capability in pursuing these interests. There is less room than before for any of the three powers to shift its position dramatically in the triangle.

113

- The competition between the two superpowers at both global and regional levels has become the center of conflict within the triangle. Gorbachev's reform program has improved the image of the Soviet Union in the West. Moscow's concessions made in the area of human rights have also reduced political tensions between the two superpowers. The internal political and economic needs in both Washington and Moscow have generated incentives on both sides for further improving their relations and making efforts to constrain their nuclear arms race. Following the signing of the INF Treaty and its promise to withdraw troops from Afghanistan by the end of February 1989, Moscow initiated a proposal to withdraw half a million troops from both Europe and Asia. So far, Washington has responded to this proposal favorably without making its own promise. Nevertheless, if Moscow did cut a half million of its armed forces in the next two years, it is unlikely that the Bush administration would be able to do the same. More importantly, Gorbachev's proposal may create serious difficulties between Washington and its NATO allies. The reduction of strategic weapons is a much more complicated issue. It is directly related to the balance of conventional forces in Europe, concerning which most European and American strategists believe that the Warsaw Pact has superiority over NATO. Whether or not the two superpowers would be able to reach an agreement on the restriction of the arms race in outer space may largely depend upon whether the Bush administration will be willing to cease the research program for the Strategic Defense Initiative (SDI) in the near future. Both the progress in technological development and the complications of U.S. domestic politics may make it difficult for President Bush to make significant compromises in this area. Gorbachev, too, is facing serious resentments from his military generals, who have expressed their concern that he may have gone too far, so that Moscow's fundamental security interests may be jeopardized. Soviet generals are particularly worried about the United States' leading position in the outer space arms race.[22] The deep distrust between the two countries, especially between their military elites, remains.
- The two superpowers may continue their sharp competition over a number of regional security issues. During the past two years, Moscow has increased its military forces, especially its navy fleet and strategic air force, in the Far East. It has not reduced its military presence in the South China Sea, where the United States

continues to face the possibility of losing its military bases in the Philippines. It is likely that the Bush administration may soon review the dynamics of the Asian-Pacific region and formulate a new strategy to protect its security interests there. In the Middle East, the competition between the two superpowers has continued, although the intensified political and military struggle between various Islamic countries and between Israel and its Arab counterparts may have overshadowed Moscow's deep involvement in the region. If the current Israeli-Arab confrontation continues to escalate and if the proposed U.S.-Palestinian talks fail to make significant progress in bringing peace to the region, it is likely that Moscow's influence in the area will naturally increase, as disappointed Arab nations may look to Moscow for help. In regard to Central America, the 101st U.S. Congress will surely make it difficult for the White House to increase its military pressure on Nicaragua. Yet the existing basic conflict between the United States and Nicaragua, which is backed by the Soviet Union and Cuba, will remain. In sum, the recent improvement in U.S.-Soviet relations has not fundamentally altered the nature of the strategic and security relationship between them. In most areas of international politics, their competition is likely to continue.

- In Eastern Europe, Moscow has already experienced and will continue to face serious political challenges from popular domestic forces. Gorbachev's reform program in the Soviet Union, if it continues, will certainly encourage most East European states to speed up their economic and political reforms. Yet the reform process in these countries is likely to increase their independence from Moscow, thereby challenging the latter's political authority and jeopardizing political stability in Eastern Europe. This potential will likely provoke political conflicts between the East and the West, notably between Moscow and Washington.

- In a number of Third World countries that have strategic significance, such as South Africa, South Korea, and the Philippines, political conflicts between local regimes and their opposition continue to provide opportunities to Moscow to expand its political and even military influence. Such developments would reinforce the competition between Washington and Moscow.

- Meanwhile, relations between China and the two superpowers have appeared less tense, more manageable and flexible. To avoid being the central target of Moscow's Far Eastern strategy, Beijing has made efforts to improve the relationship with Moscow. Meanwhile, it has played down the need for security cooperation with Washington. Yet the Sino-American military exchange program has advanced. Washington and Beijing have been cooperative on various regional security and political issues in Asia, such as support for the Afghan resistant movement, the security of Pakistan, the demand for the Vietnamese withdrawal from Cambodia, and the reduction of tensions on the Korean Peninsula. The cultural and economic ties between the two countries have expanded rapidly, and the United States is now China's third-largest trade partner. Although Beijing has continued to press Washington to reduce its arms sales and transfers of military technology to Taiwan, the Taiwan issue seems to be more manageable than before. Unless Taiwan's internal politics suddenly drive the island in the direction of independence, Sino-American relations will unlikely reverse in the near future. As a result, the foundation of Sino-American relations is no longer based only upon mutual security interests, but rather on a combination of political, economic, and strategic interests. The working relationship between Washington and Beijing has improved.

During the past few years, the Asian-Pacific region has also experienced many important changes. Economically, it continues to be the region with the highest growth rate in the world. It has become more competitive in the international market, and its share of world trade has continued to increase. Its intraregional economic transactions have expanded rapidly as well. Although the newly industrialized countries (NICs) have been hurt by the increased international protectionism in the industrial nations, they have made strong efforts to adjust and upgrade their economic structure, transforming their economies from labor-intensive ones to semi–capital-and-technology-intensive ones. The recent appreciation in the value of the yen has weakened Japan's position in the international market; and Japan's trade war with other industrial market economies is likely to intensify. Yet Tokyo's recent policy of deregulating its control over capital flow between Japan and other nations has allowed Japan to play an increasingly important role in the international financial market. This policy, in turn, is likely to restructure that market and speed up the process of integration of the economy of East Asia into the world economy at large.[23]

Politically, however, the region has presented a more complicated picture. During the past few years, the Soviet Union and its allies, notably Vietnam, have made greater efforts than the United States and its allies to develop their military capability in the region. The trends of military balance in the region have favored the Soviet Union and its allies and semi-allies, not the United States and its allies. While maintaining roughly forty divisions of ground forces along the Chinese borders, Moscow has doubled the size of its Pacific Fleet, the largest fleet it has, and significantly strengthened its tactical and strategic air force in the Far East. Moscow has also built up strong transportation, communication, and supply facilities. Thus, it is not an exaggeration to say that the Soviet Union has already built up its military capability for fighting a two-front (Europe and Pacific) war.[24]

More importantly, Moscow's strategic position in the region is stronger than ever. In Northeast Asia, it is capable of putting strong military and political pressure on both Beijing and Tokyo. Recently, by increasing its economic and military aid to Pyongyang and at the same time expanding its ties with Seoul, Moscow has deepened its involvement on the Korean Peninsula. In comparison with Beijing, Moscow is able to provide more and better weapons to Pyongyang. In Southeast Asia, the Soviet Pacific Fleet has been allowed to use bases in Cam Ranh and Da Nang bays, where it has also deployed long-distance bombers. If the United States loses its bases in the Philippines in the next few years, the Soviet Union's presence in Vietnam could be even more challenging to the stability and security of the region. Strategically, ASEAN has been weakened by the divergence of security interests among its member nations, especially between Thailand and Indonesia, and by internal political difficulties. To improve ties with Beijing, Moscow has asked Hanoi to pull out of Cambodia. Yet Hanoi has shown little flexibility on the Cambodian issue. Given the sharp conflicts between different factions of the Cambodian resistance movement, at least in the near future, it is difficult for the international community to work out a solution acceptable to all parties involved.

In South Asia, the dynamics of the strategic balance have continued to favor the Soviet Union and its strategic partner, India. Rajiv Gandhi's foreign policy has proved consistent with his mother's pro-Soviet position, although he has shown his flexibility in dealing with Washington, Beijing, and Islamabad. The overlap of political and strategic interests between the Soviet Union and India is unlikely to change in the near future, as it is deeply rooted in the balance of power in the region and India's domestic politics as well as its culture. Strategically, the Soviet-Indian security partnership serves their common interest in maintaining pressure on both Pakistan and China and in deterring further U.S. involvement in the region's security affairs. India's dependence on the Soviet Union for weapons supply and political support is unlikely to decline. Domestically, India's increased conflicts between different ethnic groups and its political instability have been and will continue to be the major political obstacles to the relaxation of tensions with Pakistan. Moscow has supplied over 80 percent of the total weapons India has imported, including some sophisticated weapons systems such as the MiG-29. Around the time of Gorbachev's trip to India in the spring of 1987, New Delhi revived the issue of territorial disputes with Beijing. This event has indicated New Delhi's uneasiness at Moscow's efforts to improve Sino-Soviet relations and with its political dependence on Moscow.[25] In December 1988, Rajiv Gandhi visited Beijing. During the meetings with his Chinese counterparts, both sides promised to reduce tensions and improve the ties between them. Nevertheless, as one Chinese South Asian specialist pointed out, the two countries have a long way to go to overcome their disputes over territory and the issue of Tibetan refugees in India, not to mention their conflicts over regional security and strategic affairs.[26]

For Beijing, the key country to serve its security interests in the region is Pakistan, a country with which Beijing has had a close relationship over three decades. Yet the death of General Zia-Ul-Haq may create further domestic political and economic difficulties in the country. Prime Minister Benazir Bhutto has expressed her willingness to expand close relations with China. Yet it remains to be seen whether she is able to manage the country's internal politics and economy. Any serious domestic political crisis may indeed jeopardize Islamabad's current pro-U.S. and pro-Chinese foreign policy. The continued military and political pressure by the Soviet Union from the north and India from the south will continue to threaten Pakistan's security and leave it with little choice but to seek the support of both China and the United States.[27] Given the nature of geopolitics and the military balance in the region, however, the effectiveness of Washington's and Beijing's deterrence against threats to Pakistan's national security will continue to be limited.

Such a security environment has worried Beijing's policy-makers. China's basic security interest is to create a relatively peaceful and stable international environment for its ongoing modernization program. Two goals are to reduce Moscow's political and military pressure on Beijing and to break up Moscow's strategic encirclement of China. It is also in China's interest to maintain the political stability of the Korean Peninsula; to reduce the possibility of a consolidated, militant "united Indochina" under Hanoi's dominance and with Moscow's backing; and to prevent Pakistan from coming under Moscow's shadow. In addition, Beijing is interested in a peaceful resolution of the Taiwan issue. Finally, Japan's great potential to transform its economic power into commensurate political or even military power is a serious issue that Beijing has to face up to in the long run.

To pursue its strategic interests, Beijing has given Moscow three preconditions for the normalization of their relations: substantial withdrawal of the Red Army from Sino-Soviet and Sino-Mongolian borders; the elimination of Moscow's political support and military aid to Vietnam's occupation of Cambodia; and the withdrawal of Soviet troops from Afghanistan. Together with Tokyo, Beijing has also been calling for the reduction of Soviet strategic weapons deployed in the Far East.

Although Moscow has recently solved some of these issues, Beijing is still facing a number of difficulties in furthering its security interests. The military balance between China and the Soviet Union favors the latter; and this situation is not likely to change in the foreseeable future. The key issue here is that while facing a well-armed Red Army with strong offensive capability, the Chinese Army has only a defensive position. The efforts that China has made to improve ties with the Soviet Union have reduced border tensions between the two countries and reopened border trade across both China's northeast and northwest borders. Moscow has not, however, made much effort to slow down its military buildup in the Far East, nor does China have much leverage to force it to do so. The removal of a few divisions of Soviet ground forces from the People's Republic of Mongolia has been well received in Beijing. Nevertheless, achieving a further reduction of Soviet armed forces along the Chinese border seems to be a long and difficult process, as Moscow does expect Beijing to make similar moves. Such a reduction of Chinese military forces would further weaken China's position vis-à-vis the Soviet Union, as the Chinese Army has far less mobility and depends more on predeployment. In addition, any significant removal of military forces along Sino-Mongolian and Sino-Soviet borders would naturally cause strong reactions from the United

States and its allies, notably Japan, thereby jeopardizing China's relations with the West and Japan as well as the current power structure in the Far East. Thus, the process of reducing military forces along the Sino-Soviet border will be a long one.

In Southeast Asia, due to the difficulties of managing its wartime economy and strong pressure from the international community, Hanoi might be willing to pull its troops out of Cambodia if Moscow would cut back its support to the Vietnamese and if the international community could work out an arrangement to prevent the Communist faction within the resistance movement from returning to power. Nevertheless, in comparison with the other two factions, the Communist faction is the strongest one within the resistance movement. It is far better armed, trained, and organized than the other two factions. So far, China is the major supplier of weapons and economic aid to the Communist faction. Even if China completely cut off its support to this faction it could still win a bloody civil war after the Vietnamese withdrawal. Improved Sino-Soviet relations have already undercut Hanoi's position in relation to Beijing. Yet, Hanoi does take advantage of the Sino-Soviet conflict. Its strong nationalism, which aims to establish a "united Indochina" under its own dominance, contributes to its relative independence of action from Moscow. Its war experience over four decades has created a militant and ambitious regime. And finally, both Hanoi and Moscow acknowledge the strategic significance of Cam Ranh and Da Nang bays to the security of Southeast Asia, if not the whole Asian-Pacific region. It will be difficult, if not impossible, for Moscow to force Hanoi to pull its troops from Cambodia at the cost of losing Vietnam as its only ally in Southeast Asia.

In South Asia, the dynamics of the security environment and the balance of power are likely to continue the present trends. The Soviet Union's withdrawal may still leave Afghanistan with a continued civil war. One possible outcome of the civil war would be the creation of a militant Islamic fundamentalist regime capable of exporting its radical ideology, thereby destabilizing regional politics and challenging China's northwest provinces, where over 3 million Muslims live and where ethnic tensions have increased during the past few years. Such an Islamic fundamentalist regime could also threaten Pakistan's political stability. In this regard, neither Beijing nor Washington can do much to help stabilize the domestic situation in Pakistan. Moreover, the existing balance of power between India and Pakistan restricts both Beijing's and Washington's efforts to secure Pakistan, nor can they expect any significant shift in India's pro-Soviet position in the near future.

What is the U.S. factor in China's security planning, including its policy toward the Soviet Union? In the Asian-Pacific region as a whole, the United States military presence is essential to counter Soviet military expansion. Sino-American political cooperation on subregional security issues in the region and the two countries' military exchange programs have served and will continue to serve China's interest in deterring any attack or military threat by the Soviet Union. Without equilibrium there will be no peace. To leave open the option of upgrading such cooperation would also strengthen Beijing's bargaining position vis-à-vis Moscow. On the Korean Peninsula, a well-planned and -managed Sino-American cooperative effort could provide the most feasible way to reduce tensions and to increase contacts between the two Koreas. It could also maintain stability and open North Korea gradually to the international community. In the long run, the process of Japan's rearmament and the development of its strategic role would shift the balance of power in the region and the world, thereby changing the nature of regional and world politics. For China, a strengthened U.S.-Japanese security relationship and U.S. military presence in the region is a safeguard against Japan becoming an independent regional military power with a strong offensive capability.

In Southeast Asia, China has made major efforts to cooperate with ASEAN, especially Thailand, to contain Vietnamese regional expansionism. Such efforts have not been institutionalized, however. Besides the historical tensions still existing between China and some of the ASEAN states, the low-key policy that Washington has taken toward Southeast Asia is the major reason. In the long run, Washington and Beijing may find it necessary to further their cooperation to work out a reasonable solution to the Cambodian issue, to contain any further Soviet-Vietnamese expansion in the region, and to prevent the Philippines from becoming a second Vietnam.

In Afghanistan there is the increased need for Washington and Beijing to coordinate their support for the resistance movement and balance different factions within it, thereby preventing Afghanistan from becoming a second Iran. It will also be necessary for them to work together to guarantee Pakistan's security and to support stability in the country. Strong political support from both Washington and Beijing is the key to preventing Pakistan from falling under Moscow's shadow. Without effective coordination between China,

Pakistan, and the United States, it would be difficult for any of them to improve their ties with India significantly. These efforts would of course begin with high-level but informal strategic consultation.

Since the early 1970s, the United States has not been a threat to China's national security, but rather the principal potential strategic partner against the Soviet Union and its allies and semi-allies, which have presented the primary direct threat to China's security. The development of political and security cooperation with Washington has increased Beijing's capacity to cope with regional security issues on China's periphery. Meanwhile, to reduce tensions and improve relations with the Soviet Union will reduce Moscow's direct military and political pressure on Beijing. It may increase Beijing's leverage in dealing with Moscow's allies and semi-allies in Asia. In addition, an improved relationship with Moscow can also protect Beijing's interests in the light of possible U.S.-Soviet détente. All in all, the dynamics of China's security environment will continue to lessen its incentive to improve significantly its ties with the Soviet Union. To reduce tensions with Moscow while continuing to develop its economic, cultural, political, and security relations with Washington and its allies would serve China's best interests.

MOSCOW'S CHINA POLICY

Moscow's China policy has the following distinct characteristics. Unlike Beijing's policy toward the Soviet Union, Moscow's attitude toward Beijing is much less influenced by the Soviet Union's domestic politics and economic development. Rather, it is mainly determined by Moscow's overall foreign policy. This is due primarily to the Soviet Union's relatively greater political stability and higher degree of institutionalization of foreign-policy–making. Its policy toward China has not been a serious issue in Soviet party politics since the middle of the 1960s. Secondly, Moscow's China policy is more consistent than Beijing's policy toward the Soviet Union. This consistency entails a certain rigidity, which explains why Moscow was unable to respond effectively to Beijing's more flexible approach to Moscow.

Finally, unlike China, the Soviet Union is a superpower with broad global political and security interests. Moscow's China policy is only a part of its global strategy, although it is viewed as central to Moscow's strategy toward the Asian-Pacific region. Given the fact that the Soviet Union's military power and global interests have rapidly expanded during the past decade, its China policy has been less determined by specific interactions with Beijing and has increasingly become a function of its global and Asian-Pacific strategy.

Generally speaking, three basic factors now determine Moscow's China policy: ideological divergence or convergence between Beijing and Moscow; economic and cultural ties between the two countries; and international politics, including the dynamics of the triangle between Beijing, Moscow, and Washington.

The post-Mao reform in China has removed most of the previous ideological barriers between Beijing and Moscow. Gorbachev and his associates have expressed strong interest in China's experience of economic reform and the open-door policy and have begun their own reform program. Since mid-1986, the Soviet press has ceased its criticism of China's domestic development. Instead, many Soviet scholars and journalists have begun to tell of China's experience of reforming its economic system and expanding its economic ties with industrial nations. Gorbachev himself has repeatedly expressed his personal support of China's reforms. The Chinese press, in turn, has widely and favorably described Gorbachev's political and economic reforms as well as his "new thinking" of international affairs. Chinese reformers are particularly interested in Gorbachev's political reform and his policy toward the history of the Soviet Communist Party, an area in which the Chinese have not been able to make much progress.[28] Although, the previous ideological obstacles that prevented Beijing and Moscow from reestablishing party-to-party relations have been overcome, because of political considerations, especially the possible effects on its relations with Washington, Beijing has been reluctant to do so.

Despite this development, a number of new ideological and political problems have appeared between Beijing and Moscow. Like reforms in most East European countries, China's economic reform and open-door policy have strong foreign-policy implications. Conservative Soviet policy-makers and scholars of China, who have strong influence within the bureaucratic establishment, have appeared to be increasingly worried about whether Chinese reforms "have gone too far." In particular, they have been anxious about the rapid expansion of Western influence in China and the danger that it may undercut China's official ideology. The increasingly expanded economic and cultural ties between China and industrial market economies will, the Soviets fear, make China even more dependent on the West, especially the United States, leading thereby to a harsher Chinese approach toward Moscow.[29]

The deep distrust between Beijing and Moscow still exists. This distrust has been exacerbated in Moscow by Beijing's active efforts to cooperate with the West, notably the United States, on security issues. Soviet scholars and policy-makers remain critical in their views of Beijing's foreign policy and security strategy, although because of tactical reasons, they no longer publicize their criticism. Such distrust is unlikely to be easily overcome by the limited relaxation of tensions between the two countries, unless the balance of power in the Asian-Pacific region and both countries' basic security interests shift fundamentally.

China has signed agreements with the Soviet Union and East European countries to receive technical assistance. Thousands of Chinese cadres and technicians who studied in the Soviet Union during the 1950s and 1960s now play key roles in various governmental and nongovernmental institutions in China. They are particularly influential among the party ideological establishment and in technocratic circles. The trade between China and the Soviet bloc is mutually advantageous: China can provide the Soviet bloc with agricultural and consumer goods; the Soviet bloc can supply China with industrial equipment. More importantly, neither China nor the Soviet bloc have to pay hard currency in their trade. Such trade is guided by both sides' central planning systems, thereby involving limited risk and instability. Prices of Chinese consumer goods are lower than those of Western countries and NICs; they are thus competitive in the markets of the Soviet bloc. Finally, it is unlikely in the near future that the Soviet bloc will launch a war of protectionism against Chinese goods. For these reasons, the trade between China and the Soviet bloc is likely to increase in the years ahead.

There are, however, some important limitations on the potential increase of Sino-Soviet trade. China's ability to export agricultural goods to the Soviet bloc is not unlimited. Although the successful agricultural reform has increased China's agricultural output significantly during the past decade, the increase appears to be slowing down. This is happening because the increase was due primarily to substantial institutional reform, but further increase of agricultural production will largely depend upon the amount of capital investment and technological development.[30] Meanwhile, the Chinese rural economy is experiencing an important transition: peasants are putting more and more capital and labor into the development of rural industry and into trade between rural and urban areas, but not into agricultural production. In fact, it has been reported that in both 1987 and 1988, China's total grain output declined sharply.[31]

Trade with the Soviet bloc amounted to about 5 percent of China's total foreign trade in two recent years.[32] Between the early 1960s and the early 1980s, trade between China and the Soviet bloc had declined significantly and the latter had stopped providing technology to China. Since the sixties, China has imported a large amount of industrial equipment and technology from Western nations and Japan. As a result, the Chinese economy has become far less dependent on Soviet technology and increasingly dependent upon Western and Japanese technology. Further, the Soviet Union no longer seems willing or able to supply the high technology that China needs for its modernization drive (notably in the computer and telecommunications industries). In sum, while Sino-Soviet trade will continue its smooth growth in the years ahead, that growth will not be faster than that of China's trade with industrial market economies. Nor will it play a significant role in influencing the political and security relationship between Beijing and Moscow.

In the area of international politics, Sino-Soviet relations have experienced some important changes during the past few years. Beijing and Moscow have appeared less antagonistic outside the Asian-Pacific region. They have been less critical of each other's policies in the Third World. Beijing has taken a "neutral" position toward U.S.-Soviet rivalry over various issues outside the Asian-Pacific region, such as the arms race between the two superpowers, and the recent developments in southern Africa, the Middle East, and Central America. Beijing has welcomed the recent U.S.-Soviet relaxation. Moscow, in turn, has avoided talking about Beijing's policies outside the Asian-Pacific region. Moscow has also encouraged East European states and Communist parties in Western Europe to develop ties with Beijing.

Within the Asian-Pacific region, however, Sino-Soviet relaxation has been limited. The two Communist powers are still in sharp conflict, especially with regard to regional security issues. For Moscow the China factor is important to both its global strategy and its strategy toward the Asian-Pacific region. Globally, Moscow is in a relatively unfavorable position within the triangle: it is faced with a stronger challenge from Washington, and the limited process of Sino-Soviet relaxation has not significantly altered the basic strategic competition between Beijing and Moscow. Thus, if Moscow failed to manage its relations with both Washington and Beijing, the latter could easily form an anti-Soviet partnership (one may add Japan and Western Europe). In the long run, Moscow has to face the possibility that the world's most populous nation may be armed with American and Japanese technology and backed by Washington and Tokyo in a challenge to its entire eastern border. This possibility is a basic reason why Moscow has not ceased its efforts to continue its military buildup in the Far East, to encircle China strategically, and to maintain effective deterrence credibility against both Tokyo and Beijing. In addition, building up its capacity to fight a "two-front war"—in Europe and the Asian-Pacific region—is Moscow's major deterrence to Washington.

The strategic importance of the Asian-Pacific region to both superpowers seems likely to increase. It is a region that has a very complicated political structure: two superpowers, two regional powers (China and Japan), and other states in regional conflict. In addition, many states in the region face serious political challenges, both domestically and internationally. Many countries in the region have had or will have political successions. Political institutions in many of these countries have undergone important transformation, thereby creating a certain political instability. The Soviet Union does not have much political and cultural access in support of its expansionism in this region, nor does it enjoy strong economic influence. The only advantage that Moscow and its allies can exploit is their increased military power. The potential political instability in the region may provide opportunities for Moscow to exercise its military power to reshape the current political structure of the region.

In Northeast Asia, Moscow and Beijing share certain common interests: to reduce border tensions between them, to maintain stability in the Korean Peninsula, and *in the long run*, to prevent Japan from becoming an independent military power with a strong offensive capability. Nevertheless, in each of these matters, Beijing and Moscow are either in competition or conflict with each other.

Will the Sino-Soviet military balance change significantly in the near future? The answer seems to be no. In terms of military balance, Soviet troops in the Far East have the upper hand over China's People's Liberation Army, not to mention the Soviet Union's superiority in nuclear weapons. The forty divisions of Soviet ground forces deployed in the Far East are far better equipped and trained, with greater mobility and fire power, a better supply system, and stronger support from air and naval forces. During the past two decades, Moscow has built a strong infrastructure, including military bases, airports, roads, and railways in the Far East. These facilities enable the Red Army to easily receive supplies and necessary support from its western front. The Soviet Pacific Fleet, which has aircraft carriers and nuclear submarines, has already developed the capacity to blockade, and land on, the northern Chinese coast. In comparison with its Chinese counterpart, the Soviet Air Force in the Far East is far better equipped with Backfire long-distance bombers and MiG-31 fighters. The pullback of a few divisions of Soviet ground forces from the Chinese border, if it occurred, would not weaken Moscow's military position in relation to Beijing. Rather, the Soviet Union will continue to enjoy a great superiority in air, naval, and nuclear attacking forces over China. Taken together, unless Moscow dramatically cuts down its strong offensive capability in the Far East, Beijing will continue to be under strong military pressure from Moscow, placing it in a weak bargaining position.

Strategically, Soviet forces (especially air, naval, and nuclear) stationed in the Far East also counter both the U.S. and the Japanese presence in the region. They defend the Soviet Union's eastern border (the Trans-Siberian Railroad is close to the Sino-Soviet border). Such a deployment supports the Soviet military presence in the South China Sea. These military missions are a part of the Soviet long-term global strategy. It is hard to imagine that limited Sino-Soviet relaxation would lead Moscow to alter its global strategy, to weaken its own capacity to compete with the United States and its allies in the Asian-Pacific region, or to reduce significantly its armed forces in the Far East.

At present, both Beijing and Moscow have an interest in maintaining stability on the Korean Peninsula, as any serious military confrontation between the two Koreas could possibly lead to a regional or even a global war. It may no longer be possible to restrict such a war to the conventional level, since the United States has already deployed tactical nuclear weapons in South Korea. Nevertheless, the dynamics of the peninsula are largely determined by its internal developments. Pyongyang will have a leadership succession in the next few years. The process or outcome of the succession may result in greater tension and more confrontations between the North and the South. It may also intensify the Sino-Soviet competition in the North. In the South, the ongoing political transition may jeopardize South Korea's political stability. This in turn might provoke a preemptive attack from the North because of the fear that Seoul would seek to escape domestic turmoil. If the current trend in the arms race between the two Koreas continues, in the next four or five years, South Korea will hold a military advantage over North Korea. Pyongyang may thus increase its military and political pressure on Seoul before the military balance is finally shifted.

Moscow is now better situated than Beijing to compete for influence in Pyongyang. It is better able to provide economic and military aid, and capable of taking a strong anti-American stand in support of Pyongyang's demands for reunification. If the ongoing U.S.–South Korean–Japanese security cooperation continues to develop, it is likely that Pyongyang will lean toward Moscow for political support and security guarantees. Since 1987 Moscow and Pyongyang have increased their security cooperation. Moscow has provided Pyongyang with MiG-25 fighters; Pyongyang, in turn, has invited Soviet fleets to visit its harbors and allowed Soviet military planes to fly over its territory. Meanwhile, Moscow has slowly moved closer to the government in Seoul. These moves have clearly shown the new Soviet leadership's strong interests in the Korean Peninsula.

During the past few years, Beijing has adjusted its previous policy toward the Korean Peninsula. It has announced that it will not support an attack by Pyongyang on the South, although it would help Pyongyang if the latter were attacked by the South.[33] Beijing has encouraged Pyongyang to open its doors and to increase its contacts with the West. Beijing has in fact endorsed the succession arrangement for Kim Il Sung's son. Since the second half of 1988, Beijing has rapidly expanded its ties with Seoul. It has opened Shandong province to South Korean investors. Businessmen and scholars from the two countries have exchanged visits. Many Chinese cities are now open to South Korean tourists. The two countries may soon open offices for economic and consular affairs in each other's capital.[34] All these moves have helped to reduce tensions between the North and the South, but they do not necessarily strengthen Beijing's ability to compete with Moscow, especially when the succession crisis takes place in Pyongyang. The last thing that Beijing wants is for North Korea, for either internal or external reasons, to become a "second Vietnam," armed by Moscow to challenge China's northeastern border.

Moscow and Beijing have different views on Japan's rearmament and U.S.-Japanese security cooperation, although neither of them wants to see Japan become a great independent military power in the future. Beijing would not strongly oppose the process of Japanese rearmament as long as it neither altered Japan's security strategy against the Soviet Union nor made Japan an independent military power with an offensive capability. U.S.-Japanese security cooperation is therefore essential, as such cooperation can guide Tokyo's strategic intent. For its part, Moscow opposes any attempt at Japanese rearmament. Closer security ties between Washington and Tokyo would certainly provoke a strong reaction from Moscow, as such cooperation would allow Washington to use Japan's rich economic and technological resources against Moscow. Finally, in the long run, if U.S.-Japanese security ties failed to prevent Tokyo from becoming an independent military power and altering its military strategy, Beijing would have little alternative but to turn to Moscow.

With respect to the Sino-Soviet conflicts, the central issue in Southeast Asia is whether Moscow will cut back its support to Hanoi. Since 1979, when China "taught" Vietnam "a lesson," Moscow has made a huge capital investment in Indochina, notably Vietnam. Since 1978 Hanoi has received over US$5 billion in aid from Moscow. Moscow's aid to Hanoi has amounted roughly to over US$3 million per day, three times the amount of its aid to Cuba. Hanoi has received a large number of advanced weapons and has built up the world's fourth-largest military power and the fifth-largest air force.[35] Over twenty thousand Soviet advisers and technicians are now working in various Vietnamese military and civilian institutions and tens of thousands of Vietnamese are receiving training in the Soviet Union. In return, Hanoi serves Moscow's strategic interests by challenging China's southern border, threatening ASEAN states'—especially Thailand's—security, and providing military bases to the Soviet Pacific Fleet and its air attack force in competing with U.S. Pacific forces. The Soviet-Vietnamese strategic alliance has been solidified.

Both globally and regionally, Soviet-Vietnamese security cooperation has great strategic significance. Globally, to have access to military bases in Cam Ranh and Da Nang bays strengthens the Soviet Pacific Fleet's strategic position vis-à-vis the U.S. Seventh Fleet, threatens Japan's supply lines, and supports the Soviet military presence in the Indian Ocean. Within the region, Soviet-Vietnamese security cooperation is an important part of Moscow's military and political pressure on China, threatening China's southern coast. It also serves Moscow's strategy in Southeast Asia, where local politics has appeared highly unstable and will continue to do so. During the next few years, the political transformation in the Philippines will likely have an important impact on the region. If the Aquino government fails to create a stable political situation, the United States may lose its military bases in the Philippines, the ASEAN alliance will face a real challenge, and the strategic map of Southeast Asia will look more favorable to the Soviet Union. If this situation occurs, the Soviet fleet and air force operating from military bases in Cam Ranh and Da Nang bays, together with well-trained and fully equipped Vietnamese troops, could be quickly sent to the Philippines if required.

Moreover, the relationship between Hanoi and Moscow is an interdependent one. Hanoi knows well its strategic value to Moscow and takes appropriate advantage of the Sino-Soviet conflict. It is also a relatively independent regime able to mobilize strong, militant nationalist sentiment. It has been fighting for decades for the goal of a "unified Indochina" under its own dominion. The serious economic crisis and the recent restructuring of the leadership in Hanoi may reduce the degree of Vietnamese militancy. But Vietnam may not complete its withdrawal from Cambodia by the end of 1990, as it promised. Since China is viewed as the principal obstacle to its ambition, Hanoi may maintain its anti-Chinese attitude.

Taken together, in Moscow's calculation, the strategic importance of Soviet-Vietnamese security cooperation may still outweigh the possible gain Moscow might obtain by cutting back its support of Hanoi. Beijing might take a more "neutral" position than at present between Moscow and Washington, but this shift would count for less, in Moscow's eyes, than its current relations with Vietnam. In the foreseeable future, therefore, there is little incentive for Moscow to pursue a policy of rapprochement with China at Vietnam's expense, nor would Hanoi be either passive or cooperative if faced with such a prospect.

The key security issue in South Asia in the years ahead for both Beijing and Washington is the security of Pakistan. A bloody civil war in Afghanistan is likely to continue. Given Islamabad's deep involvement in the Afghan war during the past ten years, the fighting will likely continue to affect Pakistan. To support the pro-Soviet Afghan government and protect its border in Central Asia, where

Muslims are in the majority, Moscow may still have to put strong political and military pressure on Islamabad, not to mention the option of reintroducing Soviet troops into Afghanistan if necessary. Even if the Afghan rebels take power, they may face internal conflict due to the sharp ideological and political differences among rebel factions. More importantly, many rebel groups are supported and financed by different Islamic states, including Iran, Iraq, and Saudi Arabia. A takeover by the Afghan rebels could result in a militant Islamic fundamentalist regime capable of exporting revolution to its neighbors, especially Pakistan. In addition, the security of Pakistan also depends on Prime Minister Bhutto's ability to manage the country's tense politics and difficult economic situation. A deep social and political crisis in Pakistan could be exploited by Moscow and India as an opportunity to further undermine the country's political stability and to force Islamabad to alter its pro-Washington and pro-Beijing foreign policy.

In the years ahead, the relationship between Pakistan and India may continue to be tense. The domestic political and racial tensions in India will continue to be an important motivation for New Delhi to seek external conflict to deflect domestic disarray. Its ambition to be the dominant power in South Asia and the Indian Ocean, and the cultural and religious stress between the two countries, will continue to accentuate the conflicts between them. Pakistan's close ties with both Beijing and Washington will continue to sustain India's strategic posture as a partner of the Soviet Union and to increase its motives to place strong political and military pressure on Pakistan.

Furthermore, the Soviet Union may also exert its own political and military pressure on Pakistan. Moscow's strategic objective is either to "Finlandize" Pakistan or to put Pakistan under its own control. Should Pakistan come under Moscow's control, China's two politically sensitive provinces, Xingjiang and Tibet, bordering the Soviet Union, Afghanistan, India, and Pakistan, will feel much more insecure. Lack of capacity to help Pakistan to preserve itself would also damage Beijing's and Washington's international credibility.

Will Moscow reduce its political support and economic and military aid to India, the key country in the region? The answer seems to be no. The Soviet-Indian security partnership serves a number of Moscow's central interests: it is an important part of Moscow's strategic encirclement of China; it allows the Soviet fleet access to a harbor in the Indian Ocean, which is essential to Soviet competition with the U.S. Sixth Fleet; and it enables Moscow to press Pakistan. This strategic partnership, moreover, has a history going back to the 1960s. During the Sino-Indian border war of 1961–62, Moscow provided New Delhi with a great deal of military aid and strong political support. Since then a large percentage of the weapons India has imported has come from the Soviet Union. Moscow has helped New Delhi build up its own defense industry, and a large number of Indian military personnel have been trained in the Soviet Union. In both Indian-Pakistani wars (1965 and 1971), the Soviet Union strongly supported India both politically and militarily, while Washington and Beijing backed Pakistan. In the Soviet-Indian Friendship Treaty, signed in 1971, soon before the second Indian-Pakistani war broke out, Moscow and New Delhi declared that the two powers will consult in time of crisis and refrain from conflict with the other.[36] This is similar to the tone used in the Soviet-Vietnamese Friendship Treaty signed in 1978, a few weeks before Vietnam's invasion of Cambodia.[37] Without Moscow's support, India cannot realize its ambition to be the dominant power in the region. As long as Sino-Indian rivalry and the Indian-Pakistani conflict continue, India will likely continue its dependence on Soviet military and political support and will try to maintain the effectiveness of the Soviet-Indian strategic partnership.

In sum, Beijing and Moscow have sharp conflicts of interests in South Asia. These conflicts are likely to continue, if not intensify, in the years ahead. As the political structure of the region continues to be unstable, Moscow will surely take geopolitical advantage of and further weaken Pakistan's security. Beijing would certainly make every effort, including the development of an informal framework of strategic cooperation with both Washington and Islamabad, to support Pakistan.

BEIJING'S BASIC POLICY OPTIONS IN DEALING WITH MOSCOW

In the years ahead, Beijing seems to have three basic policy options in dealing with Moscow. The first would be to pursue a rapid process of Sino-Soviet reconciliation. Economically, Beijing could continue to increase its trade with the Soviet bloc and to import more technology and industrial equipment from the Soviet Union, thereby increasing the degree of economic dependence on Moscow.

Culturally, Beijing could further eliminate its differences with Moscow on ideological issues and rapidly expand exchange programs with Moscow. Beijing could reduce the number of its students studying in the West and Japan, while sending more scholars and students to the Soviet bloc.

Beijing could also dramatically improve its political relations with Moscow. The two Communist parties could restore their ties; and Beijing could continue to strengthen its relations with East European states and Communist parties around the world, although a new international Communist movement is unlikely to be established. Beijing might even improve its state-to-state relations with Moscow by establishing a regular mechanism for consultations at the summit level, with both sides willing to solve the border issue and to pull back a certain number of their armed forces along the Sino-Soviet and Sino-Mongolian border. Outside the Asian-Pacific region, while continuing its competition with Moscow for influence in the Third World, Beijing might try harder to avoid disputes with Moscow and to take strong positions similar to Moscow's against Washington's Third World policy. Beijing might further distance itself from Washington and play down its common security interests with Washington. The Taiwan issue could once again become a highly emotional political backdrop to Sino-American relations.

This approach would further reduce political tensions and improve state-to-state relations between Beijing and Moscow. It would, to a certain extent, reduce Moscow's political and military pressure on Beijing. In the area of trade, China would receive more technology and industrial equipment from the Soviet bloc. More Chinese scholars and students would have the opportunity to study in the Soviet Union, where the political system and official ideology are similar to China's own, thereby presenting a far lesser challenge to the Chinese political system at home. Domestically, this approach would serve well the interests of conservatives within the party and the government and contribute to their efforts to rebuild a post-Khrushchev Soviet-type political and economic system.

This approach would further reduce conflicts between Beijing and Moscow outside the Asian-Pacific region, thereby allowing Beijing to take a more flexible position in the Third World. To a certain extent, it could also increase Beijing's bargaining power with Washington. Within the Asian-Pacific region, Sino-Soviet reconciliation would moderate their competition for influence over Pyongyang, thereby reducing the latter's incentive to lean toward

Moscow politically. This approach would put Japan in a difficult position, because Moscow would surely increase its political and military pressure on Tokyo while Beijing could become more critical of Japan's rearmament. Given the regional geopolitics and Beijing's influence on Japanese public opinion, such international pressure could strongly affect Tokyo's security planning and foreign-policy–making. In Southeast Asia, Moscow might convince Hanoi to reduce tensions with Beijing and to turn its attention south. In South Asia, Beijing could expect Moscow to reduce its pressure on Pakistan, to promise not to threaten China's western border, and to convince India to improve relations with China.

The costs of taking this approach, however, would be high. Economically, Beijing might have to change its developmental strategy from an "open door" to the West to dependence on the Soviet bloc for economic and technological assistance. China's position in the international market would thus be weakened, while Moscow would unlikely be capable of meeting China's needs to obtain highly sophisticated technology to upgrade its industrial base. Nor would the readoption of the Soviet model improve China's economic efficiency in general and its competitiveness with other nations in particular. Culturally, the younger generation and the intellectual establishment, who have been deeply alienated from the official ideology and strongly influenced by the new information imported into the country during the past few years, would likely feel greater resentment toward a rapid Sino-Soviet reconciliation, as the Soviet model is widely viewed as the symbol of political repression, bureaucratism, and economic inefficiency.

In the international arena, this approach would be unlikely to improve China's security environment significantly. Moscow would probably neither slow down its military buildup in the Far East nor stop its expansionist activities in the Asian-Pacific region, as Beijing does not have much leverage to force it to do so. More importantly, the limited withdrawal of Soviet ground forces from the Chinese border will not change the existing military imbalance between the two countries. Moscow has already built up a sufficient military infrastructure and supply system in these areas, and its deployment of air and naval forces in the Far East would unlikely be affected by an improvement in Sino-Soviet relations.

This approach would destabilize the current triangular relations between Moscow, Beijing, and Washington. It would also reshape the balance of power in the Asian-Pacific region and once again put

China in the central position in conflicts. This is because Washington and its allies in the Asian-Pacific region would react strongly to a rapid Sino-Soviet reconciliation, thereby restructuring their security strategies. As a result, under Washington's strong encouragement, Tokyo would further speed up its process of rearmament. Political tensions between Washington and its Asian allies on the one hand and Beijing on the other could be revived. Current Sino-American relations could undergo a fundamental change. Washington might pursue a new security treaty that would include South Korea, Japan, and the ASEAN nations. The current relative stability of the region would thus be undermined. Such an international environment could force Beijing to increase its dependence on Moscow, thereby further weakening its bargaining position vis-à-vis the latter.

On the Korean Peninsula, a rapid Sino-Soviet reconciliation would not necessarily reduce tensions between the two Koreas, as such a development would reduce Beijing's incentive and ability to cooperate with Washington in preventing a possible military confrontation between the North and the South. The forthcoming succession to Kim Il Sung, in addition, will naturally accentuate the competition between Beijing and Moscow for influence over Pyongyang.

In Southeast Asia, Moscow is unlikely to reduce its military presence, given its ambitious global strategy and the region's unstable political future. Hanoi might be willing to pull out all of its troops from Cambodia. Yet the war in Cambodia could continue. China's ties with ASEAN could face increased difficulties, as the changed Sino-Soviet relations could force Washington either to increase its direct involvement in the region or to encourage ASEAN to pursue an appeasement of Hanoi.

In South Asia, Pakistan's security might still be under threat, because the continued war in Afghanistan could expand. More importantly, the rapid Sino-Soviet reconciliation would probably not change India's attitude toward China, nor would it reduce Indian-Pakistani tensions. While the common security interests shared by Washington and Beijing would be jeopardized, domestic stability in Pakistan might remain under challenge. The region's political structure would become more unstable.

To sum up, to pursue a rapid Sino-Soviet reconciliation is possible, but it would demand that Beijing adjust its foreign and security policy significantly. This approach would reduce political tensions between Beijing and Moscow. It would also, however, destabilize the balance of power and the international system in the Asian-Pacific region, if not the world as a whole. China's basic security interests would thus continue to be challenged.

Theoretically, Beijing has the second policy option in dealing with Moscow. This is a "cold war" approach. Under this approach, Beijing would once again cut back its cultural and economic ties with Moscow. On the political front, Beijing could freeze both party-to-party and state-to-state relations with Moscow. Instead, it could work more closely with Yugoslavia, Romania, and those West European Communist parties that have kept their distance from Moscow and challenged Moscow's authority. At the global level, Beijing would surely move closer to Washington and actively participate in Washington's containment strategy. In the Third World, as we saw during the 1960s and most of the 1970s, such a development would likely revive serious competition between Beijing and Moscow.

In Northeast Asia, Beijing, by increasing its political support and military aid to Pyongyang, could intensify its competition with Moscow for influence over North Korea. It could also make further efforts to develop strategic cooperation with the United States, Japan, and Western Europe in order to counter Moscow's pressure. In Southeast Asia, Beijing would demand that Moscow reduce its military presence. It would also increase military and political pressure on Hanoi, pursue a tough, nonnegotiations approach toward the Cambodian issue, and seek to form an alliance relationship with Thailand. If the Vietnamese-Thai confrontation intensified, Beijing, with Washington's encouragement, would surely launch another border war against Hanoi. In South Asia, as long as Moscow continues to support the Afghan government, Beijing would continue to back the rebels. It would also encourage an increase in the U.S. military presence in the Indian Ocean and work more closely with both the United States and Pakistan against the Soviet-Indian partnership.

Moscow would surely react strongly to this approach. In terms of military balance, Beijing is still in a much weaker position than Moscow. Moscow might speed up its military buildup along the Chinese border. It might also further its efforts to encircle China strategically by increasing its political and military pressure on China and destabilizing China's peripheries. China would thus once again become the central target of Moscow's security strategy in the region. What and how much support Beijing would receive from Washington in the face of a Sino-Soviet confrontation is still an open question, not to mention that so dependent a relationship to the United States could undercut the Beijing government's domestic legitimacy. More importantly, it is not in Beijing's interest to become once again the central target of Moscow's containment strategy in the Asian-Pacific region. The increased dependence on United States political and military support would also weaken Beijing's bargaining position with Washington.

On the Korean Peninsula, a sharp confrontation between Moscow and Beijing would likely destabilize Pyongyang's politics and probably undermine the stability of the peninsula in general. If Pyongyang chose to lean toward Moscow, Beijing would face a "second Vietnam," armed by the Soviet Union to challenge China's northeastern border. Under a strong military threat from Moscow, Beijing might have to support Tokyo's efforts at rapid rearmament, which in the long run could challenge China's own security. In Southeast Asia, while the United States might continue its low-key non-direct-involvement policy and the ASEAN alliance remained weak, both politically and militarily, China might find it increasingly difficult to deal with an increased Soviet military presence and the Soviet-Vietnamese military alliance. Given the nature of the geopolitics of South Asia, an intensified Sino-Soviet confrontation would likely lead to an upgrading of Soviet-Indian strategic cooperation. In the worst case, such a cooperation could undermine Pakistan's security and threaten China's Western border.

In sum, to pursue a militant approach toward Moscow is not desirable for Beijing, as it would jeopardize China's goal of creating a relatively stable and peaceful international environment, needed for its economic development. This approach would also weaken Beijing's position in the "big" triangle and undermine the stability and peace of the Asian-Pacific region.

The third and clearly the most rational approach that Beijing could take would be to pursue a limited détente, while continuing its competition with Moscow in matters of security. It is important for Beijing to prevent any dramatic changes in the triangle between Washington, Moscow, and itself. In this case, Beijing's fundamental security goals would be to reduce the military and political pressure from Moscow while creating a relatively stable and peaceful international environment. Under this approach, Beijing would continue to expand its economic and cultural ties with Moscow, but this would not overwhelm Beijing's cultural exchange programs and economic cooperation with the Western world. Outside the Asian-Pacific region, Beijing would continue to be less critical of Moscow's foreign policy. It should not, however, pursue an "equal distance" policy between Washington and Moscow, as Moscow still presents the principal threat to China's national security. Beijing would continue to make efforts to reduce border tensions with the Soviet Union and to improve state-to-state relations, including holding summits, with Moscow. It should not reduce the demand that Moscow withdraw a substantial number of its troops along the Chinese border; slow down its military buildup, especially the strengthening of its air force, nuclear attack forces, and naval fleet; and cut its support of Hanoi's occupation of Cambodia.

With this approach, Beijing could advance its cooperation with Washington in maintaining stability on the Korean Peninsula and encourage Pyongyang to increase its participation in the international community. In the short term, Beijing might take a low-key approach toward Tokyo's rearmament, as long as these efforts would not encourage Japan to become an independent military power with a strong offensive capability. It should also advance its low-level security cooperation and military exchange programs with Washington.

In Southeast Asia, while demanding that Moscow reduce its military involvement in the region, Beijing should maintain strong military and political pressure on Hanoi as long as the latter keeps its troops in Cambodia and threatens the security of Thailand. Under Washington's encouragement, Beijing should continue its efforts to cooperate with the ASEAN states against the Soviet-Vietnamese alliance.

Beijing should continue its support of Pakistan and the Afghan rebels while trying to improve its ties with India. Should Pakistan's security come under serious challenge from either the Soviet Union or India, Beijing would surely be willing to provide all possible support to Pakistan, including direct joint operations with Washington.

To compare it with the first two options, the third option would not require Beijing to significantly readjust its current foreign and security strategies. It would contribute to the stability of the current triangle between Washington, Beijing, and Moscow, as well as that of the international system of the Asian-Pacific region. This approach would lead China's policy toward the Soviet Union in a "dual-track" direction: China would continue to improve its cultural and economic ties with Moscow and to reduce certain political tensions; at the same time, with regard to the Asian-Pacific region's security, Beijing would continue its efforts to secure China's peripheries. It would give Moscow the incentive to moderate its expansionist activities around China and to reduce its motivation to advance its strategic cooperation with Hanoi and New Delhi against Beijing. The continued Sino-Soviet conflicts would become more manageable and less likely to develop into direct military confrontation. Thus, the limited relaxation of Sino-Soviet tensions would contribute to the region's stability.

Finally, to leave open the option of upgrading its security cooperation with Washington and its allies would serve Beijing's interest in deterring Moscow's further expansionism against China. It would not, however, overwhelm the competition and confrontation between the two superpowers. More importantly, to develop the working relationship with Washington could strengthen Beijing's ability to cope with subregional security issues in the Asian-Pacific region.

SIX

CHINA'S POLICY TOWARD THE UNITED STATES

GUOCANG HUAN

Since 1982, when the Reagan administration shifted its ideology-oriented China policy and the Chinese government formed its "independent foreign policy," Sino-American relations have developed smoothly and become more manageable. Both Beijing and Washington have improved their understanding of the nature of Sino-American relations. Through expanding their working relationship, the two governments have learned to cooperate in those areas where they share certain common interests while at the same time separating, as much as possible, their disputes on other issues from their overall relations.

For its part, the Chinese government has made great efforts to expand its economic and cultural relations with the United States. Beijing has advanced its military exchange programs and effectively coordinated its policies toward subregional security issues in the Asian-Pacific region with Washington, although it has played down their common security interests. While distancing itself from the United States on many issues in international politics and economics *outside* the Asian-Pacific region and improving relations with Moscow, the Chinese government has carefully balanced its relations with the two superpowers and avoided tilting the triangle formed by the three countries' relationships.

The Chinese government has continued to ask the U.S. government to reduce its support to Taipei and to encourage the latter to open formal negotiations with Beijing. Beijing itself has also made major efforts to reduce tensions and increase contacts with Taipei. In comparison with previous years, Beijing's approach toward Taipei has been more realistic, rational, and effective. The Taiwan issue in Sino-American relations has become more manageable.

On the other hand, there have been certain weaknesses in China's policy toward the United States that have constrained the further development of Sino-American relations. Apart from the dynamics of China's domestic political and economic developments, the existing institutional gap between the Chinese and American economies has been a major cause of difficulties for American corporations doing business with China. The Chinese government has not yet learned how to deal effectively with increased U.S. protectionism against Chinese goods. Its inconsistent policy toward Sino-American educational exchange has had a strong impact on Chinese students studying in the United States.

On the political front, China's policy toward the United States has continued its transformation. The dynamics of China's domestic politics have had some impact on Sino-American political relations. Demanding fewer Sino-American political and cultural ties, the conservatives within the party and the government have been increasingly critical of the expanded Western, especially U.S., political and cultural influence among Chinese youth and the intelligentsia. The continued unrest in Tibet and some U.S. political factions' deepened involvement in the matter have caused new political tensions between the two countries. There has been a lack of institutionalization of Beijing's cooperation with Washington in subregional security issues in the Asian-Pacific region. The two countries' policy-makers have not developed joint policy-study programs to coordinate their actions in the region. The process of expanding Sino-American military exchange programs has been restricted by both countries' domestic institutions.

China's policy toward the United States has been and will continue to be a central part of Chinese foreign policy. It will continue to have a strong influence on China's relations with other parts of the world, especially the Western industrialized nations and the Soviet Union. It will also be an important component of China's overall security strategy and its foreign policy toward the Asian-Pacific basin. It has played and will continue to play an important role in shaping China's domestic politics.

Internationally, China is a regional power with global strategic importance. Its policy toward the United States will influence the trend of the triangular relations among Washington, Moscow, and itself. Given the key role that both Beijing and Washington play in the security of the Asian-Pacific region, China's policy toward the United States will also have a significant impact on the stability and balance of power in the region in the long run.

Against this background, this chapter reviews changes in China's policy toward the United States during the past few years and its nature and problems, defines China's basic interests, and then discusses the basic policy guideline that China could follow in dealing with the United States in the coming decade.

CHINA'S CURRENT POLICY TOWARD THE UNITED STATES

Current Chinese policy toward the United States has the following distinct characteristics. First of all, it is no longer a policy with a simplistic framework. Rather, the Chinese government is making strong efforts to separate, to the degree possible, those issues over which it has disputes with Washington from those in which the two countries share certain common interests. Second, in comparison to the period before 1979, when China and the United States established diplomatic relations, policy-makers in Beijing have been much better informed about various international issues, including U.S. foreign policy. They have improved their understanding of American domestic politics and its implications for Washington's policy toward China. The institutional gap between the two countries' political and economic systems has been acknowledged, although little progress has been made in narrowing the gap. The Chinese government has formed new research institutions for international relations and American studies. As a result, it is in a better position to approach different sectors of American government and society.[1]

Third, the Chinese government has made great efforts to balance its policy toward the United States and its overall foreign policy. Beijing has repeatedly announced that its U.S. policy is determined mainly by the bilateral relations between the two countries. Yet it has continued to cooperate with Washington on various regional and subregional security and political issues in the Asian-Pacific region in countering Moscow's political and military pressure. While welcoming the relaxation of tensions between the two superpowers, Beijing itself has improved ties with Moscow.

Beijing no longer regards security interests shared with Washington as the only foundation of Sino-American relations. Rather, it includes economic, cultural, and political interests shared by the two countries.[2] In addition, Beijing has effectively used its policy toward the United States to deal with other nations.

During the past few years, especially since the beginning of the 1980s, when the Chinese government recognized the necessity of reducing its economic dependence on Japan, Beijing has made great efforts to expand its economic relations with the United States. It has signed a number of trade agreements with Washington. Many Chinese ministries and trade corporations have opened offices in the United States. More and more American states and cities have established "sister relationships" with their counterparts in China, and trade fairs have been held more frequently in both countries. Establishing long-term business relationships with major American corporations has been given heavy emphasis.[3]

Due to its improved knowledge of the relationship between politics and business in the United States, Beijing has been particularly interested in expanding trade ties with American corporations through former top U.S. governmental officials. In order to enter the U.S. market, the Chinese government has sent more and more trade delegations to visit the United States. Through the press and their conversations with American officials, Chinese leaders and diplomats have openly demanded that Washington remove protectionist barriers against Chinese goods.[4] Meanwhile, in the international community, the Chinese government has been working together with other nations to criticize U.S. trade policy toward developing and newly industrialized countries (NICs).

Beijing has actively and openly approached the United States about purchasing advanced technology. Chinese leaders and diplomats have repeatedly urged Washington to reduce restrictions against the transfer of technology to China. Chinese companies have rapidly expanded their business ties with those major American corporations that are willing and able to sell technology to China. To reduce its dependence on a single supply of technology and to avoid restrictions on technology transfer to China, the Chinese government has encouraged the competition between American, European, and Japanese corporations. More and more Chinese ministries and major corporations have opened offices in the United States for contacting major American corporations and analyzing the American technology market.

Back at home, the Chinese government has offered favorable tax rates to those American corporations that bring advanced technology to China. The government has also waived import taxes on many items of technology and industrial equipment. The central government has organized a number of institutions and corporations to specialize in purchasing technology from abroad, including the United States. The State Council has set up the Office of Technology Imports to coordinate technology-import projects nation-wide.

The Chinese government has made great efforts to attract direct investment from the United States. Besides offering favorable income tax rates and other fiscal treatment, top Chinese leaders have often given direct orders to economic planning agencies to solve certain difficult problems in Sino-American joint-venture operations. To build the American business community's confidence in the Chinese market, Chinese leaders have frequently and openly confirmed their commitment to the open-door policy. The Chinese government has signed agreements with the U.S. government to protect and guarantee American investment in China. Recently, the Chinese government has begun to consider issuing bonds in the U.S. market.

In the international community, the Chinese government has actively approached a number of international financial organizations, such as the World Bank, the International Monetary Fund (IMF), and the Asian Development Bank. In these organizations, the U.S. has an important influence. It has encouraged these organizations to accept China as a member and to provide China with loans at low interest rates and with long-term repayment periods.

The second aspect of China's policy toward the United States is its educational and cultural exchange programs with Washington. During the past few years, the Chinese government has rapidly expanded its educational exchange programs with the United States. Although the government has been unable to pursue a consistent policy of sending Chinese students to America, the number of Chinese students and visiting scholars studying there has continued to increase, reaching about twenty-five thousand in 1988. Over a thousand American students and scholars are now studying or conducting their field research in various Chinese universities. Hundreds of Chinese academic institutions have established exchange relations with their counterparts in the United States. More importantly, the Chinese government has encouraged an increased number of Chinese students to study social sciences and management in America, and many American scholars have been invited to China to give lectures on these subjects.[5] There is now a new generation of Chinese foreign-policy–makers. The Chinese government has recently reached an understanding with the U.S. government that will prevent Chinese students sponsored by the Chinese government from staying in the United States upon completing their studies.[6]

The Chinese government has relaxed its control over cultural exchange programs with the United States. The two countries have exchanged hundreds of diverse cultural delegations each year. American movies, music, literature, and social sciences have been widely introduced into Chinese society. American journalists have been allowed to visit most parts of China and interview wide sections of Chinese society. To listen to the Voice of America is no longer regarded as a "political crime," although during student demonstrations, the Chinese government has accused the Voice of America of "provoking" unrests in China.

The third component of Beijing's U.S. policy is its political policy. During the past few years, Beijing has adjusted this policy significantly. Beijing and Washington have frequently sponsored exchange visits of top-level officials and expanded official channels of governmental consultation. Acknowledging the institutional gap between the two countries and the complex nature of American politics, the Chinese government has approached Washington more effectively by respecting certain American institutions and rules. In a number of cases, for instance, instead of simply putting political pressure on Washington, the Chinese government has begun to hire American lawyers to fight legal battles in American courts. Chinese diplomats have been more active than before in delivering speeches to the American public and approaching U.S. legislative bodies.

The existing gap in basic values and political systems between China and the United States has created certain difficulties between the two governments and the two societies. While insisting on its full sovereign rights to manage China's internal political affairs, Beijing has adopted a low-key approach in dealing with criticism from certain sectors of the American public on its human rights and population-control policies. Chinese diplomats and scholars have appeared on American television and have written articles for influential American newspapers, defending their government's policies. Protecting its public image in American society has been regarded by the Chinese government as a high priority in its policy toward the United States.

Major changes have taken place in China's policy toward many international issues *outside* the Asian-Pacific region, where China does not have strong and direct security interests but important political interests. The Chinese government has altered its simplistic anti-Soviet policy in the Third World (outside the Asian-Pacific region). It has become more critical toward Washington's policies in Central America and Southern Africa. China has established diplomatic relations with Nicaragua and encouraged Washington to moderate its policy toward the Sandinista government. In the Middle East, Beijing has continued to support the Palestine Liberation Organization (PLO) and Arab nations and to criticize U.S. and Israeli policies. On issues outside the Asian-Pacific region, China has increasingly voted against the United States at the United Nations. Together with other developing and underdeveloped nations, China has demanded that the United States make more efforts to reduce its trade protectionism and help the developing world.[7]

In the area of arms control, Beijing has recently taken a more "neutral" position in relation to the two superpowers, criticizing any moves made by either Moscow or Washington that may upgrade the arms race and destabilize the strategic balance between them. While encouraging Moscow and Washington to reach an agreement on the reduction of medium-range missiles in both Europe and Asia, the Chinese government has been critical of Washington's policy of developing the Strategic Defense Initiative (SDI). Since 1985, China has expressed its support for the peace movement in Europe, Oceania, and the United States.[8]

The Taiwan issue remains a key source of tension between the two governments. Beijing has continued to put political pressure on Washington to further reduce its political support of, and weapons sales to, Taipei. Top Chinese leaders and diplomats have frequently asked Washington to play a "more active role" in convincing Taipei to open direct contact and negotiate with Beijing. Moreover, Beijing has asked Washington to create more opportunities for the two sides of the Taiwan Strait to expand their informal and even formal contacts in the United States. While being increasingly worried about Taiwan's potential for moving in a more independent direction, Beijing has recently expressed its strong criticism of the goals and activities of some political groups in the United States that want to separate Taiwan from the Chinese mainland permanently.[9]

On the other hand, Beijing itself has continued to try to get closer to Taipei by reducing political tensions and increasing trade and other direct contacts with Taiwanese society. While reserving the right to use force, Beijing has significantly reduced its military pressure on Taipei. Beijing has taken a low-key approach toward Taipei's political succession to the late President Chiang Ching-kuo and the recent political struggle between the Nationalist Party or

Kuomintang (KMT) and its opposition. It has left open the option of making direct contact with the opposition, although its major interest is to expand ties with the KMT, the ruling party. Beijing has continued to encourage the expansion of economic relations, cultural exchange, and other communications between Taiwan and the Chinese mainland. Beijing has invited Taipei to return to various international organizations under the name of "China-Taipei" or "China-Taiwan."[10]

Within the Asian-Pacific region, however, Sino-American cooperation has advanced and has been consolidated. While Beijing has reduced tensions and improved cultural and economic ties with Moscow, it has nevertheless been sensitive to possible reactions from Washington to such a development and has made strong efforts to maintain the stability of the triangle between Washington, Moscow, and itself. The Soviet Union is still viewed as the principal threat to China's national security. To break down Moscow's strategic encirclement of and to reduce its political and military pressure on China are considered by Beijing as basic security and strategic goals. During its increasingly frequent consultations with Moscow, Beijing has demanded that Moscow completely withdraw its troops from Afghanistan, reduce its armed forces along the Chinese border, and stop its support of the Vietnamese occupation of Cambodia. Beijing and Moscow have reached an agreement on the territory disputes between them and have begun to work together on the issue of the Vietnamese occupation of Cambodia.[11]

Although it has played down the U.S. role in its strategic and security planning, Beijing has continued to regard the United States as a potential strategic partner against Soviet expansionism in the region. In public, Chinese officials have not recently mentioned their concerns about the increased Soviet military activities in the western Pacific. Yet for Beijing, the U.S. military presence in the region has served as the key counterfactor to the rapid Soviet military buildup, especially the Soviets' enlarged Pacific Fleet, with its strong air-attack power. Beijing has supported the Aquino government's efforts to stabilize its power, as any dramatic political changes in the Philippines could cause the expulsion of American bases from that country, thereby further strengthening the Soviet Union's strategic position and destabilizing the balance of power in the region.

Both Beijing and Washington are committed to guaranteeing the security of Thailand and Pakistan and continuing to provide weapons and economic aid to rebels in Afghanistan and Cambodia.

High-level consultations between the two governments on subregional security issues within the Asian-Pacific region and on various international issues have become more frequent and regular.[12] Beijing has coordinated its policy with Washington to balance the three factions of the Cambodian resistance movement, has expanded its cooperation with the ASEAN states, especially Thailand, and has maintained strong political and military pressure on Vietnam.

On the Korean Peninsula, Beijing has emphasized its interest in maintaining the current military balance, although, at North Korea's request, it has continued to demand the withdrawal of U.S. military forces from South Korea. Beijing has been encouraging Seoul and Washington to increase their contacts with Pyongyang and has been encouraging Pyongyang to increase its participation in the international community. This approach is regarded as the key policy in reducing the existing tensions between the two Koreas and providing alternatives to Pyongyang's present and future leadership. Since the second half of 1987, Beijing has opened its markets to Korean investors. Economic and cultural ties between the two countries have expanded rapidly.[13] On the other hand, Beijing has been critical of Washington's efforts to strengthen South Korea's military forces and in particular to deepen Japan's involvement in the security affairs of the peninsula, as such efforts will increase confrontations between the two Koreas, push Pyongyang closer to Moscow, and reduce China's leverage in competing with the Soviet Union for influence over Pyongyang.

Beijing is no longer supportive of Washington's efforts to push Japanese rearmament, since a rapid process of Japanese rearmament could undermine the current balance of power in the Asian-Pacific region and challenge China's own security.[14] Nevertheless, Beijing has continued to appreciate the U.S.-Japanese security arrangement, which can serve as the safeguard to prevent Japan from becoming an independent military power with strong offensive capability, threatening its neighboring nations.

In Southeast Asia, Beijing has concentrated on the Cambodian issue and its direct confrontation with Hanoi. While expressing its dissatisfactions with Washington's low-key approach toward the Cambodian issue, Beijing has downgraded its criticism of the increased Soviet military presence in the region. Chinese diplomats, however, have kept reminding their American counterparts about the long-term threat to the region's security and stability.

In South Asia, Beijing's key concern is the security of Pakistan, a country that has had good relations with both China and the United States and has played an important role in buffering Moscow's expansionism in the region. The death of President Zia may lead to some major shifts in Pakistan's foreign policy. Whether or not Benazir Bhutto will be able to manage the country and maintain political stability is still an open question. She may face challenges by the Pakistani armed forces as well as Islamic fundamentalists both in and outside the country. Ethnic and local politics may also intensify. Economically, Pakistan may continue to suffer from high inflation, high unemployment, low growth, low efficiency, and poverty. Externally, India, the Soviet Union, and Afghanistan may increase their political and military pressure on the new government, thereby forcing it to reduce its international commitments and to alter its policy toward the West and China. To pursue its security interests, Beijing has welcomed the U.S. military presence in the Indian Ocean and has encouraged its support of Pakistan's security. Beijing itself has made a strong commitment to Pakistan's national security. While improving its own ties with India, Beijing has taken a low-key attitude toward Washington's unsuccessful efforts to push India away from the Soviet Union.

Beijing has made strong efforts to expand its military exchange program with Washington. Visits of high-level military personnel to both countries have become more frequent. The newly established Chinese National Defense University has begun to exchange students, professors, and training materials with the National Defense University of the U.S. Army. In the fall of 1986, the first U.S. Navy vessel visited China. The number of Chinese military personnel who are studying on American campuses has continued to increase; and many of them have visited U.S. military academies.[15]

ASSESSMENTS OF CHINA'S POLICY TOWARD THE UNITED STATES

All these efforts have been effective. In the economic sphere, Sino-American trade has increased rapidly; the United States is now China's third-largest (after Japan and Hong Kong) trade partner.[16] A few hundred Sino-American joint ventures and many American banks operate in China; U.S. petroleum corporations have played a major role in the development of China's inland and offshore oil exploitation; and the United States ranks number two (after Hong Kong) on the list of foreign investors in China.[17] Washington has made strong efforts to loosen certain restrictions on the transfer of technology to China and has treated the latter differently from most Communist countries. Consequently, China has imported a substantial amount of technology (some of which has military implications), industrial equipment, and even certain weapons systems from the United States.[18]

In the international community, China has continued to pursue its image as a maker of "independent foreign policy." Its relations with various developing and underdeveloped nations, including those countries that have close ties with Moscow, have improved. Moreover, China has rapidly restored its relations with most East European nations and Communist or Socialist parties in Western Europe.

Beijing's position in the triangle between Washington, Moscow, and itself has remained stable. Sino-Soviet ties have continued to improve, although the strategic relations between them have not changed significantly. Yet this new relationship has resulted in the reduction of Moscow's political pressure on Beijing and has allowed the latter to avoid once again becoming the central target of Moscow's strategy in the region. Moscow has repeatedly expressed its willingness to improve relations with China and has made concessions by pulling out one division of troops from Mongolia, pressing Hanoi to withdraw from Cambodia, and completely withdrawing its armed forces from Afghanistan. On the other hand, however, the ongoing Sino-American military exchange programs and the two countries' strategic cooperation have strengthened Beijing's bargaining position vis-à-vis Moscow and increased its capacity to cope with subregional security issues in the Asian-Pacific region.

In general, Beijing's working relationships with Washington have become more manageable than before. Its approach to Washington and the American public have been more rational, reasonable, and thus effective. Frequent high-level consultations between Beijing and Washington have effectively improved mutual understanding and coordinated the two countries' policies in dealing with each other and with other international issues in which they share certain common interests. As a result of an improved understanding of China's political system and culture, Washington has been sensitive to Beijing's internal politics and has avoided provoking conflicts over issues such as human rights and freedom of the press.

The enlarged military exchange programs between the two armies have improved their mutual understanding. The Chinese military establishment has been far better informed about activities of the U.S. Army and other security and international issues. These developments have contributed to China's efforts to create a new generation of military officials and strategists with broad international perspectives and an understanding of modern warfare.

Meanwhile, Washington has become more sensitive than before to Beijing's interest in the reunification of Taiwan, although it has continued its policy of nondirect involvement in Beijing-Taipei relations. It has welcomed the increased contacts between Beijing and Taipei and has promised to follow the principles of the three Sino-American Shanghai Communiqués.[19] It has taken a low-key approach toward the development of Taiwan's internal politics, avoiding conflicts with Beijing in this respect. Washington supported Beijing in gaining membership in the Asian Development Bank and convinced Taipei not to leave the bank.[20] In the United States and some other locations, American academic and private institutions have initiated more international conferences attracting scholars and officials from both Beijing and Taipei.

In the area of Asian security, both Beijing and Washington have encouraged Pyongyang to open up more to the international community. Beijing's deep concerns about the future direction of Japanese security strategy have been taken into account in Washington. Under Washington's encouragement, ASEAN states, especially Thailand and Singapore, have expanded their cooperation with China. Washington has appreciated Beijing's support of the Aquino government's efforts to stabilize the Philippines' domestic politics and economy. Beijing's political and military pressure on Vietnam has been regarded by the United States and Thailand as a positive step toward the resolution of the Cambodian issue. In Afghanistan, Washington and Beijing's support of the rebels has been well coordinated. More importantly, both countries' strong commitment to the security of Pakistan has served as the key deterrent against the increased political and military pressure of the Soviet Union and India on Pakistan.

Nevertheless, there have been a number of problems in China's policy toward the United States. On the economic front, growing U.S. protectionism has presented a serious challenge to any further increase of Sino-U.S. trade. Not only has it hampered China's efforts to increase its exports of manufactured goods to the United States, but it has also hurt China's trade with Hong Kong and other Asian nations, whose imports from China have largely been financed by their own exports to the United States. Although the Chinese are now more interested in doing business with Americans, inefficiency and an incomplete understanding of the nature of the Chinese market and decision-making process have been major reasons why many American corporations have failed to compete with their Japanese counterparts in China.

For its part, China's major difficulties have occurred in the institutional gap between its own economy and the American economy. Most Chinese corporations are still not familiar with American market and business practices. The decision-making process in China is still slow, bureaucratic, and lacking in incentive. Chinese are reluctant to hire American consulting firms and to deal with small- and medium-sized American companies. Thus, there is no mechanism that can allow Chinese corporations to respond effectively to rapid changes in demand in the American market. Moreover, during the past few years, China's economic development and economic policies have been highly unstable. The inflation rate has been high. Since the end of 1984, China has had a serious shortage of foreign exchange. As a result, it has been very difficult for American investors to convert their profits made in China into hard currency. Although the Chinese have made strong efforts to reform their central planning system and managerial institutions, particularly in regard to enterprises with foreign involvements, the wide institutional gap between the two economies continues to exist. The Chinese government has adjusted its policy toward foreign-involved enterprises, but there has been a lack of effective legal institutions to protect the interests of foreign investors from local bureaucratic intervention. It has become increasingly difficult for foreign-involved enterprises to obtain the raw materials and energy supplies necessary for their operations in China. Because of the Chinese government's changed economic strategies, many projects involving foreign companies have either been delayed or canceled. Since the last quarter of 1986, political tensions in China have increased. Consequently, American investors have been discouraged from making long-term commitments to the Chinese market. These instabilities and inconsistencies have also weakened Chinese corporations' ability to enter the American market.

In many areas, the U.S. government continues to adopt certain restrictions against the transfer of technology to China, especially those that have military applications. There have been similar disputes between Washington and its European allies over the export of technology to the Soviet Union. Some ASEAN states have also complained about Washington's sales of technology to China. For its part, the Chinese still have much to learn about the international technology market. It should not depend solely on a few large corporations. In particular, Chinese are not familiar with the U.S. legal and political system with regard to the procedures involved in license applications for technology exports to China. In addition, China's limited amount of foreign exchange reserve has restricted its capacity to buy American technology.

The major obstacle to further expansion of Sino-American cultural and educational exchange programs has been the unstable nature of Chinese domestic politics. Ongoing party politics and the campaign of "antibourgeois liberalization" have strengthened bureaucratic control over cultural and educational affairs and discouraged Chinese intellectuals from expanding their personal contacts with foreigners and studying Western culture and social sciences. Such a political atmosphere has been a major reason why many Chinese students study abroad, especially in the United States, where the immigration law has made it possible for them to stay or to delay their return to China.[21] Furthermore, tensions between the Chinese government and foreign journalists have increased, which have indeed hurt China's image in the West.

In the international community, there has been increased cooperation from other developing or underdeveloped nations in regard to China's leverage in obtaining consensual and economic aid loans from the World Bank, the IMF, and the Asian Development Bank. Beijing's sharp criticism of Washington's Third World policy (outside the Asian-Pacific region) has been used by some American politicians as an excuse to demand a change in U.S. policy toward China.

Although the process of Sino-Soviet relaxation has been a gradual and limited one, many American scholars and policy-makers have been worried about its implications for the stability of the triangle formed by Washington, Beijing, and Moscow. They have been particularly worried about whether such changes would allow Moscow to remove a large part of its resources from the Chinese front to target the United States and its allies. The limited Sino-Soviet relaxation has also had strong implications for Asian security: how should Soviet expansionism in the region be contained and who should do it? The answer to these two questions may lead to a rethinking of Washington's security strategy toward the Asian-

Pacific region. So far, most American strategists have not really thought through this issue. Nevertheless, further improvement of Sino-Soviet relations may naturally stimulate discussion about this issue among American policy-makers.

The further development of the working relationship between the two governments has met certain difficulties, too. The tightened political control over Chinese public life has caused greater uneasiness among American "China hands." Privately, American diplomats have increasingly complained of their difficulties in expanding contacts with broad sections of Chinese society. The two governments have had more disputes over issues in China involving human rights, minorities, and freedom of the press. The Chinese government, for its part, has continued to protest that some American politicians have intervened in Chinese affairs by "attacking the Chinese government's domestic policy." During student and ethnic demonstrations in 1987 and 1988, Beijing accused the Voice of America and some American journalists of encouraging the dissent. In comparison with Taipei, Beijing has had far less influence on Capitol Hill.

The ongoing Sino-American military exchange programs have not been well-coordinated with both countries' strategic planning. In particular, there have been no joint research projects on security issues in which the two countries can further pursue their common security interests. The gaps in values between the two armies have also slowed down this process. Moreover, there has been a lack of mutual support between these military exchange programs on the one hand and the two countries' foreign-policy–makers on the other.

Within the Asian-Pacific region, a major problem has been that Sino-American cooperation has not been institutionalized. Although both Beijing and Washington want to maintain stability on the Korean Peninsula, they have approached the issue differently. Beijing's main emphasis has been on reducing tensions and increasing contacts between the two Koreas. In addition, expanding Pyongyang's participation has been regarded as an important instrument for changing its behavior gradually in the international community. Beijing has been particularly sensitive to the deepened Japanese involvement in the security affairs of the peninsula. For its part, Washington has encouraged expansion of contacts between Seoul and Pyongyang; it has recently expressed a willingness to develop direct and informal ties with Pyongyang.[22] Yet its key policy has been to strengthen Seoul's military power and increase its international popularity, and to develop South Korean–U.S.–Japanese security cooperation. These differences have in turn made it difficult for Beijing and Washington to coordinate their policies toward the peninsula more effectively and to further reduce tensions there.

Neither Beijing nor Washington seems to have a clear, long-term strategy regarding the security of Japan. China and other Asian nations have been alarmed by Tokyo's attitude toward the history of Japanese aggression during the first half of this century. Tokyo's decision to break Japan's defense-spending limit of under 1 percent of its GNP has invited strong criticism from those countries. They have been worried about the long-term implications of Japanese rearmament for the region's security and stability. As a result, they have been increasingly critical of Washington's efforts to encourage Tokyo to speed up its rearmament and play a greater role in regional security affairs without Washington's clear and effective guidance. The key issue here is that China and other Asian nations want to see an institutional mechanism to prevent Japan from becoming an independent military power with offensive capability that will threaten their own security. Yet Washington has not made enough efforts to reassure these countries.

In Southeast Asia, Beijing has been dissatisfied with Washington's ambiguity toward Hanoi. For Beijing, Washington's efforts to draw Hanoi away from Moscow by increasing contacts with it or even by restoring diplomatic ties can only be counterproductive. Beijing does not believe that Hanoi would be willing to significantly reduce its dependence on Moscow, nor would it completely pull out its troops from Cambodia without strong political and military pressure. The U.S. approach has thus been viewed as an appeasement that can only confuse the international community and increase Hanoi's bargaining position on the Cambodian issue. Any political solution of the Cambodian conflict will be unacceptable to Beijing if it allows the continuation of the Vietnamese occupation of that country; the only way to "solve" the issue is to force Hanoi to withdraw its troops. Therefore, apart from support for the resistance movement in Cambodia, forming a "united front" and increasing the international political pressure on Hanoi has been regarded by Beijing as a key means of pursuing its goals. Thus, Beijing has not been satisfied with Washington's low-key approach toward Vietnam. More importantly, Beijing is the only player who continues to provide weapons and economic aid to the Communist faction in Cambodia. Although it has pressed the Cambodian Communist faction to play a less public role and has made clear that it does not want to see the Communist faction return to power, Beijing has continued to be hesitant to cut off its supply of weapons to the Communist faction.

In South Asia, the key issue appears to be how to coordinate Beijing's and Washington's support for Pakistan's security and their relations with India. After Gorbachev's second trip to New Delhi, Sino-Indian territorial disputes and Indo-Pakistani border tensions have declined. Rajiv Gandhi himself visited Beijing in December 1988. Beijing's basic position has been to leave its territorial disputes with India to the future, to support Pakistani security, and, at the same time, to make efforts to improve its relations with New Delhi. The Indians have continued to be suspicious of Beijing's position, however, largely because of the progress in the relaxation of Sino-Soviet tension, India's conflicts with Pakistan, and its internal political difficulties. New Delhi continues its support of the Tibetan refugee government based in India, although during his trip to Beijing in December 1988, Prime Minister Gandhi assured the Chinese that the Indian government recognized Tibet as a part of China and would not allow Tibetan refugees to engage in any political activities against China.[23]

Washington is unquestionably committed to the security of Pakistan. Nevertheless, the military imbalance between India and Pakistan and the instability in Pakistan are compelling reasons for arguing that the United States should pull New Delhi away from Moscow by increasing its aid to India and reducing its support for Pakistan. However, due to the geopolitics of the region and India's heavy dependence on the Soviet Union, such a change in policy seems unlikely. In addition, the Indian lobby has been active in persuading Capitol Hill to adopt a tough stance toward Pakistan. These factors have made it difficult for the mainstream strategic planners in Washington to develop a long-term strategy for India and Pakistan and to coordinate its policy with Beijing, with which it shares great common interests in the region.

Finally, the Taiwan issue has continued to be troublesome, although it has become more manageable than before in the context of Sino-American relations. Beijing has continued to demand that Washington reduce its support of Taipei and play an "active role" in contributing to the reunification of Taiwan. Beijing has complained about some American politicians' strong support of Taipei and their involvement in the Taiwanese Independence Movement (TIM). Beijing has been worried about recent political developments on Taiwan and the newly formulated opposition party, the Democratic Progressive Party (DPP). Yet it does not seem to have a concrete, proper, and effective strategy to deal with the dynamics of Taiwanese politics. Both psychologically and politically, the recent tensions in China's internal politics have jeopardized Beijing's credibility and its position in dealing with Taipei.[24]

Washington's major concern seems to be to avoid any serious crisis between Taipei and Beijing and between the KMT and the DPP. It is also in its interest to prevent a possible revival of tensions between China and the United States over the Taiwan issue, as such tensions will further upset Beijing's internal politics and undermine current Sino-American relations and the stability of the region. Nevertheless, due to its domestic politics and its historic ties with Taipei, Washington has not been willing to push Taipei to the negotiating table with Beijing and to substantially reduce its support to Taipei. Moreover, an active Taiwan lobby has been one important reason why Washington has kept its commitment to Taipei. Certain political forces in the United States have continued to push Taiwan to move toward independence.

FUTURE TRENDS IN SINO-AMERICAN RELATIONS

In general, Sino-American relations are determined by both countries' domestic developments and the dynamics of the international environment. In the coming decade, each of these factors are likely to undergo important changes. These changes will have a strong impact on China's policy toward the United States.

On the economic front, it is likely that the Chinese economy will continue its rapid growth. Such a rapid growth would further reduce China's need to import agricultural goods and strengthen its capacity to export manufactured goods. As a result, China's demand for American agricultural goods may continue to decline, while its incentive to exploit the U.S. market of manufactured goods will increase. In addition, the government's efforts to pursue its program of Four Modernizations will continue to require substantial imports of technology, industrial equipment, and capital investment, especially from industrial market economies.

Although the Chinese government will continue to reform its managerial institutions, it will probably not soon introduce a radical price reform based upon private ownership of the industrial sector or a fundamental reform in the banking system. Thus, instabilities and uncertainties in Beijing's economic policies may continue. The present institutional gap between the Chinese and American economies is likely to remain. In the short term, China may be unable to build up a mechanism that would allow the country to respond to rapid changes in the international manufactured-goods market and the overseas financial market. Its ability to increase exports of manufactured goods will be constrained. Due to the decline in demand for oil in the industrial market economies and the increased competition among OPEC nations, at least in the near future, the price of oil in the international market is unlikely to jump up again. Therefore, China, whose oil accounts for 20 percent of its total exports, will continue to have a shortage of foreign exchange.

The Chinese government will surely continue to grant favorable fiscal and financial treatment to foreign investors. Foreign-involved enterprises in China will likely continue to enjoy special rights to manage their own operations. Nevertheless, they will probably continue to face high inflation, limited market shares, shortages of raw materials and energy, a relatively poorer infrastructure, and bureaucratic intervention. The high degree of political risk of direct investment in China will remain.

It is unlikely that Washington, for its part, will dramatically alter its protectionism against NICs, although it might be less tough toward Chinese goods. The Bush administration is likely to continue Reagan's economic policies toward China. Yet with their majority position at both the Congress and Senate, the Democrats may make it difficult for the White House to do so. As long as Sino-American political and strategic relations remain stable and manageable, Washington will continue to loosen its restrictions against the transfer of technology to China. Nevertheless, some controls over transfer of technology, especially those technologies that have strong military applications to China, will remain. Unless the Chinese government manages to continue its reforms and liberalization and to increase the degree of consistency in its policy on foreign investment, American investors will continue to be very cautious about the high degree of political risk of the Chinese market.

Internationally, the competition for market, technology, and capital investment between Asia's newly industrialized countries and China is likely to intensify. The key policy issue for the Chinese government will be whether it will be able to create a favorable investment environment for competing with other Asian nations. It will also be important for Beijing to contribute to Hong Kong's stability and prosperity both before and after 1997. American corporations will face more serious competition from their Japanese and European counterparts for the Chinese market.

Political relations between the two countries may experience some important changes. Beijing may soon experience a real succession to the old generation (including but not limited to Deng Xiaoping). Due to the country's current political structure and political and economic instabilities, the process of the forthcoming succession might intensify the political struggle within the party and tensions between the state and society. Although the dynamics of China's internal politics might, to some extent, destabilize its relations with other parts of the world, the country's basic national interests and its changed public opinion would likely continue effectively to constrain the ability of a post-Deng leadership from altering its foreign policy, especially its policy toward the two superpowers and the Asian-Pacific region.

In comparison with Reagan, Bush certainly knows more about international issues in general and about Asian affairs, including China, in particular. Given the dramatic changes taking place in the Asian-Pacific region and in U.S.-Asian relations, the new American president may restructure U.S. policy toward the Asian-Pacific region, including its policy toward China. In the coming decade, Taiwan will continue its fundamental social, political, and economic changes, which will have strong implications for its relations with both the Chinese mainland and the United States. While struggling with increased international protectionism against its exports, Taipei will have to make strong efforts to upgrade its national economy, thereby becoming more competitive in the international market. Under the encouragement of some political forces in the United States and Japan, the struggle between the KMT and the DPP may intensify. Practically speaking, chances that the DPP will gain power are slim. Rather, it will continue to function as an opposition to put pressure on the KMT government. Nevertheless, this struggle, if it continues to intensify, could get out of control, thereby provoking intervention by the Taiwanese army and intelligence forces.

The Taiwan Independence Movement (TIM) is another problem. So far, most of its leading activists are in fact based abroad, especially in the United States and Japan. In Taiwanese society, tensions between "mainlanders" and "natives," especially among the younger generation, have declined significantly during the past two decades. This is likely to be the general trend in the future. The TIM does not have an effective institutional base from which to pursue its goals under this current constitutional framework, nor does it gain strong support from the majority in society who would like to enjoy greater political rights but not at the cost of political upheaval. So far, the majority of DPP politicians have distanced themselves from the TIM; and both within the leadership and at the grass roots of the DPP, the "mainlanders" and "natives" share responsibility and work together. Moreover, many DPP leaders have demanded that the KMT government expand contacts with the Chinese mainland. In the international community, the TIM is unlikely to receive broad sympathy and support. The TIM could become a strong political voice only if the KMT government failed to maintain political stability or if Beijing suddenly chose once again to significantly increase its military pressure on Taipei.

If Beijing is able to continue its reform and its open-door policy, to contribute to Hong Kong's stability and prosperity effectively, and to maintain good ties with Washington, tensions between Beijing and Taipei will further decline and various contacts between them will continue to expand. This process might not lead directly to an immediate solution to the reunification question, as Taipei would have to be convinced that the post-Deng leadership will be able to continue its present policy; and the ongoing struggle between the KMT government and its opposition will continue to make it difficult for the former to pursue a rapid course in moving closer to Beijing. Nevertheless, the further increased contacts will surely enhance mutual understanding between the two sides of the Taiwan Strait, discourage Taipei from moving toward independence, and create a more favorable atmosphere for the reunification in the long run.

As part of its own strategy, Washington will likely continue its support for Taipei. It will not, however, want to encourage a revival of tensions between Taipei and Beijing. Publicly, Washington will likely continue to take a "dual track" approach: it will promise to follow the principles of the three Sino-American Shanghai Communiqués and not take the responsibility of forcing Taipei to negotiate with Beijing.[25] The strengthened Sino-American ties and declining tensions between Beijing and Taipei, however, will encourage Washington to help expand the relationship between them—although, in general, its role in this relationship will probably continue to decline. If Taiwan moves further in the direction of independence or its political stability is undermined, however, the political conflicts between Beijing and Washington may suddenly increase.

Beijing has had and will continue to have serious difficulties in dealing with minority ethnic populations in Tibet, Inner Mongolia, and Xinjiang. Although Beijing will provide more economic aid to these areas where the ethnic populations live, given Beijing's constrained financial resources and the wide income gap between these areas and the rest of China, these groups' living standards are unlikely to be raised significantly in the near future. Politically, Beijing will try its best to moderate its policies toward these areas. It is likely to provide ethnic elites more opportunities to participate in public life and to grant greater religious freedom to the population at large. Meanwhile, the Chinese government will maintain political and military power in these areas to secure political stability. Tensions between the Chinese government and the ethnic populations, however, are likely to remain.[26]

The ethnic tensions in China may become a political issue between Beijing and Washington in the next few years. The dissenting Chinese ethnic groups, notably the Tibetans, have received some sympathy on Capitol Hill as well as from the U.S. public at large. It is partially due to the Tibetan refugee government's effective lobbying and public relations activities. If the tensions in China continue to be high and if the Tibetans continue to lobby effectively in Washington, Capitol Hill may increase its pressure on the White House to press Beijing to make further efforts in reducing conflicts with the ethnic populations and improving human rights in China.

Washington will be willing to continue expanding its cultural and educational exchange programs with Beijing. It will also cooperate with the Chinese government in preventing more Chinese students from overstaying their terms in the United States. Although Washington itself will probably not play an active role in introducing Western culture into China, the expanded cultural relations between the two countries will naturally do so. Whether or not these programs develop smoothly will depend largely upon the dynamics of China's domestic politics, especially its degree of political liberalization and the relationship between the state and the intellectuals, and its general political ties with the United States.

In the years ahead, the mutual understanding between Washington and Beijing will likely be further improved. Differences in basic values and institutions between the United States and China, however, will continue to exist. These differences will have a strong impact on the working relationship between the two governments. Although the American public would generally welcome the further growth of Sino-American relations, Chinese diplomats will have to compete more effectively with their counterparts from Taipei, New Delhi, the ASEAN capitals, and Tokyo. Some American politicians, both on Capitol Hill and in the White House, may also challenge China's foreign policy. Certain sections within American society will continue to criticize China's domestic politics and put pressure on the U.S. government to downgrade its ties with Beijing. American journalists, diplomats, and scholars who are dealing with China may continue to complain about the difficulty of making contact with broad sections of Chinese society. Lack of information or a deep understanding of the Chinese government's decision-making processes and of the society at large will probably continue to be the major weakness in their dealings with China.

Outside the Asian-Pacific region, disputes or even conflicts between Washington and Beijing over certain political and economic issues may intensify. It is unlikely, for instance, that Beijing and Washington will agree with each other over issues such as the "new international economic order" and North-South relationships. Unless Washington is willing to change dramatically its current policy toward southern Africa, Central America, and the Middle East, Beijing will surely remain critical of the United States on these issues. Beijing will probably not, however, pursue an active policy of directly confronting Washington's Third World policy.

Beijing and Washington will probably continue to have disputes over arms control. Washington will probably try to convince Beijing to join international talks on arms reduction. It will also continue to put pressure on Beijing not to transfer nuclear technology to any other countries. For its part, Beijing will remain critical of the arms race between the two superpowers while keeping its independence and continuing to build up its nuclear deterrence capacity. Given the wide gap between U.S. and Chinese nuclear forces and the common threat the two countries face, it is unlikely that these disputes will get out of control. More importantly, apart from the ongoing arms race between Washington and Moscow, in the coming decade the balance of nuclear power in the Asian-Pacific region may undergo important changes: both South Korea and Taiwan might choose the nuclear option; the nuclear arms race between India and Pakistan may intensify; and Japan's attitude toward nuclear weapons might also change. Washington and Beijing may respond to these changes differently, although both of them want to maintain nuclear stability in the region.

In the coming decade, the Moscow-Washington-Beijing triangle will continue to change. At the global level, the two superpowers are most likely to continue their competition in Europe, the Middle East, and Africa, and in the arms race. Because of the Soviet Union's internal difficulties and the United States' fiscal constraints, both Gorbachev and Bush may choose to further reduce political tensions between them. Their cultural and economic ties might expand. The deep distrust between the two countries, however, is likely to remain. Moreover, their strategic relations will probably not change significantly; each country will continue to view the other as the principal threat to its national security. The two might be able to reach certain agreements over the reduction of nuclear weapons. Nevertheless, these agreements are unlikely to stop their competition in new areas, as their basic security interests are in sharp conflict and the process of technological development will continue to stimulate the arms race between them. To reduce the Soviet-American competition over regional security issues around the world would probably be even more difficult. This is because these issues always involve other nations, which may depend upon the superpowers for economic aid, political support, and military supply and, at the same time, enjoy a certain freedom of action. In addition, whereas in Europe the line between the two camps is clearly drawn and there is a relatively high degree of political stability, in many other regions where Moscow and Washington are competing politically and militarily, the division is often unclear and the degree of political instability is high. As a result, the superpower competition there is always more complicated.

If the Chinese government is able to maintain its internal stability and continue its current foreign policy, China's relations with both superpowers will probably continue to improve. In particular, it is possible for China to maintain the most favorable position within the triangle while pursuing its basic security interests effectively. Unless China's security environment changes dramatically,

Sino-Soviet tension will continue to decline; and China will be able to avoid being once again the central target of Moscow's containment strategy in the Asian-Pacific region. The Soviet Union will nevertheless still present the principal challenge to China's national security. On the other hand, it is unlikely that the United States will present a serious threat to China's national security, although the issue of Taiwan will continue to be a problem between Washington and Beijing.

Within the Asian-Pacific region, Sino-American relations are likely to experience certain important changes. This is because China's basic security interests will continue to be concerned primarily with that region, where Washington and Beijing share many common strategic interests. The potential for advancing Sino-American cooperation on subregional security issues will thus be great. On the Korean Peninsula, tensions between the two Koreas could decline if the current military balance could be maintained and Pyongyang increased its participation in the international community. For both Washington and Beijing, key security issues will continue to be how to maintain stability and prevent North Korea from leaning further toward the Soviet Union. Yet they may continue to approach these issues differently. The forthcoming succession to Kim Il Sung, the intensified political struggle between the regime and its opposition in South Korea, and a possible shift in the military balance between the two Koreas might undermine stability. In addition, the deepened involvement of Moscow and Tokyo would likely complicate security and political affairs on the peninsula.

Washington will surely continue its encouragement of Japanese rearmament and Tokyo's increased role in regional political, economic, and security affairs. It will also further expand the U.S.-Japanese security arrangement. Whether or not Washington will change its basic security strategy in the Asian-Pacific region and urge Tokyo to develop into an independent military power with a strong offensive capability remains an open question. Its answer may depend largely upon U.S.-Soviet competition at both the global and regional levels, the future dynamics of the Washington-Beijing-Moscow triangle, and other Asian nations' attitude toward Japan. Moreover, Japan's domestic politics may turn in a more conservative direction. Its strong economic and technological power would likely encourage both the Japanese government and Japanese society, especially the younger generation, to demand a greater role in regional security affairs. In this regard, Japan's unstable international environment would increase the Japanese public's feeling of insecurity.

In Southeast Asia, both Washington and Beijing will face five basic security problems: how to press Hanoi to pull out its troops from Cambodia completely; how to create a neutral Cambodia; how to insure Thailand's security; how to reduce Moscow's political influence and counter its military presence in the region; and how to help some ASEAN states to manage their internal economic and political crises. In addition, ASEAN states will most likely continue their disputes over security issues. On each of these issues, Beijing and Washington share some common interests. Both of them, for instance, will continue their full commitments to Thailand's security and continue to demand that Hanoi withdraw from Cambodia completely. Both of them will also demand that Moscow reduce its military presence in Vietnam and its strategic cooperation with Hanoi. Nevertheless, Washington's key interest is to counter Moscow's expansionism while Beijing may focus more on its confrontation with Vietnam. Beijing and Washington may continue their disputes over how to deal with the Communist faction in Cambodia. Moreover, the United States is allied with the ASEAN countries, with which (especially both Indonesia and Malaysia) China may continue to have political conflicts.

In the coming decade, tensions between India and Pakistan may remain high. As New Delhi deepens its dependence on Moscow's political support for its ambition to be the dominant power in the region, for economic aid, and for weapons supply, it may continue to challenge the security of both Pakistan and China. At the same time, it will seek to improve its ties with Washington, though not at the cost of jeopardizing its relations with Moscow. Apart from the challenge from India, Pakistan will continue to be threatened by the Soviet Union (through Afghanistan). Its internal economic difficulties may further deepen; and the political struggle between the new government and Islamic fundamentalists may intensify. In Afghanistan, Moscow's withdrawal may lead to a bloody civil war between the regime and the resistance movement. More importantly, the Islamic fundamentalists may soon control the power and extend their influence to the whole region. In sum, the region may become highly unstable. Its geopolitics will nevertheless continue to constrain both Washington and Beijing's ability to pursue their security interests effectively.

CONCLUSION: WHAT CAN BE DONE?

To pursue its national interests effectively, Beijing may adopt the following basic policies in dealing with the United States:

Economically, it is important for Beijing to form a long-term strategy based on a concrete, detailed, and careful analysis of China's domestic needs and the dynamics of the American market. This strategy must be the product of consistent and predictable government policy. This is essential for increasing the confidence of American investors in the Chinese market. The existing institutional gap between the Chinese and American economies has to be further narrowed by the Chinese government's economic reforms in the urban industrial, financial, and trade sectors. It is necessary for China to gradually establish a mechanism that would enable the country to respond effectively to changes in the American market. Such a mechanism must be based upon great decision-making power with strong incentive at the enterprise level. The government should also continue to introduce market mechanisms and to encourage the development of the private sector.

The Chinese government's financial and fiscal policies must be readjusted. To encourage China's exports to the United States, for instance, the renminbi (RMB, the Chinese currency) should be further depreciated; and prices in the Chinese domestic market must be gradually linked directly to prices in the international marketplace. Favorable conditions designed to attract foreign investment should be continued. Foreign investors' share in China's domestic market ought to be defined clearly and protected by law. They should be allowed to convert the profits they make in China into hard currency.

To enter the American market and gain more advanced technology from the United States, Beijing should continue to urge Washington to remove protectionist barriers against Chinese goods as well as restrictions against the transfer of technology to China. It will be desirable for China to encourage further competition among industrial nations to sell it technology and industrial equipment. While making greater efforts to approach systematically those small- and medium-sized American companies that are able to sell advanced technology to China, it will be increasingly important for the Chinese government or Chinese business organizations to hire U.S consulting companies to conduct market surveys and to lobby for China's interests.

In order to expand cultural and educational exchange programs with the United States, the Chinese government should adopt a liberal and consistent cultural and educational policy. Tensions between the state and society, especially the intelligentsia, should be further reduced and political control over cultural affairs must be loosened. While the Chinese government will certainly continue to ask the U.S. government to encourage Chinese students to return after studying in the United States, its major policy should be to create more favorable working and living conditions, including granting the freedom for them to go abroad again. Moreover, it is desirable to allow those students who are not sponsored by the Chinese government to choose to stay in the United States, as they will have a certain influence in American society, including in Washington, strengthening Sino-American ties in the long run.

In the international community, especially outside the Asian-Pacific region, it would not be in Beijing's interest to pursue an overall strategy against the United States. Rather, judgments should be made case by case. Beijing may remain critical of Washington's policy in regard to North-South relations, Central America, the Middle East, and southern Africa, where it does not have strong security interests, and it will continue to try to build up good relations with Third World nations in general. Yet, given its limited political and economic influence in these regions, it probably would not be in Beijing's interest to overemphasize the importance of these regions relative to its overall foreign policy. Beijing should continue to separate its disputes over these issues from other areas in which it may share common interests with Washington.

It will be in Beijing's interest to be critical of the arms race between the two superpowers, especially in regard to their competition on new weapons systems. Such competition not only threatens world peace in general but also weakens China's nuclear deterrence capability. Nevertheless, China should not initiate negotiations with the Soviet Union and the United States for the reduction of nuclear weapons. Rather, it is important for China to continue its efforts to narrow the nuclear gap between the two superpowers and itself. Within the Asian-Pacific region, Beijing should pursue a policy of nuclear nonproliferation, not transferring technology to or manufacturing nuclear weapons for any third country. It should urge Washington to put pressure on both Taipei and Seoul not to develop their own nuclear weapons. Together with Japan and other Asian nations, Beijing should continue to demand that Moscow further reduce its nuclear weapons deployed in the Far East.

Maintaining a relatively stable triangular relationship between Washington, Moscow, and itself will serve Beijing's interests. While pursuing Sino-Soviet relaxation and avoiding once again being the central target of Moscow's strategy in the region, Beijing should demand that Moscow withdraw a substantial number of troops from the Chinese border and cut its support of Hanoi's occupation of Cambodia. In addition, it is in Beijing's interest to counter Moscow's continued efforts to encircle China strategically, to destabilize China's peripheries, and to strengthen the Soviet air force and navy in the Far East. At the same time, China may advance its cooperation with the United States on security issues in the Asian-Pacific region. Independence does not mean noncooperation. Such cooperation should be based upon the principle of minimum costs for maximum benefits for both sides. Moreover, Beijing should leave open the option of upgrading such cooperation as a deterrent against Moscow's political and military pressure. Thus, it will be in Beijing's interest to encourage Washington to maintain its military presence and play the central role in countering Moscow's increased military activities in the region.

On the Korean Peninsula, while maintaining good relations with Pyongyang, Beijing may encourage Washington, Tokyo, and Seoul to expand their contacts with North Korea. It should also help North Korea increase its participation in the international community and reduce its diplomatic isolation. These efforts should be coordinated with Washington and be gradually institutionalized. Meanwhile, it will be desirable for Beijing to continue to expand its relations with Seoul. Any significant shift in the military balance between the two Koreas would likely provoke a serious military confrontation or even war. Beijing should thus discourage any external forces from helping either Pyongyang or Seoul to do so. It should discourage Washington's efforts to increase Japanese involvement in the peninsula's security affairs.

It is in Beijing's interest that the U.S.-Japanese security arrangement continue to guide Tokyo's rearmament process and its security strategy effectively. At present, it is unnecessary for Beijing to be strongly and publicly critical of Tokyo's increased efforts to build up its military if the latter does not intend to alter its anti-Soviet strategic direction. Nevertheless, together with other Asian nations, Beijing should urge Washington to discourage Japan from transforming itself into an independent military power with strong offensive capacity, undermining the balance of power in the region and threatening its neighboring nations. In this regard, to expand its cooperative security relations with Washington and to maintain the stability of the triangle formed by the two superpowers and itself will reduce Washington's incentive for encouraging Tokyo to speed up its rearmament and to play a greater role in the region's security affairs. In addition, Beijing and other Asian nations should put some direct political pressure on Tokyo.

In Southeast Asia, Beijing should discourage Washington from restoring diplomatic relations with Hanoi as long as the latter maintains troops in Cambodia. While maintaining political and military pressure on Hanoi, Beijing should reject any political solution that may allow the continuation of the latter's occupation of Cambodia. If Hanoi withdraws its troops completely from Cambodia, Beijing should stop providing weapons to the Communist faction and press the latter to work together with the other two factions to build a neutral and peaceful Cambodia. It will be essential for Beijing, together with Washington, to maintain its commitment to the security of Thailand and to continue its support of the resistance movement in Cambodia. While making efforts to improve its ties with the ASEAN states, Beijing should ask for Washington's cooperation in an effort to coordinate the two governments' policies toward Vietnam. If the Soviet Union continues to increase its military activities in Southeast Asia and to support Vietnam's military buildup, it would be in Beijing's interest to support the U.S. military presence in the region. Moreover, to maintain the stability of the region and counter Moscow's influence effectively, Beijing should help Washington stabilize the domestic economy and politics of the ASEAN nations, especially Thailand and the Philippines.

Regular high-level consultations between Washington, Beijing, and Islamabad should be developed in order to exchange views and information about security affairs in the region. Although Washington may not want to jeopardize its ties with New Delhi, such consultations would be effective in countering Moscow's threat to Pakistan and discouraging New Delhi from increasing its pressure on Islamabad. If the security of Pakistan comes under serious threat, Beijing should be prepared to support Islamabad and to urge Washington to do the same. Beijing and Washington should coordinate their policies toward Afghanistan, so that post-Soviet-occupation Afghanistan will not become a second Iran. Moreover, Beijing should not be oversensitive to Washington's approach to New

Delhi, as such an approach would probably not be effective in pushing the latter away from Moscow. Nevertheless, Beijing should be alarmed if such efforts were to weaken Washington's commitment to the security of Pakistan.

Beijing will surely continue to demand that Washington further reduce its support and sales of weapons to Taipei. It should also continue to ask Washington to create more opportunities for increased contacts between the two sides of the Taiwan Strait. Nevertheless, more emphasis should be given to Beijing's own efforts to contact directly the KMT government and broad sections of Taiwanese society. While paying more attention to studying the relationship between the KMT government and various opposition groups, Beijing should be alarmed by the deepening involvement of certain American political forces in Taiwan's internal politics, as such involvement might further undermine the political stability of the island and create a crisis that could damage Sino-American ties. Beijing should express its concern through diplomatic channels.

Finally, the best relationship is a relationship that works. Beijing may make efforts to institutionalize its working relationship with Washington by further separating their disputes from those areas in which they share common interests. It should also strengthen its lobby in Washington to promote its own interests. In this regard, those Chinese students or scholars who have studied and have chosen to stay in the United States and who are familiar with the American political system can play a key role. It will also be desirable to develop Sino-American joint research programs on various international issues, especially those concerned with subregional security issues in the Asian-Pacific region and the triangular relations between Moscow, Washington, and Beijing. Such research programs, if conducted professionally, will increase mutual understanding and help both sides form their foreign and security policies. In the long run, such efforts will create a new generation of policymakers in both countries who understand each other well and know the best way of dealing with each other. China's policy toward the United States will thus become more rational and effective.

SEVEN

CHINA AND THE KOREAN PENINSULA

YUFAN HAO

History and geography have combined to make the Korean Penin-sula vitally important to China's security. This importance lies not only in the fact that the peninsula shares a fairly long border with China's industrial heartland, the northeastern provinces, but it also stems from the convergence—and often the clash—of interests of the Soviet Union, Japan, and the United States in Korea. For the last century, Korea has served as an object of conflict and a corridor of invasion for three great powers: Russia, the United States, and Japan. Chinese support of the North Korean forces in the Korean War in 1950, in response to U.S. intervention on behalf of South Korea, together with the close ties between the leadership of the Chinese Communist Party and the Korean Workers' Party led by Kim Il Sung, which dated from the 1930s, have reinforced the impor-tance of Korea in China's policy calculations.

Since the founding of the People's Republic of China (PRC), Beijing's Korean policy has been strongly influenced by its overall security concern. The history of this security policy can be divided roughly into three periods, with Chinese–North Korean relations as its cornerstone. In the 1950s, China saw the United States as the major threat to its security. It allied itself with the Soviet Union and supported the Democratic People's Republic of Korea (DPRK) against the American-backed South Korean regime. Through the 1960s, while the United States remained a security threat, the Sino-Soviet dispute created a new threat, which included the danger that the DPRK might become an exclusive ally of Moscow and un-friendly to China. Chinese regional policy was therefore twofold: to support the DPRK in the struggle against the U.S.-backed South Koreans on the one hand, and to prevent Kim Il Sung from taking the Soviet side in the Sino-Soviet rivalry on the other.

Throughout the 1970s, China's first priority was to deal with the increasing Soviet threat to its security. For this purpose, China developed a new relationship with the United States and Japan. At the same time, Beijing carefully maintained its relations with the DPRK, though not without difficulties.[1]

Since the beginning of the 1980s, the security environment of the Northeast Asian region surrounding the Korean peninsula has been undergoing significant changes and has become fluid. All major powers seem still to support the common, minimum objective of maintaining stability in the region. There remain, however, many uncertainties concerning this sensitive and heavily militarized area. This fluid and dynamic situation has posed a serious challenge to China's regional objectives and has attracted more and more attention from Beijing's foreign-policy–makers.

What are the important recent changes in and around the Korean Peninsula? What will be China's Korean policy in the 1990s? This essay attempts to answer these questions by examining two major interrelated factors that play a pivotal role in shaping China's Korean policy: (1) the changing situation in and around the Korean Peninsula; and (2) China's fundamental policy objectives in the area. In discussing the strategic environment of Northeast Asia, this essay, by analyzing developments in and around the Korean Peninsula, will emphasize recent changes and possible trends that seem to be of particular significance to regional stability and to Chinese interests. As to the Chinese policy objectives, the essay will examine current Chinese interests in the Korean Peninsula, and how the changing situation has affected and will continue to affect Beijing's pursuit of its regional interests. On the basis of these assessments, the study will conclude with some policy recommendations.

TRENDS IN AND AROUND THE KOREAN PENINSULA

Chinese policy toward the Korean Peninsula is largely influenced by the security environment in and around the peninsula. The situation in the area could be regarded as a kind of balance of power or equilibrium in which the six parties—China, North and South Korea, Japan, the Soviet Union, and the United States—constantly interact and adjust their relationship, each trying not only to maintain and improve its position but also to prevent a dangerous new imbalance from emerging.

Since the 1980s began, challenges to the regional equilibrium have been looming on the horizon. In and around the Korean Peninsula, four trends seem particularly significant for the evolution of the security environment in general and for China's regional policy in particular: (1) the rapid Soviet military buildup in the region; (2) the improvement of Soviet–North Korean relations; (3) the unstable political situation within the peninsula; and (4) the growth of the economic and military power of South Korea.

The Soviet Military Buildup

The first and most significant trend that has challenged the balanced situation is the rapid buildup of Soviet military capabilities. The Soviets believe that the existing balance of power in this region has been more or less unfavorable to them since the 1970s, and they are determined to improve their current position by increasing their own influence and power there.

The Soviet Union's Far East policy has had three main ingredients since the 1970s: (1) to challenge the United States in East Asia; (2) to contain China in an effort to keep it weak; (3) to discourage Japan from becoming a strong military power and to prevent a Sino-U.S.-Japanese entente against the USSR. This policy of the Soviet Union was not very successful in the 1970s.[2] China entered into de facto, if very loose, cooperation with the United States and Japan. Subsequently, it has begun a modernization program that by the year 2000 could significantly increase its power. America's relations with East Asia have never been better. It has an extensive alliance system in East Asia, and has for the first time in this century maintained good relations with both China and Japan.

There are many reasons for the Soviets to believe that a rapid buildup of their military and arms assistance capability will be an effective way to change their unfavorable status. Actually, Moscow started its buildup in the late 1960s, and it has basically undergone two stages: the first, in the late 1960s and early 1970s, emphasized the rapid buildup of ground forces aimed primarily at China. The second stage involved the deployment of a new generation of intermediate-range nuclear weapons (IRBMs), a major expansion and qualitative improvement of the Pacific Fleet, and the development and extension of Soviet bases in the territories north of Japan. Its objective began to include a military capacity to counter U.S. air and navy deployment in the Pacific and interdict the sea and air lines of communications linking the United States and the region in order to neutralize potential U.S.-Chinese-Japanese cooperation.

As a result, the USSR now has a formidable array of military forces in the Northeast Asia. These include some 35 to 40 percent of its ICBM force and ballistic missile submarines (SLBMs), 25 percent of its ground forces and fighter aircraft, and more than 30 percent of its strategic bombers and naval forces.[3] Moreover, these forces have now been equipped with some of the most modern weapons in the Soviet inventory, including a Kiev-class aircraft carrier displacing 40,000 tons (the *Minsk*), an amphibious assault ship (the *Ivan Rogov*), Delta-class SSNBs (SSNB denotes a ballistic-missile-armed nuclear-powered submarine), MiG-25 Foxbat fighters, MiG-27 Flogger fighters, Tu-22M Backfire bombers, Tu-95 Bear/E bombers, and SS-20 IRBMs.[4] This Soviet buildup in the Far East has taken the USSR a considerable distance toward its goal of altering the balance in their favor. In the process, it has begun to change the basic structure of power in the region.[5]

Although the Soviet leaders for the last decade have behaved as if the Korean Peninsula was assigned a low priority in their overall East Asian policy, this attitude has undergone a gradual change recently.[6] The Sea of Okhotsk has become much more important to the USSR as a bastion area for SSBNs whose long-range missiles have been targeted on the United States since the early 1980s. Over the same period, the Soviets have been steadily augmenting the role of Northeast Asia as a platform and staging area for Soviet wartime deployment southward, to Cam Ranh Bay and the Indian Ocean.

Recent developments in Moscow suggest that the Soviet Union's policies toward East Asia are changing as Gorbachev strengthens his position. Moscow has carefully switched its strategy from relying solely on military power to expanding its influence through the promotion of trade as a policy instrument and through the reduction of tension with old adversaries.

However, given the growing geostrategic importance of Northeast Asia to Moscow, and the fundamental and long-term nature of its competition with the United States and China, the Soviets are not likely to change this current policy orientation. A strong military presence and capability in the region has simply become too important for Moscow to neglect. Therefore, although Mikhail Gorbachev may reduce the magnitude and speed of the Soviet buildup in the region, it is likely to remain a constant feature of the strategic environment through the 1990s.[7]

This qualitative and quantitative military buildup certainly does not serve China's interests in the region. First of all, it increases the threat to China's security. Second, it also could threaten the regional power equilibrium and could affect the quadrilateral relationship among the United States, Japan, China, and the Soviet Union, and the balance of forces between North and South Korea. Third, it might also increase the possibility of major Japanese rearmament efforts, which is also undesirable from China's point of view. The Soviet military buildup in the region has caused increasing concern for the Chinese leaders throughout the 1980s.

The Improvement of Soviet-DPRK Relations

Related to the rise of the Soviet expansion in East Asia is a trend toward improvement of relations between the USSR and the DPRK.[8] Over the years, these relations have fluctuated widely: from extremely close in the early 1950s, to an almost total break in the early 1960s, with varying points in between from the mid-1960s to early 1980s. These fluctuations indicated some divergence of interests and the difficulties in managing disagreements in the bilateral relations, as well as the traditional mutual distrust imbedded therein. However, strategic needs, as perceived by both sides, have held the two countries together.

The Soviet Union's interests in North Korea are primarily security concerns defined in terms of its global and regional perspective. The strengthened U.S.-Japanese and U.S.–South Korean security alliances and the possibility of a U.S.-Japanese-Chinese alliance directed against the USSR have augmented the strategic importance of North Korea to the Soviets. While Moscow's economic interests there are marginal, its political interests demand that Pyongyang not take the Chinese side in the Sino-Soviet rivalry. For North Korea, the Soviet Union has been and continues to be the principal source of economic and military aid and the guarantor, though not totally reliable, of its security in the face of the external threat. Pyongyang hopes, while maintaining its independence, that Moscow will lend full support in its political struggles with the South, including its efforts toward unification.

Throughout the 1970s, Pyongyang had tilted markedly to Beijing rather than to Moscow. It published China's attacks on the USSR, criticized Cuba, condemned Vietnam, and denounced "dominationism," which was clearly aimed at the Soviet Union. Yet at the same time, Kim Il Sung has always held open the possibility of improving relations with Moscow, and has wanted to demonstrate Korea's independence of Beijing. Against a background of

Beijing-Pyongyang strains in 1979–80, Kim Il Sung began to make cautious overtures to the Soviets, signaling a desire for improved bilateral relations. The Soviets showed little response to the North Koreans until after the death of Brezhnev in late 1982.

The Korean Air Lines incident in September 1983 and the Rangoon bombing one month later provided opportunities for the Soviets and the North Koreans to improve their relations. When a Soviet airplane shot down the KAL plane, Pyongyang, after three weeks of silence, endorsed the Moscow explanation of the incident, blaming the United States for the incident. Shortly after that, when the Rangoon bombing occurred, the Soviets published Pyongyang's defense of its position and ignored the official Burmese account.[9]

North Korean–Soviet relations have seen a steady and substantial improvement since Kim Il Sung's official visit to the Soviet Union in May 1984. Although there were no immediately visible benefits, Pyongyang began to change its attitude toward the Soviet Union afterward. One remarkable change was Pyongyang's willingness to express gratitude to the Soviets for the defeat of Japan and the liberation of Korea. For years, the Soviets felt aggrieved by the North Koreans' ingratitude for past Soviet help, for the North Koreans had attributed the liberation of Korea exclusively to the efforts of the Korean People's Revolutionary Army led by Kim Il Sung. On Liberation Day in 1984, Kim for the first time in many years praised the "liberating role played by the Soviet Union."[10] Through this expression of gratitude for Soviet help, Pyongyang attempted to remove an irritating and emotional obstacle to better relations with Moscow.

In November 1984, Soviet Deputy Foreign Minister Mikhail Kapitsa made a thirteen-day visit to Pyongyang to negotiate a new border treaty, which was signed in Moscow in April of the following year. This treaty apparently gave both countries better access to each other's territory, economically and militarily. As a result of this visit, the Soviets agreed to supply North Korea with advanced MiG-23 fighter aircraft.[11] Recent Soviet aircraft overflights across North Korea's narrow east-west corridor along the DMZ may also be a result of the border treaty.

The first vice-chairman of the Soviet Council of Ministers, Geydar Aliyev, went to Pyongyang in August 1985 to attend the celebration of the Fortieth Anniversary of Korea's Liberation. He was accompanied by the first deputy minister of defense, Marshal V. Petrov, who reportedly offered SAM-3 missiles to North Korea

(SAM—surface-to-air missile). It is worth noting that Pyongyang did not invite China to attend the ceremony, a clear indication of North Korea's tilt to the Soviets. To underscore the warming of Soviet–North Korean relations and military cooperation, three Soviet warships, headed by the flagship *Tallinn* with the first deputy commander of the Soviet Pacific Fleet aboard, arrived in Wonsan, North Korea, the first visit of a Soviet naval vessel to a North Korean port.[12]

Why did Moscow-Pyongyang relations improve so dramatically in the 1984–85 period? For Pyongyang, trends in Chinese domestic and foreign policy must have worried the North Koreans. However, more important than the China factor on Pyongyang's side were its military and economic needs. With the improvement of U.S.–South Korean relations and Seoul's scheduled receipt of F-16s from the United States in 1986, Pyongyang must have felt more keenly than ever the need for more military and economic support from Moscow.

On the Soviet side, the most important reason for developing closer relations with North Korea has been a concern over what Moscow regards as an emerging U.S.-Chinese-Japanese cooperative relationship. The beginning of military cooperation between Washington and Beijing, though so far limited, has alarmed the Soviets.[13] Moscow fears the emergence of a less favorable position for it in the Northeast Asian balance. The second reason is Soviet concern about being excluded from diplomacy relating to the Korean Peninsula. Earlier, Kim Il Sung had asked the Chinese rather than the Soviets to pass the tripartite proposal to the United States, and Washington's counterproposal of a four-party talk included China but not the Soviet Union. The improvement of relations between Pyongyang and Moscow may be considered necessary to prevent the exclusion of Moscow from decision-making regarding the Korean Peninsula.

This trend seems likely to continue, and therefore demands special attention.[14] The reported Soviet access to North Korean airspace allows reconnaissance flights against China, threatening not only the Manchurian industrial sector but also the Bohai and Yellow Sea shipping lanes and the Northern Fleet headquarters at Qingdao. The level of concessions and bargaining required by the Soviets to gain such a foothold on the peninsula underscores the rising importance of Korea in the eyes of the Kremlin leadership. It further indicates to China the Soviet desire to obtain other major privileges from Pyongyang by offering supplies of high-tech weaponry that China cannot provide.

Political Developments on the Peninsula

Political developments in both Seoul and Pyongyang have introduced an element of unpredictability into current policies and the prospects for regional stability. In North Korea, the most noticeable uncertainty is that posed by the succession of leadership. Kim Il Sung has made clear his intention of designating Kim Chong Il, his eldest son, as his successor. Kim Chong Il has attained a position in the party second only to that of his father, and several people closely identified with him have begun to appear in high positions.

Political succession is not an event but a process. Pyongyang began this process in 1973. By all accounts, it is well advanced, and at least in contrast to that of China in the Maoist period, appears relatively smooth and harmonious. A combination of circumstances—the absence of any serious rivals for power, Kim Il Sung's good health, which has provided him with a long period to prepare for the succession, the isolation of North Korea, and the approval of Beijing and Moscow—has enhanced the probability that it may be effectively accomplished even before Kim leaves the scene.[15]

Nevertheless, the succession process in the DPRK is still in progress and may well continue for many years. One key question is, how much time will Kim Chong Il need to consolidate his position and establish his own leadership credentials. Kim Il Sung enjoys the status he does today not only because of his accomplishments but also because of his success in defeating challenges from both inside and outside North Korea. Whether Chong Il is capable of strengthening his own power to a point beyond challenge is still uncertain.

There are at least three possibilities for the power transition, with three different consequences for regional stability. The first and most likely one is the success of the process. Should Kim Chong Il succeed to power, it would make likely a continuation of Kim Il Sung's policies. The idea of *Juche,* or independence in foreign policy, would remain. However, Chong Il is likely to be called upon to decide numerous important issues regarding North Korea's economic development strategy, unification, and North-South relations. When there are internal conflicting opinions, it seems that Chong Il has to make certain modifications in his father's revolutionary goals in order to ensure the smooth functioning of North Korea's political, economic, and military systems. It seems highly unlikely that Kim Chong Il will substantially change the DPRK's current orientation.

The second possibility is that the post–Kim Il Sung leadership will be a coalition government. After Kim's death, Kim Chong Il might meet opposition from more senior figures in the party and the army. A coalition might be formed after both sides make substantial compromises. In this situation, the new leaders in Pyongyang might substantially modify Kim's revolutionary tradition, especially the identification of self-reliance as a fundamental objective, and their unification strategy. There are two possibilities in these circumstances: Pyongyang's new leadership might stay on the old track defined by Kim Il Sung; or they might adopt a pro-Moscow stance and distance themselves from Beijing for economic and military reasons.

The least possible outcome is that a struggle for power might take place, with the military taking over, in the absence of agreement, when Kim Il Sung is gone. In this situation, the junior Kim or one of his rivals for power might seek to win the succession struggle by involving Moscow or Beijing in it. The Russians seem to be positioning themselves to exploit the internal divisions within the North Korean leadership.[16] The new leadership in Pyongyang might be tempted to pursue an adventurist policy against the South as a mean of strengthening their own claims, and might make substantial concessions to Moscow in exchange for military and economic aid.

Another important trend has been the growth of political instability in South Korea. This instability is rooted in the desire of the South Korean people to end the excessive personalization of politics in the South and their desire to institutionalize political democracy.

Since the early 1960s, South Korean politics has been dominated by a military dictatorship. Park Chung Hee, a military general, rose to power with a coup and ruled increasingly as a dictator for nearly two decades. In 1972 he formulated his authoritarian political system through the so-called Yushin Constitution. The National Assembly became a rubber stamp, indirect presidential elections replaced the direct vote, and in effect Park was made president-for-life. In 1979 Park Chung Hee was assassinated, and within a few months, a young military officer, Chun Doo Hwan, seized power in another coup, and the people's discontent was increased as a result of the bloodletting in a major incident in Kwangju. One-man rule has continued.

Chun's regime has not suffered any serious disorder like the Kwangju rebellion since then, and, on the surface, politics has returned to a pattern of relative stability, marked occasionally by minor demonstrations and strikes. Yet inside the society, profound forces have been moving toward putting an end to the excessive personalization of political power. Since early 1986, the political opposition has mounted a nationwide campaign urging a constitutional provision for direct presidential elections. However, Chun has refused to accept this and has asserted that the issue should be deferred until after his successor takes office.

In the legislative election in 1986, the just-formed opposition New Korea Democratic Party won nearly a third of the vote, while support for the ruling Democratic Justice Party (DJP) declined considerably. Since March 1987, thousands of people have demonstrated in the streets, and anti-American slogans have been heard frequently. This time, a rising and well-educated middle class has begun joining the opposition forces demanding political participation. It seems that the situation could lead to an end of the military rule that has persisted over the past twenty-five years.[17]

Bowing to strong pressure from the opposition, Chun finally made a concession and a direct presidential election was held on December 16, 1987. Chun's chosen successor Roh Tae Woo, the presidential candidate from the ruling party, won the election because of the disunity of the opposition forces.

However, since the Roh administration took power, South Korea has witnessed some profound changes. Seoul has made peaceful initiatives toward the North Koreans and has vigorously approached China and the Soviet Union. The inter-Korean talks resume soon. When Pyongyang demanded an end to annual U.S.–South Korean military exercises, which it views as a threat to its security, as a precondition for parliamentary talks and other proposals for inter-Korean contact, the Roh administration decided to scale back the annual exercise as a conciliatory gesture to North Korea.[18] Also, the 1988 Seoul Olympics—boycotted by the North Koreans but attended by China and the Soviet bloc—witnessed an increase in contacts between Communist countries and South Korea, leading, in the case of Hungary, to the establishment of diplomatic relations.[19]

The possible consequences of this change of political situation demand attention. Is North Korea ready to accept this dramatic change in South Korea? The change, from a military dictatorship to a more democratic rule, might increase the sense of disadvantage felt by Pyongyang, which might then take some provocative actions in this changing environment, possibly seeking to exploit the situation to achieve unification by force.

To sum up, the 1990s will be a critical period for the two Korean states. Both face unprecedented political uncertainties from these changes.

Growth of the Economic and Military Power of South Korea

The fourth trend concerns the growth of economic and military power in South Korea. South Korea's economic development has been impressive in the postwar period, while the growth rate of the North Korean economy, though it increased rapidly in the first two decades after the end of the Korean War, has slowed down since the 1970s because of the rigidity of structure and strategy, outmoded technology, and the diversion of resources to the military in response to perceived external threats.

South Korea now enjoys a more advanced economic and industrial capacity than the North. In 1984, the South Korean gross domestic product (GDP) was US$83.2 billion, while that of the North was estimated to be $39.9 billion.[20] South Korean technology is also believed to be superior to that of the North. Unless Pyongyang changes its development strategy, the present gap between the South and the North will continue to grow.

When the North and the South are compared militarily, North Korea is believed to have a considerable quantitative superiority in military equipment as a result of an intensive defense buildup during the 1960s and 1970s. In 1985, North Korea maintained a military force of 838,000 troops, 800 aircraft, and 502 vessels, while the South Korean military consisted of 620,000 troops, 440 aircraft, and 110 vessels.[21] However, upon close inspection, North Korea's numerical advantage turns out to be misleading: almost 40 percent of its aircraft consist of the outmoded MiG-15s and MiG-17s. Only MiG-21s are considered roughly equal to F-5s. Although the delivery of forty

MiG-23s by the Soviets may upgrade Pyongyang's air power, South Korea still seems to enjoy an edge. In terms of naval vessels, Pyongyang's advantage is also dubious. Sixty-two percent of its vessels are fast-attack craft equipped with guns or torpedoes, 19 percent are landing craft, and 11 percent are coastal patrol craft.[22]

South Korea has been expanding and modernizing its military forces since the middle of the 1970s (beginning twelve years later than the North), under its Force Improvement Plans I (1976–82) and II (1982–87). Its military budget has been increased substantially and is now close to 6 percent of its GNP. Though this percentage is less than that of the North, its US$4.402 billion military budget is bigger than the $4.19 billion budget of the North. After the successful completion of its two improvement plans, the South will eventually surpass the North and will remain ahead in the 1990s. This could trigger an escalation in the arms race that would further increase the possibility of destabilization in the peninsula in the 1990s.

The growing gap in economic power between the North and the South, coupled with the growth of South Korean military power, suggests that Pyongyang's leadership is confronted with some difficult choices: (1) doing nothing and watching South Korea "win the race" economically while acquiring the base for military superiority; (2) changing its approach by opening its economy to the West as China has done, soliciting capital and technology; (3) leaning further toward the Soviets in order to obtain more capital and technology from them, meshing its economy into COMECON, and partially giving up its independence; (4) taking direct or indirect military action, as many Western observers have feared, to try to undermine or set back South Korea's economic progress. The fourth option is almost impossible due to the lack of sufficient military strength in the North and the U.S. military presence in the peninsula. Recently, there are some indications that North Korea intends to choose the second of these options. A new joint-venture law enacted in North Korea in September 1984, together with the "trade development resolution" adopted by the 7th Supreme People's Assembly in January 1984, are expressions of North Korea's altered economic development strategy.[23] Kim Il Sung also showed increasing interests in contact with the United States.[24] However, both past patterns and recent trends suggest that the third alternative demands careful attention by the Chinese leadership.

CHINA'S CURRENT OBJECTIVES AND POSSIBLE APPROACHES

The trends described above are the most significant factors affecting the security environment in Northeast Asia as far as regional stability is concerned. These trends have two basic features: rising Soviet power and influence, and the increase in destabilizing factors. In the long run, these are moving in a direction not congenial to Chinese interests. What are China's regional objectives at present? How will China respond in the context of those trends in the 1990s?

China's policy toward the Korean Peninsula is largely a function of her overall foreign-policy concerns, which at present are based on the following premises:

- The Soviet Union is the main threat to China's security. From the Chinese perspective, the major goal of the Soviet Union's Asian policy is to strategically encircle and weaken China. The steady growth of Soviet ground, air, naval, and strategic forces deployed in East Asia, together with Moscow's success in expanding its influence in Indochina and Afghanistan, pose a major challenge to the PRC's security interests.
- Despite this major threat from the Soviet Union, military conflict with the Soviets is unlikely in the near future. Therefore, China does not need to increase its military buildup in any dramatic way at present. Meanwhile, a moderate reduction of tensions between Beijing and Moscow is in China's interests.[25]
- China needs a fairly long period of peace in order to modernize its economy, upgrade its industrial and defense capacity, and become strong enough to defend itself in the face of any future external threats. For this purpose, Beijing needs to create and maintain political stability and unity at home and a peaceful environment in the surrounding region.
- The United States is not a threat to China's security at present. On the contrary, it is a potential strategic partner in the face of the threat from the Soviet Union. Therefore, to maintain good relations with the United States is very important to China's interests.
- China does not want to be involved in the superpowers' global competition, in which China's relatively weak military position makes its security somewhat uncertain. Thus, it is not in China's interest to enter into an exclusive alliance with either the United States or the Soviet Union.[26]

- The principal sources of the capital and technology needed to modernize China are Japan, the United States, and West Europe.
- To have good and healthy relations, especially economic cooperation, with Japan is also very important. At the same time, China would not like to see the Japanese rearm themselves rapidly. It is not in China's interests to have a militarily strong Japan.[27]

These premises require China to pursue an independent and peaceful foreign policy. This policy in turn requires a regional policy toward the Korean Peninsula to be aimed at three basic objectives:

1. To maintain regional stability and the existing balance. Any development in and around the Korean Peninsula that might lead to instability will be regarded as adverse to Chinese interests. Considering the peninsula as an area of tension and military buildup, China hopes that tensions will be relaxed and peaceful reunification be gradually realized.
2. Given the strategic importance of North Korea, and the unique set of cultural, historical, geographical, and political ties with it, maintaining good relations with Pyongyang is crucial.
3. It is best for China's interests that the bilateral relationship between the DPRK and China be maintained in a way that will not adversely affect Beijing's overall relations with Washington and Tokyo, and if possible, its economic relations with Seoul.

China's reasons for desiring stability in Korea are obvious. A military conflict would undoubtedly impose upon the Chinese an extremely serious dilemma that Beijing is neither willing nor ready to face. Bound by explicit treaty obligations to North Korea, and repeated security commitments, and influenced by the Soviet factor, China might find it extremely difficult to refuse to assist the DPRK if a conflict were to occur. This would inevitably damage China's cooperative ties with the United States and Japan and could compromise China's economic modernization program. If the Soviet Union were to enter such an open conflict and the Soviet-DPRK defense treaty were invoked, this would further complicate and worsen China's position. Soviet influence in North Korea would increase substantially, since only the Soviets could supply sophisticated weapons for a military confrontation with U.S.-backed South Korea. Therefore, the primary objective of China's regional policy is to maintain stability and reduce tension in the Peninsula.

Beijing's overriding security interests in Korea cannot be protected without a good relationship with Pyongyang. Even if regional stability is maintained, if North Korea, like Vietnam, allies itself with the Soviets, the consequences might be as adverse to China's interests as would those resulting from instability in Korea. North Korea is the critical missing link in Moscow's chain of encirclement around China. A "second Vietnam" on the Korean Peninsula would give the Kremlin a crucial "knife" pointing at the heartland of China's industry and resources. Politically, Pyongyang's importance has loomed large within the perspective of China's current status in international Communist affairs. It is important to Chinese prestige and influence that Kim Il Sung refuse to support the Moscow-sponsored campaign against Beijing and that he cooperate with China in the Third World, especially in the context of nonaligned movements.

Among China's objectives, the most difficult one is to maintain its relations with North Korea in such a way that Sino-American relations will not be strictly circumscribed. No matter how warm its relations with China, Pyongyang's leadership has always cast a wary eye on Beijing's dealing with Washington, and it always has the Soviet card in its hands. China's political balancing act, therefore, has remained a very delicate one: to persuade the DPRK, on the one hand, that closer Sino-American relations will benefit North Korean interests and that China will do nothing to compromise Pyongyang's interests, and on the other hand to refuse to play any direct role, as the United States has hoped it would, to defuse tension. But this task has proved to be extremely difficult due to the fact that the interests of the two countries have not always converged, especially in security issues. Although consultation between the two capitals before any major policy shift is considered to be very important by Beijing's leadership, the offsetting costs remain high. Recent trends have demonstrated that Beijing wishes to seek more room to maneuver. Beijing has expanded its unofficial economic relations with Seoul, and is likely to continue its efforts to achieve a balance between supporting its longtime ally in the North and maintaining its good relations with Washington and Tokyo.

To pursue its regional objectives, China is trying to develop an international policy that counters manipulation by either superpower. Since 1982 the PRC has repeatedly declared that it "will never attach itself to any other state or bloc of states."[28] The PRC leadership will continue this effort as long as its current security perceptions remain unchanged.

Although recent trends indicate that there is some possibility that Beijing might be able to ease tensions with Moscow and distance itself from Washington, there appear to be limits as to how far Beijing is prepared to go in this respect. Beijing's posture toward the Soviet Union, and therefore the United States, is influenced by the Kremlin's stance toward China. Since Gorbachev came to power, Moscow has undergone some dramatic changes in its global foreign policy. Yet it has not reduced its military pressure on China, nor has it met Beijing's three conditions for further improvement in bilateral relations, namely, the withdrawal of troops along the Sino-Soviet and Sino-Mongolian borders, an end to Soviet support for the Vietnamese occupation of Cambodia, and the withdrawal of Soviet troops from Afghanistan. Although Moscow has pulled out one division of troops from Mongolia and has completed the withdrawal from Afghanistan, it still remains the fundamental threat to China's national security.[29]

In the 1990s, there will be continuing negotiations between China and the USSR and maybe a continuing easing of Sino-Soviet hostility. A summit meeting between Beijing and Moscow has been scheduled in 1989. Yet Moscow will continue to be China's major concern even if Beijing asserts that the immediacy of the Soviet threat has somewhat diminished in recent years. The United States no longer poses such a threat, and Sino-American relations will remain cooperative, but with areas of friction and disagreement such as the issues of Taiwan, trade, and technology transfer. The current pattern in which China is closer to the United States than to the USSR is likely to continue in the 1990s.

Beijing's basic interests in the Korean Peninsula are likely to mesh well, in a basic sense, with those of Washington during the 1990s. Both countries desire regional stability and have no interest in allowing tensions to escalate or radical change to occur in the status quo of the peninsula. However, Beijing and Washington differ on how to achieve stability. Having rejected the Carter administration's policy on the withdrawal of ground troops from South Korea, the Reagan administration stressed the importance of close U.S.–South Korean political and military cooperation for the region's stability, and attempted to strengthen the U.S. presence in the peninsula.[30] It is likely that the Bush administration will continue Reagan's policy in that area in the foreseeable future. This serves no good purpose for Beijing's leaders. It makes North Korea take a continuously hostile stance toward the United States and keeps Beijing in a very difficult position in dealing with both.

Sino–North Korean relations have been and will continue to be the cornerstone of Beijing's regional policy. Although Beijing's relations with the DPRK suffered some strains in the late 1970s due to differing perceptions of the security threat and certain domestic policies, they have been gradually restored by the strenuous efforts made by Beijing since that time.[31] During the 1980s, Beijing has conducted its relationship with North Korea reasonably well and has kept all disagreements at a manageable level. To maintain a cooperative relationship with North Korea, Beijing will continue its political, diplomatic, military, and economic support of Pyongyang in the years ahead. There is no fundamental conflict of interest between China and the DPRK. Like Beijing, Pyongyang's compelling interest at present is to reduce regional tensions and maintain stability for its economic development and its peaceful reunification scheme. China has taken every opportunity to assure the United States and Japan that Kim Il Sung has neither the intention nor the capability of invading the South and that the North Koreans are genuinely interested in easing the tension in the peninsula. At the same time, Beijing's leadership has tried to persuade Pyongyang that another Korean War would be a disaster for North Korea.

China will continue to encourage Pyongyang's independent foreign policy and its efforts to open its economy to the West, as China has done. Deng Xiaoping took Kim Il Sung to look at the celebrated Sichuan model of enterprise autonomy in 1982. This visit was designed to help Kim understand China's modernization policy and the economic reform, for the Chinese leadership sees this as a necessary step in reducing Pyongyang's dependence on Moscow and to reduce tension in the peninsula. Beijing favorably noted the DPRK's recent plan to expand its economic relations with capitalist countries, to quadruple the 1980 export rate by 1989, and to set up special export bases.[32] Even though Pyongyang is reluctant to give up its strategy of self-reliance in its development, Beijing's leaders seem confident that they can influence North Korea's future economic orientation if China's own Four Modernizations program proves to be successful.

Beijing will continue its support for North Korea's call for a withdrawal of U.S. troops from the peninsula and the ending of joint U.S.–South Korean military exercises. Many scholars in the

West seem to believe that China favors the presence of some U.S. military strength in South Korea as a condition necessary to the preservation of military balance and stability and to counterbalance Soviet military power in the region.[33] This view is fundamentally misleading. Although China sees the U.S. military presence on the Korean Peninsula as posing no threat to China's security at present, and that it might have some merit in maintaining the regional power balance and preventing the South from attacking the North, it is still, in the eyes of Beijing's leadership, a principal source of regional tension.[34] First, it has made the North Koreans feel insecure, since Pyongyang continues to regard U.S. "imperialists" and the Japanese "militarists" as their mortal enemies, who not only present the main obstacle to unification but also pose a serious threat to North Korea's security. The sense of insecurity in Pyongyang has caused the diversion of much of its limited resources to defense-oriented production. This in turn has escalated the arms race between the North and the South, and further reinforced U.S. willingness to maintain and even increase its military power there. This vicious circle is the main disruptive force in the region and makes the situation explosive and dangerous.

Second, should the North come to perceive South Korea as militarily superior, it could further turn to Moscow as the only available source for the assistance needed to defend itself. The fact that South Korea should be able to attain this position, with enthusiastic help from America, by the early 1990s, if present trends continue, makes a Pyongyang tilt toward Moscow likely. Third, this cycle has motivated the increasing Soviet military buildup in the region in order to counter U.S. power, and this increases the possibility that the superpowers might bring the Korean problem into their global competition. If that happens, it would not only raise the already high level of militarization on the peninsula, but would also make far more difficult any negotiations of the two Korean states to ease the military situation between them.

The PRC will continue to regard inter-Korean contact as a major means of increasing regional stability and of solving the Korean problem. Although the talks begun in 1987 were suspended in December 1988 and have not yet resumed, Seoul did make some significant gestures toward the North. South Korea has unilaterally withdrawn from the annual U.S.–South Korean military exercises, and Roh Tae Woo said in his New Year message that 1989 "is expected to bring a decisive moment in which the wall of confrontation between South and North Korea will be torn down."[35] This South Korean initiative is a significant step, for it may help build up the mutual trust between the two Korean states.

The inter-Korean talks appear to have at least three beneficial implications for China's interests. First, they should serve to reduce tension in the region and the possibility of military conflict. Second, they should enable the Chinese to more openly explore unofficial relations with South Korea. Hu Yaobang asserted that future direct Sino–South Korean economic ties would be "dependent on how things develop between the North and the South."[36] Third, Beijing should be able to use North Korea's proposal of a confederation arrangement with South Korea to link their own calls for a "one country, two systems" approach to the reunification of Taiwan. In February 1985, Deng Xiaoping claimed that the PRC and the DPRK shared the same approach to their national reunification.[37]

Since the beginning of the 1980s, Beijing's leadership has been testing the possibility of having some maneuvering room in its relations with North Korea. Beijing has shifted from a position that would not countenance any ties at all with Seoul to an increasingly active nongovernmental relationship. The combination of Beijing's pragmatic open-door economic policy and its efforts to separate politics and economics in its foreign policy led to a rapid growth in indirect trade between China and South Korea through Hong Kong. The total value of this indirect trade was estimated to be about US$20 million in 1979, and it increased, in spite of the North Koreans' discontent, to $1.5 billion in 1987 and is expected to reach $3 billion in 1988, while China's trade with North Korea was only $519.4 million in 1987.[38]

Besides indirect trade relations, the airplane hijacking incident of 1983 and the torpedo boat incident of 1985 provided occasions for Beijing to contact directly an unrecognized regime. The successful settlement of the two events seemed to indicate that China can deal with an unrecognized regime in a businesslike manner in a crisis situation. Chinese sportsmen have also had some contacts with their South Korean counterparts in international games. At the 10th Asian Games in 1986, China sent a team of 389 athletes even though North Korea boycotted the games.[39] South Korean industrial giant Daewoo was reported to have signed a joint-venture agreement with China and has opened an assembly plant to build televisions and refrigerators in Fuzhou.[40]

Pyongyang has not been pleased about China's contacts with

Seoul. Accordingly, China has been sensitive to Pyongyang's displeasure, and has made it clear that China will not contact Seoul officially.[41] Yet China's unofficial contact with South Korea will continue, though it will still be limited in the years ahead due to the importance of the Sino–North Korean relationship. Wherever there is a policy difference between Beijing and Pyongyang in dealing with Seoul, the PRC leadership will consult frequently with their North Korean comrades through exchanges of high-level visits.[42]

In the coming decade, Japan will become increasingly important to China. China and Japan share common apprehensions about the growing Soviet military buildup in East Asia and share an interest in maintaining peace and stability in the Korean Peninsula. However, Beijing-Tokyo relations have not been devoid of problems, including trade disputes, the issue of Japan's textbooks, and the controversy over territory. The memory of the Japanese invasion of China will continue to make Beijing wary of any signs of a revival of militarism, and Tokyo will prefer that China continue to place a low priority on military modernization. China will continue to pursue a policy of close cooperation with Japan not only to contain Soviet expansion but also to support China's economic modernization program. Beijing will continue its efforts to solve problems in relations with Japan by frequent high-level consultations and by mutual compromise. At the same time, PRC leadership will continue to hint to the Japanese that China does not want to see Japan become a military power and that any resurgence of militarism will evoke a reaction from the Chinese.[43]

FUTURE PRC POLICY

In light of China's objectives and possible approaches and the described possible trends, it would be desirable that Beijing's policy toward Korea and Northeast Asia be based on the following judgments and to move in the following directions.

China should be concerned but not excessively alarmed by the Soviet buildup in Northeast Asia. It certainly does not serve China's interest. Yet China should not worry too much about it since the major aim of the Soviet buildup is to counter the American military presence in this region, although it is also a result of Soviet fear of potential U.S.-Chinese-Japanese cooperation. China seems to have at least two options in responding to this Soviet buildup. The first is to moderately improve relations with Moscow and distance itself from the idea of military cooperation between the United States, China, and Japan. This might help reduce tension in this region, although it might also entail dangers that are inherent in appeasement. Another response would be to increase cooperative ties with the United States and Japan. This would make the efforts to counter Soviet expansion more effective and might even impel the Soviets to reevaluate their Far East policy. Some observers interpret Gorbachev's recent overture to China as the result of the fear of this possibility.[44] Although currently remaining closer to the United States than to the Soviet Union, China seems now to hesitate in making this basic decision, and is more or less in the middle between the United States and the Soviet Union.

The "three obstacles" in Sino-Soviet relations should be regarded as a touchstone indicating the Kremlin's real intentions toward Beijing. If the Soviets change their anti-China policy by removing the "three obstacles," China could cautiously choose the option of distancing itself from Washington and seeking an equidistant position between the superpowers. However, if these conditions were to be only partially met, the Soviet Union would still constitute the primary threat to China's security, and China should still maintain its close cooperative relationship with the United States. Given the basic, long-term competition between the United States and the Soviet Union and the pressing internal economic problems perceived in Beijing, Moscow has incentives to seek relief in its relations with Beijing or at least to partially prevent China from forming closer ties with Washington. Therefore, China should try to direct the current situation in ways that are less potentially explosive and more mutually beneficial. China will see its interests best served by easing tensions with Moscow, step-by-step, and at the same time by maintaining good relations with Washington. This would further improve China's already favorable position in the Washington-Moscow-Beijing triangle, and would be consistent with the thrust of China's policy interests in the Korean Peninsula.

Although economic factors have become increasingly important in bilateral relations, Sino-American relations will continue to be influenced by the Soviet factor. The attempt to deal with the expansion of Soviet military power in the region is likely to preoccupy American leaders for some years to come, although the degree of expansion might be reduced by Gorbachev's new approach. Because of the perceived cost to the United States of dealing with the Soviets

197

on its own, Washington is likely to further solicit increased support from its allies. Thus, China's value may continue to contain a special twist: if the PRC could be counted on to stand up to the Soviet challenge, it would spare America from having to bear the brunt of the fighting in the event of any military conflict. In this context, the United States can be expected to compromise its interests on issues of lesser importance in order to maintain and develop its relations with Beijing, in the interest of strengthening its efforts to deal with the Soviet Union. China should be careful, however, to avoid being accused of playing the Soviets off against the Americans.

The improvement in Soviet–North Korean relations demands special attention. But China should recognize the limits of these relations. In spite of his disillusionment with some of China's current policies, Kim Il Sung is highly unlikely to tilt totally toward Moscow, mainly because of his sense of independence and his view that the Juche idea represents North Korea's fundamental national interests, and also because of the deep-rooted divergence of interests and distrust between Moscow and Pyongyang. Among fundamental North Korean interests, the aspiration for independence has been the top priority; it is rooted in Korea's historical experience. North Korea thus will resist Soviet efforts at de facto integration. Chinese sensitivity, and Soviet insensitivity, to North Korea's desire for independence has contributed to the character of Pyongyang-Moscow and Pyongyang-Beijing relations.[45]

The Soviets always find the North Koreans intractable, ungrateful, and difficult to manage. Pyongyang has often acted in a manner contrary to Soviet wishes and has sometimes openly attacked Soviet policies. But as long as there are American nuclear weapons and F-16 fighters in South Korea, which Moscow views as a direct threat to its security, Moscow cannot treat Pyongyang harshly because of the strategic importance of North Korea. The current North Korean leadership sees the USSR as a big, threatening neighbor that would like to dominate North Korea as it does Mongolia. The North Korean leaders also recognize that they must depend on the Soviets to some extent, economically and militarily, and more importantly as the principal counter to U.S.–backed South Korea. This unavoidable dependence breeds frustration and resentment.[46] Moscow keeps North Korea on a short rein, providing neither the military nor the economic support that it would like to have. Moscow's reliability is also questionable; the historical lesson of the Korean War is still fresh in the minds of the DPRK's leadership: it was the

Chinese, not the Soviets, that came to the defense of the DPRK. These factors resulted in DPRK-Soviet relations remaining cool, and sometimes strained, for most of the last two decades, and they are likely to create obstacles to close relations in the future.

China should be prepared to accept a moderate improvement in Soviet relations with North Korea, as long as this does not threaten China's fundamental strategic and political interests in North Korea. In fact, such a trend might have three beneficial implications for Beijing. First, it could reduce the Soviet fear of being surrounded by a new containment system and excluded from the peninsula's affairs and thus compelled to resort to provocative actions via North Korea. As a result of the recent reduction of Sino-Soviet tensions, this concern has subsided considerably. Second, it would encourage Pyongyang to continue its independent policy, which serves Chinese interests better than a policy of dependence on either Moscow or Beijing. As a vital buffer to Soviet expansion, an independent North Korea is clearly of greater utility to Beijing than it is to Moscow. Third, since Moscow is not interested in an open conflict in the peninsula either, it might be helpful if the Soviets do preserve some influence and help to prevent provocative actions by either Korean state.

Although China has until very recently lagged behind the Soviet Union in semiofficial dealings with South Korea, it is clear that Pyongyang is extremely sensitive to the Chinese opening toward South Korea. This sensitivity in Pyongyang reveals the importance of China in the DPRK's policy calculations, which China should appreciate and value. China's economic contacts with Seoul should not be expanded to the extent that Sino–North Korean relations would be compromised. North Korea should always be a higher priority. China should not change its opposition to all "two Koreas" formulas—such as "cross-recognition" and the "simultaneous admission" to the United Nations. If Pyongyang modifies its position on these issues, so can China. China should be careful about dealing officially with Seoul. Any formal official contact might be regarded as an indication of China's willingness to accept the "two Koreas" idea, which in turn could be viewed in some countries as strengthening the case for "two Chinas." Seoul has indicated openly that if the PRC would establish diplomatic relations with South Korea, it would sever its relations with Taipei. Although this would further the PRC's efforts to isolate Taiwan in the world community, the cost would surpass the benefits.

Finally, China should concentrate its efforts on domestic economic development, to ensure that its modernization attempts succeed. The PRC's current GNP is estimated to be worth US$567 billion, which is a little more than one-third (or 40 percent) that of the Soviet Union. If China keeps its annual growth rate at about 7 percent, as is projected, its GNP may reach 60 percent of that of the Soviet Union in 1990 and about 86 percent by the year 2000.[47] If the PRC's modernization drive, especially its seventh five-year plan (1986–90), continues to bear fruit throughout the 1990s, it will not only increase China's economic leverage vis-à-vis the Soviets in influencing North Korea, but will also have some significant effects on North Korea's international economic orientation and its foreign policy. Economic considerations are expected to loom larger than ever before in China's policy toward the Korean Peninsula.

EIGHT

CHINA AND SOUTHEAST ASIA

XIAOBO LU

China has given high consideration to the relationship with its Southeast Asian neighbors since the founding of the People's Republic in 1949. China's relations with them, however, have undergone dramatic changes. Indonesia, one of the first nations in Southeast Asia to establish formal diplomatic ties with China, now is the least friendly among the ASEAN countries and has not yet normalized diplomatic relations. The country China once supported so strongly, with weapons and rice, in its anti-American war—Vietnam—now has become its most antagonistic opponent in the region. The world is no longer as it was in the 1950s when the Bandung Conference was held. The end of a painful war in Indochina has finished an American era in Asia; to a large exent, the balance of power between the two superpowers was much affected. Vietnam aligned itself with the Soviet Union and invaded another Communist country—Cambodia—where it has been fighting a war ever since. On the domestic scene, there have been many changes in the power structure, the most significant of which were the death of Mao and the downfall of the radical "Gang of Four," followed by the reforms launched by Deng Xiaoping. Most recently, the fall of the authoritarian regime of Ferdinand Marcos in the Philippines is yet another important development with a long-range impact on the situation of the region and the relationship between China and the countries in the region.

During a recent visit to Thailand, China's new premier, Li Peng, claimed that Sino-ASEAN relations are better than ever, and he urged further political and economic cooperation. There is no question that China has given top priority to its relations with Southeast Asian countries in the past decade. Indeed, China has been very successful in recent years in developing friendly relations with major countries in Southeast Asia. Looking into the next decade, however, there are several crucial issues yet to be addressed if China wants to maintain a successful policy toward Southeast

Asia. And the next decade will determine the fate of China's domestic program—reforms and modernization—which is in turn much affected by the international environment, especially the situation in Asia.

THE STRATEGIC SITUATION IN SOUTHEAST ASIA

Southeast Asia, a densely populated region, has grown in strategic importance since the end of World War II. Any country that seeks to become a global power will try to gain a foothold in Southeast Asia. The two superpowers have both tried hard to control the region. For a long time, Southeast Asia was within the sphere of influence of the United States. After the end of the Vietnam War, however, the United States for a while took a rather restrained policy stand. The USSR, on the other hand, invaded Afghanistan and supported the invasion of Cambodia by Vietnam, its closest ally in the region. The USSR strengthened its military might in Asia, directly threatening the American military bases in the Philippines and the security of the sea-lanes. During the period from the late 1970s to the present, the USSR has successfully opened the route to the Indian Ocean through the South China Sea by gaining the bases at Cam Ranh Bay and Da Nang in Vietnam. The Soviet naval force in this region has been greatly strengthened: two aircraft carriers were put into service in the Pacific Fleet and some thirty surface ships and submarines, and several dozen aircraft, including Backfire bombers, are routinely stationed in Southeast Asia.[1]

In the past seven years, the Soviet Union has concentrated on consolidating and developing its military bases in Indochina. Moscow has given a great deal of military aid to its regional ally, Vietnam. Before 1975, total Soviet military aid to Vietnam was around US$400 million. After the invasion of Cambodia in 1978, aid was almost doubled. From 1978 to 1984, US$5 billion of military aid and $4 billion in economic aid were given to Vietnam by the Soviet Union.[2] The Soviet military bases in Vietnam today have not only a routine complement of aircraft and warships, but also a large intelligence-monitoring network covering communications in all of Southeast Asia, Southern China, and part of the Indian Ocean. This greatly enhances the strategic positions of the Soviet Union in Southeast Asia: (1) the sea-lanes from the Pacific to the Indian Ocean are more open to the Russians; (2) the Russians have gained the ability to choke off the sea route in the South China Sea and attack the Strait of Malacca; (3) they are able to oversee and threaten the American bases in the Philippines—Clark and Subic—and the American base in Guam; (4) they threaten Southeast Asia politically and psychologically.

In the past two years or so, there have been some signs that the Soviet Union, with the reform-minded Mikhail Gorbachev taking over power, has been softening its aggressive posture in the world and in the region. Not only has it pulled its army out of Afghanistan and offered to dismantle its SS-20 missiles aimed at China, it also has agreed that it is time to settle the Cambodian issue and is willing to begin pressing Vietnam to pull out in accordance with a set timetable. Obviously, these major changes in Soviet policy toward Asia are an important part of Gorbachev's overall readjustment in foreign policy. The first public appearance of Gorbachev's new Asian policy came in July 1986. In his watershed speech in Vladivostok, Gorbachev explicitly expressed the Soviet intention to expand economic relations with the ASEAN and Pacific countries. In November, the Soviet Union, for the first time, was an observer at the meeting of the Pacific Economic Cooperation Conference (PECC), a nongovernmental body founded to promote Asian-Pacific economic cooperation. Moscow has expressed its interest in becoming a full member of PECC.[3] In September 1988, Gorbachev proposed a seemingly more conciliatory plan for Asia, taking further steps to show Moscow's concern for peace in Asia and the Pacific. In a speech in Krasnoyarsk, he offered to relinquish the Soviet naval base in Vietnam if the United States would agree to eliminate its bases in the Philippines, to freeze the deployment of Soviet nuclear weapons in the Asian-Pacific region, and to transform the USSR's treaty-violating radar complex in Siberia into an international space center.[4]

With Reagan's "peace through strength" strategic policy, the United States has also once again been strengthening its strategic positions in Southeast Asia. To counter the growing Russian influence, the goal of the United States is to maintain its military advantage in the region and to curtail the increase of Soviet forces by supporting ASEAN so that vital sea-lanes can be kept open. The United States, to reach this goal, has improved its military bases in Southeast Asia and the Pacific. It has also upgraded the quality of its Pacific Fleet. Cruise missiles, Trident submarines, and new F-14 jet fighters have been deployed. Relations between the United States and non-Communist countries in Southeast Asia and China have been strengthened over the past ten years to balance Soviet power in the region. In recent years, the Reagan administration has increased military aid to the ASEAN nations. In 1978 it amounted to US$162.5 million. In 1984 it was $326.6 million.[5] On the other hand, the United States has also been trying to avoid direct involvement in the region, especially on the Cambodian issue.

Although the future of the strategic situation in Southeast Asia looks brighter than ever, one should not be overoptimistic. The intention and sincerity of Moscow's new Asian policy is yet to be tested. The response of the United States, led by a new administration, is important. The direction and concrete steps of Chinese policy toward the region will also be of great significance in the next decade. After the Cambodian conflict took place, China's strategic position in the region was enhanced. It has been playing a major role. To China the threat of Soviet hegemonism has been a crucial security problem in its backyard, and the United States has not responded strongly enough. It seems China would like to see a more active U.S. involvement.[6]

The United States also has to face the question of the future of the military bases in the region. Will it be able to keep the bases? Would it like to make a deal with the Russians, as the latter have proposed? Clearly, the steps these three major players take in the next few years will to a large degree determine whether there is peace or war in the region. Considering the developments toward the end of the 1980s, one should be cautiously optimistic about the future of the security of Southeast Asia in the 1990s.

THE CAMBODIAN ISSUE

Vietnamese troops invaded Cambodia in December 1978, over ten years ago. Finally, the problem shows some signs of being solved. However, the war against the Vietnamese occupation still drags on painfully. Vietnam has for a long time dreamed of a "grand Indochina federation" under its control, but only with Cambodia's internal instability did Vietnam get a chance to realize its dream. On the military front, the anti-Vietnamese forces of the Khmer Rouge, the National Sihanoukist Army (NSA), and the Khmer People's National Liberation Front (KPNLF) of Son Sann have fought vigorously for the past ten years. However, this coalition force of some

70,000 has been facing almost the same number of troops of Heng Samrin, backed up by over 140,000 Vietnamese soldiers. In the past dry seasons, the Vietnamese troops have launched major attacks on the resistance forces, but without much success.

On the other hand, despite the fact that the three forces formed a coalition Government of Democratic Kampuchea (GDK) in June 1982 and a joint military command headquarters in the summer of 1985, the great disparity in strength and the internal divergence among the three allies has resulted in the failure of the resistance forces to successfully drive the Vietnamese out solely by military means. As the Cambodian war continues, and with their own domestic difficulties growing, the Vietnamese have gradually realized that the occupation is a great burden. Vietnam has forced itself into a very difficult double-front situation. A political solution has turned out to be the best way for all the parties involved. However, the Vietnamese have been trying in recent months to secure a non–Khmer Rouge government after its withdrawal. If it is not possible to exclude the Khmer Rouge, then Vietnam desires a secondary role for it.

Nineteen eighty-eight was a year of positive development so far as the Cambodian issue is concerned. Vietnam has agreed to a final withdrawal by the end of 1990. Most recently, Hanoi announced that it would complete the withdrawal by late 1989. Whether it can meet this deadline or not, this should not be taken as a hollow gesture. Since the mid-1980s, Vietnam has begun preparing for the postwithdrawal era. It has certainly realized that a prolonged military occupation is impossible. Meanwhile, Vietnam has also tried to perpetuate its nonmilitary influence on the future Cambodian political framework. The greatest efforts have been in its "Vietnamization" drive to colonize the country before it withdraws its troops. Currently, the Vietnamese are able to put themselves in both administrative and military posts in the Heng Samrin regime. They seek to assimilate the Cambodians, sending thousands of their citizens into the occupied country. This Vietnamese immigration began quietly in 1979 and became open and intensive after 1982. More than seven hundred thousand Vietnamese citizens are reported to have moved into Cambodia by the end of 1985. In Phnom Penh and the region to its east, more than 60 percent of the population is Vietnamese.[7]

The Cambodian situation has been the focus of concern among countries throughout the region. In China's view, "the Cambodian issue concerns not only Cambodia but has a direct bearing on peace and security in Southeast Asia. . . . Hanoi's regional hegemonist behavior is looked upon with anxiety by the world community."[8] To a great extent, the Cambodian issue has shaped China's relations with the countries of the region. It has also brought the non-Communist countries of Southeast Asia much closer to China after the normalization of relations in early 1970s. Since China regards Soviet support of Vietnam as a major security threat, it firmly links the settlement of the Cambodian question with the normalization of Sino-Soviet relations. In April 1985, Deng Xiaoping even hinted to Moscow that if the Russians pressured Vietnam to withdraw from Cambodia, China would be willing to accept the presence of Soviet bases in Vietnam.[9] This shows how much significance the Chinese leaders have given to the issue and how eager they are to see the problem solved. Despite the early Soviet refusal to bring the Cambodian issue into the bilateral relations, China has insisted that Moscow played an important role when the conflict initially occurred, and it can play a key role in bringing the war to an end if it is willing to do so. In the past twelve months or so, both Moscow and Beijing have moved in the direction of solving the Cambodian problem with a political solution and thus toward a full normalization of relations after some thirty years. The respective foreign ministers have exchanged visits, paving the way for a summit meeting of Deng and Gorbachev in 1989.

China's position on the Cambodian issue underwent some changes in recent years. While continuing to provide military aid to the anti-Vietnamese forces, it now endorses a political settlement with a four-party coalition government. China even agrees to join the international supervision and guarantee of peace after the withdrawal of the Vietnamese.[10] Although some observers argue that China has been pushing the development of the issue toward the solution it desires most—the military defeat of the Vietnamese and their puppet regime—the fact is that China has been very accommodating to the proposals of the GDK.

For China there are both advantages and disadvantages in a rapid settlement of the problem. The threat of Vietnam and the resistance war in Cambodia have generated closer relations between China and the non-Communist ASEAN countries, whose leaders are essentially very skeptical of China's intentions and roles. Behind a determined anti-Vietnam united front, there exists a deep-rooted fear of possible "Chinese expansionism." As long as the war continues, China, seen as a balancing power by the ASEAN countries, can hope to maintain close ties with these nations. The ASEAN nations have not had a chance to test China's policy in a peaceful and neutral Southeast Asia. The Cambodian issue certainly has served as an interim issue to fill in the gap, at least in the short run. There are signs that the countries that have maintained strong ties with China in the past decade, not to mention long-antagonistic Indonesia, began wondering what kind of role China would play with the disappearance of the Cambodian issue.

However, time does not favor the Vietnamese; their own domestic problems and the strong resistance forces in Cambodia now offer more practical hope for a quick settlement than before. So long as the issue is alive, China will have a bargaining chip in dealing with the Soviet Union and Vietnam. For Hanoi the Sino-Soviet rapprochement, with the Cambodian issue "becoming a pawn," according to Vietnamese Foreign Minister Nguyen Co Thach, represents a danger of being caught in between.[11] While Beijing waits to see how Moscow is going to exert pressure on Hanoi, Hanoi may be eager to reach a solution soon.

Vietnam has the heavy burden of sustaining a large military force, which severely hinders its economic development. With a population of 63 million, Vietnam has a regular army of more than 1 million plus nearly 3 million in reserve and quasi-military units, making it, per capita, the world's largest national military force. In the past ten years, Vietnam's economy has largely depended on Soviet aid. The Russians have been involved in 250 projects and the USSR today counts for 64 percent of Vietnam's trade. Under the 1985–90 Soviet five-year plan, aid to Vietnam is set at 8–9 billion rubles (US$12.8–14.4 billion).[12] However, it is not unlikely that Moscow would not maintain that level and would cut the aid. Besides, since the invasion of Cambodia by Vietnam, major countries like China, the United States, Japan, and the ASEAN nations have enforced an economic embargo against Vietnam.

Although it is not yet very clear whether the reformists among Hanoi's top leaders can win over the conservative faction, the need and desire for reform is apparent today. Slowly and painfully, Hanoi, led by a leader from the new generation, Nguyen Van Linh, started moving toward normalization of relations with China and the United States. In an unusual move in late 1988, Hanoi amended its 1980 constitution, which explicitly denounced China, the United States, and Japan as enemies. Now the names of these nations are replaced by vague terms such as "colonialist" and "imperialist."[13]

Serious problems for China also remain if the Cambodian question is not solved soon. As a nation engaged in vigorous economic development, China needs a peaceful environment. The war in Indochina poses a great danger to China's security. In this respect, China shares vital interests with ASEAN. For the ASEAN countries—all marine states—the increased Soviet naval presence is a source of imminent danger. A Singaporean observer said, "More dangerous has been the ability of the Soviet Union to gain basing rights in Vietnam and Cambodia."[14] If the straits were blocked, the regional trade the ASEAN nations rely on would languish and all of East Asia would be "vulnerable to political blackmail." To many ASEAN countries, economic survival depends on maintaining their vital sea lines of communication between the Indian and Pacific oceans.

Another possibility is that the longer the war in Cambodia drags on, the less patient the anti-Vietnam ASEAN nations may become and the more likely they would split on the issue. In this scenario, China would face a less friendly ASEAN and a troublesome Indochina at the same time, and there is no guarantee that some less enthusiastic ASEAN countries would not spell out their own terms for compromise with Hanoi.

Finally, though China has given as much military and economic support as possible to the resistance forces and tries to keep the coalition together, at some point the three forces may fall apart. Some may even make deals with the Vietnamese and Heng Samrin if the war is not won in the near future. The controversial Khmer Rouge has been the target, from time to time, of the other forces, who want to exclude it from any future coalition.

Thus, Chinese leaders have to consider the positive and negative consequences of a quick political settlement. China has to make its long-range goals clear—what kind of neutral government in Cambodia it wants to see after the complete withdrawal of the Vietnamese troops. Given the fact that the Soviet Union would not unilaterally give up the bases already gained in Vietnam, can a neutral Cambodia survive next to a regional giant? How can the three (maybe four, if Heng Samrin's forces are included) parties share power when a political solution is finally reached? What relationship should China have with the Khmer Rouge after power is taken jointly? Another interesting question, though, is the future role of the United States in the region in the next decade if, as the trauma of the Vietnam War diminishes, the ASEAN nations seek strong ties with Washington to balance the powers in the region. For the Chinese leaders, there are several policy options to choose from. The most dramatic alternative is to make some kind of compromise with the Soviet Union, which may in turn put pressure on Vietnam. But this means China has, to a great extent, accepted the status quo in Cambodia. It seems that China and the Soviet Union are moving toward a substantial improvement of relations and China now prefers a political solution to the use of military means. For this option, China would definitely require that Cambodia remain neutral and nonaligned, free of any foreign control.

With the possibility of political settlement in sight, the international community has begun to be concerned about the political framework after the Vietnamese withdrawal. The main concern is that the vacuum would be filled by the Khmer Rouge. This is likely to be the focus of the problem in the next few years. It is not likely that China would try to put a single, dominant Khmer Rouge in power. It is both risky and unrealistic for China to do so. Not only the ASEAN nations would oppose the dominance of the Khmer Rouge; international public opinion would also be against it. China would avoid antagonizing ASEAN nations and the West, who have been very critical of the Khmer Rouge, after the problem of withdrawal disappears. On the other hand, as Zhao Ziyang made clear, China would not allow any attempt to exclude the Khmer Rouge from future coalition governments.

THE ATTITUDE OF THE ASEAN NATIONS

The Cambodian issue has also had a great impact on the foreign policies of the non-Communist countries of ASEAN. While Vietnam and Laos turned to the Soviet Union for support and became its allies, the ASEAN nations have improved their regional cooperation and have more or less sided with China on the issue. They call for a quick withdrawal of the Vietnamese forces from Cambodia and the return of an independent government in that country. They have remained united in their efforts to achieve this in the United Nations and elsewhere. In March 1986, the coalition government of Democratic Kampuchea proposed an "eight-point political solution" to end the civil war rapidly. The resistance forces agreed to negotiate with Vietnam to allow it to withdraw its army in two periods set by agreement, and expressed their willingness to talk with the Heng Samrin government to find out a way to set up a quadrilateral coalition government. The proposals immediately received support from ASEAN and China, but were rejected by Hanoi. During the ninteenth meeting of the ASEAN foreign ministers in Manila in June 1986, ASEAN nations unanimously supported the proposals and called for reconsideration by Vietnam.

However, in meeting the Vietnamese threat, the ASEAN countries have different interests and thus their policy stands will not always be identical. Nor should there be any illusion that ASEAN will be solidly united in policies toward Indochina when the situation becomes more complicated. China realizes this.

Thailand, immediately threatened by the presence of the Vietnamese forces across the Thai-Cambodian border, is the country least friendly to Hanoi and the closest to China. To Bangkok, it is already very clear from the past experience of border fighting with the Vietnamese that Hanoi desires to swallow Thailand into its own sphere of influence some day. To ease the tension and risk, Thailand has relied on China's commitment to contain Vietnam. China even assured Thailand that if the Vietnamese invade Thailand, it will launch another "punishment" at the southern border.

Since the historic day in 1975 when Thailand's senior statesman Kukrit Pramoj signed a diplomatic normalization pact with the late Chinese premier Zhou Enlai, Sino-Thai relations have come a long way. From a convergence of interests in opposition to the Vietnamese occupation of Cambodia, which has formed the cornerstone of bilateral political cooperation, the relationship has expanded in recent years to cover the economic and military fields. The number of formal and semiformal exchanges jumped from 61 in 1979 to some 722 in 1986.[15] Leading Thai personalities—including Princess Maha Chakri Sirindhorn, former Prime Minister Prem Tinsulanonda, and former Army Supreme Commander General Arthit Kamlang-Ek—have been to China in recent years, while most key Chinese leaders have visited Bangkok in return. After this flurry of exchange visits by senior officials from both sides, the bilateral ties reached a high point when Li Peng chose Thailand to be the first foreign country he would visit after becoming premier in 1988.

Bangkok needs to foster friendly ties with Beijing; Chinese pressures along the Sino-Vietnamese border are the only effective deterrent against any Vietnamese military adventures into Thailand. There are also indications that the two countries are moving closer in military cooperation, but it is premature to speculate on how far the military ties will go. Given that the bulk of the Thai armed forces' weaponry is based on U.S. systems, the possibility of a significant shift toward Chinese arms in the foreseeable future can be ruled out.

Despite claims by Thai officials that other ASEAN countries have come around tacitly to accept the close Sino-Thai relationship, the Indonesians and Malaysians have continued intermittently to voice their concern, albeit discreetly. The Indonesian-Malaysian position is perhaps best summed up by a senior ASEAN diplomat who stated: "Vietnam's intransigence has given them no other choice [but to go along with the Thai position]. This is not an acceptance as such but more a realization of Thailand's need [to depend on China] as present realities dictate. But as and when the Vietnamese become more flexible, they would expect the Sino-Thai relationship to loosen up, and Bangkok to be more accommodating with Hanoi."[16] Here the actual strategic thoughts of the ASEAN nations, including Thailand, cannot be clearer.

Indonesia and Malaysia have traditionally regarded China as the long-term security threat to Southeast Asia. Indonesia in particular has made frequent and friendly overtures to Hanoi in the past, though its perceived role as a bridge between ASEAN and Vietnam has taken on a conspicuously low profile since the much-publicized visit to Jakarta by Vietnamese Foreign Minister Nguyen Co Thach in early 1984 when he rejected Indonesian President Suharto's offer to mediate a settlement of the Cambodian conflict.[17]

The ASEAN countries on the whole view China as a balancing power in the region to contain Vietnam and the Soviet Union, but as a short-range rather than a long-term ally because of the differences in ideology, internal instability, and ethnic problems. Therefore, in the next decade more American involvement in the region's affairs would be favored and welcomed by the ASEAN countries. An ASEAN conference in 1986 concluded that "the United States must undertake an aggressive effort to assist the nations [in the region] in order to free their resolve and resources for a settled response to the long-term Soviet threat to their vital interests."[18] Some countries, such as Indonesia, even think the United States is a reluctant player, and they want it to resume a formal relationship with Hanoi so that an alternative to Vietnam's total dependence on the Soviet Union might be found and an ultimate settlement reached. However, American politicians and scholars seem to be cautious. Many of them see the necessary role of the United States in the region but warn against the role of regional hegemonist in Southeast Asia that it played in the 1960s.[19]

In this context, China must make it clear that while seeking to play a key role in regional affairs it will not interfere in any internal affairs of the ASEAN nations and sincerely wishes to establish enduring relationships with them. It should let the ASEAN countries understand that what China needs is a peaceful southern flank unendangered by any superpower or regional power. China shares their fundamental objective of keeping Southeast Asia a peaceful and neutral region free from any dominance by regional or outside powers. China would find it alarming if one of the ASEAN nations came under Soviet influence.

Policy-makers in Beijing seem to have realized the problems that are likely to occur after the Cambodian issue is resolved and have started preparing for the new situation. During his visit to Bangkok, Premier Li Peng revealed China's new "Four Principles for Sino-ASEAN Relations." This new policy statement is obviously meant for Sino-ASEAN relations after the Cambodian issue has been settled and includes the following principles: (1) peaceful coexistence despite differences in social and political systems; (2) antihegemonism; China will not seek to be a hegemonist power; it will not interfere in the domestic affairs of the ASEAN countries; (3) further development of economic relations; (4) continuing support of regional cooperation and initiatives from ASEAN.[20] These principles are by no means novel, but they do reflect China's concern about future relations with ASEAN nations after the settlement of the Cambodian issue. Undoubtedly, China attaches great importance to its relations with ASEAN and it is in the vital interest of both sides to maintain peace and prosperity in Southeast Asia.

SINO-ASEAN ECONOMIC RELATIONS

During a visit to four ASEAN countries in 1986, Chinese Vice-Premier Tian Jiyun stated that the major purpose of his visit was to probe new fields and new ways to develop further trade, economic, and technological cooperation between China and the ASEAN countries. He proposed that (1) friendship and economic cooperation complement each other—friendship can lead to cooperation and cooperation may promote friendship; (2) it is not enough to make trade deals only—China welcomes and encourages investment and industrial cooperation; (3) to further broaden the scope of economic cooperation, China and the ASEAN countries should start item-to-item trade in addition to currency transactions.[21] China's attention to developing economic cooperation will continue, since both China and ASEAN need to enhance their domestic economy and international trade.

Economic development in the ASEAN nations in the past decade or so has been fairly rapid. In the 1970s, the economic growth rates of the ASEAN countries were among the highest in the world. The annual average growth rate of ASEAN was 7.4 percent, twice as high as the world average rate. In the early 1980s, though the world economy slowed down, the ASEAN economy still kept its pace.

The impressive economic growth in most ASEAN countries has facilitated the strengthening of economic ties between China and ASEAN nations. Since the early 1980s, Sino-ASEAN economic and trade relations have developed rapidly. In 1985 the total value of Sino-ASEAN trade was US$3.22 billion, eighteen times that of 1971. ASEAN has become a major trading partner of China. Although China's trade relations with the ASEAN countries began in the early years of the People's Republic, there was no real expansion of the relationship until the mid-1970s when China normalized diplomatic relations with some of the ASEAN nations. Sino-Filipino trade was valued at US$330 million in 1980, and Sino-Thai trade increased in value from US$122 million in 1975 to an estimated $800 million in 1988.[22] In 1987 the total value of Sino-Singaporean trade reached a record high of US$2.25 billion. By June 1988, Singaporean businesses had invested in 170 ventures in China, with a total value

ECONOMIC GROWTH RATES OF ASEAN COUNTRIES (PERCENTAGE)

	1978–82	1983	1984	1985	1986	1987
Indonesia	6.8	3.5	4.5	1.8	3.2	—
Philippines	5.4	1.5	− 5.5	− 3.95	1.5	5.05
Thailand	6.5	5.8	5.9	4.1	—	7.0
Malaysia	6.9	5.6	6.9	2.8	—	2.5
Singapore	9.0	6.1	8.2	− 1.7	1.9	3.4
Brunei	—	—	—	—	—	—

Sources: *ASEAN Security 1985*, by Research Institute for Peace and Security (Tokyo: Brassy's Defense Publishers). The figures of 1986 and 1987 are from *Asian Survey*, vol. XXVIII, no. 2 (February 1988).

of US$400 million. Direct trade between China and Indonesia has been resumed after some twenty years, and the value of annual trade is currently around US$100 million. In addition, China and Indonesia also conduct trade via Hong Kong and Singapore. In 1985 alone, 814 Chinese delegations concerned with trade and economic affairs visited the ASEAN countries.[23]

However, even with the progress made in the past decade, Sino-ASEAN economic relations are not very impressive. Sino-ASEAN trade accounted for only 1.5 percent of the total foreign trade value of ASEAN in 1984. Trade with China accounts for 1.5 percent of the value of Malaysia's foreign trade.

The major obstacle in the way of future trade and economic cooperation between China and the ASEAN countries is their similar export structures. Almost all the countries except Singapore have to rely on agricultural products, raw materials, oil, and low-tech industrial products. Malaysia, for example, exported minerals that made up 13.8 percent of the total export in the first season of 1985; oil and petroleum products made up 18.9 percent, and agricultural products 24.5 percent. These three kinds of major export items already held 57.2 percent of the total Malaysian export.[24] In Indonesia, crude oil and petroleum products accounted for 76.3 percent of 1984 exports.[25] If it is likely that Chinese light industrial products, such as textiles, can enter Southeast Asia, and Malaysian palm oil and rubber enter China, other major items of each others' export can hardly be traded off. On the contrary, there are some areas in the world market where China may have to compete with some ASEAN countries. For instance, Japan was traditionally a big market for Indonesian oil. Since Japan increased oil imports from China, Indonesia began to feel threatened by Chinese competition. The Japanese, on the other hand, "use" Chinese oil to cut the price of Indonesian oil. Indonesia is certainly very unhappy about this. Other items such as rice, tin, and textile products do not arouse much competition currently, but in the future they may all be problems since both sides export large amounts.

ASEAN countries vary in the significance they attach to future economic relationships with China. To some, regional interorganizational cooperation is a priority. At the ASEAN foreign ministers' meeting held in Kuala Lumpur in July 1985, Malaysian Prime Minister Mahathir Mohamad said that the potential of the ASEAN market is four times larger than that of the Chinese market.[26] Acting on this assumption, it would be understandable for businessmen and investors of the ASEAN countries to explore the ASEAN market rather than to invest and trade with China. In addition, during his visit to China in November 1985, Mahathir urged ASEAN businessmen to invest in ASEAN countries and he also urged the Chinese to support this practice. The slow speed and small scale of the ASEAN investment in China have become a problem in Sino-ASEAN economic relations. Despite several investment promotion agreements—including one on investment-capital protection signed by Chinese President Li Xiannian in March 1985 and another on double-taxation avoidance signed by Chinese Vice-Premier Tian Jiyun in October 1986—overall Thai investments in China have yet to reach a substantial scale. During his visit to three other ASEAN nations, Tian Jiyun called for more investments by these countries in China.

China clearly wants to expand economic relations with the ASEAN countries. It has taken substantial steps to promote and facilitate such relations, to balance the trade in which China has had a surplus, and to attract investments from the ASEAN nations. Besides traditional import items from Southeast Asia, China has agreed to buy some items that are not badly needed. When the Thai economy was battered by severely depressed world rice prices, China signed a US$43 million rice-and-maize deal with Thailand in early 1986.[27]

In November 1986, China agreed to purchase an extra thirty thousand tons of Thai glutinous rice and twenty thousand tons of green mung beans—despite the fact that it is exporting similar products to India and Japan.[28]

This policy indeed shows the wisdom and foresight of the Chinese leaders. It also proves to be fruitful. A steady, friendly relationship is more important than simply gaining more dollars. China has successfully conducted its trade with Thailand, Singapore, and some other ASEAN countries after solving problems in this way. However, even taking into account Thai Foreign Minister Saddi's optimistic statement that "through friendly joint efforts we may endeavour to avoid clashes as far as is practical," China has to face the fact that the current export structures on both sides make further large-scale economic and trade relations difficult. In the long run, China itself will suffer from trade deficits with such major partners as the United States and Japan and from a serious shortage of hard currency. It cannot afford to take on the burden of purchasing commodities it does not badly need. The best solution is twofold.

First, China must concentrate on attracting more investment, technology transfer, and services such as banking, port management, and hotel construction and management from the ASEAN countries. With the economic reforms expanding to a broader arena, experienced ASEAN businessmen and managers may find a potential Chinese market. China, then, cannot just wait to see if they are coming, but must rapidly facilitate a favorable climate for foreign investments. In the short run, it may be necessary for China to let foreign investors make money at a relatively high cost to China. We can well expect that if the economic reforms continue to be carried out and more legislation is enacted to protect foreign investments, there will be more investors coming from the ASEAN countries. Without such steps, any call for more foreign investment and cooperation will be nothing but hollow words.

Second, China has to restructure its export: the current heavy reliance on basic manufactured products and raw materials has already hurt China in many ways. Falling oil prices cost China some US$3 billion in 1986. Strategic export restructuring may take a long time, but the sooner this is done, the greater incentive China will have to strengthen economic and political relations with the ASEAN countries.

THE INTERNAL DIMENSION OF SINO–SOUTHEAST ASIAN RELATIONS

The strategic situation and economic development in Southeast Asia are not the only factors that affect relations between China and the ASEAN countries. There are three internal factors that determine such relations, as well.

First, the internal stability of the countries involved. In the past ten years, China has been undertaking a courageous experiment, or a "second revolution," to use the words of many China watchers. The modernization program has resulted in some changes in China's foreign policy. The first shift is from an externally oriented foreign-policy line to an internally oriented one. The former took "the liberation of the whole of mankind" as "our own sacred task." Proletarian internationalism was the basis of China's foreign policy then. As a result, China's policy toward Southeast Asia was to support the Communist insurgencies. After 1979, and especially after the major readjustment in 1982, China's foreign policy became more internally oriented. National interests prevailed. Foreign policy became a tool serving domestic economic development. "Without a peaceful world," Deng said, "we cannot reach our goals. So it is our sincere hope that in twenty and even seventy years there will be no war. Then we may develop our economy in a relaxed manner."[29] Obviously, the major objective of China's foreign policy is to have a favorable international environment, peaceful and stable.

The second change in foreign-policy guidelines is the change in the overall outlook of the contemporary world by the Chinese leaders. In the later years of Mao's leadership, the world was seen as a "barrel full of explosives"; a war, regional or global, might break out anytime. "The enemies are deteriorating, we are growing stronger day by day," Mao claimed. Guided by this understanding, Chinese foreign policy was conducted on a "class struggle" base. However, since the early 1980s the outlook of the Chinese leaders on the issue of war and revolution has changed. Hu Yaobang made this clear when he stated that "although the shadow of a new world war still exists now, the possibility of preventing it from happening is growing year by year."[30] As a result of this change, a large number of defense industries have shifted either totally or partially to civilian production. According to the head of the National Defense Science, Technology, and Industry Commission, by the year 1990 the number of consumer products made by the defense industries will be three times the number in 1980. Further evidence of the change was the discharge of a million PLA servicemen by early 1987. In the past few years, military spending has been tightly controlled. Defense spending now accounts for less than 10 percent of total government expenditures.

The third change lies in China's pragmatic attitude in separating state-to-state relations from the relations of parties. The Chinese Communist Party has gone further than before to make national interests superior to ideological interests when dealing with countries of different political and social systems, especially the ASEAN countries. It has stopped "exporting" revolution to other countries, including the neighboring ASEAN countries. The CCP has made it clear that it is wholly up to the Communist parties of other countries to decide their own course and means of revolution. This is particularly significant to the ASEAN nations who complained, frequently before and even sometimes after the normalization of relations with the PRC, that the Communist insurgencies in their countries were inspired and supported by China. The recent rapprochement between China and the Soviet Union also illustrates this change of attitude.

The reforms have brought positive changes in Chinese society. The economy has grown rapidly. But due to the existence of a transitional dual-track system, a large population, a bureaucracy that always resists liberal measures, and lack of rule by law, the reforms are encountering serious problems within the party and in the society. To many people, the reforms are not satisfactory. They complain about soaring consumer prices and the corruption of party and government officials. Some people are simply not used to the new systems after some forty years of eating from the "iron rice bowl." We have reasons to be concerned about the possibility of future instability in China. The student demonstrations in late 1986 and after the death of Hu Yaobang in April 1989 are signs of unrest. The next few years will be one of the most crucial periods in China's history. It will face such problems as how much further the economic reforms and political reforms (if any) should be carried; how to counter the growing inflation while not hurting the economic growth and overall reform; who will be in charge after Deng and, more critically, will China return to the old system? It is not impossible that we may see some instability in China in the next decade, but one sure thing is that today's Chinese people are not the same as they were twenty years ago or even ten years ago when they were so easily guided and mobilized for political campaigns. Certain kinds of tensions between the elite and the masses, and among different segments of the elite, may possibly occur. The society, the system, and the ideology will all come under serious tests in the next decade.

In the next ten years, countries in Southeast Asia will also have to confront possible internal instability. The Aquino government in the Philippines not only has to consolidate its victory by overcoming the challenge of the discordant military leaders and strong opposition, but also has to reconstruct an economy that was on the edge of collapse when Marcos fled the country. So long as the Aquino government retains its popular support and is able to handle the economic problems, conditions in that country will remain relatively stable. However, given the dominant power of the military and the strong political challenges from various opposition forces, Aquino must gain substantial control of the army. Otherwise, it is possible that a military coup would endanger the current civilian order.

Longtime rulers Prime Minister Lee Kuan Yew of Singapore and President Suharto of Indonesia will retire in the next decade. Thailand and Malaysia will hold new elections. Will these countries remain politically stable while their economies continue to grow? It is hard to predict, though recent development in most ASEAN countries shows more encouraging signs. Some of them, such as Indonesia and Malaysia, have mixed ethnic-religious insurgency problems. Military fighting is still going on in the Philippines and Malaysia. The next decade may see some opposition parties take power. In countries like Indonesia and Thailand, the possibility of a military coup can not be ruled out.

Another problem affecting the internal stability of the ASEAN nations is the insurgencies. In the Philippines, the Communist forces have been very strong in their military struggle against the government. After Mrs. Aquino took power, the New People's Army agreed to a cease-fire for a period of time. But the problem is by no means solved. Malaysia, and to some extent Thailand, have similar problems. Since the reforms in China began, the Communist insurgencies in the region have become more independent. Some have softened their stands. Though China has repeatedly claimed that it will not intervene in others' domestic affairs and now maintains only moral ties with the Communists in Southeast Asia, these countries are very sensitive about the matter. Although it is likely that the insurgencies will continue, it is quite unlikely that they will cause serious political crises in the foreseeable future. Still, China should continue the current policy toward party-to-party relations to further convince the ASEAN countries of its sincere intentions.

Neither China nor the ASEAN countries want to see each other in an unstable situation. No domestic instability in the region will be in the interests of the countries concerned. To China, instability in the ASEAN countries could bring in more superpower intervention and change the balance of power. If China changes its foreign policy as a result of a fundamental change in its overall policy or if there is domestic instability, the deep-rooted fear of China's intentions will resurface in the ASEAN countries.

Leadership changes in Hanoi have even more profound significance. Although it is still too early to presume that the new party leader, Nguyen Van Linh, who replaced Trong Chinh in December 1986, will shift from the fundamental policies of the previous leadership, certain adjustments in economic policies, and even in foreign policy, can be counted on. Since the invasion of Cambodia, the

Vietnamese economy has deteriorated to the edge of crisis. It is estimated that in the past five years Hanoi's defense spending amounted to approximately US$4.5 billion, meaning an annual average expenditure of over $800 million. It counted for 50 percent of the total annual national spending. By now, Hanoi has a debt of more than US$6 billion.[31] Experts believe the Vietnamese economy is ten to twenty years behind most of the ASEAN countries. Although Hanoi has realized its difficulties and launched an economic reform in 1981, it has not yet gone very far nor been very successful. In the past several years, there have been quite a few political purges at the highest level. Some high party and government officials were ousted and replaced. The members of the Politburo and the ministers changed dramatically. The struggle between the growing faction of reformists, led by Nguyen Van Linh, and the conservatives is not over. The next few years will see the result of this power struggle, which in turn will have a profound impact on regional affairs.

Even if the reformists in Hanoi wanted to introduce some new policies, they would not see them implemented quickly because of likely resistance from cadres and the army who have already started complaining. To the Vietnamese, the essential issue is how to wind up the painful and long-lasting war in Cambodia as soon as possible. It pays a high price to keep its hand in that country. Hanoi's dilemma is that while desiring indirect control over its weak neighbor and a strengthening of its domestic economy, it is not willing to give up its dream of an Indochinese federation under its control. And it wants its puppet regime under Heng Samrin to be able to stand on its own feet. It is hard to engage in a genuine national reconstruction as long as a heavy burden is carried.

Another dimension of Sino-ASEAN relations is the question of the ethnic Chinese. The issue is by no means a new one. It has been a serious issue in relations between China and many ASEAN countries, especially Indonesia and Malaysia.

Today there are some 30 million ethnic Chinese living outside of China, who may be put into two major categories—those who still have not given up their nationality as Chinese and have not been naturalized, and those who are citizens of the countries they reside in. Most of them live in Southeast Asia, where a great majority of them are citizens of the local country. For instance, in the Malaysian population, the Chinese make up 35 percent, the next largest ethnic group to the Malays (50 percent). In Singapore, the Chinese comprise 77 percent of the population. In Thailand there are 3 million Chinese (both Thai citizens and aliens), constituting 13 percent of the total Thai population.[32] In all these countries, although the Chinese may be a minority group (as in Indonesia), they are generally successful and play an important role in the local economy. In these countries, ethnic problems always combine with problems of religion and insurgency. Thus, the ethnic-Chinese issue has always been a very complicated and touchy one.

Traditionally, "blood lineage" was a major factor in the treatment of the ethnic Chinese in Southeast Asia by the Chinese government. The overseas Chinese, regardless of whether they were naturalized or not, were all treated as *hua qiao*. Due to domestic racial and religious conflicts, ethnic Chinese have often been made scapegoats by local governments. China has reacted strongly to these anti-Chinese moves. The ethnic Chinese themselves have kept their traditions and customs, and their strong ties with China, especially when they found themselves vulnerable to the majority ethnic groups. When the Communist insurgencies arose in the 1960s, the tension between the ethnic Chinese and other ethnic groups and between China and the ASEAN countries was at its peak. In some countries, such as Malaysia and Thailand, the ethnic Chinese were involved in the insurgencies. The spate of bomb explosions in the Chinese-controlled business complexes in Jakarta and the Malay-Chinese ethnic riot in 1969 in Kuala Lumpur are obvious manifestations of this kind of ethnic tension in those states.

Since the new policy toward the relatives and property of the overseas Chinese was implemented in 1978, the PRC government has once again won support from many overseas Chinese in Southeast Asia. Economic development in China has attracted some investment and assistance from them. But at the same time, the governments of the Southeast Asian countries are still cautious. To some extent, they grow even stronger due to the increased communication between the ethnic Chinese and the PRC. In the next decade, China faces a dilemma: on the one hand, it needs the substantial attention of the overseas Chinese in its modernization drive, especially those who are successful business people, and it must protect the interests of those who are not naturalized citizens of the country they reside in. It is also hard to cut all emotional links between those naturalized citizens and China, where they may still have many relatives. On the other hand, wariness and suspicion over possible close ties between China and the ethnic Chinese in their countries still exists. China, on the whole, has to be very cautious over the extent to which it woos the Chinese in Southeast Asia in the new, developing era.

The picture of future Sino–Southeast Asian relations is encouraging overall. The positive changes in the world in the late 1980s will have a great impact on the situation in Southeast Asia in the next decade. However, China can not delude itself that relations will be easily maintained. Issues such as Cambodia, Communist insurgencies, and the ethnic Chinese may all pose great difficulties for China. Some problems likely to occur in the region that will need attention: political arrangements in Cambodia after the Vietnamese withdrawal, the territorial dispute over the islands in the South China Sea (the Nansha or Spratly Islands), and the new role of the United States in the region. Keen efforts by all the countries in the region to reduce tension and peacefully settle disputes are still necessary. A genuine and enduring mutual understanding and trust needs to be built up. China must understand how deeply Southeast Asian countries fear and distrust it. China's major task is to remove such fear and distrust.

ASEAN has claimed that it wanted Southeast Asia to become a "peaceful and neutral zone free from outside intervention of any sort." Many years have passed, and the region is still not peaceful. Neither of the two superpowers is committed to the support of this goal. Can the Cambodian problem be settled soon? Can Southeast Asia become a neutral zone after it is solved? I doubt it. But it is certainly in the best interest of China if there can be a peaceful, neutral, and friendly Southeast Asia.

NINE

CHINA'S THIRD WORLD POLICY

ZHIMIN LIN

China's Third World policy has always been a difficult subject. Compared with other aspects of its foreign policy, China's positions on Third World affairs tend to be more rhetorical than substantive, often more general than specific. However, as China began to reshape its international strategy in the early 1980s, it has taken several concrete steps to revise its Third World policy.[1]

China has dropped almost completely the revolutionary component, which used to be the dominant tone, from its policy statements related to Third World issues. When Zhao Ziyang visited four Latin American countries (the first visit of its kind) in 1985, he called for deideologizing international relations.[2] His words were not taken as a mere gesture to China's relatively new friends there but a genuine reflection of the country's new orientation in domestic and international affairs.

China has begun to show more sensitivity to the problems of the developing nations. Unlike before, when typical Third World difficulties such as poverty, prolonged economic stagnation, and constant domestic unrest were indiscriminately attributed to the damaging consequences of ex-colonial rule or the vicious effects of the world capitalist system, China now stresses equally, if not more, the role of mismanagement on the part of Third World governments themselves and their inappropriate use of foreign models, including those strongly influenced by China's own development in the past.[3] While the term "Third World" is still widely in use in the Chinese press, the phrase itself has less to do with the original Chinese interpretation of a united, progressive world and a world of hope. More often the media depict the Third World as a divided, problem-ridden one with a highly uncertain and even gloomy future.

China has become increasingly used to conventional methods in dealing with its Third World friends. The days when China was willing to throw a substantial amount of money into a handful of countries in order to fulfill its moral and political commitment to the so-called course of the Third World are gone. Most economic exchanges between China and developing countries are now conducted on strict business terms. China even maintains a significant trade surplus with many Third World countries. For the first time in history, China is not just selling arms to a number of these countries, but is openly viewing this as an ordinary practice in international relations. While China continues to provide a limited amount of economic assistance to several Third World countries, it is now a net recipient, rather than a supplier, of foreign aid.[4]

Concerning political relations and China's treatment of regional conflicts, the changes are even more dramatic. Until recently, China has not treated individual events happening in the Third World in their own right. Very often, the lines between friends and enemies were drawn depending on China's broad strategic concerns. Now the new catchphrase is "case-by-case," even though this approach may imply some inconsistencies in China's overall relationships with the two superpowers. For example, ever since the Soviet invasion of Afghanistan in 1979, China has remained one of the main supporters of Afghan resistance groups fighting against the Soviets and the regime they support. At the same time, however, China was not hesitant in condemning publicly the U.S.-backed rebels in Nicaragua who were fighting against the pro-Soviet Ortega government.

To understand the full significance of this development in China's foreign policy, it is useful to explore three basic questions: What is the historical background of the above changes? What has been altered so far and what is the nature of the recent policy shift? And finally, what is the implication of this ongoing development for the future of China's Third World policy?

THE NEED FOR CHANGE: LESSONS FROM HISTORY

Over the last three decades, policy-makers in China adopted three different strategies or policy schemes in dealing with the Third World issue: the "peaceful coexistence" approach in the 1950s, the "revolution" approach in the 1960s, and the "grand alliance" approach in the 1970s. None of these three strategies has survived the test of history. Still, their influence remains, their impact is still visible and significant. Current and future Chinese Third World policies will inescapably be compared with these three predecessors.

Peaceful Coexistence

The peaceful-coexistence strategy adopted in the early and mid 1950s had its intellectual roots in the 1940s. In the days immediately following World War II, Mao had raised the notion of the existence of an "intermediate zone." Instead of forecasting an imminent clash between the United States and the Soviet Union, as many people had expected when the Cold War began, Mao asserted that the real battlefield lay in the vast zone that separates the two giant rivals, a zone that "includes many capitalist, colonial and semi-colonial countries in Europe, Asia and Africa."[5]

This notion, though not fully developed into a sophisticated theory at that time, was important to China's later conceptualization of the world's political and economic structure in general and the Third World problem in particular. From the very beginning, the Chinese leaders were nurtured with a tripartite perspective of international relations. Contrary to Stalin's dichotomous, two-camp view of the world, one in which the Soviet Union was supposedly the natural leader of one of the camps, Mao's stress on the existence and importance of a third force opened a way for China to develop its own identity in international affairs. Such a tripartite world map allowed China to maintain its ideological agreement with the Soviet bloc while claiming membership in another group of states with whom China shares more, in terms of historical experience and international stature. Moreover, this tripartite notion helped to articulate a ground on which China could advance its own influence legitimately. Theoretically, there was an area which by Chinese definition belongs to neither the Soviet Union nor the United States. China's presence in this area would therefore not only serve China's own interests but the interests of the socialist world as well. The fact that China had never completely given up this tripartite orientation—even in the early 1950s, when it announced its famous "leaning to one side" policy (toward the Soviet Union)—highlights the value of this notion to Chinese leaders.

The notion had its inherent weaknesses though. For example, the general nature of this sweeping demarcation did not help China much in selecting specific policy alternatives, especially where China's immediate interests, such as in border disputes, were involved. The notion also encouraged some illusions that deeply rooted differences among Third World countries would become secondary concerns because of the countries' identical location in the world economic and political structure. However, given the normative and practical utilities of the notion, it came as no surprise that, once China had consolidated its domestic control and secured the economic and military support of the Soviet Union in the early 1950s, its first articulated Third World policy—the peaceful-coexistence policy—rested on premises that drew heavily upon this tripartite perception.

The Five Principles of Peaceful Coexistence were first mentioned by Zhou Enlai in his interview with a visiting Indian delegate in 1953.[6] They subsequently appeared in Sino-Indian and Sino-Burmese statements concerning their border talks in 1954. Later these principles became the standard themes in China's stated policy toward other Third World countries.

As a doctrine, peaceful coexistence means a set of commendable rules of international behavior. As a strategy, however, it revealed that the main concern of China at that time was to help create a united, self-conscious, anticolonialist, and anti-imperialist coalition among newly independent states. Such a broad coalition was expected to help China break out of its isolation and establish its unique position in world politics. To this end, China was willing to tone down its ideological differences with many Third World countries and to rely largely on reconciliatory policy postures as the basic means of approaching Third World countries.

Parallel to China's internal quest in the mid-1950s for a period of low political tension and high concentration on economic growth, the peaceful-coexistence strategy was fairly successful in its first stage. It helped China to establish initial relations with some of its neighbors. It assisted China in winning its first major diplomatic victory during the 1955 Bandung Conference.[7] However, the strategy failed to serve as a viable foreign-policy framework for China. In the late 1950s, the "wind" began to change. China was unable to take advantage of the momentum generated at the Bandung meeting to establish more extensive relations with Third World countries. Even worse were the increasing conflicts with countries with which China had managed to open up relatively good relations in the previous period. China's relations with India, for example, deteriorated substantially in the late 1950s. China had invested considerable effort in the early 1950s to improve its relations with India, with the hope of securing its southern border and showing the world the unity of the two largest Third World countries. Yet a series of events ranging from rebellion in Tibet and disputes along the common borders threw the one-time harmonious Sino-Indian relationship into a long period of open hostility. In short, the adverse results in the late 1950s raised serious doubts about the appropriateness of the low-key and conciliatory strategy of peaceful coexistence.

Several domestic and international factors had also contributed to the downfall of the strategy. The first was the increasing radicalization within China. The Anti-Rightist Campaign of 1957 and the fever of the Great Leap Forward made such a "soft" foreign-policy line politically neither appealing nor necessary. Second, China's earlier hope to maintain a stable and less hostile international environment began to vanish as a result of the second Taiwan Strait crisis in 1958.[8] The United States subsequently stepped up its efforts to build a series of treaty organizations to "contain" China. China's efforts to maintain good relationships with other Asian nations became increasingly difficult. Finally, the emerging Sino-Soviet split after the late 1950s made it impossible for the Chinese to call for the general unity of the Third World without distinguishing the "pro-Soviet" Third World countries from the "pro-Chinese" ones.

In retrospect, two lessons must have seemed particularly painful to the Chinese leaders. First of all, the Third World is by no means a unitary entity, as China wishfully perceived. The common aspirations that hold the Third World together, such as the need for political independence, are not strong enough to overcome all differences. Second, and more important, each member of the Third World has its own order of interests. The individual countries may well become united under certain circumstances, but as China itself has learned all too well, once they are caught in a situation in which their perceived priorities are in conflict with their obligations as member states of the Third World, few of them seem to be willing to give up the former for the latter. A timely and careful review of Third World policy based on these lessons would have helped China to develop a more sensible approach. However, when the lessons were actually learned, they were learned from a very different perspective, as the subsequent revolutionary strategy attests.

The Dominance of Revolution

Internal and external developments in the early 1960s created an atmosphere in which a revolution-based strategy toward the Third World became particularly attractive. The first was the rapid escalation of tension between China and the Soviet Union. If the conflict between the two countries in the fifties had been more or less confined to ideological differences, during the early sixties the focus gradually shifted to issues that were of great importance to national security and international positions.[9]

The impact of this shift was twofold. On the one hand, as the number of Soviet divisions along the common border increased from less than ten in the late 1950s to more than thirty in the early 1960s, and as the Soviet leaders openly challenged the correctness of China's domestic and international policies, Beijing leaders concluded as early as 1963 that a total break with Moscow was inevitable.[10] As a result, China, from the early 1960s on, stepped up its efforts to "stake out its own geographical areas of interest on the international scene."[11] On the other hand, because of the strong Chinese criticism of the alleged "sell-out" of Third World interests by the "revisionist" Soviet Union led by Khrushchev, the thrust of China's new Third World policy could hardly be anything but a more radical policy scheme. Partly to respond to the split and partly to challenge Soviet dominance, China adopted a distinctively revolution-based Third World policy throughout the rest of the sixties.

The second development was the independence movement in Africa. In the early 1960s, the delayed decolonization had finally reached its peak in that continent. In 1960 alone, seventeen African countries became independent. This development, while it had little to do with China's initiative, gave the country a rare opportunity to put its new strategy into practice. Unlike many Asian countries, whose independence was accompanied by the heritage of a well-developed social and economic infrastructure handed over by their ex-colonial rulers, most newly independent African states were much more open to new social and economic models that would not just give them guidance but a sense of aspiration and confidence in building a new nation. A major developing country, China's ambitious development plan and remarkable achievements in the early postrevolution years and its subsequent development could hardly be overlooked by these eager searchers.

Prompted by increased domestic and international pressures and attracted by the opportunities in Africa, China tried hard to implement the new version of its Third World policy. Unlike the peaceful-coexistence strategy, whose meaning was rather vague and whose implementation was highly fragmented, this "revolution strategy" tended to be more concrete and its execution more systematic.

The new strategy had two major components. One was China's determination to increase both symbolic and substantial support to those countries fighting for independence or undertaking various forms of struggles against the "reactionary" regimes. Of course, this did not mean that China would automatically back all self-proclaimed revolutionary movements. According to Peter Van Ness, in 1965 (the peak year of the revolution strategy), China endorsed revolutionary armed struggle "in only 23 of a possible total of some 120 developing countries."[12] In fact, during this period most material aid went to a few select states whose experience bore more similarities to China's own past—Vietnam and Algeria, for example. However, this policy's explicit and strong endorsement of revolution and national independence left few doubts that China would have supported more countries if it had been able to do so.

Another component of the revolutionary strategy was China's strong advocacy of and support for a development strategy of self-reliance. According to the then-prevailing Chinese view, the struggle for political independence by a Third World country would remain incomplete unless it was followed by a nationalized and self-sufficient economy. For that purpose, newly independent states had to find a development strategy distinctive from those offered by the imperialist West or the equally misleading ones suggested by the revisionist East. To support its argument, China was willing, in addition to its own practice along this line, to assist other Third World states with various forms of economic aid even though the country itself was far from rich in such resources.

China's new strategy worked relatively smoothly in Africa. Zhou Enlai's highly publicized visit to eleven African and Asian countries in late 1963 and early 1964 represented a breakthrough in China's relations with the African countries. Never before had China been so positively received by so many Third World countries. The dominant theme of Zhou's visit—the call for a new, independent, and prosperous Africa—was warmly received, along with a number of small but effective aid programs.[13] Six more African countries had established diplomatic relations with China in that year alone. Some of them have since become China's closest friends in Africa, such as Tanzania and Zambia.

In Asia, however, the balance sheet was less clear. At the state-to-state level, the major diplomatic victories China managed to achieve included the signing of border treaties with many neighboring states: Burma, Nepal, Pakistan, Afghanistan, and Mongolia.

Unfortunately, relations with India did not work out that way. A key state in China's previous Third World policy, India, with its neutralism once warmly received but now being openly criticized by China as nothing but a disguised antirevolutionary scheme, found itself at war with China in 1962. Furthermore, China's more militant Third World policy, especially the call for domestic revolutions, fueled some deep-rooted suspicions among its Asian neighbors. With the exception of a few countries such as Indonesia and North Vietnam, the reactions from most Asian countries to China's hard-line policy were negative. Lin Piao's famous 1965 article on the universal application of "people's war" seemed to have further confirmed their wariness. In fact, in the first half of the sixties, the only neighboring state with which China managed to establish a new and good relationship was Pakistan. Even that achievement was prompted more by the latter's fear of India than by the influence of China's revolution strategy.

By the mid-1960s, there were increasing signs that the revolutionary strategy was falling apart. In Southeast Asia, the bloody coup in Indonesia in 1965 led to a break in diplomatic relations with China. China lost one of its few remaining political allies in the region. In the same year, the second Asian-African Conference was aborted on the eve of its opening as a result of a coup in the host country—Algeria. China had hoped to use the forum to revitalize the revolutionary spirit of the Third World that was seen to have eroded since the late 1950s. Even in Africa, where the revolutionary strategy had been reasonably well received earlier, the news was hardly better. The initial enthusiasm for learning the Chinese model was replaced by a more sober appreciation of its limitations. A series of coups had driven many leaders who had close ties with China out of power.[14] On the eve of the Cultural Revolution, China's diplomats were expelled from a number of African countries, some of which even went so far as to suspend diplomatic relations with China.

The ill fate of the revolutionary strategy raised an inevitable question: what had gone wrong? It seems that two problems associated with such a strategy were largely to blame. First was the problem of overreaching. Committing itself to a broadly defined goal of revolution, China was forced to become involved in areas where it had very few or only indirect interests. The strong ideological component of the revolutionary strategy severely limited China's freedom of selecting the proper priorities and developing effective means to implement them. The more China was involved, the more expensive but less effective the strategy seemed to be. The second problem was miscalculation. By relying on an ideologically based strategy, China vastly underestimated the degree of complexity of the Third World and third world issues. For example, one of the dominant themes in China's policy statements during that period was the need for a concerted Third World struggle against both revisionism and imperialism. However, given the fact that most developing countries used to have or would like to continue to have some special relationship with one or the other of the two superpowers, that call could only serve to alienate China from a great number of those countries. Parallel to this was China's overly optimistic assessment of the general international trend and its ability to influence it. Similar to its predecessor, the revolutionary strategy reflected the Chinese leaders' belief that a strong surge in the Third World movement could soon lead to some sweeping changes in which developing countries would be the main beneficiaries. Mao, for example, asserted that the more chaotic international affairs were, the better the result would be for the world's people. Some of these highly inflated estimates became the key arguments supporting the formation and execution of the revolution strategy.

The strategy was in many ways a policy blunder. In a country where official foreign policy was rarely criticized, the revolutionary strategy was one of those which received both official and scholarly denunciations in subsequent years. By the late 1960s, a new Third World strategy was in the making.

United Front

The new strategy—a strategy that was based fundamentally on the concept of a united front against the Soviet Union—was part of a major foreign-policy turn in China during that period. Once again, domestic needs and international pressures worked together to prompt the change.

Domestically, the heyday of the Cultural Revolution was over. After more than two years of nationwide disorder and chaos, Mao finally decided that it was time to restore a certain degree of order while continuing the revolution. As a result, various government agencies, including the foreign-policy apparatus, were gradually returning to normal modes of functioning. The relative tranquility on the domestic front gave Mao and other top Chinese leaders a chance to consider some more threatening developments abroad, especially the Soviet invasion of Czechoslovakia in 1968. This event and the rise of tension along the Sino-Soviet borders were given top attention by Chinese leaders. In fact, the invasion to a certain extent helped to end the most violent phase of the Cultural Revolution, for Mao was reportedly worried that continued chaos at home might give the Soviets a pretext to apply the so-called Brezhnev Doctrine to China.[15] The border clash with the Soviet Union in March 1969 accelerated the reorientation process. According to some recent Chinese sources, shortly after the clash senior Chinese leaders began to seek fundamental changes in China's foreign policy in order to offset the overwhelming threat from the north.[16] In addition to the change toward the USSR was a somewhat modified perception of the United States. A United States weakened, ideologically if not militarily, as a result of the protracted Vietnam War was seen as less threatening to China. Moreover, the United States' growing concern over the unprecedented expansion of the Soviet Union coincided quite nicely with China's predominant concern. The subsequent Nixon-Kissinger overtures to China, on the other hand, made it possible to shift China's international strategy of opposing both superpowers to one of opposing the Soviet Union while treating the United States as an implicit ally.

The practical implications of this reorientation were enormous. In addition to the Sino-American rapprochement, the road to most advanced countries was cleared. Political and economic relations with the West flourished during the final years of Mao's rule. In 1973, for example, China decided to purchase about US$4.3 billion worth of industrial equipment from the West,[17] the largest such step taken since China received Soviet aid to build its industrial base in the 1950s. The improved relationship with Washington also helped Beijing establish new contact with "pro-U.S." developing countries. In two years (1971–72), twenty-four Third World countries opened or resumed diplomatic relations with China. Simply put, the major shift in China's foreign policy in the early 1970s put China into a much better position to carry out its Third World policy.

After the initial focus on the Sino-U.S. rapprochement, part of Mao's attention was turned to the task of creating a more systematic and theoretical basis for the new policy. The result was his famous "three worlds theory."[18] The theory was first spelled out by Mao in his talk with the visiting president of Zambia, Dr. K. D. Kaunda in early 1974. Later it was formally pronounced by Deng Xiaoping at the Third Special Session of the U.N. in 1974.[19]

Scholars have different views on the meaning of the theory and its real bearing on China's concrete Third World policies. Some tend to view the theory as a device used primarily to support China's call for an alliance against Soviet expansionism.[20] Others see it as an indicator through which the shift of priorities in China's foreign policy since the mid-1970s can be measured.[21] Still others have paid little attention to it.[22]

In reality, the theory has served different functions over different periods. In the early 1970s, it was introduced as a theoretical preparation for the major turn in China's foreign policy. It was also used to offset some of the negative feelings some Third World countries had in regard to the rapprochement and the subsequent close ties between China and the United States. But quickly the theory became a handy device to justify China's concentration on the Soviet Union, and no longer both the Soviet Union and the United States, as the number-one enemy. The famous editorial in *People's Daily* in 1977 transformed Mao's views into a theory.[23] By symbolically putting the Soviet Union and the United States into the same category (the "First World"), but essentially emphasizing in the argument that the former was a more dangerous threat to Third World countries, China was able not simply to call for a stronger Third World vis-à-vis the other two worlds, but to pave the way for the later advocacy of an informal alliance that would include China and other developing countries, most of the Second World—Western Europe and Japan—and the United States in a well-coordinated struggle against Soviet expansionism.

Such a united-front–based strategy had two clear implications for China's Third World policy. In a broad sense, the strategy tied that policy even more closely to its strategic concerns vis-à-vis the two superpowers. Third World policy in this sense became more derivative. It also became less coherent. If China's overall relations with the two superpowers changed, so did the focus and approach of its Third World policy.

In terms of relations with individual developing countries, one of the most striking characteristics of the united-front strategy was the tendency to value these relations primarily according to the degree of a country's "Soviet connections." Those who allied with or supported the Soviet Union were automatically considered adversaries and those who didn't were considered friends. Throughout the 1970s, two themes were often used by China to justify such a black-or-white approach. One was the conviction that because of the weakening of the United States, the USSR had become the only rising and therefore more immediately threatening hegemon. To target anything other than Soviet hegemonism would do a disservice to the world's people. The other was the assertion that the Third World, because of its complexity and strategic importance, was the focus of Soviet expansion. Unlike U.S. imperialism, whose nature was well understood by developing nations, the new Soviet expansionism was less exposed and thus more insidious. It was therefore necessary for Third World countries to "wake up" and submit themselves to the need of building a broad coalition to contain the thrust of Soviet expansion.

Relying on such a rationale, China adopted a two-way but complementary approach toward Third World issues during most of the 1970s. On the one hand, China used almost every available occasion to show its strong opposition to any moves that might help the Soviet Union gain ground in the Third World. China reacted strongly against India's intervention in Bangladesh in 1971 and subsequent actions, warning that such moves would ultimately benefit the Soviet Union.[24] China was equally, if not more, critical, of a series of Soviet actions in Africa and Asia during the mid-1970s, such as the Soviet-Cuban involvement in Angola in 1975 and the Soviet-backed coup in South Yemen in 1977. On the other hand, China was noticeably receptive to events that helped to undermine the Soviets' global influence, sometimes at the risk of contradicting some of their own long-valued principles or practices. For example, China retained its formal relationship with Chile after a bloody coup in 1973 led to the death of the elected president, Salvador Allende, who himself was an old friend of China. Contrary to its longtime practice of standing with the majority of Arab countries, China accepted with even certain warmth the Egyptian-Israeli peace treaty in 1977, a move that was condemned by most Arab nations at that time. The main reason: with the strong U.S. initiative, the move helped keep Soviet influence out of the Middle East. China responded similarly to events in Somalia, Zaire, and the two Yemens in the late seventies.

The united-front strategy reached its peak in the wake of the Soviet invasion of Afghanistan. After that, the factors that made such a strategy attractive began to show their fundamental limitations. By the early 1980s, the strategy had to be dropped.

The most obvious weakness of the strategy was its overreliance on close relations between China and the United States and parallel interests or actions. The illusion of an implicit Sino-U.S. alliance broke down when in its early days in power the Reagan administration seemed to have taken a more pro-Taiwanese stance than its predecessors. While the policy shift on the part of the U.S. did not escalate into a major confrontation between the two countries, it became the direct cause of China's disenchantment with its previous Third World policy. There were other more deeply rooted weaknesses inherent in the policy, too. For example, after being put into practice for a number of years, the united-front strategy often proved to be too simplistic. To base its policy largely on one factor—whether or not the Soviet interest was hurt—China had once again underestimated the need for some developing nations to develop close ties with the Soviet Union primarily for their own interests, economic or geopolitical. To insist on the anti-Soviet criterion helped alienate a large number of Third World states. Furthermore, the striking parallel between the Chinese and American positions on many Third World issues, especially those associated with regional conflicts, aroused suspicion or even resentment from some developing countries, which openly or privately viewed it as evidence of China's increasing deviation from its claimed Third World position.

There was perhaps an even more fundamental motivation for China to drop the grand alliance strategy. As the Chinese concentrated more and more on domestic reform and the modernization drive, to invest huge resources in direct conflict with the Soviet Union in some peripheral areas became increasingly unsupportable. Since many of the benefits of the earlier strategy of grand alliance were exhausted, such as the normalization of diplomatic relations with the United States, to continue such a policy would increase costs without adequate return. For example, to draw a clear line between those who were pro- or anti-Soviet Union prevented China from expanding relations with nations that are subject to Soviet interests. Although significant improvement of relations with the Soviet Union was not a possibility in the early 1980s, to go the other way obviously was seen as detrimental to China's efforts to seek a more stable international environment and, if possible, one more favorable to China's interests. Besides, the deradicalization process on the domestic scene made harsh anti-Soviet propaganda outdated.

Because of these complicated calculations, China decided to undertake another major shift in its Third World policy, though gradually.

THE THRUST OF CHANGES: THE REALITY OF THE PRESENT

Some Background

The end of Mao's era and his policies of political mobilization represents a real watershed in the post-1949 history of China. According to the not exclusively Marxian view that internal and external affairs are intimately related, the revolutionary change in China's domestic system should certainly alter its foreign policy. And indeed it has. In 1982, China adopted a new "independent" foreign-policy line during the 12th National Congress of the Chinese Communist Party.

The exact meaning and nature of this new policy remain a focus of scholarly debate. The basic motivation to stress independence (a de facto repudiation of the previous grand alliance strategy) obviously came from two sources. One is China's understandable promotion of a more peaceful and cooperative international environment. Such a setting is crucial to protect China's modernization drive from being disrupted by unwanted external disturbances; to lessen pressure on China to expand its defense spending so that more resources can be used to assist domestic reform; and to justify domestically the overwhelming concentration on economic affairs. The other is China's intention to increase sharply its participation in normal international economic interactions. It is hoped that these exchanges will provide the country with growing opportunities in trade, inflow of foreign investment, access to advanced technology, and managerial expertise, all of which are essential in China's reform effort. A low-key and economic-centered foreign policy was thought to be necessary to facilitate these exchanges. To translate these key concerns into concrete policy choices, China has, since the early 1980s, reevaluated and rearticulated its basic positions on international relations. The result was what Deng Xiaoping called the two major shifts *(zhuan bian)* in China's foreign policy: the shift from a policy based on the belief that world war is inevitable to the conclusion that such a war can be postponed, if not avoided, for a long period of time; and the abandonment of the practice of drawing policy lines based solely upon a country's connection with the Soviet Union.

These shifts shook the premises of China's previous policies toward the Third World. Changes are inevitable, though by no means easy. Over the last few years, one of the central parts of China's Third World policy initiatives has been the efforts to develop a new policy package that, hopefully, can meet both domestic needs and international concerns.

International Stability and Moral Commitment to the Third World

China's overwhelming concern for international stability has produced a dilemma in its Third World policy: how to realize China's current goals without deviating too far from its stated agreement with the Third World on the necessity of transforming the existing world economic and political system to make it more favorable to developing countries.

Stability has seldom been a priority in China's previous policies toward the Third World. In fact, in all three strategies mentioned above, changes were preferred to the status quo. In other words, as China became more and more interested in benefiting from its contact with the existing international system, there has been an inevitable conceptual gap between what China wants now and what it traditionally promises to do as a self-proclaimed member of the Third World.

Solving this dilemma has proven to be rather difficult. China has yet to provide a comprehensive rationale for its new Third World policy. However, through various and sometimes confusing official remarks, two arguments have been stressed. One is to draw a fine line between what China regards as the long-term goals of the Third World and the urgent needs and necessities in the short run. In theory, China still insists that major changes in current international arrangements, such as those of international trade and finance, are essential especially in the long run to help poor Third World countries escape from their backwardness.[25] On the other hand, when discussing specific measures, China shifts its emphasis to the question of how to meet the more urgent needs of the present. For example, China argues that the gap between poor and rich countries has increased. To speed up their economic development, Third World countries have to learn how to utilize and not simply reject the existing system. Dialogue and cooperation, especially among themselves, are considered to be more useful in Third World efforts to "catch up."[26] To do so, Third World countries need more stability than disruption even if that means prolonging the life of the existing unequal system for a period of time.

Realistically, according to the prevailing Chinese view, many Third World countries will have little chance of realizing their development goals unless they incorporate their own efforts with help from outside.[27] In other words, the North-South conflict notwithstanding, the relationship between the two sides is no longer seen as necessarily adversarial or mutually exclusive. In addition to what Samuel Kim called a shift in China's image of the international economic system from "the *dependent* model to the trilateral model of interdependence,"[28] China now puts more emphasis on the potential benefits than on the negative consequences associated with such interactions. Deng Xiaoping himself made this point when he said, "If China's trade is doubled, from $50 billion up to $100 billion, that means China is able to consume more capital and goods. If it is doubled again, China can consume even more. Doesn't that mean the solution to the problem of finding markets for the advanced countries?"[29] The benefits China can gain through international economic exchanges are equally stressed. Over the last ten years, China has become the fastest-growing trading power among developing countries.[30] The recently announced "outward economy strategy" *(wai xiang jing ji zhan rei)* indicates a further push toward internationalizing the Chinese economy.

To be sure, China is not unaware of possible backlashes associated with integration into the world economy. The rise of trade protectionism, the fluctuation in international monetary markets, and the unstable prices of major Third World exports such as oil— all will have adverse effects on Third World countries such as China. Yet China sees no alternative to working with the North and increasing internal cooperation among Third World states, at least in the short run.

The second argument China has used to solve the dilemma between long-term and short-term goals is to draw a distinction between changes China considers necessary and those that may have damaging repercussions. To call for international stability does not imply that China will oppose all change. On the contrary, in order to maintain long-term stability and minimize negative consequences associated with international exchanges, some changes are considered inevitable and necessary. For example, the 1973–74 oil crisis and the subsequent price hike were welcomed by China as a clear indication of what it called the rising power of the Third World.[31] The 1979 oil price increase provided concrete benefits to China, because the country had increased its oil exports dramatically after the mid-1970s. The move was again warmly applauded. However, the oil glut and the sharp drop in oil prices since 1983 forced China to take a more sober view of this issue. The lowered price of oil cost China about US$3 billion in revenue in 1986 alone.[32] As a result, China began to attach much less political significance to such developments and to focus on working out ways to stabilize the oil market and prices by voluntarily freezing or even cutting its oil exports.

In regard to political changes, China's view is more complex. On the one hand, China still strongly supports national movements, especially those in South Africa and the Middle East. On the other hand, civil and regional wars are no longer automatically seen as agents of necessary changes in the Third World. The emphasis now is on negotiations and peaceful settlement. For example, China used to consider international peacekeeping forces as nothing but instruments with which the major powers could interfere in Third World countries. With this new emphasis on lessening tension, China is now an even stronger advocate of the more extensive use of negotiations in settling regional conflicts such as the one in Cambodia.

To draw these two distinctions does not solve the above dilemma completely. In fact, suspicion and criticism of China's new positions have been on the rise in certain Third World countries. For the current pragmatic leadership in Beijing, however, these theoretical formulations have at least constituted a basis on which the current Chinese treatment of Third World issues can be justified and carried out.

Economic Centrality and Its Accommodations

If policy changes can be measured by how they alter priorities, the growing centrality of economic concerns in China's recent relations with developing countries illustrates how much the nature and characteristics of China's Third World policy have been changed.

Parallel to China's emphasis on international stability, its new Third World policy has put overwhelming weight on the economic dimension. This is in sharp contrast to the previous policies, which were motivated primarily by political considerations.

Take China's economic aid, for example. As we saw earlier, economic aid used to be one of the most important means China had to support its Third World strategies. In a number of cases, the decisions to aid certain countries were made even at the obvious expense of domestic considerations of capacity and need. The percentage of government spending that went to various aid programs ran as high as 6.7 percent in 1972, 7.2 percent in 1973, and 6.3 percent in 1974, the peak years in the history of PRC aid to the Third World.[33] Given the urgent need of China during that period to restructure the economy, which had suffered badly during the early years of the Cultural Revolution, these figures were by any standards much too high even for a well-developed economy, and the decisions to provide such amounts of aid could only be explained in political terms.

This is no longer the case. Even before the Maoist era was formally ended, Chinese leaders decided they could no longer afford such aid programs and began to scale them down. Due in large part to the breakdown of relations with Vietnam, Laos, and Albania, the three largest recipients of Chinese aid, China's economic assistance to Third World countries has dropped sharply since 1977. Chinese aid to the Third World reached a record low in 1982, totaling only US$40 million. In 1983 the figure rose to US$230 million, or about half a percent of the total government budget.[34] However, compared with the US $2.5 to $3 billion spent annually in the early and mid-1970s, the increase was hardly impressive. Chinese leaders have promised on different occasions to increase their aid to Third World countries as China becomes more prosperous.[35] Given the lessons learned from the past and the increasing domestic competition over resources, it is very unlikely that economic aid will return to its central position in China's policy toward the developing countries. Even if the amount of aid is to grow in the future, it will more likely be based on what Chinese officials now call the principle of "mutual benefit" rather than a return to the old de facto practice of making a one-way contribution.

In contrast to the decline of enthusiasm for providing one-way economic aid, China has made great efforts to promote bilateral trade based on conventional terms. Trade is now the most important aspect of China's growing relations with Third World countries. This is consistent with China's overall emphasis on international trade as a major means to boost its economy. According to one Chinese estimate, every 100 million RMB worth of exports will bring in 12,000 new jobs, 35 million RMB in taxes, and many other benefits.[36] For a country that badly needs foreign currency to buy advanced equipment and technology and to pay off the debt it accumulated as a result of large-scale foreign borrowing, an increase in exports is also a key to long-term economic safety and prosperity. It is no wonder that Chinese leaders are now in the habit, while traveling, of devoting a large portion of their time and energy to wooing new customers or trading partners. Zhao Ziyang's tour of Latin America in 1985, for instance, produced fifteen new economic agreements.[37]

However, the actual results of the promotion of trade with Third World countries have been rather modest. The table indicates the amount and distribution of China's trade with the Third World by regions.

While it is difficult to detect a general trend, two things are clear. First, the growth rate of trade between China and the Third World has been much slower than the 22.5 percent annual increase in China's total trade turnover from 1979 to 1985. Second, the share of trade with Third World nations in China's total trade has decreased steadily. Several factors in particular contributed to this relatively poor performance despite the Chinese leaders' strong commitment. First, the drive to increase Chinese exports came during a period when many Third World countries were facing serious payment problems. The worldwide trade boom of the early 1970s ended with a serious slowdown in the late 1970s and early 1980s. Huge debt problems together with slower growth and a shrinking world market for a number of major Third World goods severely limited the ability of some developing nations to buy Chinese products. Second, the nature of Chinese export products is a major obstacle to the rapid growth of exports to other developing countries. The bulk of China's goods sold to these countries are textile and light industrial products. While there is a continued market for this group of goods, expanding sales has become increasingly difficult. More and more developing countries are now producing and exporting the same items China produces. In some rapidly develop-

CHINA'S TRADE WITH THE THIRD WORLD

	Totals, in Million US$			% of China's Total Trade
	Africa	Latin America	Asia	
1982	1,526	1,511	6,406	23.1
1983	1,203	2,035	5,976	21.4
1984	1,234	1,653	7,424	19.3
1985	880	2,570	8,275	16.8
1986	1,000	2,000	8,036	14.9

*Excluding Japan and Hong Kong.
Sources: *Statistical Yearbook of China*, 1985, 1986, 1987 (Longman Group [Far East]).

ing countries, there has been a shift in consumer interest from traditional goods to more sophisticated commodities such as cars, which China is not yet able to provide. On the contrary, because of the industrial restructuring in many advanced states, China found it easier to expand its exports of the above goods to these countries rather than to sell them to Third World states.

In dealing with these difficulties, China has over the past years taken several countermeasures. For example, there has been a renewed interest in barter trade so that trade can be expanded with countries that are short of foreign exchanges. China has increased its production of goods that are high in demand, such as electronic goods, machine tools, and agricultural machines, so that it can maintain and expand its share in the Third World market. China has concentrated on areas where it had few or no trade relations before. Latin American countries, for example, are the main target of China's new trade "offensive." By 1987 twelve Latin American countries had signed trade agreements with China. In 1984, for example, Sino-Brazilian trade reached a value of more than US$800 million, surpassing the amount of Chinese trade with most Asian countries. Although trade with Latin America accounts for only 5 percent of China's overall trade, there have been increasing indications that China has chosen that part of the world as an important market for Chinese goods, services, and technology in the coming years.

Despite these efforts, China's trade relationship with other Third World countries has not been growing as fast as was expected. Partly reflecting the anxiety that China might not be able to reap all the benefits of its open-door policy, recent Chinese commentaries suggest that the government needs a more aggressive foreign policy that takes "economics as command."[38] Such a policy will undoubtedly increase the pressure on China to seek more trade opportunities as it develops relations with Third World countries.

Another indication of the shift of focus from political to economic relationships is China's new willingness and enthusiasm for adopting more flexible forms of economic cooperation. Service export and labor contracting, for example, are becoming more and more important in China's relations with certain developing countries. Traditionally, labor service provided by China was restricted to those services required by the Chinese aid request made by local governments. In recent years, China has spent considerable efforts on promoting the export of labor service by actively participating in international bidding for construction projects, offering a variety of services, including consulting and sharing expertise. By the end of 1988, China had signed about fifteen hundred contracts with over eighty states, a majority of them Third World countries. The export of labor power and other services now contributes over US$5 billion a year to China's overall balance of payments.[39] In recent years, China has been the largest recipient of direct foreign investment among all developing countries.[40] While China received most of the investment from advanced countries, it has shown increasing interest in attracting capital investment from other Third World countries. Financial cooperation between China and some oil-rich Middle East countries, for example, has been flourishing in recent years, with Kuwait taking the lead, and now some initial efforts have been made to draw Saudi Arabia into the circle.[41]

Other forms of economic interaction, such as technology transfer, are also being promoted to tap the economic potential of China's relations with Third World countries. At the same time, Beijing has increased its involvement in the so-called "South-to-South" or intra–Third World cooperation. Such cooperation ranges from creating various regional organizations, to organizing all kinds of associations of producers or consumers, to promoting multilateral consultations and special treatment available only to a certain category of Third World countries. Although a Third World country itself, China has long abided by a policy of not participating directly in regional cooperative organizations. There have been signs, however, that such an approach may have changed. In addition to China's already active role in a number of Asian and Pacific organizations, it is now seriously considering a recent invitation from the U.N. Group of 77 to work more closely with them. If accepted, it could mean a breakthrough in China's long-standing practice of supporting but not participating in Third World organizations. China also increased its involvement in some small-scale but more specific intra–Third World projects. It hosted the 1981 Beijing Conference on South-to-South Consultation and two other major Third World conferences on technological cooperation that were designed exclusively to expedite technological assistance between developing countries. So far, China has offered ninety-eight such programs, on topics ranging from agricultural development to energy-saving techniques, while receiving forty-six programs from other Third World countries.[42]

The growing centrality of economic relations has provided China's Third World policy with the substance it badly needed in order to translate the policy from mainly a political commitment to an enterprise that provides the country with concrete benefits and solidly based influence. In this sense, whether China can develop a viable Third World policy for the next decade depends largely on the ultimate benefits of the above changes.

Bilateral Relations and Regional Policies

A solid Third World policy cannot stop at merely defining broad concerns; it also has to develop specific and differentiated regional and bilateral policies. As part of the general overhaul of its Third World policy, China has in recent years substantially modified its treatment of bilateral and regional issues.

As a policy guideline, China clarifies its principal approach to bilateral and regional issues as follows: (1) China will not try to interfere in any Third World countries' domestic affairs. More specifically, China will not try to divide the Third World along ideological lines, nor will it object to an individual country's right to decide its relations with other countries, including those with the two superpowers. (2) China will make a clear distinction between what it calls "party-to-party" relations and the relations between states. On the one hand, China has in recent years increased its contacts with various parties or political groups. By the end of 1987, it had established or resumed formal relations with over two hundred such parties and groups.[43] On the other hand, however, China has insisted that these relations be restricted to moral and ideological affairs. Largely to allay the long-held suspicions of a number of Southeast Asian countries, Chinese leaders have made this a central point every time they have visited these countries. (3) China will not discriminate against any Third World country in its overall relations with the Third World. It will continue to develop closer relations with "old" friends. At the same time, special efforts will be made to improve relations with countries that have had either few or only hostile relations with China in the past.[44]

To translate these proclaimed principles into concrete actions, China has, in the past several years, taken separate steps to reshape its relations with countries in different regions—Asia, Africa, and Latin America.

ASIA. Among China's relations with the three continents where most of the Third World countries are located, the relations with Asia are perhaps the most complicated and bear the least resemblance to the above policy stances. China's policies toward individual Asian states are more reflective of national security concerns than what their broad Third World policy suggests.

In China, Asia seldom has to be considered as one region. More often it is divided into a number of subregions, such as Northeast Asia, Southeast Asia, South Asia, the Near East, or the Middle East, with each of these areas enjoying quite a different level of attention from foreign-policy–makers in Beijing. Traditionally, China's policy toward these areas seems to have followed two rules: the more strategically important the region is, the more attention it will receive; and the more that a relationship with a country or region requires attention to security concerns, the less emphasis is put on the economic dimension of that relationship. Although far from conclusive, there have been signs that these laws have been broken.

First, while the first rule remains basically true, the content of what constitutes strategic importance has been modified. For example, the Northeast was the traditional focus of China's national security concerns. But in recent years, such focus has gradually shifted to Southeast Asia or even South Asia. Behind this shift was not so much a change in terms of military balance, as people traditionally believed, but a growing realization among Chinese leaders that strategic interests are more than security in the narrow sense and include the maintenance and expansion of an economic and technological edge that helps to attain a regional structure that is least threatening to a country's long-term stability and prosperity. Compared with the Northeast, where the power structure is quite fixed, Southeast and South Asia contain more uncertainties or opportunities that China can use to promote its own interests through more involvement in these regions. This explains why China has invested so much energy in improving relations with India, which resulted in an Indian prime minister visiting China in 1988 for the first time in almost thirty years. Although the trip did not create a breakthrough on the most thorny bilateral issue—the border dispute—the development is in itself an indication of China's shifting emphasis in dealing with its neighbors.

Another interesting development in this respect was China's remarkable efforts to become engaged in Middle Eastern affairs. In

249

1979, when Deng Xiaoping was asked about China's attitude toward the changes in Iran, his answer was, "Our influence there is little or close to zero."[45] Eight years later, the same answer could be completely different. By maintaining close ties with both Iraq and Iran during the war period, China is now in a position to play a special role in the region. One American observer of Chinese foreign policy recently wrote, "For the first time Washington needed Chinese support to achieve its objectives in the Middle East."[46] Although China's exact objectives in the Middle East remain unclear,[47] it seems China has enlarged its definition of strategic interests to include concerns over the immediate need to secure markets or funds to lay the ground for a future active Chinese role in the region. It is perhaps because of these redefined goals that China reacted unusually quickly to the beginning of direct talks between the U.S. and the PLO by holding the first meeting between Chinese and Israeli foreign ministers early in 1989.

The second rule lost even more relevance in China's recent relations with Asian countries. Not only has its trade volume with South Korea far surpassed that with North Korea, but there have been reports that China is now considering resuming and increasing trade with Vietnam should the latter honor its timetable to withdraw its troops from Cambodia.

These changes—the reordering of strategic concerns based on a broadened perception of China's short- and long-term interests and the reduction of the interference of purely strategic concerns in normal economic relations—have already reshaped and will continue to reshape China's relations with Asian countries in a very significant way.

AFRICA. To many, Africa seems to be the biggest loser as a result of the new policy China has adopted since the early 1980s. Previous Sino-Africa relations had been built upon three key factors: (1) *China's aid.* African countries as a group ranked second to Asia in the amount of aid received from China. One Chinese official estimated that by 1983 each African country had received on average US$313 million worth of aid from China;[48] (2) *Mutual moral and political support.* For years, when it came to issues like its return to the U.N., China could count on African states for support most of the time. Similarly, China has been one of the most vocal supporters of the political demands of African nations, ranging from the calls to establish a new international economic order to the struggle against apartheid; (3) *The Soviet connection.* Containment of Soviet expansion in Africa has long been a major factor in making policy concerning China's relations with individual countries. China's policy toward Angola was a clear example of this.

However, because of the recent changes in China's foreign policy in general and in its Third World policy in particular, all these factors have lost their prominence in China's policy considerations. There have already been some complaints from the local media that China has overlooked its traditional friends in its new policy initiatives.[49] Politically, this may not be true. In recent years, senior Chinese leaders have frequently traveled to a large number of Third World states. According to the distribution of these visits, there has been no evidence that China has chosen to neglect Africa. On the contrary, Chinese leaders seemed particularly sensitive in balancing these visits. In 1985, for example, there was an almost even distribution of such visits: Hu Yaobang, then general secretary of the CCP, visited four South Pacific countries; Li Xiannian, the head of state, visited Burma and Thailand; Zhao Ziyang went to four Latin American countries; Tian Jiyun, a senior vice-premier, traveled to five African nations; Yao Yilin, another senior vice-premier, went to three Middle Eastern countries. If we take into account Zhao Ziyang's eleven-nation tour of Africa in 1983 and the large number of African leaders who have visited China, we get the impression that in the realm of foreign relations, Africa remains high on China's list of priorities.

The more serious problem in Sino-African relations, however, has to do with stagnant economic relations between the two sides. Part of the cause of the problem was the increasing reluctance on the part of China to offer special treatment to African countries. When Zhao Ziyang visited Africa in 1983, he was reported to have written off 100 million RMB worth of debt Zaire owed to China.[50] But beyond that, the trip did not bring many new aid programs. Under Beijing's new emphasis on domestic development, it is very unlikely that China will be willing to substantially increase its economic assistance to African countries, since some of them have already surpassed China in terms of per capita income. The challenge to Chinese leaders therefore is to find alternatives to the previous bases of the Chinese-African relationship without committing itself to new and costly undertakings.

Chinese leaders seem fully aware of the above dilemma. A number of steps have been taken to improve the situation. One is to invite African leaders to visit China more frequently for political consultations. In the first quarter of 1987, for example, twelve African leaders visited China, by far the largest group in this category. Furthermore, Chinese leaders often chose to make major policy statements during these meetings so that the political significance of these occasions could be highlighted. Another step is to increase China's participation in small- and medium-sized projects in Africa. Unlike some previous projects, such as the building of the expensive Tanzania-Zambia railway, these projects are more affordable. For example, China recently has promised to help establish several centers in Africa to train local agricultural, technical, and managerial personnel.[51] Finally, China seems to have adopted a more "evenhanded" approach toward African states. Traditionally, China's efforts in Africa tended to concentrate on countries that were either ideologically radical or politically "pro-Chinese." The new policy calls for the development of relations with almost all African countries, with special emphasis on cultivating closer relations with states with which China has had little contact before, such as the Ivory Coast and Liberia.

How effective these measures are remains to be seen. Compared with the past, China's new approach toward African countries is low-keyed, yet substantially more balanced.

LATIN AMERICA. Compared with its treatment of Africa, China's enthusiasm for improving relations with Latin American countries and the initial results of that improvement are astonishing. After having almost no formal relations with the region (with the exception of Cuba) throughout the 1950s and 1960s, China now has opened diplomatic relations with twenty-one countries that account for over 90 percent of the population and four-fifths of the total GNP of Latin America. China has provided aid to a half dozen states and signed trade agreements with twelve countries in Latin America. In 1988 China's trade with Latin America was more than double that with Africa. More important, there have been increasing signs that the trade figures will continue to rise. China and Peru, for example, are now studying the possibility of coinvesting in some major mining projects. If implemented, China will become the major trading partner of Peru. Sino-Brazilian cooperation in the production of military equipment such as aircraft and electronic devices is unique in China's relations with the Third World.

The political relationship between China and Latin America is also good. China has long been a supporter of many of the region's political or economic demands, such as the 200-mile fishing-zone rights, the nuclear-free zone declaration, and the eleven debtor-nation group's demand for renegotiation of payments. Second, geographic remoteness used to be a major factor in keeping the two parties apart. But this remoteness also means that China has had fewer discords with Latin American countries than with Asian. When Zhao Ziyang visited Latin America in 1983, the main thrust of his talk was about the bright future rather than the past. In recent years, there has been a significant increase of top-level visits between China and Latin American states.

However, there are a number of obstacles that have to be removed in order to achieve real breakthroughs. The lack of mutual understanding is one of them. China has recently increased its efforts to train adequate personnel who are capable of promoting bilateral relations or helping to design regional policies. Furthermore, the debt crisis hit Latin America the hardest. Although the direct impact of the debt problem on Sino–Latin American trade is minimal given the small amount of turnover, the negative consequences of such a problem—Mexico's overall trade has stagnated for a number of years while Brazil's shrank several billion dollars—may eventually put a serious restraint on the fast growth of this trade.

Evaluations

This brief overview of China's policy toward the Third World during the 1980s has revealed some of the main characteristics of the new policy:

- The new policy is more pluralistic than its predecessors. Unlike the revolution strategy or the united-front strategy, which tended to rest China's relations with the Third World countries on a single premise, the new policy gives sufficient attention to factors other than strategic or ideological concerns. China, in dealing with Third World issues, whether bilateral or regional, has become more sensitive to the existing variant situations, more adaptive, and is concentrating more on opportunities than on declared principles. While such an approach often causes confusion, and the actual results are less impressive than those China achieved in terms of its growing relations with advanced capitalist and socialist countries, it helps China to maintain its ties (as in Africa) or increase contact (as in Latin America) with Third World countries at a time when the available resources are drastically reduced.

• The new policy is more domestically oriented. If there is one feature that exemplifies the change in the nature of Chinese foreign policy, it is certainly this. Despite public statements that suggest otherwise, the formation and implementation of China's new policy toward the Third World is motivated by direct domestic demands, such as the need for capital and markets. Political commitments become relevant only if they are in accordance with the country's self-interests. This does not suggest that previous policies were motivated solely by altruistic reasons. However, the overwhelming emphasis on economic ties and benefits puts the new Third World policy more in line with the kind of policies China adopted in dealing with other nations.

• The new policy is more effective and more difficult to manage. Because of the above changes, the current Third World policy seems to be more effective than any previous policies in a number of ways. First, it has been less costly. Secondly, it has helped to deliver more tangible benefits to China's domestic undertakings, and to maintain and in some cases expand its influence (as in the Middle East). Finally, the new flexibility and pragmatism implied by the new policy has helped to open a wide range of options through which, if continued efforts are made, China can expect to further expand its relations with the developing countries in a mutually beneficial manner.

However, the cost of success is also substantial. One of the major problems resulting from recent policy changes is the increasing difficulty of managing the more diversified and multiple-channel relationships the changes have brought about. In addition to confusion and perceivable inconsistency, a minor blunder such as China's sale of arms to Middle Eastern countries can often have serious repercussions. A serious challenge, therefore, is how to narrow the gaps between rhetoric and actual policy, between ambitious plans and effective means, and between the increasing complexity of relationships and the lack of adequate institutions and personnel to manage them.

THE FUTURE OF CHINA'S THIRD WORLD POLICY

The past has taught, and China seems to have learned, that the Third World is not a unitary entity. Its political, cultural, and economic diversity makes it impossible to use any simple strategy in dealing with its many states. This diversity and the complications arising from it have caused China to face the limitations on its influence in the Third World and to modify its ambitions accordingly. Moreover, the effectiveness of China's policy initiatives toward the Third World depends not only on its own calculations, but even more on the responses of the targeted developing nations. To overestimate China's ability to influence the course of the Third World is utterly unprofitable. On the other hand, the experience of recent changes has indicated that the Third World is an area in which China still possesses huge potential for maneuverability. China's concentration on economic modernization and domestic affairs need not exclude its active role in Third World affairs. On the contrary, provided that a careful and balanced policy package is available, both China's short-term and long-term interests in world affairs can be promoted by its strengthened relations with other developing countries.

To develop such a policy is by no means easy, as the history of the last three decades reveals all too well. Whether or not China will be able to pursue an effective Third World policy depends primarily on how it defines its interests and appreciates the constraints.

China's basic interests in the Third World for the next decade have two distinctive aspects. On the one hand, the nature of China's modernization programs and its major security concerns suggest that its main interests in external affairs in the next decade will continue to lie in its relations with the West and the East, not the South. Even within the broad category of China's relations with Third World countries, a large portion of its attention will be given to its ties with more immediate neighbors.

On the other hand, China's interests in the Third World as a whole remain substantial. Politically, to continue China's strong support for the common cause of the Third World serves two purposes. China's willingness to maintain its identity with the Third World will certainly improve its image among most developing countries and help to ward off criticism that by integrating itself into the current international economic system China's role as an independent force in the international arena has been weakened. At the same time, to be closely allied with Third World countries is consistent with China's overall objectives in world affairs. In fact, the two most frequently addressed themes in China's foreign-policy statements—the need to promote peace over conflict and to aid development, including that of the Third World—require China to look more carefully into issues with which the developing countries are deeply involved. A world of peace and prosperity is unthinkable unless major problems the Third World is facing are addressed. China's recent call to establish a new international economic *and* political order reflects a reconfirmation of this belief.[52]

In a more practical sense, a strengthened political relationship with the Third World will provide China the support it needs especially during the next decade, when China is expected to play a larger role in a number of international and regional issues such as arms control and the settlement of regional conflict.

Economically, as China continues its current reform effort and open-door policy, the development of various types of economic relations with Third World countries will remain an essential part of China's new international economic strategy. In an era when politics is economics and economics has largely to do with foreign economic relations, focusing on economic issues that have direct bearing on its modernization program has been and should be the centerpiece of China's new Third World policy. In the short run, trade with developing countries not only widens the market but provides the trade surplus China needs to partially offset the deficit resulting from its trade with advanced countries. The inflow of investment from Third World countries and the transfer of technology contribute directly to China's development. In the long run, such strengthened economic relations will help to enhance China's international position and to increase the available resources it needs in order to become a real world economic power. Furthermore, the relatively low level of current economic interaction between China and other Third World countries suggests that there are huge potentials to be explored.

Finally, there are reasons to believe that China's strategic interests in the Third World may also grow. Recent years have already witnessed a two-dimensional effort on the part of China to adjust its strategic concerns in a changed world. On the one hand, there has been considerable movement to diffuse conflict with the Soviet Union so that the direct strategic threat can be reduced. On the other hand, there has been a tendency to broaden the definition of "strategic interest" to include areas where China has little direct interest at the moment but, as the capacity of the Chinese economy grows, where its involvement will certainly expand (such as the Middle East). China does not have to follow the superpower example of commiting itself to extensive military and regional arrangements, but in order to secure its flourishing economic ties with these regions, China will have to participate more actively in regional negotiations or cooperative efforts.

To sum up, it would be wrong to conclude that Third World issues will play no more than a peripheral role in China's future foreign policy. Nor would it be fair to predict that the proportion of its energies China devotes to its relations with the Third World countries will decline as it bids for more integration into the existing international system. Yet to define these interests is one thing; to promote them in an effective way is another. The latter requires a clear and realistic understanding of the constraints the country faces and what possible policy means are available to maximize China's interests under these constraints.

The first constraint is, of course, the increasing complexity of the Third World itself. On one hand, the Third World is getting poorer as a whole. On the other hand, it has become more differentiated internally than ever before. A small group of countries recently considered developing countries have now become newly industrialized countries. But a large number of them remain poor; some of them are even worse off than before. According to a recent World Bank report, the real growth of GNP of developing countries in the first half of the 1980s is 3.46 percent, slightly over half of what it was in the previous fifteen years.[53] The income gap between developing and advanced countries more than doubled between the early 1950s and the mid-1970s. The share of exports from developing countries in the world market was down from 28 percent in 1980 to less than 19 percent in 1986.[54] Other issues, such as the debt crisis and persistent low prices for major Third World exports, are also threatening the future of many Third World countries. Such a bleak picture increases the difficulties China has in dealing with the Third World. The slower growth, for example, means fewer opportunities to expand economic relations. The worsening domestic situations can lead to more crises in Third World countries, which may in turn cause violent fluctuations in the international system, something China's current leaders do not want to see.

The Third World is also more differentiated. Today there are probably more conflicts than common ground among many developing countries. For the Chinese leaders, this means that a viable Third World policy has to address both the general problem the Third World faces and the specific issues that affect individual states. In other words, to coordinate different aspects of its Third World policy becomes increasingly crucial to its success. This problem is further complicated by the fact that no matter what, China's policy toward the developing nations will always have a superpower factor behind it. The strong anti-Soviet orientation of the 1960s and 1970s to a large degree dictated China's Third World policy during those years. In recent years, there have been more clashes between China and the United States over a number of symbolic and substantiative issues concerning the Third World. As China becomes more and more deeply involved in regional issues, these conflicts could lead to adverse effects on China's relations with other countries: witness the strong U.S. reaction to China's sale of antiship weapons to Iran and intermediate-range ballistic missiles to Saudi Arabia.

In short, China is now dealing with a more divided Third World. To be effective, China's new Third World policy has to be more discriminating on the one hand, and better coordinated on the other. Although not entirely impossible, the complexity is such that China is likely to take a trial-and-error approach that means more ad hoc decisions and, very likely, more mistakes. How China deals with this challenge will to a large degree determine the final outcome of the new policy.

The second major constraint on China's Third World policy is the limited resources that it can invest in its efforts to develop relations with Third World countries. This has been a problem all along. Writing in 1981, Harry Harding said that "despite its enormous size and population, China has relatively few material resources to devote to its policy toward the Third World."[55] Seven years later, this assessment is still valid, if not more so. At least in the short run, China will not have much more to offer than it does now. A more productive Third World policy therefore requires more effective use of the existing resources.

However, despite some of the recent innovations and improvements we mentioned above, the efforts to carry out a more efficient Third World policy has been impeded by several factors. It is true that because of its longtime commitment to the cause of the Third World, China can partially substitute material support with moral or political support. Yet, as one Chinese official put it, you cannot always send good wishes without providing substantial evidence.[56]

China at some point will have to increase its aid to certain key developing states if it wants to maintain the basic momentum in its relations with the Third World. China's ability to effectively implement its new policy is seriously compromised by the country's lack of sufficient personnel who know Third World issues well and are capable of generating feasible policy recommendations and of then putting those policies into practice. For example, despite government efforts, the study of the Third World as a major field in China has been actually declining. Even the limited resources available are mostly used in areas where relations with more advanced countries are the prime concern. Unless immediate measures are taken, China's new Third World strategy, however promising in rational analysis, may not ultimately turn out to be what it should be.

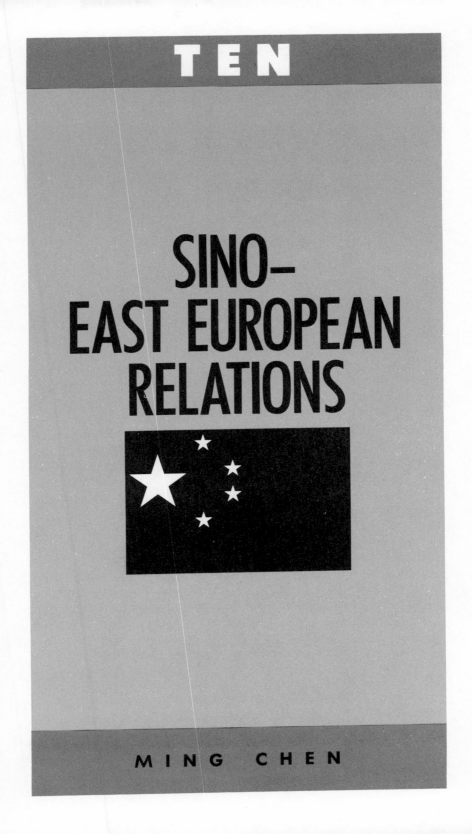

TEN

SINO–
EAST EUROPEAN
RELATIONS

MING CHEN

INTRODUCTION

China's relations with Eastern Europe have shown remarkable progress in the post-Mao period. While strengthening its special ties with Romania and Yugoslavia, China has conspicuously improved its relations with the five loyalist East European countries—Poland, East Germany, Hungary, Czechoslovakia, and Bulgaria[1]—and has renewed some contacts with Albania.

Both sides have displayed a marked interest in developing relations. During 1985 and 1986, there was an unusually frequent high-ranking diplomatic exchange between China and the majority of the East European countries.[2] But what has motivated China to warm up again, and at such a tempo, its long cooled-off relations with the five loyalist East European countries, while also greatly strengthening its traditional ties with Romania and Yugoslavia? And what are the major motives on the part of East European countries for promoting their relations with China? What are the characteristics of their present relations? Finally, what will be the general trend of development in their relations? These questions will be discussed in the following sections.

Generally speaking, the first decade of China's relations with Eastern Europe (from 1949 to 1959) could be compared to their honeymoon, in which China, as a member of the socialist family headed by the Soviet Union, maintained a close relationship with almost all of the Communist East European countries except for Yugoslavia, whose development constituted a deviant model of building up socialism. During this period of close cooperation, China was a leading trade partner of these countries, and they in turn joined the Soviet Union in helping to build China's industrial base almost from scratch.

For the majority of the Chinese leaders at that time, Eastern Europe was both remote and unfamiliar. As a consequence, they

263

depended heavily on Soviet views of East European problems. One example was the ostracism of the so-called Yugoslav revisionist clique from the socialist family. Tito looked in vain to Mao Zedong for an ally in resisting pressure from Stalin.[3] The unrest in Eastern Europe in the wake of de-Stalinization in 1956 involved the Chinese as an intermediary between the discontented East Europeans and Krushchev, who was then too weak to handle both domestic power struggles and East European unrest simultaneously. During his trip to Eastern Europe in the winter of 1956, Zhou Enlai canvassed for the solidarity of the Soviet-led socialist family. While the Chinese prevented the Russians from militarily crushing the Polish uprising of 1956, they urged the Soviets to invade Hungary to restore Communist rule. Nineteen sixty, when open Sino-Soviet disputes broke out, was a watershed in Sino–East European relations, which ended China's honeymoon with most of the East European countries, except for Albania and Romania.

RAPPROCHEMENT WITH THE LOYALISTS

For a long time, China's relations with East Germany, Czechoslovakia, Bulgaria, Poland, and Hungary, the so-called loyalists, involved a minimum of trade and cultural exchanges. Experts and economic aid from those countries were withdrawn from China in 1960, together with such assistance from the Soviet Union. Soviet arguments were piously published by their media, while the Chinese view was unfairly treated. Some countries were more active than others in vilifying the Chinese, sometimes even outdoing the Soviet Union. Czechoslovakia, for example, went so far as to expel Xinhua News Agency correspondents from Prague in 1963, much to the anger of Beijing.[4] The reasons for this almost unified support for the Soviets were varied, but two were particularly important: The first was the Soviet domination over Eastern Europe. At the Bucharest Conference in 1960, for instance, Khrushchev exerted such strong pressure on East European countries that they did not even venture to approach China. Second, the Chinese position was too radical to be acceptable among most East Europeans. Mao's apocalyptic vision of an atomic war with imperialism sent shivers down the spines of East Europeans and dampened any possible enthusiasm for Beijing.[5] To make matters worse, the Chinese talked only to the converted, seldom trying to influence even potential sympathizers. Thus, in their fight for allies against the Russians, the Chinese became "their own worst enemies."[6]

During the late 1970s and early 1980s, relations did not notably improve. Beijing and Moscow, though interested in improving relations, were involved in a series of incidents that created friction between them. One was China's punitive invasion into Vietnam in early 1979. All of the loyalist countries without exception joined Moscow in condemning China and stiffened their stance toward improving ties with China. Even Hungary's János Kádár, with whom China had achieved the most progress, assailed China in uncommonly harsh terms.[7] The other was the Soviet invasion of Afghanistan in late 1979, which in the eyes of the Chinese constituted "a severe challenge, comparable to the invasion of Czechoslovakia in 1968."[8] For the first time in the postwar period, the Soviet Union sent its troops beyond the East European realm, using the Brezhnev Doctrine as a pretext. The Chinese called off further negotiation with the Soviets, thus dimming immediate prospects with the East Europeans.

Not until 1983 did Chinese relations with the five East European countries begin to undergo marked improvement. With the further implementation of the open-door policy, China gradually restored exchanges with the loyalist East European countries in the fields of the arts, sports, journalism, tourism, and others. There were exchange visits between the vice ministers of foreign affairs of China and the five loyalist countries. Later, the Chinese and East European foreign ministers began to hold regular talks during the annual session of the U.N. General Assembly. This was soon followed by exchanges at the level of vice-premier, and recently even heads of state.[9] China also signed long-term trade agreements and established bilateral committees on trade and economic, scientific, and technological cooperation with these countries.[10] According to official Chinese sources, in the coming five-year period, the value of trade between China and the member states of COMECON will reach US$32.6 billion, of which trade with the Soviet Union will account for more than half, or $16.38 billion, Romania $6.5 billion, Poland $3 billion, East Germany and Czechoslovakia each $2.1 billion, Hungary $2 billion, and Bulgaria $468 million.[11]

China has maintained a specific interest in developing its relations with Hungary, which has been adopting a rather mild position toward China and making progress in its economic reforms. Besides Hungary, China achieved significant improvement in its relations with Poland and East Germany as well. The Chinese and Polish vice-ministers of economics exchanged visits in 1985. The vice-chairman of the Chinese National People's Congress, Wang Renzhong, visited Poland in 1985; and in return, Polish Parliamentary Marshal Roman Malinowski went to China in June of 1986. Wojciech Jaruzelski's visit in September of 1986 was the first top-level visit to China from the loyalist circle in more than twenty years. In 1984 China signed a ten-year agreement on economic, trade, scientific, and technological cooperation with Poland, and the two governments set up a committee to implement the agreement. The exchange of goods in 1985 was 2.8 times that of 1984.[12] Also, China and Poland set up general consulates respectively in Shanghai and Gdansk.[13] In the case of East Germany, there have also been frequent exchange visits of senior officials. East German Party leader Erich Honecker was the second top leader in the loyalist circle to visit China in 1986.[14]

China's policy toward the loyalist East European countries is determined mainly by two factors: China's domestic political and economic developments, and its relations with the Soviet Union. Since the death of Mao and the downfall of his radical followers in 1976, the new leadership in China has pursued an increasingly pragmatic policy that focuses on a search for development programs capable of realizing the Four Modernizations by the end of the twentieth century. The new Chinese foreign policy, influenced by these domestic policy shifts, adopts an international posture, which is closer to the developing countries, a bit more aloof from the United States and its Western allies, and less antagonistic to the Soviet Union. It was within this general framework that China began to seek détente with the Soviet Union and develop relations with other pro-Soviet socialist countries.

Politically, China has undergone a process of reassessing the character of the loyalist regimes. In his report to the 12th National Congress of the Communist Party of China on September 1, 1982, then General Secretary Hu Yaobang devoted a whole chapter to the significance of China's independent foreign policy. He pointed out that the Five Principles of Peaceful Coexistence are applicable to China's relations with all countries, including socialist countries.[15] This gave a clear signal that China was ready to improve relations with socialist countries, though he did not specify which countries were socialist besides Romania, Yugoslavia, and North Korea. However, then Premier Zhao Ziyang's routine government work report in 1983 offered the answer. Having observed the "friendly feelings" that the Chinese people cherished for the East European people, Zhao indicated that China's relations with those countries would continue to improve and expressed a growing Chinese interest in the achievements and experience in their "socialist construction," thereby acknowledging openly the "socialist" character of those countries.[16] In the last few years, Chinese officials have emphasized time and again to visiting East European officials that China's policy of opening up to the outside world would mean opening up to both Western capitalist countries and East European socialist countries.[17]

Not only has China reassessed the character of the loyalist regimes, but also the role of those states in the international arena. The Chinese have given up their old view of these countries as being the vassals of the Soviet Union, and instead have emphasized that they constitute an important force in safeguarding peace.[18] China now seeks to promote Sino-Soviet détente through a wider cooperation with those East European countries.

The Chinese overture also represents a significant effort to increase Chinese influence among foreign Communist parties.[19] In his report to the 12th National Congress of the CCP, Hu Yaobang expressed the willingness of the Chinese party to develop its relations with other Communist or working-class parties in strict conformity with Marxism and the principle of independence, complete equality, mutual respect, and noninterference in each other's internal affairs.[20] The Chinese had followed the restoration of party ties with Yugoslavia during Tito's visit to China in 1977 with exploratory contacts with some of the major West European Communist parties, leading to the restoration of party relations with the Italian Communist Party in 1980 and with the French Communist Party in 1982. As for the loyalist East European parties, the Chinese slowly built contacts with the East German party beginning in 1982, and to a slightly lesser extent with the Hungarian Communist Party.[21] By 1987 the Chinese party had resumed party-to-party relations with all the loyalist parties.

Since China and the East European countries all follow Communist ideology, there were fewer political and ideological side effects for China to be concerned with as a result of developing ties with East European countries. While maintaining an open-door policy to the West, the Chinese leadership has been very watchful for the invasion of Western ideas—the so-called "spiritual pollution"—and its perceived dreadful consequences. The Chinese leadership has repeatedly made it clear that while absorbing advanced science and technology, universally applicable ways of administration and management, and healthy cultures from countries throughout the world, including developed capitalist countries, China should reject capitalist thinking and social systems that maintain exploitation and suppression, and all the "ugly and rotten things" of capitalism.[22] This attitude partially helps explain the Chinese refusal to join Western governments in condemnation of the Polish suppression of Solidarity in 1981. The Chinese leadership showed a certain distaste for Solidarity lest a comparable independent trade union might emerge in China. The organization of the Chinese economy and the structures of Chinese enterprises may differ in certain important respects from those of loyalist Eastern Europe, but there are sufficient similarities for Chinese leaders to fear the emergence of a similar movement in their own country.[23]

Economically, through the long-term agreement on barter trade with East European countries, China exchanges its agricultural products, raw materials, and textile goods for steel and industrial equipment from Eastern Europe and is thus able to avoid the kind of trade friction that has developed with Japan, the United States, and other Western countries, while reducing its dependence on the West by dispersing its trade markets. For example, with regard to textiles, while protectionism is on the upsurge in the United States, the Soviet Union and the East European bloc have become the second largest market for Chinese textile products.[24]

In addition to the benefits of trade, China has found herself in need of closer cooperation in the fields of science and technology. Chinese officials openly acknowledge that science and technology have developed rapidly in Eastern Europe in the past twenty years, with some areas reaching advanced world levels. In recent years, China and the East European countries have been exploring ways for further cooperation in these fields. Proposals range from the transfer of scientific and technological results and cooperation in soft science to the holding of academic symposiums. At present, there are approximately three hundred cooperative science and technology projects between China and East European countries, involving coal mining, machine manufacturing, agriculture, environmental protection, water conservation, geology, construction, food processing, railways, chemicals, electronics, and meteorology.[25] Moreover, some old equipment of the 1950s from the Soviet Union and East European countries has needed to be fixed up and furnished with spare parts. According to Chinese estimates, around three thousand technological items from the East European countries are needed to transform existing enterprises.[26]

The economic benefits that China may enjoy also include experience in socialist construction in Eastern Europe. In this regard, Hungary has attracted special attention from the Chinese for its outstanding achievements in industrial production, foreign trade, and some other fields. The reason lies in the systematic program that Hungary has implemented to rationalize its management, such as stimulating production efficiently in accordance with the market and endowing enterprises with their proper right of self-autonomy and management. There have been exchanges of experience in economic reform. While sending groups of experts to study reform in Hungary, China has also invited Hungarian economists to visit China. For instance, from October 24 to November 24 of 1985, a group of leading Hungarian economists visited China for a scholarly exchange on economic problems.[27] In his trip to Hungary in 1987, Zhao Ziyang expressed his hope of learning from Hungarian experience.[28] Meanwhile, the Chinese may also benefit from studying their problems, such as the debt crisis prevalent in Eastern Europe, as China itself is inevitably bound to encounter some of those problems on its own way to modernization.[29]

The majority of the loyalist East European countries also have good reasons to improve their ties with China. The major obstacle to improved relations, Soviet opposition, seems to have been removed. Strictly speaking, East Europeans had no basic conflict of national interests with the Chinese. The most important reason for their unanimous siding with the Soviet Union in the Sino-Soviet split was the pressure from Moscow. For the Soviets, the Sino-Soviet split enhanced their traditional stake in Eastern Europe. In a real sense, Eastern Europe provided not only the physical basis but also the ideological justification for the Soviet Union's claim to superpower status, both toward the West and toward the rest of the developing and Communist world.[30] Therefore, the Soviets could hardly tolerate any different positions among its East European partners with regard to the Chinese Communists, who challenged Soviet ideological authority. None of those countries could depend on China to counterbalance Soviet pressure. China was a regional power, far from Eastern Europe. As then Chinese Premier Zhou

Enlai once remarked to a Yugoslav journalist, "Faraway water cannot put out fires."[31]

Beginning in the early 1980s, both the Soviet Union and China displayed increasing interest in improving relations with each other, while Soviet-American relations were apparently deteriorating during the first few years of the Reagan administration. The Soviet Union wished to strengthen its bargaining position vis-à-vis the United States by speeding up the process of détente with China. The Soviets regard the rapprochement between post-Mao China and East European governments as part of their own drive for closer ties with the Chinese.[32]

After a period of substantial development during the early 1970s, economic growth in loyalist Eastern Europe slowed drastically and almost ceased by 1980. In contrast to the 1971–75 plan period when "produced national income" in Eastern Europe grew at an average of 7.3 percent per year, the growth rate in the 1976–80 period dropped to about half of that, or 4 percent. Poland, the largest East European country, managed only a 1.6 percent average annual gain. By 1981 there was an overall negative growth rate in the East European bloc.[33] Moreover, most of those countries are carrying a growing burden of foreign debt. Poland's total debt in convertible currency, for example, stood at US$29.3 billion in December 1985.[34] This severe economic recession desperately needs to be reversed. And China is now carrying out an open-door policy, devoting major efforts to developing the economy. Having similar economic systems, East European countries would find in China a good partner for economic and trade cooperation. One consideration of importance is the balance of trade. Most of the loyalist East European countries have serious problems in that area and profitable new trade agreements with China would help control their trade imbalance. China is a very good source of consumer goods, such as textiles, which are in short supply in Eastern Europe. And Eastern Europe would also have an excellent market in China for its machine tools, which are not very popular in the West.

CONSOLIDATED TIES WITH YUGOSLAVIA AND ROMANIA, AND SIGNS OF A THAW WITH ALBANIA

China has for some time maintained a close relationship with Yugoslavia and Romania. Since Mao's death, exchanges at the level of party, government, army, and people have been extremely frequent. In 1978, on the tenth anniversary of the Soviet invasion of Czechoslovakia, the chairman of the Chinese Communist Party and premier, Hua Guofeng, visited Romania and Yugoslavia and signed agreements with both of them on the establishment of intergovernmental committees on economic, scientific, and technological cooperation. They also signed protocols on trade and cooperation in other fields.[35] This was soon followed by the visit in 1983 of the succeeding general secretary of the Chinese Communist Party, Hu Yaobang.

After the Soviet invasion of Czechoslovakia, China began to mend its fences with Yugoslavia, the chief target of Chinese ideological attack for many years and yet an East European country free from Soviet domination. To China after 1968, struggle against the menace of social-imperialism was to take precedence over the ideological disputes with revisionists. In February 1969, the first Yugoslav government delegation in nine years arrived in Beijing and negotiated a trade protocol on March 17. In November of the same year, Yugoslavia upgraded its diplomatic relations with China to the ambassadorial level, and set up a direct shipping line to China in February of 1970. The visit to China by Yugoslav Secretary of State for Foreign Affairs Mirko Tepavac in June of 1971 led to the inauguration of the first Yugoslav industrial exhibition in Beijing in December of that year. Belgrade was chosen as a link in China's international airline network. In 1975, when the chairman of the Yugoslav Federal Executive Council, D. Bijedic, visited China for the first time in many years, Mao praised President Tito for standing up to oppression and showing firmness as strong as iron.[36]

In 1977 Yugoslav President Tito paid an official and friendly visit to China at the invitation of the Chinese government. By then both sides had given up completely their long-term ideological discord. Tito's visit was highly appreciated in China. *People's Daily* commented that Tito's visit would promote the development of the just united struggle against hegemonism waged by various peoples, and the progressive cause of national liberation and social emancipation in various countries.[37] In 1980, when Tito died, the Chinese government sent a delegation led by Hua Guofeng to attend his funeral. Hua praised Tito as a great Marxist and an outstanding proletarian revolutionary.[38]

China's relationship with Romania, on the other hand, is one of a tested friendship. After the Sino-Soviet polemics broke into the open in the early 1960s, Romania was the only East European country to publish both sides of the argument, most notably the exchange of public letters between the Soviet and Chinese Communist parties, thus maintaining some neutrality in the conflict.[39] The essence of the Romanian position, as Kenneth Jowitt has rightly summed up, was that relations between ruling Communist parties and governments should be based on cooperation, with the right of dissent and nonparticipation, rather than on the principle that all decisions should be made unanimously.[40] These viewpoints were beyond doubt highly appreciated by the Chinese Communists, who considered Romanians close friends at the Bucharest Conference.

For the past twenty years and more, the two nations have signed agreements and conducted extensive cooperation in a wide variety of areas ranging through politics, economy, science and technology, culture, sports, public health, journalism, and international tourism. Since 1971 President Ceauşescu has paid four official visits to China; three of them were made after Mao's death (1978, 1982, and 1985). None of the other East European heads of state can possibly beat his record. On the occasion of Ceauşescu's fourth visit, Chinese President Li Xiannian guaranteed once again that China would never swerve from its policy of developing full-fledged Sino-Romanian relations. Diplomats in Beijing noted that China's reception of its Romanian guest went far beyond the conventional red-carpet welcome accorded to a visiting leader.[41]

The common strategic interest China shares with the two Balkan countries has obviously been the main reason for the three to strengthen their ties with each other: a nonaligned Yugoslavia and an independently minded Romania in the backyard of the Soviet Union have been and will continue to be of special significance to China in its efforts to counter the Soviet drive for domination and expansion; and on the other side, the two countries find their close ties with China an important chip in their bargaining with the Soviet Union for more political and economic benefits, though they can never rely on China for any substantial support to counter Soviet military intervention.

China, Romania, and Yugoslavia have also shared an intense interest in economic cooperation. Romania was the thirteenth-biggest importer of Chinese goods and the fourteenth-biggest exporter to China in 1983,[42] while China was among the top ten principal trading partners of Romania in the same year.[43] Although China and Yugoslavia are not each other's major trading partners, the two countries have an increasing interest in expanding their economic cooperation. Furthermore, China has cultivated a deep interest in the Yugoslav model of building a socialist economy, which is characterized by the direct participation of workers in enterprise management and the endowment of private enterprises with rights of self-autonomy. Through the efforts of more than twenty years, Yugoslavia has gradually worked its way into the ranks of the industrially developed countries. The Chinese leaders have repeatedly emphasized the Yugoslav experience in creating a system of socialist self-administration.[44]

As for China's relations with Albania, there are already signs of a thaw after a period of almost ten years. In 1983 trade relations were restored, and the two countries' vice-ministers of foreign trade exchanged visits.

Albania used to be the staunchest ally of China in the Sino-Soviet split. It obtained substantial economic aid from China after it broke relations with the Soviet Union in early 1960. According to Chinese official sources, Albania received more than one hundred items of economic and military aid. Beijing spent more than US$5 billion on Albania and sent more than six thousand engineers and technicians.[45] Sino-Albanian discord could be traced back to the Kissinger secret visit to China in 1971. As far as Albania was concerned, China had abandoned its dual role in the struggle against both the Soviet revisionists and the U.S. imperialists by seeking détente with the United States and supporting both NATO and the Common Market,[46] thereby losing its revolutionary militancy. But the open split took place after Mao's death and the downfall of the Gang of Four in 1976. In the Notes from the Central Committee of the Albanian Party of Labor in 1978,[47] China was grouped with the United States and the Soviet Union. The Notes supported the view that Enver Hoxha, Albania's leader, allied himself with China's Gang of Four and was unable to accept Hua Guofeng and Deng Xiaoping.[48] In response to the escalating Albanian diatribe, China suspended all military and economic aid to Albania and withdrew its military and economic experts.[49] Tirana immediately retaliated by suspending, in September of the same year, bilateral trade, as well as scientific, technological, and cultural cooperation between the two nations.

After the death of Enver Hoxha in 1985, fifty-nine-year-old Ramiz Alia took power. He was faced with the problem of how to expedite Albania's economic development. During the four decades when Enver Hoxha controlled Albania's domestic and foreign policy, progress did occur in the economy and in education, but Albania lagged behind its immediate neighbors. In fact, the economic gap between Albania and other European nations has now widened. Hoxha's isolationism as well as his system of highly centralized management have delayed the country's technological development to the extent that Albania is now in a position much inferior to that of its neighbors.[50] During the past few years, the Albanian government has been tacitly readjusting its domestic and foreign policies, somewhat revising its ways in order to increase its international contacts. In December 1985, an Albanian vice minister of foreign trade arrived in Beijing and signed an agreement on trade and payments for the period from 1986 to 1990.[51]

THE FUTURE DYNAMICS OF SINO–EAST EUROPEAN RELATIONS

Over the next few years, there are three possible trends in China's relations with the loyalist East European countries. The first could be the rapid rapprochement between China and the whole Soviet and East European bloc on the one hand, and quickly soured relations between China and the West on the other. The realization of this possible trend would be largely determined by developments within China. The internal strife around the political and economic reforms has become so sharp in recent years that a series of reshufflings has taken place within the party and the government, which first led to the dismissal of some leading reformers from their posts, such as Hu Yaobang in early 1987, and then to a major frustration of conservatives in the 13th National Party Congress in October of the same year. As reform still has an extremely tortuous road ahead, it is possible that the conservative school may take over power within the party and the government.

In such a case, the current reform would be reoriented. Political control would be tightened, and China would probably reexamine its open-door policy. Politically, China would cut back its ties with the West while strengthening its cooperation with the whole Soviet and East European bloc, although the alliance relationship that China enjoyed with the latter countries during the 1950s would not likely be reestablished. Economically, such a change would bring about a dramatic increase in trade between China and Soviet-bloc countries, and the latter would greatly increase their supply of technology and industrial equipment to China; in contrast, China's economic activities with the West would be greatly reduced. And China would study more seriously East European models of economic reform while playing down the role of the Western model. Culturally, China would regard the Soviet and East European bloc as a major source for training its students and cadres, if not the only one. China would try by every means to get rid of the influence of Western ideology and bourgeois culture. In sum, China's door would be more open to the East and less open to the West.

Yet as long as the basic conflict over national interests between China and the Soviet Union is not thoroughly resolved, China is not likely to consider any sort of partner relationship with either the Soviet Union or its East European allies. In addition, given the present scope of its cooperation with the West, China could not afford to cut all its Western economic ties. Since the inauguration of the open-door policy, for example, a few thousand joint ventures with the West have been successfully launched and the influx of Western capital is expected to reach US$20 billion by 1990.[52]

The second possible trend is the dramatic deterioration of relations between China and the loyalist East European nations as a result of the escalating conflict between China and the Soviet Union. In spite of his initiatives to promote détente with the West and with China, Mikhail Gorbachev will not likely give up Soviet control over Eastern Europe. In a speech to the Central Committee of the Soviet Communist Party immediately after his appointment as general secretary, Gorbachev affirmed his determination to "preserve and strengthen in every way the fraternal friendship of our closest friends and allies—the countries of the great socialist community."[53] On the other hand, the loyalist East European countries will still be highly dependent on the Soviet Union for energy and trade. If Moscow were to put new restrictions on energy exports to its East European partners or to demand that they significantly reduce their trade surplus vis-à-vis the Soviet Union, their economies could be gravely undermined. In addition, they are extremely vulnerable to any major Soviet military action.

The possibility of a renewed Sino-Soviet conflict can hardly be totally excluded, even though the Soviet Union has made some efforts toward overcoming the major barriers (i.e., the Soviet troops stationed along the Sino-Soviet and Sino-Mongolian borders, the Soviet invasion of Afghanistan, and the Soviet support of the Vietnamese aggression against Cambodia) that Beijing put forward.

Should this trend come true, Beijing and Moscow would heighten their contention in Eastern Europe. While working more closely with Romania and Yugoslavia, Beijing would try to stir up the troubled water. Besides bringing up old topics such as the Soviet economic exploitation and hegemonistic practice in that area, Beijing would find new opportunities in the Polish dilemma and the succession problems in the coming years. The military suppression by the Polish authorities in December 1981 put the situation under temporary control, but it failed to solve the structural problems, which may give rise to new crises. For the foreseeable future, Poland is likely to remain a political tinderbox in the area, one that could ignite a chain reaction among the rest of the East European countries, thereby making Soviet control more difficult. To make things worse, the heads of a number of East European nations, who have been in power for a long period, are now already over seventy. The imminent change in leadership may have a destabilizing effect, particularly if several leaders depart simultaneously.

Under the present circumstances, the new Soviet leadership, however, will continue to encourage its East European allies to take a lead in warming up their relations with China so as to help bring about a breakthrough in Sino-Soviet détente, which would, in their eyes, greatly improve their position in dealing with the Americans. They have been very active in recent years in making overtures to China, including an offer to withdraw a substantial number of Soviet troops from Mongolia,[54] the withdrawal of all the Soviet troops from Afghanistan, and the Soviet pressure upon Vietnam to withdraw from Cambodia.[55] But no matter how much relations between China and those countries may improve, the latter will not be expected to venture into the independent position that Romania and Yugoslavia have taken in regard to Sino-Soviet interaction. Should Sino-Soviet détente catch a cold, the East European countries' relations with China will immediately sneeze. The Chinese are fully aware of their situation and are prepared to deal with the mutual relations "objectively,"[56] without expecting too much of them.

The third and most likely possible trend is the continuation of the ongoing process of rapprochement between China and the loyalist East European countries, without estranging China from the West. Such a trend takes the successful continuation of the current reform as an indispensable precondition, as failure of the reform may bring China closer to the East. The new Chinese leadership that emerged from the 13th National Party Congress in 1987 seems to be determined to carry out China's open-door policy and to push ahead the current reform program. The second most important precondition is the blessing of Moscow, without which any substantial progress in China's relations with the loyalists would be difficult. In the foreseeable future, Gorbachev would continue to promote Sino-Soviet détente and, as a part of his *perestroika* and *glasnost,* would promise more freedom for his East European allies—as long as this freedom would not constitute a serious threat to Moscow's authority over those allies—and would encourage their varied forms of reform on the basis of their individual experiences.[57]

Under such circumstances, China would most likely continue to stress the priority of "economic diplomacy" characterized by foreign-affairs efforts serving "peace, development, and the Four Modernizations." Economic cooperation takes precedence over political relations, and the former's success will promote the latter.[58] China would play down the role of ideology even if it maintains close party-to-party relations with all those countries. China's goal is to mobilize all the positive factors both in the West and in the East to help realize its modernization program. Therefore, China would carefully maintain a balance between its relations with both major blocs.

On the East European side, the era of consumerism is clearly over. The problem of economic growth will be high on the agenda of the East European leaderships for the next decade. Most Western experts foresee a general continuation of slow annual growth of 2 to 3 percent for the first half of the 1990s. As a resumption of the high growth rates of the early 1970s is highly unlikely, several countries could fall back into the crisis or near-crisis conditions of the early 1980s.[59] Their trade positions with both the West and the Soviet Union will continue to deteriorate, posing significant problems for these countries. In addition, Western banks are likely to be much more cautious about lending to Eastern Europe. Consequently, East European countries will find it much more difficult to obtain credit to expand their production capacity and finance their debt service. Therefore, economic considerations will remain high on their agenda in foreign relations. The main thrust of their relations with China will thus lie in the field of economic cooperation, though political relations will be correspondingly elevated.

With the continued economic recession, many East European countries may find it increasingly desirable to experiment with less rigid mechanisms to restructure their economies. This trend has been boosted by Soviet *perestroika* and *glasnost* and Gorbachev's enthusiastic encouragement of his East European allies to conduct wide reforms within the bloc. East European countries are becoming more and more interested in China's experiences in introducing market mechanisms, the expansion of the private sector, and economic cooperation with the West. History also shows that attempts to reform the economies in those countries usually help increase the tendency toward political independence from the Soviet Union.

Such a tendency, however, could not possibly lead to the sudden and complete loss of Soviet domination, since the Soviet Union will tolerate independent tendencies only within the scope of the integrity of the bloc. Any attempt to break away from the bloc in one strike, as the 1956 Hungarian rebellion did, would without doubt be ruthlessly suppressed by the Soviet military, in spite of Gorbachev's expressed interests in lessening Soviet control of those countries.

China, Romania, and Yugoslavia will continue to value and to consolidate their traditional ties because of their common strategic and security concerns. Their relations will remain largely free from the influence of Sino-Soviet interaction.

There are, however, unstable factors in the two countries that may deprive China of its two most trustworthy friends in Eastern Europe in the coming years. Yugoslavia is now entangled in a number of difficulties. In late 1985, foreign debt stood at US$20.7 billion. The rate of inflation reached 79.5 percent in 1985, the highest level in Europe.[60] Violent regional conflicts and various ethnic rivalries have been aggravated by the general decline in living standards throughout Yugoslavia. These developments may lead to the erosion of Yugoslavia's independent foreign policy, turning on a green light for added Soviet influence.

Romania too, will probably have increasing difficulties in the coming years. Although the country succeeded in reducing its total foreign debt from a record US$10.2 billion at the end of 1981 to $4 billion in 1985,[61] it now faces growing public dissatisfaction and work stoppages as a result of the austere measures it resorted to for accomplishing this, such as curtailment of imports and domestic consumption. Romania's policy is not likely to change radically as long as Ceauşescu is in power; however, once he passes away, there is a possibility that the country may move toward unity with the Soviet Union in foreign policy. China may then lose its only foothold within the Soviet Bloc.

As for China's now frozen relations with Albania, their future will be largely decided by Albania. Under the present circumstances, any dramatic thaw is unlikely. Although Ramiz Alia has made moves to improve Albania's relations with its neighbors and to increase foreign trade, this does not necessarily suggest that he intends to stage a turnabout in domestic or foreign policy. A radical departure from Hoxha's path in the foreseeable future may prove politically too risky. All things considered, Hoxha's domestic and foreign policies succeeded in maintaining Albania's independence and in promoting its economic modernization, though in a very sluggish way. Furthermore, China's new economic policy is ideologically unacceptable to the Albanians. Finally, Albania is now in a position to endure the consequences of economic self-reliance that it could not have withstood without Chinese assistance in 1961.[62] Therefore, there is little impetus for Albania to promote its relations with China in a dramatic manner, not to speak of returning to the "good old days," when they were close comrades-in-arms. While China has kept its door open to this poorest European country, Ramiz Alia's Albania has only shown limited interest in resuming a trade relationship with its former partner.

CONCLUSION: CHINA'S POLICY OPTIONS

Among the three possible trends, the third and the most likely one is obviously the most favorable to China. In the first, China would lose its independent stance, and its role in the international arena would be correspondingly reduced. Moreover, Washington and its Western allies would cut back or even completely suspend financial and technological aid to China. As for the second, it would be both costly and risky for China to escalate its conflict with the Soviet Union. China's cooperation with loyalist East Europe would come to a halt, and all the accompanying political and economic benefits would be lost, so China would have to rely more deeply on the West, even to the extent of seriously harming its own national interests. The third possible trend, however, would leave China in its favorable position in the triangle of the Soviet Union, the United States, and China, as well as in the triangle of the Soviet Union, loyalist Eastern Europe, and China, so that China would have much more maneuverability in dealing with the other two sides in the two triangles. Therefore, it is in China's interest to help maintain the present tendency of both domestic and international developments.

To do so successfully, China should continue to keep a good balance in its relations with the West and the East. China's foreign policy should be genuinely independent. While developing its ties with the Communist East European states, China should continue to play down the significance of a common ideology and base its contacts with the ruling East European Communist parties firmly on national interests rather than on ideological cohesion. China should avoid any forms of military cooperation with those countries so as not to frighten its Western partners. In the coming decade, further cooperation between China and the West will continue to play a key role in helping realize China's modernization program. China will continue to depend much more heavily on the West than on the East for funds and advanced technology. Any attempt to return to the kind of relations it had with Eastern Europe in the 1950s will be extremely harmful to China's interests.

Second, China should keep a balance in its relations with the loyalist East European countries and the Soviet Union. On the one hand, China should continue to promote its economic and political relations with those countries, thereby affecting the centrifugal tendencies of those countries away from the Soviet Union; on the other, it should not take open and active advantage of any discord between Moscow and those countries, as it did constantly during the past two decades. In the coming years, Soviet domination over the loyalist countries will not likely be so weakened as to collapse in the face of external or intrabloc challenges. Any vigorous challenges from China will lead to a renewed Sino-Soviet cold war, thus ruining China's relations with those countries, while severe challenges from those countries will lead to harsh reactions from Moscow, such as political and economic pressure and possible military invasion, therefore also having unfavorable impacts on China's relations with both the Soviet Union and the loyalist countries.

In terms of its relations with Yugoslavia and Romania, China should continue to strengthen its traditional ties with them, helping to tide them over the present difficulties through expanded cooperation with preferential terms, because a stable Yugoslavia and Romania will remain an important asset for China in maintaining and expanding its interests in this area while curtailing the Soviet influence. This assistance, however, should not take the form of large-scale free economic aid, which could on the one hand impose too much of a burden on China's already strained economy and on the other weaken the very basis of its independence. Historical experience also shows that this kind of aid can produce very negative results, as, for example, in China's relations with Albania and Vietnam.

As for its ties with Albania, China should continue to leave its door open to this poorest European country, which is still dominated by a rigid ideology and strong nationalism. Although it may conduct some moderate readjustment, Alia's Albania will largely preserve the legacy of Enver Hoxha in the coming years. While maintaining only some trade relationship with Albania in the foreseeable future, China can at least be consoled with the fact that the continual existence of an independent Albania in the Balkan Peninsula will accord with China's interests.

ELEVEN

BEIJING'S POLICY ON HONG KONG

ZHIDUAN DENG

In September 1982, Beijing issued a strongly worded statement after British Prime Minister Margaret Thatcher's China visit initiated an unsuccessful talk on the Hong Kong 1997 issue:

> It must be pointed out that these treaties which involve the Hong Kong area were products of British imperialism's "gunboat policy" and invasion of China in the 19th century. These treaties, which were forced on the Chinese people, provide an ironclad proof of British imperialism's plunder of Chinese territory. The Chinese people have always held that these treaties are illegal and therefore null and void. . . . Whoever today tries to cling to these unequal treaties will only awaken the memories of the British imperialist invasion of China in the minds of the people in China, Britain, and the whole world.[1]

When Britain's Queen Elizabeth II and her husband Prince Philip visited China four years later, in October 1986, two years after an agreement on Hong Kong had been signed, they were given a warm reception wherever they went in the country. Deng Xiao-ping, the most prominent figure in China's post-Mao political picture, greeted the queen by saying, "Please accept welcome and regard from an elderly Chinese. The fine weather in Beijing also shows a sign of welcome to you."[2] The Chinese press declared that the queen's visit represented a milestone in the history of Sino-British relations.[3]

Apparently, the reason the queen could enjoy such a compliment while her prime minister could not was Beijing's satisfaction with the agreement on Hong Kong signed by the two sides in 1984. As Deng indicated, with the settlement of the Hong Kong issue, the task facing China and Britain is to develop their cooperation and friendship.

What will be Beijing's next statement regarding the Hong Kong issue when the British leader visits China in the near future? Between now and 1997, there remains less than a decade of transition before China regains its sovereignty over Hong Kong. During this period, Beijing's policies regarding Hong Kong will become increasingly crucial. After several years of efforts, a draft of the Basic Law for Hong Kong was announced on April 28, 1988, in Beijing. During the following five months of opinion polling in both mainland China and Hong Kong, the lawmakers collected more than seventy thousand comments from individuals and social groups regarding the draft.[4] According to Beijing, revisions and adjustments of the draft will be made in reference to the comments and suggestions.[5] It appears that, from this time on, a basic framework for the social, legal, political, and economic systems of post-1997 Hong Kong is coming into being. In the face of such a situation, local residents in the territory will feel increasingly pressured to decide their future settlement. Likewise, foreign investors will be better aware of potential benefits and risks in the Hong Kong market. The Taiwan regime will have more knowledge with which to respond to Beijing's call for reunification. China watchers around the world will also have more evidence with which to analyze Beijing's credibility and capability in the post-Mao era. And finally, the Chinese leaders will have to take more responsibility for what happens in Hong Kong, for better or for worse. Thus, in the following years Beijing will be challenged to demonstrate its capacity and readiness to regain sovereignty over Hong Kong. From this point, analysis of China's forthcoming policies on Hong Kong in the next decade is of both academic and practical importance.

This paper speculates on Beijing's Hong Kong policies in the next decade by examining the factors upon which the policies have been and will be made, such as Beijing's perception of the issue, its political and economic needs in regard to Hong Kong, its limitations in dealing with the issue, and its considerations of policy benefit and costs. It is the author's understanding that Beijing's policies on Hong Kong are products of interactions among all the factors stated above. Therefore, the author will incorporate as much as possible these factors when dealing with different aspects of the issue, although they will still be discussed individually in the paper.

The structure of the paper is fivefold: (1) China's positions in the development of the issue; (2) the interest factors underlying China's positions; (3) Beijing's strategies toward Hong Kong; (4) the limitations and dilemmas facing Beijing with regard to the issue; and (5) Beijing's possible policies in the next decade.

It is important to point out that Beijing's Hong Kong policy, like all policies, is subject to change according to China's political situation and the mentality of the Chinese leadership. To a great extent, China's domestic situation in the next decade will be a decisive factor influencing its policy on Hong Kong. During the post-Mao period, China's political and economic situation has undergone dramatic changes. The desire for economic and political reforms seems to have dominated Chinese politics up to the end of 1986. The "antibourgeois liberalization" campaign in early 1987 and the reshuffling of the leadership were signs of an increased conservative influence in China. The current leadership, with Zhao Ziyang as the party general secretary, Li Peng as the premier, and Deng Xiaoping behind the scenes but having the last say in politics, is paying more attention to administrative and economic efficiency than to political democratization in China. In this regard, if Beijing can keep its promises of not extending the political changes from the mainland to Hong Kong and if, as Zhao pointed out, China will not do anything harmful to the stability and prosperity of Hong Kong,[6] what has thus far been successful in the Hong Kong settlement will probably continue along its way. But if the Chinese political situation suffers from a serious setback in the next decade, the future of Hong Kong, like that of China as a whole, will be overshadowed by political uncertainty. As Zhang Wuchang, professor of economics at Hong Kong University, comments, "If China continues its 'open door' policy, it will be the most positive factor to Hong Kong. The future of China is the future of Hong Kong."[7]

BEIJING'S POSITIONS AND THE DEVELOPMENT OF THE ISSUE

The negotiations between Beijing and London over Hong Kong can be divided basically into three phases. The first phase began when the issue was raised by the British government in 1982 and lasted until the signing of the Sino-British agreement on Hong Kong in 1984. During this period, Beijing formulated its policy on Hong Kong, stood up to the British tough position over the question of sovereignty, and succeeded in getting concessions from London. The second phase of interactions was between the date of the Joint Declaration and mid-1985. The smooth relations between Beijing and London over this period were symbolized by the approval of the agreement by both sides and the founding of the Joint Liaison Group. Meanwhile, Beijing embarked on its full-scale political and economic penetrations in the territory. In the third phase, beginning in late 1985, Beijing accused the British government of "deviation" from the Joint Declaration over the issue of political reforms in Hong Kong. Also, Beijing speeded up its efforts to draft the Basic Law, hoping to institutionalize political development in the territory. With the British making further concessions regarding the political system in Hong Kong, Beijing has considerably increased its influence upon local affairs.

In general, Beijing's basic positions, as indicated in both the Joint Declaration and the Basic Law draft, involve four aspects: first, sovereignty over Hong Kong; second, maintenance of Hong Kong's social and political stability; third, continuation of prosperity in the territory; and fourth, maintenance of the current system and life-style in Hong Kong, labeled as "one country, two systems" after China resumes its authority. Since the Hong Kong issue was first raised in 1982, Beijing has made great efforts to interpret these positions, to crystallize them through various actions and policies, and finally to put them in the draft of the Basic Law.

To the Chinese leaders, sovereignty over Hong Kong appears to be the most important principle involved in the issue. Seemingly, Beijing's strong stance in this respect has not so much to do with its Communist nature as with the notion of national integration. In the early stages of negotiation between China and Britain from the late 1982 to early 1983, Mrs. Thatcher insisted that the British rights drawn from the three nineteenth-century treaties concerning Hong Kong be ensured and that the issue of the colony be settled "legally."[8] This position appeared to have enraged Beijing, which saw the treaties as unequal and humiliating. To counter the British position, Beijing insisted that London's acknowledgment of China's sovereignty over Hong Kong be the basis on which to negotiate the issue.[9] Beijing also rejected London's stance that the "British presence" in Hong Kong after 1997 is a condition for stability and prosperity of the region as a "de facto renewal of the unequal treaties."[10] During the whole process of negotiation, Beijing made its position clear: the principle of sovereignty is not negotiable. It appears that Beijing was so attached to the issue of sovereignty that it was ready to stand up to London by any means, even at the expense of Hong Kong's economy.

Maintenance of Hong Kong's social and political stability has been another of Beijing's major positions over the issue. It is obviously in China's interest to resume sovereignty over the territory without facing serious local instability. But at the very beginning of the discussions, the Chinese leaders were well aware of the fact that the Hong Kong issue would bring about different kinds of instability in the area. To Beijing, therefore, if the issue could be settled in the earliest possible time, the situation in Hong Kong would be least endangered. Thus, when the confrontations between Beijing and London led to a series of panics in Hong Kong, the Chinese government accused London of being unable to ease the instability in the territory. In addition, Beijing increased its pressure on Britain, saying that China would announce its plans for Hong Kong unilaterally if no agreement was reached quickly, and even that China might resume sovereignty before 1997 if "special problems" such as "turmoil" arose in Hong Kong.[11]

In the Joint Declaration, Beijing and London agreed that the Hong Kong government bears responsibility for preserving the social stability of Hong Kong during the transitional period. It is clear that Beijing's notions of stability basically rest on maintenance of Hong Kong's current social and political system. To Beijing, methods taken by the Hong Kong government to improve the efficiency of administration are welcome, but any changes of social or political structure that will possibly lead to instability in Hong Kong are not acceptable. Since the declaration, a major political event in Hong Kong has brought about serious concerns among the Chinese leaders and even triggered another dispute between Beijing and London.

The event that bothered Beijing involved the political reforms planned by the British government. Early in July 1984, the Hong Kong government issued a green paper titled "The Further Development of Local Representation in Hong Kong," proposing that certain seats in the Legislative Council (LEGCO) be decided by local election.[12] In late November of that year, a formal document, or white paper, was announced. The paper suggested a shift from the previous appointive system to an elective system through several steps in the following three years.[13] To the British, since the transfer of sovereignty over Hong Kong to Beijing is a given, the best they can do for the people in Hong Kong appears to be to develop a local political structure that will enable the local population to exercise a certain influence in the politics of this future special administrative region. To create a representative authority in Hong Kong during the transitional period, in March 1985 Hong Kong held the first election for district legislative members. In October an indirect election of twenty-five unofficial LEGCO members was held. In March 1986 the City Council membership was elected.[14] According to the initial plan of the Hong Kong government, if possible, a direct general election of LEGCO would be held in 1988 after the political reform was reviewed in 1987.

Beijing's attitude toward the political reform in the territory has been considerably negative. On different occasions, Chinese officials criticized such reforms as deviations from the Sino-British agreement.[15] The political reform appears to worry the Chinese leaders because it raises the possibility of new instability in the territory. Since the elections in recent years have stimulated a considerable degree of party politics in Hong Kong, the Chinese leaders are apparently concerned about the development of a situation that they feel will be difficult to handle in the future. In Beijing's view, since the Joint Declaration stipulates the creation of a Basic Law to regulate the future of Hong Kong, what is developing in the territory should not conflict with the forthcoming Basic Law. In the face of tremendous pressure from Beijing, the Hong Kong government had to cancel its plan for the direct LEGCO election in 1988 and decided to postpone it until the early 1990s.

The third position Beijing holds is that prosperity in Hong Kong must be preserved. After decades of development, Hong Kong's economy has become one of the miracles of Asia. Subjectively, since the Hong Kong issue was raised, the Chinese leaders have demonstrated concerns that this "golden goose" would be damaged by different negative factors. Frustrations in the Hong Kong market such as the decline in the value of the Hong Kong dollar, economic panic caused by the move of the Jardine group from Hong Kong to Bermuda, and a series of local business bankruptcies are matters of serious concern in Beijing's policy considerations. While putting pressure on the British government to maintain the economic order in the area, Beijing has been careful not to contribute to the local business instability by excessive policies. In the face of a considerable outflow of local capital,[16] Chinese officials have tried from time to time to convince businesses in Hong Kong that maintenance of prosperity in the territory is also the major policy consideration in Beijing and that the capitalist market should continue to operate after China regains its authority.[17] At the same time, China has increased its commercial and financial investment in Hong Kong in recent years to create new sources of funds for local manufacturers and real estate developers. Moreover, to maintain the stability of the local monetary system, Beijing has joined the Hong Kong government in bailing out certain financially troubled banks, including Hang Lung Bank, the Overseas Trust Bank, Jia Hua Bank, and You Lian Bank.[18] In October 1987, the stock market of Hong Kong was at the edge of collapse because of the worldwide stock market crash. Among the efforts taken to save the local monetary system from trouble, the Bank of China provided about US$54 million in standby credit.[19] Another effort has been Beijing's approach to the local "patriotic businessmen," in the hope that they can contribute to the preservation of prosperity in Hong Kong. It appears that, since Beijing has won over the British in the issue of sovereignty and managed to influence local affairs in Hong Kong, the question of how to maintain prosperity in the territory is becoming predominant in the Chinese policy agenda.

The continuance of the current system and life-style in Hong Kong after 1997, as China's fourth position, represents Beijing's basic perception of the territory. Although the Chinese leaders have said that this position is "one of respect for history,"[20] the implications go far beyond the understanding of the issue from a historical point of view. It appears that the Chinese leadership is well aware of the fact that there are substantial social, economic, and political differences between China and Hong Kong. If Beijing arbitrarily imposes on the area a system incompatible with local conditions, the current dynamics in the society will be undermined and the local resistance will become strong. Also, maintenance of the current system in Hong Kong is and will be in the interest of China's reunification with Taiwan. Such economic and political considerations, both in the short term and the long term, motivate Beijing to apply this experimental model of "one country, two systems" as a solution to the future of Hong Kong.

INTERESTS UNDERLYING BEIJING'S POLICIES

Over the years, in the development of the Hong Kong issue, several factors appear to have contributed to Beijing's policy considerations. These factors, having crystallized Beijing's basic interests in previous years, will apparently continue to underlie China's positions in the next decade.

In the first place, the principle of national integration served not only Beijing's interests in the Hong Kong issue, but also laid a basis for handling the issues of Macao and Taiwan later. Actually, while Beijing was negotiating with London over Hong Kong, it also faced the task of dealing with Portugal on the future settlement of Macao, an issue that had been put aside for several years because of Chinese domestic instability. In 1974 Portugal offered to return Macao to Beijing. This was declined by the Chinese leaders. In the following year, Beijing signed an agreement with Lisbon allowing Portugal to continue its rule over Macao.[21] But when the Hong Kong issue was brought up after the Chinese domestic situation had improved, the time for China to settle the Macao issue also came. Three years after the Sino-British Joint Declaration, the Macao issue was settled to Beijing's great satisfaction. Four rounds of negotiation between China and Portugal in less than a year, from June 1986 to March 1987, were reportedly colored by friendly and cooperative attitudes on both sides.[22] Being well aware of Beijing's strong position on the issue of sovereignty, Lisbon did not bother attempting to bargain with Beijing in this regard. On March 26, 1987, both sides signed a Joint Declaration regarding the future of Macao.[23] By the terms of the agreement, Beijing will resume sovereignty over Macao in 1999.

Although the Taiwan question does not involve regaining sovereignty from a foreign government, the essential appeal in Beijing's drive for reunification with Taiwan also rests on the notion of national integration. Beijing's "one China" position on the Taiwan issue, which it has held for nearly forty years, has not been based solely on nonrecognition of the Nationalist (or Kuomintang) legitimacy, but more important, on the notion that China as a country cannot be dismembered. There is good reason to believe that Beijing will, as it has repeatedly stated, resort to military force if Taipei announces its independence. In this regard, had Chinese leaders given any concession to London over the issue of national integration, it would have seriously undermined Beijing's position of reserving the right to take justifiable action over the Taiwan issue.

Second, Hong Kong is of vital economic importance to China. China receives over 35 percent of its annual foreign earnings from exports to and through Hong Kong and from investment there. As China has substantially increased its exports since 1980, Hong Kong plays the important double role of consumer of Chinese goods and entrepôt between China and its global trading partners. For example, Hong Kong enjoys thirteen favorable advantages in U.S.-Chinese entrepôt trade, including roles in training Chinese managers and analyzing policy changes in China, technology transfer, availability of China experts, banking service support, connections to Chinese trading companies, geographic location, housing facilities, information collection, international communications, and recreation facilities.[24] Apparently, Hong Kong also merits these advantages in commercial connections between China and many other countries. In 1986 China's exports to Hong Kong amounted to about US$7 billion,[25] second only to Japan, the largest exporter in value to the area. In 1987 Chinese exports to Hong Kong increased to a value of US$12.5 billion and made the territory China's largest trading partner, with the total bilateral trade value totaling US$20.6 billion, followed by Japan with US$16.5 billion.[26] Hong Kong is also one of the best places for China's overseas investments. In 1986 China's investments in Hong Kong topped US$5 billion, ranking first in foreign investment in the area.[27]

Not only has Hong Kong provided China with an ideal market for exports and investment, but the territory has also helped China's modernization by making a great number of investments, by providing an infusion of technology and managerial skills, and by exporting goods to the mainland. From 1980 to 1984, direct foreign investment in China totaled about US$1.38 billion; Hong Kong contributed about 80 percent of the total.[28] In 1986 Hong Kong investment in China was over HK$10 billion, an increase of 83 percent over 1985.[29]

The territory also plays an important role as an access point for foreign investments flowing to China. Hong Kong has long been considered an excellent location for the regional headquarters of foreign firms. Since 1984 an increasing number of foreign companies have announced plans to establish new regional offices in Hong Kong. A major reason was the fact that some viewed Hong Kong's increasingly close ties with China as providing an opportunity to approach the unfamiliar Chinese social and economic setting.[30]

Third, Hong Kong has been playing an important role in Beijing's "unofficial" approaches to Taiwan and countries that have no diplomatic relations with China. In recent years, Beijing has exercised its relatively successful "economic diplomacy" in Hong Kong. Countries such as Indonesia and South Korea have substantially increased trade with China through Hong Kong.[31] Despite the fact that Taipei prohibited local businesses from dealing with China for decades, indirect trade between the mainland and Taiwan via the Hong Kong market has increased in recent years. In 1983 the total value of trade between the two was reportedly US$265 million. It increased by more than 100 percent in 1984 to a value of US$554 million. In 1985 trade between the mainland and Taiwan reached US$1 billion.[32] Politically, Hong Kong has provided Beijing with an ideal site for settling disputes. In 1985 representatives of both Beijing and Seoul met in Hong Kong to discuss the issue of a Chinese torpedo boat trespassing in South Korean waters.[33] Also, in mid-1986 officials from Beijing and Taipei gathered in Hong Kong for the first time in more than thirty years to settle the China Airlines incident that occurred when a pilot of the Taiwanese airline defected to the mainland and left his colleagues and the plane to be claimed by Taipei.[34] Since early 1987, Hong Kong has become a key channel for the increasing number of people who hold Taiwanese passports and want to visit China. Under growing domestic pressure, in July 1987 the Taipei authorities lifted the ban on direct trips to Hong Kong from Taiwan in order to facilitate a "detour" to the mainland for "unofficial business."[35] Because of its traditional status as politically neutral, Hong Kong has provided both Beijing and Taipei with a theater in which to perform more flexible policies toward each other and in foreign relations. From this point of view, it will also be in China's interest to maintain the status quo in Hong Kong.

Finally, the model of "one country, two systems," which Beijing applies to solve the problem of Hong Kong, represents China's long-term interest of national integration. In the Joint Declaration signed by Beijing and Lisbon regarding the future of Macao, the settlement basically followed the Hong Kong model. According to Beijing, the use of "one country, two systems" in solving the Macao issue was another great success after Hong Kong, and the two settlements will generate far-reaching impact on the regime and the people of Taiwan.[36]

Early in the late 1970s, prior to the emergence of the Hong Kong transfer issue, Beijing began calling for reunification with Taiwan. Despite Beijing's continuous offensive, the resistance of the Taiwan regime remains strong. Realistically, more than three decades of separation between the mainland and Taiwan, considerable social and economic differences between the two sides, and the continuance of a strong anti-Communist attitude in Taiwan make it difficult for Beijing's drive to achieve immediate success. Moreover, unlike the Hong Kong and Macao issues, Beijing has little dominant influence upon the Taiwan question. In this situation, the "one country, two systems" solution to the Hong Kong problem appears to be the only feasible basis upon which Beijing can work on the Taiwan issue. Therefore, whether Beijing can successfully implement such a model in Hong Kong will be a crucial factor in its efforts to "achieve national integration."

BEIJING'S STRATEGIES REGARDING HONG KONG

Based on its interests and objectives, Beijing has gradually hammered out a set of policies to shape the political and economic development of Hong Kong.

Alignment of Beijing, London, and Local Big Business

Early in its negotiations with London, Beijing declined the British position of "a three-legged stool," that any Sino-British agreement on Hong Kong had to be acceptable to three parties: the Chinese government, the British Parliament, and the people of Hong Kong. Judging from Beijing's activities in recent years, it seems that the Chinese leaders are well aware of the fact that, without local support, particularly that of influential firms and individuals, maintenance of stability and prosperity in Hong Kong will not be ensured. Actually, since the cloud over the question of sovereignty was cleared, Beijing has made great efforts to win the support of important figures in Hong Kong and has established its own "three-legged stool," an alignment between Beijing, London, and the local elites to influence the affairs in Hong Kong.

Since the Joint Declaration, cooperation between China and Britain has developed smoothly in spite of certain disagreements over various issues. The Sino-British Joint Liaison Group has reached agreements on Hong Kong's future status in the General Agreement on Tariffs and Trades (GATT), the International Monetary Fund (IMF), the Asian Development Bank, and other international agencies,[37] as stipulated in the Joint Declaration. Both sides have also settled the issue of Hong Kong resident certificates after 1997.[38] The Sino-British Land Commission has solved the problem of land leases that continue to be valid after 1997.[39] So far, Beijing appears to be happy with the help and concessions of London that have enabled China to increase its influence over the development of the Hong Kong issue.

Beijing's efforts to win local support are relatively concentrated in the politically and economically influential circles in Hong Kong. A major strategic consideration taken by the Chinese leadership in this respect seems to be that, to maintain stability and prosperity in Hong Kong, it is crucial to work with the local elites because of their deep-rooted connections in the territory. Moreover, those who are enjoying political and economic prestige in local affairs will more likely accept Beijing's position of maintaining the status quo in Hong Kong.[40] As controversies occurred between 1986 and 1987 over the political reforms in the area, Beijing took the position that apprehensions among local businessmen would lead to instability and therefore discouraged the development of party politics in Hong Kong.

Beijing has also developed numerous close ties with important firms in the territory. In recent years, China has built a cordial relationship with the Hong Kong and Shanghai Banking Corporation (HKSBC), the largest and most influential bank in the area. Beijing granted permission for HKSBC to set up a branch in China, the first such foreign bank office. The Bank of China has arranged syndicated loans with the HKSBC to help finance foreign direct investments and development projects inside China. Meanwhile, the relationship between Beijing and the Hong Kong General Chamber of Commerce, the most influential lobbying group in the territory, has been intimate in the recent years. Since the Chamber of Commerce represents over twenty-six hundred domestic businesses from all branches of commerce and industry and holds membership in the International Chamber of Commerce, its close ties with China have apparently channeled Beijing's influence over local businesses.

In the Chinese National People's Congress (NPC) and the Chinese People's Political Consultative Conference (CPPCC), there are some fifty seats occupied by the Hong Kong delegates. These Chinese-appointed delegates are from Hong Kong's major functional sectors, such as banking, business, and commerce.[41] In recent years, these representatives in both the NPC and the CPPCC have become major objects of Beijing's efforts to influence local affairs. Besides the dual memberships of some of these delegates in the Basic Law Drafting Committee (BLDC) and the Basic Law Consultative Committee (BLCC), Beijing also invited some other local elites into these two lawmaking bodies to expand the "patriotic united front."[42] Moreover, outstanding Chinese entrepreneurs such as Sir Y. K. Pao and Henry Fok were often invited to China to consult with Chinese officials on major policies.

Financial and Commercial Penetration

To China, Hong Kong is unmistakably a golden goose. Its great potential for helping China's modernizations have drawn strong Chinese desires of "gold rushes" to the territory. Since the late 1970s, a major effort in China's foreign economic affairs has been the increasing financial and commercial penetration of Hong Kong. This economic policy will surely continue in the following years.

Several years of efforts have brought China its economic power in Hong Kong. The three main Chinese economic groups, namely China Resources, the Bank of China Group, and China Merchants have become business giants in the local economy. China Resources, which is under the direct control of China's Ministry of Foreign Economic Relations and Trade, claims to have fifty-odd wholly owned subsidiaries and some fifty other jointly owned firms, handling about 70 percent of all Chinese products sold in Hong Kong.[43] The Bank of China Group, with thirteen associated banks, is second in size only to the HKSBC. China Merchants has some two hundred companies with total assets of more than US$1 billion.[44]

China's economic activities in Hong Kong thus involve major sectors such as banking, stockbroking, trade, real estate, manufacturing, transportation, and service. There are now an estimated one thousand mainland companies based in Hong Kong.[45]

One of the most significant developments in China's economic penetration is local investment, particularly that in banking, stockbroking, and manufacturing. Apart from the money fed to financially troubled banks, investments in manufacturing represent a substantial amount of Chinese capital in the territory. In 1983 China began its first industrial joint venture in Hong Kong.[46] Since then Chinese investments have increased substantially. Up to 1987, China has reportedly established some thirty manufacturers in Hong Kong, with total investments of nearly US$150 million.[47] China Resources has also invested in the construction of the local infrastructure, such as transit and shipyard facilities. Since 1986 Chinese economic groups have become increasingly active in local stock markets. In 1986 the Bank of China Group and an agent bank of China International Trust and Investment Corporation have on six occasions issued securities worth several hundred million U.S. dollars.[48] China Resources has also issued a significant amount of securities in the market. It is estimated that these Chinese economic

297

groups are going to become increasingly involved in the local stock market in the following years.

In trade, China's exports to Hong Kong have sharply increased since 1980. The annual growth rates between 1982 and 1985 were over 20 percent, and exports from 1985 to 1986 increased an estimated 40 percent.[49] In 1987 the value of Chinese exports to Hong Kong surpassed the sum of Chinese exports to its other four major trade partners, namely Japan, the United States, West Germany, and the Soviet Union.[50]

Speedup of Basic Lawmaking

Among all the strategic considerations, the Basic Law appears to be the most important and urgent to the Chinese leadership. The terms Beijing and London reached in the Joint Declaration are only general principles regarding the future of Hong Kong and certain procedural matters. Specific questions concerning Hong Kong's future political system, its relationship with the central government, its foreign relations, its administration, and many other issues remain unsolved. Moreover, pending the creation of the Basic Law, different interpretations of Beijing's ideas will remain major sources of undesired results in the local affairs of Hong Kong. To Beijing, it is therefore necessary to have the Basic Law completed as soon as possible.

To create the Basic Law, Beijing has established the BLDC, composed of 58 members (28 from Hong Kong), and the 180-seat BLCC. Since the first BLDC meeting on July 2, 1985, the writing of the Basic Law has been a major concern in Beijing's schedule. On April 22, 1986, the BLDC worked out a draft of the Basic Law framework.[51] After six months, the third meeting of the BLDC achieved substantial progress on major aspects.[52] It was originally hoped that the Basic Law would be completed in four or five years,[53] but the lawmaking process has gone faster than expected. Some members of the drafting committee even jokingly said that they "have overfulfilled the assigned task."[54]

Practically, completion of the Basic Law at the earliest possible date will meet several of Beijing's objectives. In the first place, most China watchers are used to sensing China's policy tendencies through comments and opinions expressed by Chinese officials on formal as well as informal occasions. This has generated great pressures on Beijing in its external contacts. In particular, due to the

298

sensitive nature of the Hong Kong issue, inappropriate expression of China's intentions could create a sudden panic in the society. There have been reports that several times the Hong Kong market suffered a shock because of the probably excessive comments made by Chinese officials.[55] Under such pressure, a comprehensively and explicitly expressed law will surely serve Beijing's purpose of avoiding misunderstanding or misinterpretation of the Chinese policy.

Second, having gradually worked out a design for the future political system in Hong Kong, Beijing has a more obvious reason to exercise influence over political development in the territory. Apparently, there exist differences between the Chinese leadership and some political groups in Hong Kong.[56] Thus, despite their willingness to accept such suggestions as the separation of the executive, legislative, and judicial branches of the government in Hong Kong, as well as the highly autonomous status of the local authorities, the Chinese leaders are apparently not interested in experiencing a system of Western representative democracy in the area. In this respect, a Basic Law established well before the 1997 transfer date will generate a somewhat regulative impact on local political development. Moreover, to ease local apprehensions about policy changes in Beijing, it would be better if the law could be created earlier.

After less than three years of effort, Beijing completed a preliminary draft of the Basic Law for comments and suggestions. The draft includes the relationship between the central government and Hong Kong as a special administrative region, the basic rights and obligations of local residents, the political system, the economic system, education, culture, religious affairs, foreign affairs, and regulations concerning interpretation and revisions of the Basic Law.[57] In the debates and comments following the inception of the draft, there have been four major concerns regarding the future of Hong Kong, including the degree of autonomy, freedom and democracy, the economic environment, and human rights. As planned, members of the BLDC and BLCC have solicited a broad range of opinion, especially in Hong Kong. But how much the draft will be revised remains to be seen.

Maintaining Hong Kong's International Connections

Having been ensured sovereignty over Hong Kong after 1997, Beijing has made increasing efforts to maintain Hong Kong's status in the international economy. With regard to Hong Kong, Beijing does not seem to have trouble in separating the issue of sovereignty from the former colony's special international connections, as long as the region will be under the flag of "China, Hong Kong." On the contrary, maintaining and facilitating all these connections will better serve China's economic interests. In addition to its rights as a contracting party in GATT, as a member of the British Commonwealth, and its formal membership in the Asian Development Bank, Hong Kong also enjoys rights to participate in the Agreement Regarding International Trade in Textiles, the Multi-Fiber Agreement (MFA). It is an associate member of the Economic and Social Commission for Asia and the Pacific of the United Nations and a formal member of the Asian Productivity Organization (APO).[58] Bilaterally, Hong Kong maintains certain independent commercial and financial arrangements with a number of countries. For instance, the region has its own export quotas to the United States. Some of them, like that on textiles, are several times larger than those of China.[59] All these connections between Hong Kong and the outside world have provided China various advantages, as noted before. Moreover, Beijing is also well aware of the fact that the international connections of Hong Kong have been crucial factors contributing to the economic success of the region. In recent years, Hong Kong's global status has been stressed both in the Chinese official press and on diplomatic occasions.

PRESSURES AND LIMITATIONS

In actual practice, policies often have limitations. There usually exist certain gaps between strategic objectives and policy results. Beijing's efforts regarding the Hong Kong issue are no exceptions. Apparently, there are still a number of difficulties and policy limitations that the Chinese leaders will have to overcome in the following years.

Beijing's Penetrations Versus Local Apprehensions

A major problem facing Beijing has been local apprehensions about the future of Hong Kong. The change in Hong Kong's status is from a free-market economy to a region under the control of a Communist government that has presided over five revisions of the

Chinese constitution as well as several political and economic catas-trophes. Among the population of Hong Kong, a significant portion are immigrants or refugees from the mainland and their offspring. In varying degrees, most of these people maintain negative attitudes toward the frequent policy changes and the politicized social life in China. Furthermore, used to the apolitical and utilitarian culture in Hong Kong, many people naturally fear being under the control of a Communist government.

Unlike London and the Hong Kong government, these people do not have official commitments to the smooth transition of sover-eignty to Beijing. They are free to move away from the colony if opportunities are available. Apparently because of the Hong Kong 1997 issue, the territory has witnessed in recent years a substantial outflow of local capital and human resources in spite of the increas-ing inflow of foreign investment. It is estimated that about 30,000 people moved out of Hong Kong in 1986, and about 40,000 in 1987. The annual number of Hong Kong emigrants in the next several years will likely climb to 50,000. These emigrants have mainly tar-geted three countries, namely the United States, Canada, and Aus-tralia. Since 1983, the annual number of emigrants from Hong Kong to the United States has been more than 8,000, with the exception of 1986. In 1987, the number of immigration visas that the Canadian government granted to Hong Kong applicants reached 22,000, an increase of 150 percent compared with the figure for 1986.[60] About half of these emigrants reportedly have college equivalent or higher degrees and more than half are professionals, managerial staff, or skilled workers. The massive outflow of people has caused a serious brain drain from Hong Kong. Many business and academic institu-tions have suffered because of the departure of professionals and skilled staffs. The HKSBC, for instance, lost 8 percent of its admin-istrative staff to foreign emigration in 1987.[61] Although there are no official statistics, unofficial information indicates that local capital reinvestment in Hong Kong, normally between 10 and 12 percent, reached only 5 percent in the spring of 1986.[62]

The local unease seems to have been fostered by China's direct penetration in the area. In the economic realm, owners of small and middle-sized businesses in Hong Kong are reportedly worried by the fact that the increasing number of state-owned Chinese eco-nomic entities will undermine regular operations of the local mar-ket.[63] Under British rule, the Hong Kong government has traditionally maintained a laissez-faire economic policy. Furthermore, even though there are some economic tycoons in the territory, the markets in Hong Kong remain highly competitive. However, as state economic activities expand, some people fear that the regular operation of the economy will be damaged.[64] Beijing's direct control of the local market will also become salient because of its economic power in Hong Kong. Politically, expansions of Chinese institutions both in size and number have also brought to the area an increasing number of people with official backgrounds. This situation will lead to changes of the existing political culture and way of life in Hong Kong.

In the face of the local apprehension, Beijing may need to consider the cost and benefit of its policy in this respect. On the one hand, it is undoubtedly true that the Chinese economy can benefit substantially from its increasing influence in Hong Kong. On the other hand, however, the continued flow of population from Hong Kong will lead to a deterioration in the quality of the human resources in Hong Kong and cause great harm to the local economy.

International Pressures

Because of Hong Kong's historical status and its international connections, the issue of the transfer of sovereignty over it has been of an international nature since its beginning. First of all, the issue is dealt with between China and Britain, both sovereign countries. In Paragraph Seven of the Joint Declaration, Beijing accepts the usage of the word "agree" regarding the implementation of the declaration and hence allows the document signed by both sides to be considered as an international agreement.[65] Under a principle of international law, both parties of the agreement should enjoy the equal rights of interpreting the document. Even though the current British government has given concessions to Beijing over the controversial questions, its positions are seemingly based on pragmatic considerations of the recent interests in their bilateral relations. Currently, London still maintains its right to interfere in the social and political development of Hong Kong during the transitional period. In mid-1988, the British Parliament decided to hold sessions to debate the Basic Law draft. Beijing maintained that the writing of the Basic Law is primarily a Chinese domestic matter and it is not appropriate for a foreign parliament to hold debates on it. However, according to the Parliament, the Basic Law should accord with the principles of the Sino-British Joint Declaration. As a party to the declaration, Britain has rights and obligations to make comments and suggestions concerning the Basic Law. In addition to the debates, London also raised questions concerning the court of last instance and the number of Chinese troops to be stationed in Hong Kong after 1997.[66] Moreover, in the future, if the Sino-British relationship deteriorates or Beijing takes certain excessive actions regarding Hong Kong, a considerable number of questions of this type would still be subject to argument. From this point of view, Beijing's policies on Hong Kong are still legally under external surveillance.

More important, Hong Kong's international economic connections have brought China under the pressure of those countries that have significant interests in the territory. As the third-largest monetary center in the world, Hong Kong contains offices of a large number of multinational banks and financial institutions. Among 152 major banks in Hong Kong, 116 of them are foreign.[67] The involvement of foreign firms in Hong Kong banking and finance has increased sharply in the past several years. In 1986, Dai-Ichi Kangyo, Japan's largest bank, took over a local bank—Chekiang First Bank.[68] The inflow of foreign capital of this type is expected to increase in the following years.

Hong Kong also enjoys a top reputation in warehousing and transportation. It has the second-largest container port in the world. The territory also has one of the largest international airports on the earth. In addition to the substantial foreign economic activity already prevalent in the territory, in recent years Hong Kong has also seen increasing foreign investment in various economic sectors. Among the countries that are the major sources of that investment, many of them are of crucial importance in Chinese foreign policy. The United States, China's greatest concern in international relations, has the largest proportion of foreign investment in Hong Kong with 54 percent of the total. (China is not included in this accounting.) Japan, with 21 percent, stands second. Although the British have withdrawn a significant amount of capital from Hong Kong in recent decades, the country still occupies third place with 7 percent.[69] These three countries together account for over 80 percent of the total foreign investment in the region. This situation, having contributed to the economic miracle of Hong Kong, also generates great pressure on Beijing. Since the economy in Hong Kong has been so closely related to the world market, what happens in the area will immediately and directly resound elsewhere in the world.

To maintain Hong Kong's international connections, the United States and the European Council have agreed that Hong Kong will remain a member of GATT.[70] Many international organizations are also considering Hong Kong's membership after 1997. The development of this situation suggests that the question of Hong Kong's future is no longer a domestic issue, nor a matter between China and Britain. The concerns of various countries regarding the situation in Hong Kong make Beijing more cautious in its policies. If those policies cause serious damage to Hong Kong's economy, China will surely face international dissatisfaction.

The Pressure of the Taiwan Issue

Since the model of "one country, two systems" is designed not only for Hong Kong and Macao, but also for Taiwan, the success of the Hong Kong experiment is of crucial importance in Beijing's overall program of national integration. The difficulty Beijing is facing with regard to Taiwan lies in the fact that the situation is quite different from that in Hong Kong or Macao. Beijing did not have much trouble bringing Lisbon into an agreement based upon the Hong Kong model, to return sovereignty over Macao to China. But its influence in the Taiwan issue is far from being dominant. From this view, as long as Beijing attempts to use the Hong Kong model to lure Taiwan, it will be under pressure to maintain its credibility in its Taiwan bid. First, it cannot afford to let the economy in Hong Kong go downhill. Second, the model must not fail in maintaining local stability, since it will also disgrace Beijing's credibility.[71] Third and most important, Beijing must keep all its promises, either in the Joint Declaration or in other official statements, to retain the capitalist system in Hong Kong for fifty years and to allow a high degree of local autonomy. Failure to do so can only bring about more doubts and resistance in Taiwan to Beijing's offer.

Limitations

The history of political development has demonstrated several facts with regard to the building of political systems. First, it shows the difficulty when people design political systems and hope that such systems can precisely meet their objectives in the future. For various reasons, political developments in most Communist as well as most Western democratic countries turn out to have "deviated" from what their advocates desired. Second, it shows that the difficulties will be greater when people design political systems for other societies, even if the designed systems are of the same nature as that of their designers. British colonial history and the U.S. experience in Japan after World War II suggest that these designed systems, imposed on different cultures, social customs, and ways of life, are more vulnerable and more subject to change than indigenous systems.

Third, it appears to be most difficult for people to design for other societies a political system different from their own. Beijing's efforts in making the Basic Law seemingly fall in this category. What adds to the difficulty facing China, as Beijing admits, is the fact that such an effort is unprecedented. Therefore, the limitations in this respect cannot be overlooked.

Even though it may be true that the lawmakers in Beijing will try to be realistic and unbiased to the greatest extent possible, unavoidable factors such as ideology, political positions, values, and specific interests will still affect the objectivity of the lawmaking process. Besides, technically there exists a question of how well the lawmakers understand a society so different from China's. Before the Hong Kong issue arose, the Center for Hong Kong and Macao Studies in Guangdong province was probably the only academic institute in the country engaged in systematic research on Hong Kong. Most studies of the region were done by foreign trade companies solely for marketing purposes. *Economic Studies,* the earliest journal in its field to be published and one of the most influential, did not have even one article on Hong Kong during a long period between 1955 and 1985.[72] No doubt there has been an increase in understanding of Hong Kong society in recent years in both academic and policy-making circles. But lack of the kind of in-depth knowledge of the region required in lawmaking remains a problem. Moreover, despite the significant number of Hong Kong delegates in the BLDC and the BLCC, their representation of local interests is still limited. Beijing has repeated that it will do its best to incorporate the interests of various social sectors in the Basic Law, but this is only an expression of Beijing's willingness. Whether the forthcoming law can realize this intention remains a question to be answered.

The limitations also involve China's internal political situation.

As many Chinese leaders and academicians have pointed out, Chinese political systems for a long time suffered from lack of laws, a low level of institutionalization of political life, and inadequate political democracy. Although post-Mao Chinese political development has yielded considerable achievements, the situation leaves much to be desired. China's economic reforms have brought forth the necessity of political reforms in the country, but resistance is reportedly strong. Even what the reformers have advocated is relatively conservative and often frustrated because of various social and political obstacles to the reforms. These political limitations in China's domestic development are apparently reflected in the formulation of the Basic Law. For instance, in designing the future political system for Hong Kong, there is consensus only in the form of separation between the legislative, executive, and judicial branches of government. But the accountability of officeholders to the people, a more important question in political life, has been overlooked.

POLICY OPTIONS IN THE NEXT DECADE

In sum, several conditions can be highlighted regarding Beijing's policy options in the next decade. By its efforts in the recent past, Beijing has managed to bring local affairs in Hong Kong under control. If nothing unexpected happens in the next few years, the situation will generally develop along the path as Beijing wishes. Moreover, in recent years a relatively conservative political force composed of local elites has gathered in the territory.[73] These people, sharing interests with Beijing in maintaining the status quo in Hong Kong, are going to play important roles in what Beijing defines as the system of "self-administration by the Hong Kong people" after 1997. On the other hand, Beijing is still facing a considerable number of difficulties and limitations. Furthermore, there are increased domestic and international pressures upon Beijing's policy considerations. Years ago, the Chinese leaders accused the British and some local Chinese in the area of using the economic issues to put pressure on Beijing. Now, because of the Chinese economic involvement in Hong Kong, China's interests have increased its own commitments to local development. Internationally, the image created by the post-Mao Chinese leadership also needs to be polished by China's own achievements. Finally, China, not anyone else, is the party which is going to have Hong Kong after 1997. Any damage to this "golden goose" at the present time is not desirable for the future.

Based on these factors, it appears that Beijing will continue its efforts to maintain stability and prosperity in Hong Kong. Moreover, it will probably make certain policy adjustments to cope with the existing difficulties. In general, China's policy options will involve the following aspects.

Increasing the Political Roles of Local Elites

Over the issues of political development in Hong Kong, a significant number of politically conservative local elites have gradually gathered their interests. While small in number, these people are influential in local politics and economy. Some of them occupy seats in the legislative or executive bodies in Hong Kong. Some have interests in connections with China. Over the controversies concerning the political development in Hong Kong, many of these people fear that introduction of Western representative democracy in the territory will negatively affect their current interests.[74] In general, this conservative side prefers a future political system that can best protect the status quo in Hong Kong.

Since mid-1985, some local people have put forth detailed suggestions for the future political system in Hong Kong. After the Cha Chiming proposal[75] in 1985, a group in the BLCC that represents business and industrial sectors in Hong Kong turned out a proposal signed by fifty-seven persons. Later a supplementary suggestion by seventy-one members was made.[76] The basic principle of these proposals, different from that of a "democratic group" in Hong Kong, suggests a relatively centralized system to maintain the high efficiency of bureaucratic administration.[77] This position appears to satisfy Beijing's objective concerning the local political system after 1997. In the following years, Beijing will continue to support this political system. In recent years, the number of Hong Kong delegates have increased both in China's National People's Congress and the Chinese People's Political Consultative Conference. These delegates are mostly influential figures in different circles in Hong Kong. Because of their backgrounds, these people are able to play important roles in connecting Beijing's desires with local affairs. In the future, Beijing will continue to offer more such positions to the local elites. Meanwhile, members of LEGCO, EXCO (the Executive Council), and the district councils in Hong

Kong will be contacted more frequently and befriended by Chinese officials. On the other hand, to ease the apprehensions among many residents, Beijing might refrain from direct interference in local affairs. Meanwhile, Beijing's strategic emphasis might shift to an increasing influence on local elites.

To establish a more efficient legislative body during the transitional period, in mid-1988 the Hong Kong government undertook a substantial reshuffling of the membership of LEGCO. As a result, only nine of the twenty-two originally appointed members retained their positions. The government is going to appoint eleven new members to fill out the reconstituted body. The remaining nine original members are seemingly of similar social and political backgrounds. They are mostly middle-aged, politically conservative and often in line with the government, and were educated either at the British universities or at Hong Kong University. Despite their ideological differences, these people are able to communicate with the democratic groups in Hong Kong. It is people of such background that the government is looking for to fill the eleven open seats. Such a change in LEGCO indicates that to lay a base for future "self-administration," the Hong Kong government is making an effort to nurture a group of relatively young and charismatic elites who can represent the interests of the middle and upper classes but are also able to connect with other sectors of the society.[78] It seems that this move of the Hong Kong government is acceptable to Beijing. In the first place, the new group of legislators will be able to last through the transitional period and their experience will be useful for the administration after 1997. Second, such a change is unlikely to create social and political instability, since it is not done through elections. And third, although these people are not pro-Beijing, most of them are not oriented toward democracy either. Based on these considerations, it is likely that Beijing will maintain its positive attitude toward the legislative reshuffles, and will probably make considerable efforts to influence this emerging group of young political elites.

Reducing Local Resentments and Apprehensions

Even with the support of local elites, Beijing will still have limitations in relieving the feeling of alienation among other social sectors. To maintain prosperity in the area, China will have to win the confidence of important social sectors such as professionals, academicians, managers, and public bureaucrats. How this is to be done remains a crucial question in Beijing's policy consideration. Such people, who were mostly educated either in local Western-oriented schools or in Western countries have been heavily influenced by Western democratic thought. During the previous political reforms in Hong Kong, many of them demanded a system of popular political participation, a democratic process for airing views, and the accountability of authorities to the voters. In recent years, increasing numbers of people of this kind have made efforts to settle abroad. Undoubtedly, a massive outflow of these educated groups would bring great harm to Hong Kong's economy.

To ease the resentment among this social group, Beijing will probably make certain concessions in regard to the local political system, especially over the question of representative government. For instance, having convinced the Hong Kong government to give up its plan of direct elections of LEGCO in 1988, Beijing will likely compromise with them regarding the elections scheduled in the early 1990s. Since the Basic Law will be completed by that time, Beijing will be less worried that the situation will be out of control as a result of elections. Also, Beijing will, at least on the surface, pay attention to local opinions about the political system in Hong Kong. In August 1988, a discussion regarding the Basic Law was held in Beijing between certain leading members of the BLDC and delegates of Meeting Point, an influential Hong Kong–based pressure group composed of prominent social activists and academics. During the discussion, the Chinese lawmakers expressed their willingness to consider many of the factors held to be important by Meeting Point, when writing the Basic Law, such as explicit regulations in the Chinese Constitution to guarantee Hong Kong's political and social system, provisions in the Basic Law to empower the chief executive of the future special administrative region to make final decisions without the interference of the central government, and the rights of local courts to interpret the Basic Law.[79] It appears that the concessions given by Beijing will more or less ease the local resentments in Hong Kong.

Moreover, to reduce local political and social tensions, Beijing will likely take steps to balance the interests of different social sectors in Hong Kong. Regarding the Basic Law, Beijing has maintained that it should be acceptable not only to business and the middle class, but also to the grass roots of Hong Kong. Based on the criticism that the executive council provided by the Basic Law, like the current EXCO, is an inefficient, elitist body, Beijing will probably reconsider the necessity of its existence. Also, Beijing will likely take into account the negative feeling among the lower social classes about the role of the "electoral college" in Hong Kong's future political system.

In addition to numerous promises that the current social system and life-style in Hong Kong will not be changed after 1997, Beijing will take further actions to ease local apprehensions about China's takeover of the territory. A possible move will be to adjust the Chinese gesture to the local system. Recently, Xu Jiatun, head of the Chinese Xinhua News Agency in Hong Kong, published an article calling for a reevaluation of capitalism. In his article, Mr. Xu used Hong Kong as an example to illustrate the contributions made by capitalist society to the global social and economic development. He suggested that there are many valuable things that China should learn from Hong Kong, including market operations, business management, monetary policies, economic environment, the legal system, and public administration.[80] Such a compliment to Hong Kong stands in stark contrast to Beijing's previous concern that the increasing contacts with Hong Kong have also had an unhealthy influence on the mainland's social and political life. Mr. Xu is commonly considered to be a Chinese representative in Hong Kong. His comments and opinions are usually seen as indications of Beijing's policy toward the territory. The fact that Mr. Xu expressed his admiration for Hong Kong so openly is a signal of forthcoming moves by Beijing to calm the local apprehensions.

Further Utilizing Hong Kong for Domestic Development

Beijing will continue to attract investment and technology from Hong Kong for China's economic development. Over the past few years, China has established along its southeast coast various special economic zones (SEZs). According to Beijing, these SEZs are going to play a role as transitional areas between foreign markets and Chinese inland markets. In recent years, many SEZs have developed close ties with Hong Kong.[81] As the latter is undergoing a transformation to a more highly capitalist and technologically intensive economic structure, its previously well-established industries, such as garment and toy manufacturing and daily consumer goods production, are gradually moving to China, which has substantial labor sources. Meanwhile, many SEZs have also arranged different kinds of joint ventures with Hong Kong businesses in certain highly technological programs. Additionally, China is attracted to sources of foreign capital, especially those that attempt to approach the mainland through Hong Kong. To maintain the role of Hong Kong as an access point for the inflow of foreign capital, China will surely continue its efforts to develop close ties between the mainland and Hong Kong.

In the face of protectionist policies adopted by the United States and Western Europe, China will continue to increase exports to Hong Kong. During the economic modernization drive, many export-oriented industries have been established and well developed in China. In addition to the efforts to seek markets in the Western countries, China will maintain Hong Kong as the largest consumer of its exports and further utilize the area for entrepôt trade to Taiwan, South Korea, and other countries that do not have direct trades with China.

Meanwhile, Chinese monetary and financial institutions will further strengthen ties with their counterparts in Hong Kong. In recent years, many Chinese enterprises have been engaged in stock markets and real estate both on the mainland and overseas, particularly in Hong Kong. In 1987, the real estate market in Hong Kong attracted $806 million from China,[82] about 16 percent of the Chinese investment in the territory. In January 1988, the Bank of China announced its plans to further expand its brokerage business in Hong Kong.[83] As a major monetary center of the world, Hong Kong will surely continue to provide many conveniences and opportunities for Chinese monetary development in the following years.

Hong Kong, Beijing, and Taiwan

Partly because of Beijing's continuous efforts and partly because of Taiwan's policy adjustments, direct contacts with Taiwan have increased substantially in the last several years. In addition to the use of numerous mutual harbors by fishermen from both sides, hundreds of thousands of people have gone to visit their relatives on the mainland. Since the 13th Congress of the Nationalist Party, the Taiwanese government has further loosened its control over contacts between the two sides of the strait. On July 12, 1988, the Taiwan Olympic Committee announced its willingness to send a delegation to participate in the Asian Games that will be held in Beijing in 1990.[84] Meanwhile, some commercial, cultural, and sports institutions are allowed to send members to the mainland to take part in different meetings and activities. Such decisions indicate that Taiwan is beginning to give up its policy of noncontact with Beijing.

If such direct contacts between the mainland and Taiwan continue to increase in the coming years, the role of Hong Kong as a channel to China will decrease. In fact, there have already been some signs of this. For instance, because it is slow and expensive to get a visa from Hong Kong, some Taiwanese and Taiwan-based airlines have decided to change their flight routes to certain Southeast Asian countries such as Singapore and the Philippines.[85] Meanwhile, the number of Taiwanese visitors traveling to China via Amoy, Fujian province, during the first half of 1988 increased to more than twenty thousand, three times as many as in the whole year of 1987.[86] The Chinese government has eased its regulations so that visitors from Taiwan no longer need to be present in Hong Kong to apply for visas. It appears that, since the future situation will likely provide people from both sides with more opportunities for direct contact, Beijing will reduce the importance of Hong Kong in this respect.

However, the political importance of Hong Kong in Beijing's reunification attempt will remain. Beijing will continue to stress the feasibility of the "one country, two systems" model for its Taiwan bid. Hong Kong will still be the base for China to approach Taiwan. As contacts between the two sides increase, Beijing will take further steps in its reunification efforts, such as establishment of certain joint committees and organizations for mutual interests. In this respect, Hong Kong will still be able to provide the ideal "third party's place" for such organizations. In August 1988, delegates from both the mainland and Taiwan met in Hong Kong and reached an agreement to set up a joint committee for commercial arbitration.[87] It appears that more and more bodies of this kind will be established in the near future and Hong Kong will be most likely considered as their base.

Seeking International Support

International support on the Hong Kong issue is of significant importance to Beijing. Economically, Beijing needs recognition of Hong Kong's post-1997 status from various international organizations. Besides, maintenance of foreign interests in the territory appears to be a crucial factor contributing to stability and prosperity in Hong Kong. Politically, if Beijing succeeds in convincing international opinion of the feasibility of "one country, two systems" as a solution to the Hong Kong problem, it will provide Beijing with a favorable climate in which to deal with other issues, especially that of the reintegration of Taiwan. In recent years, Chinese leaders have frequently explained their positions concerning the above-stated solution to foreign listeners. Apparently, this effort of winning international support will continue to be a major policy concern of Beijing in the coming years.

Meanwhile, Beijing will continue its efforts to widen the scope of Hong Kong's foreign relations. In August 1988, the Sino-British Joint Liaison Group agreed that after 1997 Hong Kong will be allowed to establish agreements independently with foreign countries on the extradition of escaped criminals. According to Beijing, although such agreements are of the nature of international law and usually dealt with between sovereign states, the reason for the Chinese government to give Hong Kong the power to handle these affairs lies in its special status in the international community.[88] It can be predicted that in the near future more agreements will be reached within the Liaison Group regarding Hong Kong's international relations.

ABBREVIATIONS

ANZUS Treaty: A security alliance including Australia, New Zealand, and the United States.

ASEAN: Alliance of Southeast Asian Nations, a security alliance including Indonesia, Thailand, Singapore, Malaysia, and the Philippines.

BLCC: Basic Law Consultative Committee, a high-level consultative body on Hong Kong's future basic law, whose members include representatives from Hong Kong.

BLDC: Basic Law Drafting Committee, a committee which is controlled by the Chinese government and includes representatives from Hong Kong for drafting Hong Kong's basic law for post-1997, when Hong Kong is to be turned over to China.

CCP: Chinese Communist Party, the ruling party in China.

COMECON: Council for Mutual Economic Assistance, a Soviet-dominated economic organization including most Communist countries.

CPPCC: Chinese People's Political Consultative Conference, China's high-level political consultative body, dominated by the Chinese Communist Party.

EEC: European Economic Community, which includes sixteen West European nations.

DMZ: Demilitarized Zone, the nonmilitary zone between North Korea and South Korea.

DPP: Democratic Progressive Party, the most influential opposition party in Taiwan.

DPRK: Democratic People's Republic of Korea, the official name of North Korea.

GATT: General Agreement on Tariffs and Trade, an international economic organization including most non–centrally planning countries in the world.

GDP: Gross Domestic Product.

GNP: Gross National Product.

HKSBC: Hong Kong and Shanghai Banking Corporation, the largest private banking group in Hong Kong.

ICBM: Intercontinental ballistic missile.

IMF: International Monetary Fund.

INF Treaty: A treaty between the United States and the Soviet Union on reducing intermediate-range nuclear weapons.

KAL: Korea Air Lines, the official South Korean airline.

Khmer Rouge: The Communist resistance movement in Cambodia.

KMT: Koumintang, the Nationalist Party, the ruling party in China between 1927 and 1949 and in Taiwan since 1949.

KPNLF: Khmer People's National Liberation Front, the Cambodian resistance movement led by Son Sann.

LEGCO: Legislative Council, the legislative body of Hong Kong.

MRBM: Medium-range ballistic missile.

NATO: North Atlantic Treaty Organization, a security alliance, whose sixteen members include the United States, Canada, and fourteen other Western nations.

NICs: Newly Industrialized Nations, countries that have industrialized since World War II.

NPC: National People's Congress, the legislative body of the People's Republic of China.

NSA: The National Sihanoukist Army, the Cambodian resistance movement led by Prince Sihanouk.

OECD: Organization of Economic Cooperation and Development, an international economic organization whose twenty-four members include the United States, Canada, Japan, and most West European nations.

PECC: Pacific Economic Cooperation Conference, an international forum focusing on economic issues in the Pacific. Its members include the United States, Canada, Japan, and many other Asian nations.

PRC: People's Republic of China, China's official name.

RMB: Renminbi, "people's currency," the currency of the PRC. In mid-1989, one RMB Yuan = US$ 0.26.

SAM: Surface-to-Air Missile, a Soviet-made antiaircraft missile.

SDI: Strategic Defense Initiative, often called "Star Wars," a U.S. anti-nuclear-weapon system still in its research stage, planned to be deployed in outer space.

SEZs: Special Economic Zones, special districts designed to attract direct foreign investment in China. China's four SEZs are in Shenzheng, Xiameng, Zhuhai, and Shantou.

SLBM: Sea-launched ballistic missile.

TIM: Taiwan Independence Movement, a political movement aimed at Taiwan's independence from China.

Warsaw Pact: A security alliance led by the Soviet Union and including six other East European nations.

INTRODUCTION: CHINESE FOREIGN POLICY
YUFAN HAO AND GUOCANG HUAN

1. *Chinese Business Review*, May–June 1988, pp. 55–57.
2. Robert Sutter, *Chinese Foreign Policy After Mao* (New York: Praeger, 1986), pp. 3–6.
3. Joseph Camilleri, *Chinese Foreign Policy* (Seattle: University of Washington Press, 1980), p. 3.
4. Golam W. Choudhury, *Chinese Perception of the New World* (Lanham, Md.: University Press of America, 1978), p. 1.
5. See Zhihai Zhai and Yufan Hao, "China's Decision to Enter the Korean War: New Light from Chinese Sources," *China Quarterly*, forthcoming.
6. Camilleri, *Chinese Foreign Policy*, p. 9.
7. Michael B. Yahuda, *China's Role in World Affairs* (New York: St. Martin's, 1978), pp. 24–28.
8. Harry Harding, "China's Changing Role in the Contemporary World," in Harry Harding, ed., *China's Foreign Relations in the 1980s* (New Haven: Yale University Press, 1986) p. 210.
9. *Ibid.*, pp. 207–8.
10. Kenneth Lieberthal, "Domestic Politics and Foreign Policy," in Harding, *China's Foreign Relations*, p. 44.
11. Michael Yahuda, *Toward the End of Isolation: China's Foreign Policy after Mao* (London: Macmillan, 1983), p. 131.

ONE: SECURITY IN THE ASIAN-PACIFIC REGION
WEIQUN GU

1. The U.S. sent out "nuclear signals" on four occasions in this region after the end of the Second World War, through the deployment of strategic aircraft to the Western Pacific: once in August 1953 around the end of the Korean War; twice during the offshore islands crises between mainland China and Taiwan in August 1954 and July 1958; and during the *Pueblo* crisis in January 1968. See Barry M. Blechman and Stephen S. Kaplan, *Force Without War* (Washington, D.C.: Brookings Institution, 1978), p. 48. The fifth time was in 1969 when the Soviet Union made a nuclear threat against China.
2. Historically, naval warfare has been an important feature of conflict in this region. China was opened up by the British Navy. Japan was opened up by the U.S. Navy. The Spanish-American War of 1898, the Sino-Japanese War of 1894–95, and the Russo-Japanese War of 1904–5 were essentially naval wars. Naval and air warfare constituted a central part of the military confrontation

in the Asian-Pacific region during the Second World War. The Japanese attack on Pearl Harbor and seizure of Southeast Asia and numerous islands in the Pacific, the U.S. "island-hopping" effort, and the U.S. air raids on Japan from China and from Pacific air bases and aircraft carriers are all important examples. The same is true with the Korean War and the Vietnam War. The Inchon landing operation staged by the United States during the Korean War was carried out with the support of 300 ships (including 6 aircraft carriers, 1 battleship, 18 minesweepers, 76 landing ships, and 66 transports) and 500 aircraft of different classes, which guaranteed sea and air dominance. During the Vietnam War, the main forces of the U.S. Seventh Fleet were permanently present off Vietnamese shores. Of the 17 strike aircraft carriers of the U.S. Navy, 15 took part in combat operations; of 9 helicopter carriers, 6 took part; also 48 of 58 of the guided missile ships—cruisers, frigates, and destroyers—and 163 of 179 destroyers. See Sergei G. Gorshkov, "The Sea Power and the State," in George E. Thibault, ed., *The Art and Practice of Military Strategy* (National Defense University of the United States, 1984), pp. 247, 249.

3. Field Marshal Montgomery once said that "the first principle of war is not to try to walk to Moscow." Bernard Brodie, *War and Politics,* (New York: Macmillan, 1974), p. 85.

4. Richard H. Solomon, ed., *Asian Security in the 1980s* (Cambridge, Mass.: OG and H Publishers, 1980), p. 28.

5. George Quester, lecture at Maryland University, August 1986.

6. Speech by Mikhail Gorbachev in Vladivostok, July 28, 1986.

7. Alison Broinowski, *Understanding ASEAN* (New York: St. Martin's, 1982), app. E, Kuala Lampur Declaration.

8. Michael Doyle, "Kant, Liberal Legacies, and Foreign Affairs," in *Philosophy and Public Affairs,* vol. 12 (Summer 1983), pp. 205–35.

9. Speech by Gorbachev, Moscow Television Service, July 28, 1986.

10. Gorbachev's speech at Vladivostok, July 28, 1986.

11. Mao Zedong's testament to Hua Guofeng, which was used by Hua as the basis for the legitimacy of his succession.

TWO: CHINA AND THE TRIANGULAR RELATIONSHIP

HONGQIAN ZHU

1. Richard W. Stevenson, *The Rise and Fall of Détente: Relaxations of Tension in US-Soviet Relations, 1953–84* (Champaign: University of Illinois Press, 1985), p. 25.

2. See Wang Jisi, "An Appraisal of US Policy Toward China: 1945–1955 and Its Aftermath," *American Studies* (Beijing: Institute of American Studies), vol. 1, no. 1 (Spring 1987), pp. 40–68; see also A. Doak Barnett, *China and the Major Powers in East Asia* (Washington, D.C.: Brookings Institution, 1977), pp. 175–93.

3. For a detailed study of "the China Lobby" and domestic influence, see Ross Y. Koen, *The China Lobby in American Politics* (New York: Macmillan, 1960); Stanley D. Bachrack, *The Committee of One Million: "China Lobby" Politics, 1953–1971* (New York: Columbia University Press, 1976); and Leonard A. Kusnitz, *Public Opinion and Foreign Policy: America's China Policy 1949–1979* (Westport, Conn.: Greenwood Press, 1984).

4. Robert G. Sutter, *China-Watch: Toward Sino-American Reconciliation* (Baltimore: Johns Hopkins University Press, 1978), pp. 47–62.

5. See, for example, Secretary of State John Foster Dulles's speech "Our Policies Toward China," June 28, 1957 (Press release, Department of State, Public Service Division, Series S, no. 58, June 28, 1957).

6. For an example of the Soviet concern about the Chinese opposition, see a brief account in Stevenson, *The Rise and Fall of Détente*, pp. 74–77.

7. See, for example, "Sino-Mali Joint Communiqué," January 21, 1964, *Peking Review*, January 31, 1965, p. 9.

8. Henry Kissinger, *The White House Years* (London: Weidenfeld and Nicolson, Michael Joseph, 1979), pp. 173, 183–184.

9. Ibid., p. 222.

10. Banning Garrett, "The United States and the Great Power Triangle," in Gerald Segal, ed., *The China Factor: Peking and the Superpowers* (London: Croom Helm, 1982), pp. 78–80.

11. Stevenson, *The Rise and Fall of Détente*, p. 156.

12. Huan Xiang, "On Sino-U.S. Relations," *Foreign Affairs*, vol. 60, no. 1 (Fall 1981), p. 49.

13. Lowell Dittmer, "The Strategic Triangle: An Elementary Game-Theoretic Analysis," *World Politics*, vol. XXXIII, no. 4 (July 1981), p. 490.

14. See, for example, William G. Hyland, *Soviet-American Relations: A New Cold War?* (Santa Monica, Calif.: Rand Corporation, 1981); Michael Cox, "From Détente to the 'New Cold War': The Crisis of the Cold War System," *International Studies*, vol. 23, no. 3 (Winter 1984), pp. 265–91; and also Phil Williams, "Détente and U.S. Domestic Politics," *International Affairs*, vol. 61, no. 3 (Summer 1985), pp. 431–47.

15. John Gaddis, "Containment: Its Past and Future," *International Security*, vol. 4, no. 4 (Spring 1980), p. 79.

16. Williams, "Détente and U.S. Domestic Politics," p. 434.

17. Robert G. Kaiser, "U.S.–Soviet Relations: Goodbye to Détente," *Foreign Affairs*, vol. 59, no. 3, 1980, p. 507.

18. For an account of Carter's policy in this period, see Michel Oksenberg, "A Decade of Sino-American Relations," *Foreign Affairs*, vol. 61, no. 1 (Fall 1982), pp. 175–95.

19. Oksenberg, "China Policy for the 1980s," *Foreign Affairs*, vol. 59, no. 2 (Winter 1980–81), p. 318.

20. For a Chinese view on this, see Huan Xiang, "On Sino-U.S. Relations," pp. 36–37.

21. Garrett, "The United States and the Great Power Triangle," p. 94.

22. Robert S. Ross, "International Bargaining and Domestic Politics: U.S.-China Relations Since 1972," *World Politics*, vol. XXXVIII, no. 2 (January 1986), p. 278.

23. For the Soviet view on the triangle, see Gerald Segal, "The Soviet Union and the Great Power Triangle," in Segal, ed., *The China Factor*, pp. 67–69.

24. George D. Knight, "China's Soviet Policy in the Gorbachev Era," *Washington Quarterly*, vol. 9, no. 2 (Spring 1986), p. 106.

25. See Hu Yaobang, "Create a New Situation in All Fields of Socialist Modernization—Report to the 12th National Congress of the Communist Party of China," *Beijing Review*, September 13, 1982, pp. 29–33.

26. Robert A. Scalapino, "Strategic Issues in U.S. Policies Toward Asia," in John Bryan Starr, ed., *The Future of US-China Relations* (New York: New York University Press, 1981), p. 151.

27. Huan Xiang, "On Sino-U.S. Relations," p. 39.

28. Rajan Menon, "The Soviet Union in East Asia," *Current History*, vol. 82, no. 486 (October 1983), p. 315.

29. Arthur Schlesinger, Jr., "Foreign Policy and the American Character," *Foreign Affairs*, vol. 62, no. 1 (Fall 1983), pp. 6–8.
30. Ibid, p. 15.
31. See, for example, *Beijing Review*, April 22, 1985, p. 6, and January 6, 1986, p. 14.
32. Since this strategy is aimed at promoting relationships with both countries, it should be distinguished from the notion of "card playing."
33. This term is borrowed from some American observers. See, for example, Donald S. Zagoria, "The Moscow-Beijing Détente," *Foreign Affairs*, vol. 62, no. 4 (Spring 1983), pp. 853–73; William E. Griffith, "Sino-Soviet Rapprochement?" *Problems of Communism*, March-April 1983.
34. See *Beijing Review*, April 28, 1986, p. 8.
35. Mike Wallace's September 2, 1986, interview with Deng Xiaoping, *People's Daily* (overseas ed.), September 8, 1986.
36. Ibid.
37. For a view on this, see Zhang Yebai, "Some Comments on the Development of US-Soviet Relations in the 80's," *American Studies*, vol. 1, no. 1 (Spring 1987), pp. 69–78.
38. See, for example, *Beijing Review*, January 6, 1986, pp. 14–15.
39. Fang Min, "U.S.-Soviet Relations," *Beijing Review*, January 20, 1986, p. 15.

THREE: CHINA'S FOREIGN ECONOMIC POLICY

QINGGUO JIA

1. Zhu Chengjun, "The New Page in China's Relations with East Europe," *Outlook* (overseas ed.), October 20, 1986; Yin Ch'ing-yao, "Peking-Moscow Relations: An Analysis," *Issues and Studies*, no. 3 (March 1986).
2. Li Peng, "Report on Work of the Government," *Beijing Review*, April 25, 1988, p. 21. According to earlier customs statistics, the nation's 1987 total import and export value amounted to US$79.9 billion. *Zhongbao*, January 2, 1988.
3. Li Peng, "Report," p. 21.
4. Ibid.
5. Ibid.
6. "Communiqué of the Statistics of 1986 Economic and Social Development," *Beijing Review*, March 2, 1987.
7. Luo Xuejuan, "China Develops Overseas Joint Ventures," *China Market*, no. 7 (1986), p. 9.
8. Xue Muqiao, "Comments on the Reform of the System of Foreign Trade," in *Guoji Maoyi* (International Trade), no. 3 (1986), pp. 4–5; Satoshi Imai, "Reform of China's Foreign Trade System," *China Newsletter*, no. 56 (1986), pp. 2–7, 22.
9. Wei Yuming, "Try to Create a New Situation in Our Effort to Utilize Foreign Capital," *Guoji Maoyi*, no. 1 (1984), p. 4; Wu Jie, "Foreign Capital in China—A Brief Review," *China Market*, no. 7 (1986), p. 10.
10. Zhang Zhongji, "End of Turmoil Brings Economic Growth," *Beijing Review*, June 12, 1988, p. 20.
11. *Beijing Daily*, February 3, 1988.
12. *Guoji Maoyi*, no. 6 (1986), p. 5. These include, among others, "The Law of the People's Republic of China on Joint Ventures Using Chinese and Foreign Investment" in July 1979; "Regulations Governing Supervision and Control

of Foreign Vessels by the People's Republic of China" on August 22, 1979; "Provisional Regulations Governing Export License System of the Administrative Commission on Import and Export and the Ministry of Foreign Trade" in May 1980; "Regulations of the People's Republic of China on Special Economic Zones in Guangdong Province" on August 26, 1980; "The Income Tax Law of the People's Republic of China Concerning Joint Ventures with Chinese and Foreign Investment" on September 10, 1980; "Interim Regulations of the People's Republic of China Concerning the Control of Resident Offices of Foreign Enterprises" on October 30, 1980; "Provisional Regulations for Foreign Exchange Control of the People's Republic of China" on December 18, 1980; "Economic Contract Law of the People's Republic of China" on December 13, 1981; and "Regulations of the People's Republic of China on the Exploitation of Offshore Petroleum Resources in Cooperation with Foreign Enterprises" on January 31, 1982. *Collection of Laws and Regulations of China Concerning Foreign Economic and Trade Relations* (Beijing: China Market Publishing Corp., 1983). More recently, "The Law on Foreign Enterprises" and "Provisions of the State Council Encouraging Foreign Investment" were added to the list.

13. Teng Weizao, "Socialist Modernization and the Pattern of Foreign Trade," in Xu Dixin et al., *China's Search for Economic Growth: The Chinese Economy Since 1949* (Beijing: New Word Press, 1982), p. 172.

14. Wei Yuming, "Try to Create a New Situation," p. 4.

15. Colina MacDougall, "Economic Report: The Chinese Economy in 1976," *China Quarterly*, no. 70 (June 1977), pp. 355–70.

16. Peter Drysdale, "The Pacific Basin and Its Economic Vitality," in James W. Morley, *The Pacific Basin* (New York: Capital City Press, 1986), pp. 11–12, 15. In strict economic terms, the numbers for per capita income do not necessarily reflect the actual physical economic well-being of countries. However, the way Chinese read them elevates their importance in influencing decision-making in China. Studying the Chinese treatment of per capita income figures, one is often amazed at the degree of importance the Chinese have given them, particularly since the introduction of the open foreign economic policy. Even Deng's goal for China's development for the period before the year 2000 is to a large extent measured in terms of per capita income. "Deng Xiaoping on Domestic Reforms, the Open Policy and Peaceful Development," *Outlook* (overseas ed.) November 3, 1986, p. 5.

17. *Xinhua Yuebao*, January 1979, pp. 1–2. Deng Xiaoping also believes that the Japanese economic take-off resulted from their bold and appropriate use of foreign capital. "Deng Xiaoping on Domestic Reforms," p. 6.

18. Yin Ching-yao, "Peking-Moscow Relations: An Analysis," in *Issues & Studies*, no. 3 (March 1986); Zhu Chengjun, "The New Page in Sino-Eastern European Relations," *Outlook* (overseas ed.) October 20, 1986, pp. 5–6.

19. *Xinhua Yuebao*, February 1985, p. 89.

20. Liu Shulong, "Summary of Foreign Investment Absorbed by China," *China Market*, no. 1 (1986), pp. 19–11.

21. Ibid.

22. Ibid., p. 10; Zhang Zhongji, "End of Turmoil," p. 21.

23. *Xinhua Yuebao*, November 1985, pp. 72–73.

24. Kazuko Mohri, "China's Economic Reform, Open-Door Policies Headed for Systematization—4th Session of 6th National People's Congress," *China Newsletter*, no. 63, (1986), p. 6.

25. Yan Ren, "Main Characteristics of China's Seventh Five-Year Plan," *China Market*, no. 6 (1986), p. 12.

26. "Zhao on Coastal Area's Development Strategy," *Beijing Review,* February 8, 1988, pp. 14–19.
27. "Deng Xiaoping on Domestic Reforms," *China Market,* no. 6 (1986), pp. 6–7.
28. According to *Jingji Daobao,* during the first six months of 1986, the contracts China signed for direct foreign investment amounted to $1.24 billion, 20 percent less than that during the first six months of the previous year. *Jingji Daobao,* no. 34 (1986), p. 27.
29. Ibid.
30. "Provisions of the State Council Encouraging Foreign Investment," *Beijing Review,* October 27, 1986, pp. 26–28.
31. For example, Jiangsu province (see *Jingji Daobao,* no. 35 (1986), p. 28) and the city of Dalian (see *Jingji Daobao,* no. 33 (1986), p. 27).
32. *China Market,* no. 5 (1986), p. 9.
33. Chung-Tong Wu and David F. Ip, "Forsaking the Iron Rice Bowl: Employment and Wages in China's Special Economic Zones," *Asian Journal of Public Administration* (Hong Kong), vol. 7, no. 2 (December 1985) pp. 216–24.
34. Qing Yuandao, "The File of Hitachi Fujian: Another Case of Joint-Ventures Between China and Foreign Countries," *The Nineties,* April 1986, pp. 25–28.
35. *Xinhua Yuebao,* July 1985, p. 83; ibid., August 1985, pp. 89–93, 94.
36. Yu Yulin, "Unhealthy Tendencies Among Chinese Communist Cadres," *Issues and Studies,* no. 1 (January 1986).
37. "Deng's (Second) Thoughts," *Asiaweek,* April 5, 1987, p. 14.
38. Yu Yulin, "Unhealthy Tendencies."
39. "Deng's (Second) Thoughts," p. 14.

FOUR: CHINESE NUCLEAR STRATEGY

XIAOCHUAN ZHANG

1. Following the successful launching of China's first ICBM, a group of three satellites with a single carrier rocket was launched successfully on Sept. 20, 1981. It was a technological breakthrough in the development of China's strategic and tactical guided missiles. See *China Official Annual Report 1982/83,* edited by New China News Co. (Hong Kong: Kingsway International Publications, 1982), p. 390.
2. *Guangming Daily,* January 22, 1983.
3. Su Yu, *Great Victory for Chairman Mao's Guideline on War* (Beijing: Foreign Language Press, 1978), p. 15.
4. Hu Yaobang, in *China Daily,* June 12, 1986.
5. *Beijing Review,* July 28, 1986, p. 4. For more detail, see "PLA Priorities: Disarmament and Development," *Beijing Review,* no. 43 (October 27, 1986), p. 16; see also Bradley Hahn, *China Business Review,* July-August 1985.

   The PLA has spent the equivalent of more than US$5 billion on nuclear weapons development alone since 1960. Production of nuclear materials probably accounts for more than half of that figure, with the rest going into research, development, fabrication, and testing. Even though this amounts to only a small fraction of government expenditure, the program absorbed a considerable portion of the country's raw materials, production capacity, and most proficient manpower at a time when other sectors of the national economy also had great need.
6. Xinhua News Agency, July 20, 1982, in FBIS-CHI-82-141-K2-4.

7. Ibid.
8. *People's Daily* (overseas ed.), June 27, 1986.
9. Harry G. Gelber, *Technology, Defense, and External Relations in China, 1975–1978*, (Boulder, Colo.: Westview Press, 1979), p. 68.
10. Gong Xuan, in *People's Daily*, May 31, 1978.
11. Zhao Ziyang, speech at the meeting on defense science, technology, and industry; see FBIS-CHI-18-JUNE-86-K2; also Hu Yaobang, in *People's Daily*, June 12, 1986.
12. Ibid.
13. IISS, *Strategic Survey, 1985–1986*, p. 155.
14. IISS, *Military Balance, 1985–1986*, p. 113; *Military Balance, 1987–1988*, p. 145; SIPRI, *Yearbook 1987*, p. 35; *Jane's Weapon Systems 1987–1988* (London: Oxford University Press, 1987), p. 3.
15. IISS, *Military Balance, 1987–1988*, pp. 115–16.
16. SIPRI, *Yearbook 1985* (London: Taylor & Francis, 1985), p. 69.
17. Col. Trevor N. Dupuy, et al., *The Almanac of World Military Power*, 4th ed. (San Rafael, Calif.: Presidio Press, 1986), p. 103.
18. Richard Nations, "Joining the League," *Far Eastern Economic Review*, April 24, 1986.
19. For more detail, see reports in *People's Daily* and *PLA Daily*, October 2 and 3, 1984.
20. *Beijing Review*, July 28, 1986, p. 4; *Beijing Review*, September 7, 1987, p. 17; for details of each year's military expenditure, see state budget: *International Financial Statistics*, November 1984 (Washington, D.C.: IMF, 1984).
21. *Beijing Review*, October 27, 1986, p. 16.
22. Hu Yaobang, speech at the Royal Institute of International Affairs, in *People's Daily*, June 12, 1986.
23. SIPRI, *Yearbook 1985*, p. 257.
24. The efforts in this respect, like the Chinese Navy's buildup, are in accordance with the active defense strategy, currently maintained by the Chinese government. See *People's Daily* (overseas ed.), April 5, 1987.
25. Bradley Hahn, in *China Business Review*, July-August 1985.
26. Norman Polmar, *Strategic Weapons* (New York: National Strategy Information Center, 1982), p. 71.
27. Even a greatly expanded effort could still be construed exclusively within the context of a deterrent rather than a war-fighting posture. See Jonathan D. Pollack, "China as a Military Power," in *Military Power and Policy in Asian States* (Boulder, Colo.: Westview Press, 1980), p. 73.
28. Paul Godwin, *The Chinese Defense Establishment: Continuity and Change in the 1980s* (Boulder, Colo.: Westview Press, 1983), p. 24.
29. Hua Di, "Nuclear Strategy and Arms Control from a Chinese Point of View," a paper presented at the AAAS Annual Meeting, Boston, February 11–15, 1988.
30. *Beijing Review*, May 27, 1985, p. 19.
31. *Washington Post*, April 4, 1988.
32. *People's Daily*, August 6, 1988.
33. *People's Daily*, July 28, 1988.
34. *New York Times*, July 16, 1988; *People's Daily*, August 8, 1988.
35. *New York Times*, December 3, 1984.
36. Harry G. Gelber, *Technology, Defense, and External Relations in China, 1975–1978* (Boulder, Colo.: Westview Press, 1979), p. 65.
37. *Far Eastern Economic Review, Asia 1978 Handbook*, p. 35.

FIVE: SINO-SOVIET RELATIONS

GUOCANG HUAN

1. *China Daily* (Beijing) January 7, 1989; A. T. Sheikh, "Gorbachev's Policy Towards Afghanistan and Pakistan," *Asian Survey*, vol. XXXVIII, no. 11 (November 1988), pp. 1170–87.
2. *Centre Daily News* (New York), December 7, 9, and 10, 1988.
3. *World Economic Herald* (Shanghai; the title is often translated as *World Economy Herald*), November 7; 1988, *Far East Economic Review*, April 21, 1988, pp. 22–23; and *People's Daily* (Beijing), October 14, 1988, and December 30, 1988.
4. *People's Daily*, September 29, 1988, December 8, 1988, and December 17, 1988.
5. *People's Daily*, December 29, 1988.
6. *World Economic Herald*, November 14, 1988; and *New York Times*, January 16, 1989.
7. *People's Daily*, December 30, 1988.
8. *Beijing Review* (Beijing), vol. 30, no. 15 (April 1, 1987), pp. 11–13.
9. International Institute for Strategic Studies (London), *The Military Balance (1988–1989)*, pp. 30–47, 146–47.
10. Zhao Rukuan and Yang Tireng, "Views On Some Policy Issues During the Ten Years' Reform," *World Economic Herald*, December 3, 1988; and Xueliang Ding, "The Disparity Between Idealistic and Instrumental Chinese Reforms," *Asian Survey*, vol. XXVIII, no. 11 (November 1988), pp. 1117–39.
11. *People's Daily*, January 2, 1989.
12. *Far East Economic Review*, December 22, 1988, pp. 12–13; *World Economic Herald*, December 19, 1988.
13. *People's Daily*, October 1, 1988.
14. M. C. Ross, "Changing the Foreign Trade System," *China Business Review* (Washington, D.C.) May-June 1988, pp. 34–37; *Asian Wall Street Journal* (Hong Kong), December 19, 1988.
15. *People's Daily*, October 8, 1988, and January 10, 1989.
16. *Cheng Ming* (Hong Kong), January 1989, pp. 6–9, 15.
17. *People's Daily*, December 13, 1988.
18. *World Economic Herald*, December 3, 1988, and December 26, 1988; and *Far East Economic Review*, December 22, 1988, pp. 12–15.
19. *People's Daily*, October 19, 1988.
20. *The Nineties* (Hong Kong), July 1988, pp. 34–47; *Cheng Ming*, November 1988, pp. 8–10.
21. *World Economic Herald*, October 14, 1984.
22. G. Duffy and J. Lee, "Soviet Debate on 'Reasonable Sufficiency,'" *Arms Control Today*, vol. 18, no. 8 (October 1988), pp. 19–22.
23. *Asian Wall Street Journal*, December 9, 1988; and *Japan Economic Journal* (Tokyo), December 10, 1988, p. 10.
24. IISS, *The Military Balance, 1988–1989*, pp. 30–47.
25. *People's Daily*, October 22, 1988, and January 16, 1989.
26. *Far East Economic Review*, January 5, 1989, pp. 10–11; *People's Daily*, January 10, 1989, December 20, 1988, and December 22, 1988; and *New York Times*, January 3, 1989.
27. *New York Times*, December 4, 1988; and *Far East Economic Review*, January 5, 1989, p. 11.
28. *World Economic Herald*, June 4, 1988; July 11, 1988; November 21, 1988; and November 28, 1988.

29. Qian Qisheng, "A Year of Improving the International Situation," *People's Daily*, December 17, 1988; and *World Economic Herald*, December 3, 1988.
30. The World Bank, *China: Long-Term Issues and Options, Annex B: Agriculture to the Year 2000: Perspectives and Options*, 1985, pp. 93–100.
31. *World Economic Herald*, November 4, 1988, and December 26, 1988.
32. *People's Daily*, January 25, 1989.
33. *Wall Street Journal*, November 25, 1983; and *Meizhou Yuaqiao Ribao* (New York), June 27, 1984.
34. *New York Times*, November 26, 1988.
35. International Institute for Strategic Studies, *The Military Balance 1988–1989*, pp. 180–182.
36. *Asian Survey*, vol. XII, no. 2 (February 1972), p. 93.
37. *Asian Survey*, vol. XIX, no. 1 (January 1979), p. 89.

SIX: CHINA'S POLICY TOWARD THE UNITED STATES
GUOCANG HUAN

1. See, for instance, A. D. Barnett, *The Making of Foreign Policy in China* (Boulder, Colo.: Westview Press, 1985), chaps. 1, 2, and 3; and *China Directory*, 1987 and 1988, (Tokyo: Radio Press).
2. U. A. Johnson, G. R. Packard, and A. D. Wilhelm, Jr., *China Policy in the Next Decade*, Report of the Atlantic Council of the United States Committee on China Policy (Boston: OG & H., 1984), chap. 1; and Fei Xiaodong, "An Interview with Ambassador Winston Lord," *World Economic Herald*, (Shanghai), November 28, 1988.
3. *People's Daily* (Beijing), May 28, 1987, and October 13, 1988; and *China Business Review* (Washington, D.C.), May–June 1988, pp. 56–57.
4. *People's Daily*, October 19, 1988.
5. *People's Daily*, October 8, 1988, December 30, 1988, and January 10, 1989.
6. *World Journal* (New York), November 14, 1988.
7. Ibid.
8. *People's Daily*, October 6, 1988; B. S. Glaser and B. N. Garrett, "Chinese Perspective on the Strategic Defense Initiative," *Problems of Communism*, March–April 1986, pp. 28–44; and Liu Yuaqiu, "China and Neutron Bomb," unpublished research paper.
9. *People's Daily*, December 20, 1988; and Ma Feibai, "Deng Xiaoping Begins to Be Impatient," *The Journalist* (Taipei), December 26, 1988, pp. 78–80.
10. Guocang Huan, "Relationship Between the Two Sides of the Taiwan Strait and Taipei's Policy Towards the Mainland," *The Nineties* (Hong Kong), July 1988, pp. 74–75; and *People's Daily*, December 30, 1988.
11. *People's Daily*, October 14, 1988, and December 30, 1988; *World Economic Herald*, November 7, 1988; and *Far Eastern Economic Review*, April 21, 1988, pp. 12–13.
12. Ibid.
13. *Hong Kong Economic Times*, December 12, 1988, p. 1.
14. *Beijing Review*, vol. 30, no. 4. (January 26, 1987), pp. 11–12, and vol. 30, no. 3 (January 19, 1987), pp. 11–12.
15. In 1988, for instance, there were at least fifty or more Chinese military personnel studying political science and international relations on various American campuses. The number of those studying science and technology was much

greater. Since 1987, the Chinese National Defense University and the National Defense University of the U.S. Army have built up a regular exchange program.

16. *China Business Review*, May–June 1988, p. 57.
17. Ibid., pp. 10–25; and *People's Daily*, October 19, 1988.
18. *World Journal*, January 5, 1989.
19. *China Times Weekly* (Taipei), January 5, 1989, pp. 13–15.
20. *People's Daily*, January 7, 1989.
21. *World Journal*, January 11, 1989.
22. *People's Daily*, January 7, 1989.
23. *People's Daily*, December 20, 1988, and December 22, 1988; and *New York Times*, January 3, 1989.
24. *The Nineties*, January 1989, pp. 42–53; and *People's Daily*, January 3, 1989, and December 31, 1989.
25. *World Journal*, March 3, 1989.
26. *The Nineties*, March 1988, pp. 53–55.

SEVEN: CHINA AND THE KOREAN PENINSULA

YUFAN HAO

1. For a useful assessment of recent Sino–North Korean relations, see Chae-jin Lee's "China's Policy Towards North Korea: Changing Relations in the 1980s," in Robert Scalapino and Hongkoo Lee, eds., *North Korea in a Regional and Global Context* (Berkeley: University of California Press, 1986), pp. 190–240. I am indebted to Chae-jin Lee for a number of ideas and points raised in his article.
2. Donald Zagoria, ed., *Soviet Policy in East Asia* (New Haven: Yale University Press, 1982), pp. 1–27.
3. Paul Dibb, "Soviet Capabilities, Interests and Strategies in East Asia in the 1980s," *Survival*, July-August 1982, p. 155.
4. See Institute of International Strategic Studies (IISS) *Military Balance, 1985–1986* (London: IISS, 1986).
5. Norman D. Levin, "Strategic Environment in East Asia and US-Korea Security Relations in the 1980s," *Rand Note*, March 1983, p. 3.
6. See Harry Gelman and Norman D. Levin, *The Future of Soviet–North Korean Relations* (Rand Corporation, October 1984).
7. See Levin, "Strategic Environment," p. 5.
8. For a useful assessment of Soviet–North Korean relations, see Young C. Kim, "Pyongyang, Moscow and Peking," *Problems of Communism* November-December 1978; Gelman and Levin, *The Future of Soviet–North Korean Relations;* and Ralph Clough, "The Soviets and the Two Koreas," in Zagoria, ed., *Soviet Policy in East Asia* (New Haven: Yale University Press, 1982).
9. China published the Burmese accounts side by side with the North Koreans' defense; see *People's Daily*, August 1983.
10. See Foreign Broadcast Information Service (FBIS), August 16, 1984, p. C1.
11. See London IISS report of May 3, 1985, as cited in the *Korean Herald*, May 5, 1985.
12. Richard Nation, "Love Boat to Wonsan," *Far Eastern Economic Review (FEER)*, August 29, 1985, p. 22.
13. For U.S.–Chinese military relations, see Edward Ross, "US–China Military Relations" (a presentation to the Heritage Foundation, January 1986); see also

Jonathan Pollack, *The Lesson of Coalition Politics: Sino-American Security Relations*, (Rand Corporation, February 1984).

14. At the invitation of Gorbachev, Kim Il Sung arrived in Moscow on October 22, 1986; see *People's Daily*, October 23, 1986.

15. See Chong-sik Lee, "The Evolution of the Korean Workers' Party and the Rise of Kim Chong Il," in Robert Scalapino, ed., *North Korea Today;* see also Byung Chul Koh, "Political Succession in North Korea," *Korea & World Affairs*, vol 8, no. 3 (Fall 1984).

16. See Gelman and Levin, *The Future of Soviet–North Korean Relations.*

17. See *Washington Post*, May 5, 1986.

18. See *Washington Post*, January 6, 1989.

19. See "Trading Comrades," *FEER*, December 8, 1988, pp. 20–21.

20. See IISS, *Military Balance, 1985–1986.*

21. Ibid., pp. 126–27.

22. Ibid., p. 127.

23. See Byung Chul Koh, "China and the Korean Peninsula," *Korean and World Affairs*, Summer 1985, pp. 254–79.

24. See *New York Times*, April 5, 1987.

25. See "Vice Premier Li Peng on Foreign Relations and Domestic Policy," *Outlook, (Liaowang)* April 28, 1986, p. 4.

26. See Peng Di, "Changes in Chinese Foreign Policy?" *Outlook*, March 17, 1986, p. 3–4.

27. In addition to the strong response to the Japanese textbook issue, the Chinese media have been reporting more general "unfavorable" trends in Japan. For a recent commentary, see Li Nan, "What Does the Fujio Issue Tell Us?" *Outlook*, September 22, 1986, p. 27.

28. See "Foreign Minister Wu Xueqian on Foreign Policy and the International Situation," *Outlook*, December 9, 1985, pp. 11–13.

29. See Gorbachev's Vladivostok speech in the *Washington Post*, July 28, 1986.

30. See Paul D. Wolfowitz, "Recent Security Developments in Korea," U.S. Department of State, Bureau of Public Affairs, *Current Policy*, no. 731, August 12, 1985.

31. Domestically, Beijing began to downgrade the role of the late Chairman Mao and to attack the cult of personality, which could not have pleased Kim Il Sung, the object of a cult in North Korea. In foreign affairs, China greatly improved its relations with the DPRK's chief adversaries, the United States and Japan.

32. See *People's Daily*, January 28, 1984.

33. Some even argue that Beijing welcomes an American presence to counter both the Soviets and the Japanese. See William R. Heaton, "America and China: The Coming Decade," in William Buckingham, Jr., ed., *Defense Planning for the 1990s* (Beijing: National Defense University, 1984), pp. 221–38.

34. See *Guangming Daily*, October 6, 1986; see also Tao BinWei, "Observations on the Korean Situation," *Beijing Review*, no. 38, September 23, 1985, p. 16–18.

35. See *Washington Post*, January 6, 1989.

36. This was first revealed by *Nihon Keizai Shimbun*, November 26, 1984; cited here from Jonathan Pollack, "China's Changing Perception of East Asian Security and Development," *Orbit*, Winter 1986, p. 787.

37. See Xinhua Fe. 3, and FBIS—China, Feb. 4, 1985.

38. See *FEER*, December 8, 1988, pp. 20–21.

39. See *People's Daily*, September 19, 1986; and *Washington Post*, September 18, 1986.

40. See Jae Ho Chung, "South Korea-China Economic Relations," *Asian Survey*, vol. XXVIII (October 1988), p. 1042.

41. Foreign Minister Wu Xueqian flew to Pyongyang during the hijacking crises to reaffirm China's disapproval of any two-Koreas "machination"; President Li Xiannian visited the DPRK soon after the Seoul Asian Games. See *People's Daily*, May 20, 1983; and *Guangming Daily*, October 3, 1986.

42. Li Xiannian said to Kim during his recent visit: "We have a good tradition that leaders of both countries love to visit each other frequently like very close relatives. Mao and Zhou did this, and we will continue to do this"; see *People's Daily*, October 6, 1986.

43. See Wang Zhaoguo's speech at the Conference on Sino-Japanese Friendship in the 21st Century, *People's Daily*, September 23, 1986, p. 6.

44. See Gregory Knight, "Soviet China Policy in the Gorbachev Era," *Washington Quarterly*, Spring 1986.

45. See Gelman and Levin, *The Future of Soviet-North Korea Relations* (Rand Corporation, 1984).

46. See Ralph Clough, "The Soviets and the Two Koreas."

47. See Dwight Perkins, "The Economic Background and Implications for China," in Herbert Ellison, ed., *The Sino-Soviet Conflict: A Global Perspective* (Seattle: University of Washington Press, 1982), pp. 91–111; see also *Beijing Review*, February 28, 1983.

EIGHT: CHINA AND SOUTHEAST ASIA

Xiaobo Lu

1. See International Institute for Strategic Studies, *Military Balance, 1985–1986* p. 30.

2. *Pacific Defense Report*, May 1985.

3. *Christian Science Monitor*, December 18, 1986.

4. *Christian Science Monitor*, September 19, 1988.

5. *Asian Affairs*, Winter 1984.

6. See the *Christian Science Monitor* interview with the Chinese foreign minister, Qian Qichen, October 11, 1988.

7. *Beijing Review*, May 5, 1986, p. 11.

8. *China Daily*, March 27, 1986.

9. *Far East Economic Review (FEER)*, March 20, 1986. p. 69.

10. *Christian Science Monitor*, October 11, 1988.

11. *Asiaweek*, December 2, 1988, p. 25.

12. *FEER*, November 10, 1988, p. 23.

13. *People's Daily*, December 28, 1988.

14. *Christian Science Monitor*, December 18, 1986.

15. *FEER*, December 11, 1986, p. 34.

16. Ibid.

17. *FEER*, March 22, 1984, p. 17.

18. *Christian Science Monitor*, December 18, 1986.

19. See Gareth Parter, "Cambodia: Sihanouk's Initiative," *Foreign Affairs*, vol. 66, no. 1 (Spring 1988).

20. *People's Daily*, November 12, 1988.

21. *Outlook (Liaowang)*, November 10, 1986, p. 26.

22. *FEER*, December 11, 1986.

23. *Outlook,* March 24, 1986, p. 28.
24. See *Malaysian Statistical Bulletin,* January–March 1985.
25. See *Monthly Statistical Bulletin* (Central Bureau of Statistics, Jakarta, Indonesia), October 1984, p. 43.
26. *Min Pao Monthly,* vol. 21, no. 2 (February 1986).
27. *FEER,* February 13, 1986, pp. 25–26.
28. *FEER,* December 11, 1986, pp. 28–29.
29. *Outlook,* September 16, 1985.
30. *Guangming Daily,* May 3, 1986.
31. *Outlook,* August 25, 1986.
32. *The Voice of the Overseas Chinese (Hua Sheng Bao),* June 3, 1986.

NINE: CHINA'S THIRD WORLD POLICY

Zhimin Lin

1. The author wishes to express deep gratitude to Dr. Peter Van Ness, Dr. Andrew Nathan, Dr. Guocang Huan, and Mr. Yufan Hao, among many others, for their comments and suggestions. Special appreciation is extended to Mr. Edward Fox, who, in various ways, has contributed to the completion of this paper. I alone, however, am responsible for the contents.
2. See *People's Daily,* November 2, 1985.
3. For two good illustrations, see *The World Economy (Shi Jie Jing Ji),* (Beijing), no. 12, 1981, pp. 11–14; *World Affairs (Shi Jie Zhi Shi)* (Beijing), no. 18, 1984, pp. 2–3.
4. *People's Daily,* January 4, 1989.
5. See *Selected Works of Mao Tse-tung,* vol. 4 (Beijing: Foreign Language Publication House, 1965), p. 98.
6. See *Dao Nian Zhou Enlai* (In Memory of Zhou Enlai) (Beijing: Ren Min Chu Ban She, 1986), p. 493.
7. See, for example, Lillian G. Harris, *China's Foreign Policy Toward the Third World* (New York: Praeger, 1985), pp. 20–22.
8. In August 1958, China bombarded and blockaded Jingmen Dao (Quemoy), an offshore island occupied by KMT troops. This action was followed by massive U.S. naval and air deployment to the Taiwan Strait. The exact motivation of this act is not yet clear. But its implications for Sino–U.S. relations were substantial. For a Chinese interpretation, see Wang Bingnan, *Zhong Mei Jiu Nian Hei Tan Hei Gu* (Review of Nine Years of Sino-American Negotiations) (Beijing: Shi Jie Zhi Shi Chu Ban She, 1985), pp. 68–74.
9. A recent Chinese book on then Foreign Minister Chen Yi revealed some of the inside details of the process. He Xiaoru, *Yuan Shuai He Wai Jiao Jia* (Marshal and Diplomat) (Beijing: PLA Literature Press, 1985), esp. pp. 52–68.
10. Ibid., p. 82.
11. Peter Van Ness, *Revolution and Chinese Foreign Policy,* (Berkeley: University of California Press, 1970), p. 13.
12. Ibid., p. 82.
13. He Xiaoru, *Yuan Shuai He Wai Jiao Jia* p. 159.
14. See Harish Kapur, *The End of Isolation: China After Mao* (The Hague: Martinus Nijhoff Publishers, 1985), p. 138.
15. See Michel Oksenberg, "A Decade of Sino-American Relations," *Foreign Affairs,* vol. 61, no. 1 (Fall, 1982), pp. 175–77.

16. In late 1969, Mao asked Marshal Ye Jianyin and several other senior military leaders to review China's strategic position and options. See *People's Daily*, October 30, 1986.

17. See *Zhong Hua Ren Min Gong He Guo Jing Ji Da Shi Ji* (The Chronology of Major Economic Events of the People's Republic of China) (Beijing: China Social Science Press, 1984), pp. 505–6.

18. According to this theory, the United States and the Soviet Union belong to the First World; Europe, Japan, and other advanced industrial states to the Second; and the developing countries to the Third. China itself, while a socialist state, is a Third World country.

19. For a full text of the speech, see *Beijing Review*, 1974, supplement no. 15.

20. Harry Harding, "China and the Third World," in Richard Solomon, ed., *The China Factor* (Englewood Cliffs, N.J.: Prentice-Hall, 1981), pp. 266–70.

21. Samuel Kim, "China and the Third World: In Search of a Neorealistic Theory," in Samuel Kim, ed., *China and the World: Chinese Foreign Policy in the Post-Mao Era* (Boulder, Colo.: Westview Press, 1984), pp. 183–86.

22. For example, Lillian G. Harris talked very little about the theory in her major work on China's Third World policy, *China's Foreign Policy Toward the Third World*.

23. For the text of the editorial, see "Chairman Mao's Theory of the Differentiation of the Three Worlds Is a Major Contribution to Marxism-Leninism," *Beijing Review*, November 4, 1977, pp. 10–43.

24. In fact, one of the accusations China made during the mid-1970s was that the Soviet Union had a "south-bound" strategy, and actions such as those India took were part of a big expansion plan.

25. Deng Xiaoping recently renewed his call for the establishment of a new international economic *and* political order. See *People's Daily*, October 6, 1988, and December 17, 1988.

26. See, for example, Zhao Ziyang, "Report of the Drift of the Seventh Five-year Plan," *People's Daily*, March 28, 1986.

27. *People's Daily*, December 23, 1986.

28. Samuel Kim, "China and the Third World," p. 187.

29. See *Outlook* (Liaowang) (Beijing), no. 18, 1985, pp. 10–11.

30. According to Nicholas Lardy, China's share of world trade has doubled in ten years and China has become an important trading market for a number of industrialized or newly industrialized economies; see his *Economic Policy Toward China in the Post-Reagan Era* (National Committee on United States–China Relations, 1989), p. 4.

31. "Petroleum Exporting Countries: Joint Struggle Wins New Victory," *Beijing Review*, no. 4, 1974, pp. 14–15.

32. *People's Daily* (overseas ed.), November 7, 1986.

33. *Zhong Hua Ren Min Gong He Guo Jing Ji Da Shi Ji*, pp. 544.

34. Harris, *China's Foreign Policy Toward the Third World*, pp. 97–98.

35. See, for example, Chen Muhua, "The Current Reality and Perspective of China's Foreign Economic and Trade Work," *Theory Monthly (Li Lun Yue Kan)* (Beijing), no. 8, 1984, pp. 1–9.

36. *World Economy*, no. 10, 1985, p. 6.

37. *Outlook*, no. 46, 1985, pp. 5–6.

38. See for example, *World Economic Herald* (Shanghai), December 5, 1988.

39. *People's Daily*, January 3, 1989.

40. Lardy, *Economic Policy Toward China in the Post-Reagan Era*, p. 4.

41. In 1982 and 1983, Kuwait provided China with loans totaling 43.6 million dinars (about US$150 million) to finance four projects in China. A Sino-

Kuwaiti investment committee was set up in early 1985. See *Beijing Review*, no. 3, 1985.

42. *People's Daily*, November 11, 1986.

43. *People's Daily*, December 14, 1988.

44. For some recent Chinese interpretations of these positions, see Xue Mouhong, "The New Situation in Our Country's Diplomacy," *Red Flag* (Hong Qi) (Beijing), no. 6, pp. 19–27; and Peng Di, "Has China's Foreign Policy Changed?" *Outlook*, (overseas ed.), March 17, 1986, pp. 3–4.

45. *World Affairs*, no. 5, 1979, pp. 4–5.

46. Robert Ross, "Foreign Policy in 1987: Independent Rhetoric, Pragmatic Policy," in Anthony Kane, ed., *China Briefing, 1988* (Boulder, Colo.: Westview Press, 1988), p. 52.

47. For a recent Chinese discussion of the subject, see Zhongqing Tien, "China and the Middle East: Principles and Realities," *Middle East Review*, Winter 1985–86, pp. 7–16.

48. See "Interview with Gong Dafei, Vice Foreign Minister for African Affairs," *Africa Report*, March-April, 1984, pp. 20–22.

49. Ibid.

50. John Copper, "China and the Third World," *Current History*, September 1983, p. 247.

51. *Beijing Review*, no. 29, 1986, pp. 26–27.

52. For some recent Chinese official comments on this issue, see Qian Qichen, "A Year of Major Improvement in the International Situation," *People's Daily*, December 17, 1988.

53. World Bank, *World Development*, (New York: Oxford University Press, 1986), p. 24.

54. *People's Daily*, December 12, 1988.

55. Harding, "China and the Third World," p. 279.

56. Chen Muhua, "The Current Reality and Perspective of China's Foreign Economic and Trade Work," p. 8.

TEN: SINO–EAST EUROPEAN RELATIONS
MING CHEN

1. These five countries have been called loyalists in the West because they have faithfully followed the general Soviet international stand, especially in regard to the Sino-Soviet disputes.

2. In 1985 Chinese Vice-Premier Li Peng visited Eastern Europe twice, covering all five loyalist countries. He was the highest-ranking Chinese official to visit those five countries in over twenty years. This was followed by the visits of Foreign Minister Wu Xuegian and Vice-Chairman of the Chinese National People's Congress Liao Hansheng to some countries in Eastern Europe in 1986. In the same period, senior officials from Eastern Europe came to China one after another. Among them were J. Obdouski, chairman of the Polish Council of Ministers; Svatopluk Potáč, Czechoslovak deputy prime minister; Nicolae Ceauşescu, Romanian president and general secretary of the party; Gunther Kleiber, deputy chairman of the German Democratic Republic's Council of Ministers; N. Suković, vice-chairman of the Yugoslav Federal Executive Council; Jaromír Obzina, Czechoslovak deputy prime minister; and Horst Sindermann, president of the People's Chamber of East Germany. The year 1986 witnessed the two most prominent visits to Beijing from the loyalist Eastern Europe in more than twenty years, those of General Wojciech Jaru-

zelski, the head of Poland, and German Democratic Republic leader Erich Honecker; the latter restored party-to-party relations with China.

3. A. Ross Johnson, "Yugoslavia and the Sino-Soviet Conflict: The Shift of Triangle, 1948-1974," *Studies in Comparative Communism*, vol. 7 (Spring-Summer 1974), p. 185.

4. *Peking Review*, July 21, 1963, p. 4; August 2, 1963, p. 5; and August 30, 1963, p. 9.

5. M. Kamil Dziewanowski, "China and East Europe," *Survey*, vol. 77 (Autumn 1970), p. 71.

6. Karel Kovanda, "China and Eastern Europe," in Chun-Tu Hsueh, ed., *China's Foreign Relations* (New York: Praeger, 1982), p. 115.

7. "Hungarian Situation Report," *Radio Free Europe*, vol. 19 (October 5, 1979).

8. William G. Hyland, "The Sino-Soviet Conflict: Dilemmas of the Strategic Triangle," in Richard H. Solomon, ed., *The China Factor: Sino-American Relations and the Global Scene* (Englewood Cliffs, N.J.: Prentice-Hall, 1981), p. 146.

9. In the past two years, all the top leaders of the loyalists have paid visits to China, while Zhao Ziyang, then premier and acting general secretary of the party, visited all the five countries in 1987.

10. *China Daily*, May 27, 1980.

11. *Ta Kung Pao*, December 24, 1985.

12. *China Daily*, September 23, 1986.

13. *Shi Jie Zhi Shi Nian Jian* (World Affairs Annual) (Beijing: World Affairs Publishing House, 1982), p. 448.

14. *Washington Post*, December 20, 1985.

15. Hu Yaobang, "Create a New Situation in All Fields of Socialist Modernization," *Beijing Review*, September 13, 1982, pp. 29–33.

16. Zhao Ziyang, "Report on the Work of Government," *Beijing Review*, July 11, 1983, p. xxiii.

17. *Ta Kung Pao*, March 31, 1985.

18. Deng Ziaoping, "Political Structural Reform Is Necessary," *China Daily*, September 4, 1986.

19. Robert G. Sutter, *Chinese Foreign Policy: Development After Mao* (New York: Praeger, 1986), p. 170.

20. Hu Yaobang, "Create a New Situation," p. 32.

21. Sutter, *Chinese Foreign Policy*, p. 170.

22. "Resolution on the Guiding Principles for Building a Socialist Society with Advanced Culture and Ideology," *People's Daily*, September 29, 1986.

23. Michael Yahuda, *Towards the End of Isolationism: China's Foreign Policy After Mao* (New York: St. Martin's, 1983), p. 194.

24. *Ta Kung Pao*, December 24, 1985.

25. Wang Gang-yi, "China Seeks Cooperation with East Europe," *China Daily*, August 14, 1986.

26. Chen Muhua, "On Trade with Eastern Europe," *Beijing Review*, September 3, 1984, pp. 16–17.

27. World Economy Monthly, *(Shi Jie Jing Ji)* (Beijing), December 1983, p. 28.

28. *Ta Kung Pao*, June 17, 1987.

29. See for reference, Zhang Shubao, "Can China Cope with the Peak Period of Paying Back Its External Debt in the 1990s?" *World Economic Herald (Shi Jie Jing Ji Dao Bao)*, May 23, 1988, p. 6.

30. Edwina Moreton, "The Triangle in Eastern Europe," in Gerald Segal, ed., *The China Factor: Peking and the Superpowers* (New York: Holmes & Meier Publishers, 1982), pp. 127–28.

31. William E. Griffith, "China and Europe: 'Weak and Far Away,'" in Solomon, *The China Factor*, p. 159.

32. *Time*, November 3, 1986, p. 42.

33. See Jan Vanous, "East European Economic Showdown," *Problems of Communism*, vol. 31 (July-August 1982).

34. *The Europa Year Book* (London: Europa Publishers, 1986), p. 2141.

35. See *Peking Review*, August 25, 1978, pp. 6-17, and September 1, 1978, pp. 4-14.

36. "A Milestone in Sino-Yugoslav Relations," *Peking Review*, September 1, 1975, p. 7.

37. *Peking Review*, September 2, 1977, p. 6.

38. *Beijing Review*, May 19, 1980, p. 3.

39. See Robert R. King, "Rumania and the Sino-Soviet Conflict," *Studies in Comparative Communism*, vol. 5 (Winter 1972), pp. 373-93.

40. Kenneth Jowitt, *Revolutionary Breakthrough and National Developments: The Case of Romania* (Berkeley: University of California Press, 1971), pp. 234-35.

41. "Ceauşescu in Beijing: Friendship Renewed," *Beijing Review*, October 21, 1985, p. 61.

42. *The Europa Year Book*, 1986, p. 723.

43. *The Europa Year Book*, 1986, p. 2202.

44. *China Daily*, August 7, 1986.

45. *Shi Jei Zhi Shi Jian* (World Affairs Annual), 1982, p. 420.

46. Dorothy Grouse Fonta, "Recent Sino-Albanian Relations," *Asian Survey*, vol. 21 (Autumn 1975), p. 143.

47. The Notes are translated into English in B. Szajkowski, ed., *Documents in Communist Affairs*, vol. II (Cardiff: University College Cardiff Press, 1979).

48. Michael Kaser, "Albania's Self-Chosen Predicament," *World Today* (London), vol. 35 (June 1979), p. 260.

49. "On China's Forced Cessation," *Peking Review* July 21, 1978, pp. 20-23.

50. Elez Biberaj, "Albania After Hoxha: Dilemma of Change," *Problems of Communism*, vol. 34 (November-December 1985), pp. 32-34.

51. *Ta Kung Pao*, December 4, 1985.

52. *Financial Times*, February 3, 1986.

53. *TASS*, March 11, 1985.

54. *China Daily*, July 31, 1986.

55. See Nayan Chanda, "A Troubled Friendship: Moscow Loses Patience with Hanoi over the Economy and Cambodia," *Far Eastern Economic Review*, June 9, 1988, pp. 16-19.

56. See "Belgrade Radio Interviews Qian Qi-chan," *Belgrade Domestic Service in Serbo-Croatian*, April 13, 1986.

57. See, for example, Gorbachev's speech from his recent trip to Czechoslovakia as quoted in *Ta Kung Pao*, April 12, 1987.

58. *Wen Wei Pai* (Hong Kong), December 18, 1985.

59. John P. Hardt and Richard F. Kaufman, "Policy Highlights: A Regional Economic Assessment of Eastern Europe," in John P. Hardt and Richard F. Kaufman, eds., *East European Economies: Slow Growth in the 1980s* (for the U.S. Congress Joint Economic Commission) (Washington, D.C.: Government Printing Office, 1985), p. xiii.

60. *The Europa Year Book*, 1986, p. 3019. Unemployment averages about 15 percent but tops 30 percent in some areas. Roger Thurow, "Tito's Legacy," *Wall Street Journal*, May 8, 1986.

61. *The Europa Year Book*, 1986, p. 2197.

62. Patrick F. R. Artisien, "Albania in the Post-Hoxha Era," *World Today*, June, 1985, pp. 109-110.

ELEVEN: BEIJING'S POLICY ON HONG KONG

ZHIDUAN DENG

1. "China's Stand on Hong Kong Issue Is Solemn and Just," Foreign Broadcast Information Service (FBIS), October 1, 1982, p. E1; also, *Beijing Review,* October 11, 1982, p. 10. The three treaties concerned refer to (1) the Treaty of Nanking, signed by the British government and the Chinese government of the Qing dynasty on August 29, 1842, by which the island of Hong Kong was ceded to Britain; (2) the Convention of Peking, signed on October 24, 1860, under which Kowloon was ceded to Britain; and (3) the Convention for the Extension of Hong Kong, signed on June 9, 1898. The main part of Hong Kong, the New Territories, was leased to Britain for ninety-nine years under this last convention.

2. "Top Leaders Urge Development of Sino-UK Relations," *China Daily* (Beijing), October 15, 1986, p. 1.

3. "Historic Moment in China-UK Links," *China Daily,* October 13, 1986.

4. *People's Daily,* October 3, 1988.

5. *People's Daily* (overseas ed.), April 29, 1988.

6. Ibid., March 29 and April 1, 1987.

7. *The Nineties (Jiushi Niandai Yuekan)* (Hong Kong), May 1986, p. 59.

8. James C. Hsiung, "The Hong Kong Settlement: Effects on Taiwan and Prospects for Peking's Reunification Bid," *Asian Affairs,* Summer 1985, p. 48.

9. Frank Ching, *Hong Kong and China: For Better or for Worse* (New York: China Council of the Asia Society and the Foreign Policy Association, 1985), p. 13.

10. T. L. Tsim, "1997: Peking's Strategy for Hong Kong," *The World Today,* January 1984, p. 38.

11. *Keesing's Contemporary Archives,* vol. XXX, January 1984, p. 32626.

12. Ching, *Hong Kong and China,* pp. 52–53; and for more details, see *Keesing's,* 1984, pp. 33095–96.

13. Ching, *Hong Kong and China,* p. 53; and *Keesing's,* 1984, pp. 33660–61.

14. *The Nineties,* April 1985, pp. 54–56; see also S. E. Finer, "Hong Kong 1997: When the Kissing Has to Stop," *Political Quarterly,* July-September 1985, p. 266.

15. *The Nineties,* December 1985, pp. 14–15.

16. For details, see Loyti Cheng, "An Economic Analysis of Capital Flight in Hong Kong," *International Law and Politics,* vol. 17 (1985), pp. 583–716.

17. Tsim, "1997," p. 44.

18. *The Nineties,* May 1986, pp. 61–62, 64.

19. *Maclean's,* April 11, 1988, p. 35.

20. *Far Eastern Economic Review (FEER),* August 25, 1983, p. 14.

21. Hsiung, "The Hong Kong Settlement," p. 47.

22. *People's Daily,* April 3, 1987.

23. *Beijing Review,* March 30, 1987, p. 4.

24. K. C. Mun and T. S. Chan, "The Role of Hong Kong in United States–China Trade," *Columbia Journal of World Business,* Spring 1986, pp. 70–71.

25. *People's Daily,* December 3, 1986.

26. "A Report on China Delivered by the Central Intelligence Agency, US," *China Spring (ZhongGuo ZhiShuen)* (New York), August 1988, pp. 49–50.

27. *China Spring,* September 6, 1986.

28. Piers Jacobs, "Hong Kong and the Modernization of China," *Journal of International Affairs,* Winter 1986, p. 70.

29. *People's Daily*, February 25, 1987.
30. *Business Asia*, October 18, 1985, p. 336, and November 8, 1985, p. 357.
31. Trade between China and South Korea via Hong Kong was estimated to be about US$160 million in 1983 and $350 million in 1984.
32. *China Trade Report*, February 1986, p. 1.
33. *The Nineties*, June 1986, p. 29.
34. Ibid., pp. 30–32.
35. Ibid., October 1987, p. 70.
36. *People's Daily*, April 3, 1987.
37. Ibid., November 29 and December 18, 1986.
38. Ibid., November 29, 1986.
39. Ibid., January 9, 1986.
40. *The Nineties*, December 1986, pp. 18–20.
41. *FEER*, August 1, 1985, pp. 24–25.
42. Ibid.; see also Dennis Duncanson, "Hong Kong, China-Repossession and Penetration," *The World Today*, June 1986, pp. 105–6.
43. *FEER*, November 20, 1986, p. 27.
44. Ibid.
45. Basil Caplan, "Hong Kong: Ten Years to Go," *The Banker* (London) December 1986, p. 15.
46. T. B. Lin, "Foreign Investment in the Economy of Hong Kong," *Economic Bulletin for Asia and the Pacific* (United Nations), December 1984, p. 77, n. 3.
47. *People's Daily*, June 29, 1986.
48. Ibid., December 11, 1986; see also Caplan, "Hong Kong," pp. 17–18.
49. *People's Daily*, December 26, 1986; and C. E. Beckett, "Hong Kong's China Market," *China Business Review*, September-October 1985, p. 43.
50. *China Spring*, August 1988, p. 49.
51. *People's Daily*, April 23, 1986.
52. Ibid., December 3, 1986.
53. Ibid., July 6, 1985.
54. Ibid., December 1, 1986.
55. For instance, after Xu Jiatun, head of the Xinhua News Agency in Hong Kong, angrily denounced the political reform taking place in Hong Kong as "deviation" from the Joint Declaration, the next day the Heng Seng stock market index fell by nearly 50 percent. See *The Nineties*, December 1985, p. 15, and *Keesing's*, March 1986, p. 34242.
56. *FEER*, November 13, 1986, pp. 13–14.
57. *People's Daily*, April 29, 1988.
58. Joseph Y. S. Cheng, *Hong Kong: In Search of a Future* (Hong Kong: Oxford University Press, 1984), p. 19.
59. Ibid.
60. *The Nineties*, May 1988, pp. 40–41.
61. Ibid., p. 41.
62. Ibid.
63. Ibid., May 1986, pp. 64–65.
64. Ibid.
65. Cheng, *Hong Kong*, p. 83, app.
66. *The Nineties*, April 1988, p. 32.
67. Caplan, "Hong Kong," p. 17.
68. Ibid.
69. Mun and Chan, "The Role of Hong Kong in United States–China Trade," p. 67; see also Lin, "Foreign Investment in the Economy of Hong Kong," pp. 96–97.

70. *People's Daily*, July 19, 1985.
71. Hsiung, "The Hong Kong Settlement," p. 50.
72. *Outlook (Liaowang)* (Beijing), March 3, 1986, p. 22.
73. *FEER*, September 18, 1986, pp. 12–13; see also Lowell Dittmer, "Hong Kong and China's Modernization," *Orbis*, Fall 1986, pp. 534–35.
74. *The Nineties*, September 1986, pp. 33–34.
75. *Asia 1986 Yearbook, FEER*, pp. 141–42.
76. *The Nineties*, December 1986, p. 18.
77. Ibid.
78. Ibid., August 1988, pp. 40–41.
79. Ibid., September 1988, pp. 64–65.
80. *People's Daily*, September 5, 1988.
81. Jacobs, "Hong Kong and the Modernization of China," p. 70.
82. *Maclean's*, April 11, 1988, p. 35.
83. Ibid., p. 34.
84. *People's Daily*, July 14, 1988.
85. *The Nineties*, May 1988, pp. 58–59.
86. *People's Daily*, July 15, 1988.
87. *The Nineties*, September 1988, p. 6.
88. *People's Daily*, August 27, 1988.

CONTRIBUTORS

Ming Chen, currently a Ph.D. candidate in the Department of Political Science at the National University of Australia, received an M.A. in international studies from the University of Denver. He was formerly a research fellow at the Institute of International Studies of the Ministry of Foreign Affairs in Beijing.

Zhiduan Deng, currently a Ph.D. candidate in the Department of Political Science at Pennsylvania State University, is a graduate of Fudan University in Shanghai, where he studied international politics, and holds an M.A. in international relations from George Washington University.

Weiqun Gu, currently a Ph.D. candidate in the Department of Government at Harvard University, was formerly a research fellow at the Center for International Studies, the State Council, Beijing.

Yufan Hao is currently a research fellow at the Center for International Affairs, Harvard University, and a Ph.D. candidate in the School of Advanced International Studies at Johns Hopkins University. He is a graduate of Nanjing University in China and has had articles published in *China Quarterly* and *Asian Survey*.

Guocang Huan, currently a Senior Fellow of the Atlantic Council of the United States in Washington, D.C., graduated from the Graduate School of the Chinese Academy of Social Sciences, Beijing. He holds an M.A. degree in international economics from the University of Denver, another M.A. in political science from Columbia University, and a Ph.D. in political science from Princeton University. He has been a research fellow at the Brookings Institution, a John Olin Postdoctoral Fellow at the Center for International Affairs, Harvard University, a visiting professor at Columbia University, and a visiting fellow at the Harry S. Truman Institute for the Advancement of Peace, Hebrew University of Jerusalem. His articles have been published in the *New York Times, Foreign Affairs, Foreign Policy, Problems of Communism,* and many other publications.

Qingguo Jia, currently an assistant professor in the Department of International Politics and a research fellow at the Institute of International Studies at Beijing University, received a Ph.D. in political science from Cornell University. He was formerly an assistant professor in the Department of Political Science at the University of Vermont, and a research fellow at the Brookings Institution.

Zhimin Lin, currently a Ph.D. candidate in the Department of Political Science at the University of Washington, received an M.P.A. from the Woodrow Wilson School at Princeton University. He graduated from Fudan University in Shanghai, where he was later an instructor in the Department of International Politics.

Xiaobo Lu, currently a Ph.D. candidate in the Department of Political Science at the University of California, Berkeley, is a graduate of the Institute of Foreign Affairs in Beijing and was formerly an instructor there.

Xiaochuan Zhang, currently a Ph.D. candidate in the Department of Government and Politics at the University of Maryland, College Park, holds an M.A. in international relations from Johns Hopkins University, and was formerly a research fellow at the Institute of Contemporary International Relations in Beijing.

Hongqian Zhu, currently a research fellow at the Brookings Institution and a Ph.D. candidate in the Department of Political Science at the University of Michigan, was formerly a research fellow at the Institute of American Studies of the Chinese Academy of Social Sciences in Beijing.

INDEX

339